Why Stock Markets Crash

Why Stock Markets Crash

Critical Events in Complex
Financial Systems

D I D I E R   S O R N E T T E

PRINCETON UNIVERSITY PRESS
Princeton and Oxford

Copyright © 2003 by Princeton University Press

Published by Princeton University Press, 41 William Street,
Princeton, New Jersey 08540

In the United Kingdom: Princeton University Press, 3 Market
Place, Woodstock, Oxfordshire OX20 1SY

Fifth printing, and first paperback printing, 2004
Paperback ISBN 0-691-11850-7

The Library of Congress has cataloged the cloth edition of this
book as follows

Sornette, D.

Why stock markets crash : critical events in complex
financial systems / Didier Sornette.

p.   cm.

Includes bibliographical references and index.

ISBN 0-691-09630-9 (alk. paper)

1. Financial crises—History. 2. Stocks—Prices—History.
3. Financial crises—United States—History.
4. Stock exchanges—United States—History.
5. Critical phenomena (Physics). 6. Complexity (Philosophy).
I. Title.

HB3722.S66 2002

332.63′222–dc21   2002024336

British Library Cataloging-in-Publication Data is available

This book has been composed in Times

Printed on acid-free paper. ∞

pup.princeton.edu

Printed in the United States of America

20   19   18   17   16   15   14   13

ISBN-13: 978-0-691-11850-5 (pbk.)

ISBN-10: 0-691-11850-7 (pbk.)

Contents

      "Tronics" Boom

269   The Nasdaq Crash of April 2000

275   "Antibubbles"
276   *The "Bearish" Regime on the Nikkei
          Starting from January 1, 1990*
278   *The Gold Deflation Price Starting in
          Mid-1980*

279   Synthesis: "Emergent" Behavior of the
      Stock Market

Chapter 8   281   Speculative Bubbles in
BUBBLES, CRISES,   Emerging Markets
AND CRASHES IN   285   Methodology
EMERGENT MARKETS
281   286   Latin-American Markets

                         295   Asian Markets

                         304   The Russian Stock Market

                         309   Correlations across Markets: Economic
                               Contagion and Synchronization of
                               Bubble Collapse

                         314   Implications for Mitigations of Crises

Chapter 9   320   The Nature of Predictions
PREDICTION OF   325   How to Develop and Interpret
BUBBLES, CRASHES,   Statistical Tests of Log-Periodicity
AND ANTIBUBBLES
320   329   First Guidelines for Prediction
                         329   *What Is the Predictive Power of
                                   Equation (15)?*
                         330   *How Long Prior to a Crash Can
                                   One Identify the Log-Periodic
                                   Signatures?*

                         334   A Hierarchy of Prediction Schemes
                         334   *The Simple Power Law*
                         335   *The "Linear" Log-Periodic Formula*

Preface

Like many other people, I find the stock market fascinating. The market's potential for lavish gains and its playful character, made more attractive with the recent advent of the Internet, resonates with the gambler in us. Its punishing power and unpredictable temper make fearful investors look at it sometimes with awe, particularly at times of crashes. Stories of panic and suicides following such events have become part of market folklore. The richness of the patterns the stock market displays may lure investors into hoping to "beat the market" by using or extracting some bits of informative hedge.

However, the stock market is not a "casino" of playful or foolish gamblers. It is, primarily, the vehicle of fluid exchanges allowing the efficient function of capitalistic, competitive free markets.

As shown in Figure 0.1 and Table 0.1, the total world market capitalization rose from $3.38 trillion (thousand billions) in 1983 to $26.5 trillion in 1998 and to $38.7 trillion in 1999. To put these numbers in perspective, the 1999 U.S. budget was $1.7 trillion, while its 1983 budget was $800 billion. The 2002 U.S. budget is projected to be $1.9 trillion. Market capitalization and trading volumes tripled during the 1990s. The volume of securities issued was multiplied by 6. Privatization has played a key role in the stock market growth [51]. Stock market investment is clearly the biggest game in town.

A market crash occurring simultaneously on most of the stock markets of the world as witnessed in October 1987 would amount to the quasi-instantaneous evaporation of trillions of dollars. In values of

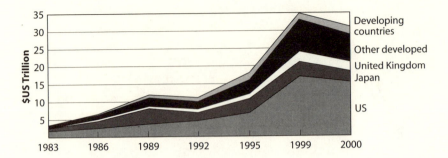

F<small>IG</small>. 0.1. Gross value of the world market capitalization from 1983 to 2000. From top to bottom, the developing countries are shown as the top strip, other developed countries (excluding the United States, Japan, and the United Kingdom), the United Kingdom, Japan, and the United States as the bottom strip. One trillion is equal by definition to one thousand billion or one million million. Reproduced with authorization from Boutchkova and Megginson [51].

October 2001, after almost two dismal years for stocks, the total world market capitalization has shrunk to a mere $25.1 trillion. A stock market crash of 30% would still correspond to an absolute loss of about $7.5 trillion dollars. Market crashes can thus swallow years of pensions and savings in an instant. Could they make us suffer even more by being the precursors or triggering factors of major recessions, as in 1929–33 after the great crash of October 1929? Or could they lead to a general

T<small>ABLE</small> 0.1

The growth of world stock market trading volumes (1983–1998) (value traded in billions of U.S. dollars)

Countries	1983	1989	1995	1998	1999
Developed countries	1203	6297	9170	20917	35188
United States	797	2016	5109	13148	19993
Japan	231	2801	1232	949	1892
United Kingdom	43	320	510	1167	3399
Developing countries	25	1171	1047	1957	2321
Total world	1228	7468	10216	22874	37509

Note the Japan bubble that culminated at the end of 1990: around this time, the trading volume on Japanese stock markets topped that of the U.S. market! The bubble started to deflate beginning in 1990 and has lost more than 60% of its value. Also remarkable is the fact that the market trading volume of the United States is now more than half the world trading volume, while it was less than a third of it in 1989.

Reproduced with authorization from Boutchkova and Megginson [51].

collapse of the financial and banking system, as seems to have been barely avoided several times in the not-so-distant past?

Stock market crashes are also fascinating because they personify the class of phenomena known as "extreme events." Extreme events are characteristic of many natural and social systems, often refered to by scientists as "complex systems."

This book is a story, a scientific tale of how financial crashes can be understood by invoking the latest and most sophisticated concepts in modern science, that is, the theory of complex systems and of critical phenomena. It is written first for the curious and intelligent layperson as well as for the interested investor who would like to exercise more control over his or her investments. The book will also be stimulating for scientists and researchers who are interested in or working on the theory of complex systems. The task is ambitious. My aim is to cover a territory that brings us all the way from the description of how the wonderful organization around us arises to the holy grail of crash predictions. This is daunting, especially as I have attempted to avoid the technical, if convenient, language of mathematics.

At one level, stock market crashes provide an excuse for exploring the wonderful world of self-organizing systems. Market crashes exemplify in a dramatic way the spontaneous emergence of extreme events in self-organizing systems. Stock market crashes are indeed perfect vehicles for important ideas needed to deal and cope with our risky world. Here, "world" is taken with several meanings, as it can be the physical world, the natural world, the biological, and even the inner intellectual and psychological worlds. Uncertainties and variabilities are the key words to describe the ever-changing environments around us. Stasis and equilibrium are illusions, whereas dynamics and out-of-equilibrium are the rule. The quest for balance and constancy will always be unsuccessful. The message here goes further and proclaims the essential importance of recognizing the organizing/disorganizing role of extreme events, such as momentous financial crashes. In addition to the obvious societal impacts, the guideline underlying this book recognizes that sudden transitions from a quiescent state to a crisis or catastrophic event provide the most dramatic fingerprints of the system dynamics. We live on a planet and in a society with intermittent dynamics rather than at rest (or "equilibrium" in the jargon of scientists), and so there is a growing and urgent need to sensitize citizens to the importance and impacts of ruptures in their multiple forms. Financial crashes provide an exceptionally good example for introducing these concepts in a way that transcends the disciplinary community of scholars.

At another level, market crashes constitute beautiful examples of events that we would all like to forecast. The arrow of time is inexorably projecting us toward the undetermined future. Predicting the future captures the imagination of all and is perhaps the greatest challenge. Prophets have historically terrified or inspired the masses by their visions of the future. Science has mostly avoided this question by focusing on another kind of prediction, that of novel phenomena (rather than that of the future) such as the prediction by Einstein of the existence of the deviation of light by the sun's gravitation field. Here, I do not shy away from this extraordinary challenge, with the aim of showing how a scientific approach to this question provides remarkable insights.

The book is organized in 10 chapters. The first six chapters provide the background for understanding why and how large financial crashes occur.

Chapter 1 introduces the fundamental questions: What are crashes? How do they happen? Why do they occur? When do they occur? Chapter 1 outlines the answers I propose, taking as examples some famous, or shall I say infamous, historical crashes.

Chapter 2 presents the key basic descriptions and properties of stock markets and of the way prices vary from one instant to the next. This frames the landscape in which the main characters of my story, the great crashes, are acting.

Chapter 3 discusses first the limitation of standard analyses for characterizing how crashes are special. It then presents the study of the frequency distribution of drawdowns, or runs of successive losses, and shows that large financial crashes are "outliers": they form a class of their own that can be seen from their statistical signatures. This rather academic discussion is justified by the result: If large financial crashes are "outliers," they are special and thus require a special explanation, a specific model, a theory of their own. In addition, their special properties may perhaps be used for their prediction.

Chapter 4 exposes the main mechanisms leading to positive feedbacks, that is, self-reinforcement, such as imitative behavior and herding between investors. Positive feedbacks provide the fuel for the development of speculative bubbles, preparing the instability for a major crash.

Chapter 5 presents two versions of a rational model of speculative bubbles and crashes. The first version posits that the crash hazard drives the market price. The crash hazard may skyrocket sometimes due to the collective behavior of "noise traders," those who act on little information, even if they think they "know." The second version inverts the logic and posits that prices drive the crash hazard. Prices may skyrocket sometimes, again due to the speculative or imitative behavior of investors. According to the rational expectation model, this outcome automatically entails a corresponding increase of the probability for a crash. The most important message is the discovery of robust and universal signatures of the approach to crashes. These precursory patterns have been documented for essentially all crashes on developed as well as emergent stock markets, on currency markets, on company stocks, and so on.

Chapter 6 takes a step back and presents the general concept of fractals, of self-similarity, and of fractals with complex dimensions and their associated discrete self-similarity. Chapter 6 shows how these remarkable geometric and mathematical objects enable one to codify the information contained in the precursory patterns before large crashes.

The last four chapters document this discovery at great length and demonstrate how to use this insight and the detailled predictions obtained for these models to forecast crashes.

Chapter 7 analyzes the major crashes that have occurred on the major stock markets of the world. It describes the empirical evidence of the universal nature of the critical log-periodic precursory signature of crashes.

Chapter 8 generalizes this analysis to emergent markets, including six Latin-American stock market indices (Argentina, Brazil, Chile, Mexico, Peru, and Venezuela) and six Asian stock market indices (Hong Kong, Indonesia, Korea, Malaysia, Philippines, and Thailand). It also discusses the existence of intermittent and strong correlation between markets following major international events.

Chapter 9 explains how to predict crashes as well as other large market events and examines in detail forecasting skills and their limitations, in particular in terms of the horizon of visibility and expected precision. Several case studies are presented in detail, with a careful count of successes and failures. Chapter 9 also presents the concept of an "antibubble," with the Japanese collapse from the beginning of 1990 to the present taken as a prominent example. A prediction issued and advertised in January 1999 has been until now borne out with remarkable precision, correctly predicting several changes of trends, a feat notoriously difficult using standard techniques of economic forecasting.

Finally, chapter 10 performs a major leap by extending the analysis to time scales covering centuries to millenia. It analyzes the whole of U.S. financial history as well as the world economy and population dynamics over the last two millenia to demonstrate the existence of strong positive feedbacks that suggest the existence of an underlying finite-time singularity around 2050, signaling a fundamental change of regime of the world economy and population around 2050 (a super crash?). We are probably starting to see signatures of this change of regime. I offer three leading scenarios: collapse, transition to sustainability, and superhumans.

The text is complemented by technical inserts that sometimes use a little mathematics and can be skipped on first or fast reading. They are offered as supplements that go deeper into an argument or as useful additional information. Many figures accompany the text, in keeping with the proverb that a picture is worth a thousand words.

The story told in this book has an unusual origin. Its roots go all the way back, starting in the sixties, to the pioneering scientists, such as Ben Widom (professor at Cornell University), Leo Kadanoff (now professor at the University of Chicago), Michael Fisher (now professor at the University of Maryland), Kenneth Wilson (now professor at Ohio State University and the 1982 Nobel prize winner in physics), and many others who explored and established the theory of critical phenomena in natural sciences. I am indebted to Pierre-Gilles de Gennes (College de France and the 1991 Nobel prize winner in physics) and Bernard Souillard (then a director of research of the Ecole Polytechnique in Palaiseau, at the French CNRS-National Center of Scientific Research), for a most stimulating year (1985–86) in Paris as their postdoctoral fellow, where I started to learn to polish the art of thinking about critical phenomena and to apply this field to the most complex situations. I also cherish the remarkable opportunity of broadening my vision of scientific applications offered by the collaboration with Michel Lagier of Thomson-Sintra Inc. (now Thomson-Marconi-Sonars, Inc.), which began in 1983 during my military duty and continues to this day. His unfailing friendship and kind support over the last two decades have meant a lot to me.

In 1991, while working on the exciting challenge of predicting the failure of pressure tanks made of Kevlar-matrix and carbon-matrix composites constituting essential elements of the European Ariane 4 and 5 rockets and also used in satellites for propulsion, I realized that the rupture of complex material structures could be understood as a cooperative phenomenon leading to specific detectable critical behaviors (see chapters 4 and 5 for the applications of these concepts to financial crashes). The power laws and associated complex exponents and log-periodic patterns that I shall discuss in this book, in particular in chapter 6, were discovered in this context and found to perform remarkably well. A prediction algorithm has been patented and is now been used routinely with success in Europe on these pressure tanks going into space as a standard qualifying procedure. I am indebted to Jean-Charles Anifrani (now with Eurocopter, Inc.) and Christian Le

Floc'h of the company Aerospatiale-Matra (now EADS) in Bordeaux, France (the leader contractor for the European Ariane rocket) for a stimulating collaboration and for providing this fantastic opportunity.

A few years later, Anders Johansen, Jean-Philippe Bouchaud, and I realized that financial crashes can be viewed as analogous to "ruptures" of the market. Anders Johansen and I started to explore systematically the application of these ideas and methods in this context. What followed is described in this book. In this adventure, Johansen, now at the Niels Bohr Institute in Copenhagen, has played a very special role, as he has accompanied me first as my student in Nice, France for two years and then as my postdoc for two years at the University of California, Los Angeles. A significant portion of this work owes much to him, as he has implemented a large part of the data analysis of our joint work. I am very pleased for having shared these exciting times with him, when we seemed alone against all, trying to document and demonstrate this discovery. The situation has now evolved, as the subject is attracting an increasing number of scholars and even more professionals and practitioners, and there is a healthy debate characteristic of a lively subject, associated in particular with the delicate and touchy question of the predictability of crashes (more in chapters 9 and 10). I hope that this book will help in this respect.

I also acknowledge the fruitful and inspiring discussions and collaborations with Jorgen V. Andersen, now jointly at University of Nanterre, Paris and University of Nice, France, who is now working with me on an extension of the models of bubbles and crashes described in chapter 5. I should also mention Olivier Ledoit, then at the Anderson School of Management at UCLA. The first model of rational bubbles and crashes described in chapter 5 owes a lot to our discussions and work together. Other close collaborators, such as Simon Gluzman, Kayo Ide, and Wei-Xing Zhou at UCLA, are joining in the research with me on the modeling of financial markets and crashes. I must also single out for mention Dietrich Stauffer of Cologne University, Germany, who has played a key role as editor of several international scholarly journals in helping our iconoclastic papers to be reviewed and published. Witty, concise to the extreme, straightforward, and with a strong sense of humor, Stauffer has been very supportive and helpful. He has also been an independent witness to the prediction on the Japanese Nikkei stock market described in chapter 9.

I am also grateful to Yueqiang Huang at the University of Southern California, Per Jögi and Matt W. Lee at UCLA, Laurent Nottale of the Observatoire Paris-Meudon, Guy Ouillon at the University of Nice, and Hubert Saleur and Charlie Sammis at the University of Southern California for stimulating interactions and discussions on the theory and practice of log-periodicity. I am indebted to Vladilen Pisarenko of the International Institute of Earthquake Prediction Theory and Mathematical Geophysics in Moscow, who provided much advice and numerous insights on the science and art of statistical testing. I am grateful to Bill Megginson at the University of Oklahoma for help in getting access to data on the world market capitalization. Cars Hommes, at the Center for Nonlinear Dynamics in Economics and Finance at the University of Amsterdam, and Neil Johnson at Oxford University, U.K., acted as referees on a preliminary version of the book. I thank them warmly for their kind and constructive advice. I thank Jorgen Andersen and Paul O'Brien for a critical reading of the manuscript. I met Joseph Wisnovsky, the executive editor of Princeton University Press, at a conference of the American Geophyical Union in San Francisco in December 2000. From the start, his enthusiasm and support has been an essential help in crystallizing this project. Wei-Xing Zhou helped a lot in preparing the fractal spiral picture on the cover, and Beth Gallagher performed a very careful and much appreciated job in correcting the manuscript.

I gratefully acknowledge the 2000 award from the program of the James S. McDonnell Foundation entitled "Studying Complex Systems." Last but not least, I am grateful for the support of the French National Center for Scientific Research (CNRS) since 1981, which has ensured complete freedom for my research in France and abroad. Since 1996, the Institute of Geophysics and Planetary Physics and the Department of Earth and Space Sciences at UCLA has provided new scientific opportunities and collaborations as well as support.

I hope that at least some of the joy, excitement, and wonder I have enjoyed during this research will be shared by readers.

Didier Sornette
Los Angeles and Nice
December 2001

Why Stock Markets Crash

CHAPTER 1

FINANCIAL CRASHES: WHAT, HOW, WHY, AND WHEN?

WHAT ARE CRASHES, AND WHY DO WE CARE?

Stock market crashes are momentous financial events that are fascinating to academics and practitioners alike. According to the academic world view that markets are efficient, only the revelation of a dramatic piece of information can cause a crash, yet in reality even the most thorough post-mortem analyses are typically inconclusive as to what this piece of information might have been. For traders and investors, the fear of a crash is a perpetual source of stress, and the onset of the event itself always ruins the lives of some of them.

Most approaches to explaining crashes search for possible mechanisms or effects that operate at very short time scales (hours, days, or weeks at most). This book proposes a radically different view: the underlying cause of the crash will be found in the preceding months and years, in the progressively increasing build-up of market cooperativity, or effective interactions between investors, often translated into accelerating ascent of the market price (the bubble). According to this "critical" point of view, the specific manner by which prices collapsed is not the most important problem: a crash occurs because the market has entered an unstable phase and any small disturbance or process may have triggered the instability. Think of a ruler held up vertically on your finger: this very unstable position will lead eventually to its collapse, as a result of a small (or an absence of adequate) motion of your hand or due to any tiny whiff of air. The collapse is fundamentally due to the unstable position; the instantaneous cause of the collapse is secondary. In the same vein, the growth of the sensitivity and the growing instability of the market close to such a critical point might explain why attempts to unravel the local origin of the crash have been so diverse. Essentially, anything would work once the system is ripe. This book explores the concept that a crash has fundamentally an endogenous, or internal, origin and that exogenous, or external, shocks only serve as triggering factors. As a consequence, the origin of crashes is much more subtle than often thought, as it is constructed progressively by the market as a whole, as a self-organizing process. In this sense, the true cause of a crash could be termed a systemic instability.

Systemic instabilities are of great concern to governments, central banks, and regulatory agencies [103]. The question that often arose in the 1990s was whether the new, globalized, information technology–driven economy had advanced to the point of outgrowing the set of rules dating from the 1950s, in effect creating the need for a new rule set for the "New Economy." Those who make this call basically point to the systemic instabilities since 1997 (or even back to Mexico's peso crisis of 1994) as evidence that the old post–World War II rule set is now antiquated, thus condemning this second great period of globalization to the same fate as the first. With the global economy appearing so fragile sometimes, how big a disruption would be needed to throw a wrench into the world's financial machinery? One of the leading moral authorities, the Basle Committee on Banking Supervision, advised [32] that, "in handling systemic issues, it will be necessary to address, on the one hand, risks to confidence in the financial system and contagion to otherwise sound institutions, and, on the other hand, the need to minimise the distortion to market signals and discipline."

The dynamics of confidence and of contagion and decision making based on imperfect information are indeed at the core of the book and will lead us to examine the following questions. What are the mechanisms underlying crashes? Can we forecast crashes? Could we control them? Or, at least, could we have some influence on them? Do crashes point to the existence of a fundamental instability in the world financial structure? What could be changed to modify or suppress these instabilities?

THE CRASH OF OCTOBER 1987

From the market opening on October 14, 1987 through the market close on October 19, major indexes of market valuation in the United States declined by 30% or more. Furthermore, all major world markets declined substantially that month, which is itself an exceptional fact that contrasts with the usual modest correlations of returns across countries and the fact that stock markets around the world are amazingly diverse in their organization [30].

In local currency units, the minimum decline was in Austria (−11.4%) and the maximum was in Hong Kong (−45.8%). Out of 23 major industrial countries (Autralia, Austria, Belgium, Canada, Denmark, France, Germany, Hong Kong, Ireland, Italy, Japan, Malaysia, Mexico, the Netherlands, New Zealand, Norway, Singapore, South Africa, Spain, Sweden, Switzerland, United Kingdom, United States), 19 had a decline greater than 20%. Contrary to common belief, the United States was not the first to decline sharply. Non-Japanese Asian markets began a severe decline on October 19, 1987, their time, and this decline was echoed first on a number of European markets, then in North American, and finally in Japan. However, most of the same markets had experienced significant but less severe declines in the latter part of the previous week. With the exception of the United States and Canada, other markets continued downward through the end of October, and some of these declines were as large as the great crash on October 19.

A lot of work has been carried out to unravel the origin(s) of the crash, notably in the properties of trading and the structure of markets; however, no clear cause has been singled out. It is noteworthy that the strong market decline during October 1987 followed what for many countries had been an unprecedented market increase during the first nine months of the year and even before. In the U.S. market, for instance, stock prices advanced 31.4% over those nine months. Some commentators have suggested that the real cause of October's decline was that overinflated prices generated a speculative bubble during the earlier period.

The main explanations people have come up with are the following.

1. **Computer trading**. In computer trading, also known as program trading, computers were programmed to automatically order large stock trades when certain market trends prevailed, in particular sell orders after losses. However, during the 1987 U.S. crash, other stock markets

that did not use program trading also crashed, some with losses even more severe than the U.S. market.

2. **Derivative securities**. Index futures and derivative securities have been claimed to increase the variability, risk, and uncertainty of the U.S. stock markets. Nevertheless, none of these techniques or practices existed in previous large, sudden market declines in 1914, 1929, and 1962.

3. **Illiquidity**. During the crash, the large flow of sell orders could not be digested by the trading mechanisms of existing financial markets. Many common stocks in the New York Stock Exchange were not traded until late in the morning of October 19 because the specialists could not find enough buyers to purchase the amount of stocks that sellers wanted to get rid of at certain prices. This insufficient liquidity may have had a significant effect on the size of the price drop, since investors had overestimated the amount of liquidity. However, negative news about the liquidity of stock markets cannot explain why so many people decided to sell stock at the same time.

4. **Trade and budget deficits**. The third quarter of 1987 had the largest U.S. trade deficit since 1960, which together with the budget deficit, led investors into thinking that these deficits would cause a fall of the U.S. stocks compared with foreign securities. However, if the large U.S. budget deficit was the cause, why did stock markets in other countries crash as well? Presumably, if unexpected changes in the trade deficit are bad news for one country, they should be good news for its trading partner.

5. **Overvaluation**. Many analysts agree that stock prices were over-valued in September 1987. While the price/earning ratio and the price/dividend ratio were at historically high levels, similar price/earning and price/dividends values had been seen for most of the 1960–72 period over which no crash occurred. Overvaluation does not seem to trigger crashes every time.

Other cited potential causes involve the auction system itself, the presence or absence of limits on price movements, regulated margin requirements, off-market and off-hours trading (continuous auction and automated quotations), the presence or absence of floor brokers who conduct trades but are not permitted to invest on their own account, the extent of trading in the cash market versus the forward market, the identity of traders (i.e., institutions such as banks or specialized trading firms), the significance of transaction taxes, and other factors.

More rigorous and systematic analyses on univariate associations and multiple regressions of these various factors conclude that it is not at all clear what caused the crash [30]. The most precise statement, albeit somewhat self-referencial, is that the most statistically significant explanatory variable in the October crash can be ascribed to the normal response of each country's stock market to a worldwide market motion. A world market index was thus constructed [30] by equally weighting the local currency indexes of the 23 major industrial countries mentioned above and normalized to 100 on September 30. It fell to 73.6 by October 30. The important result is that it was found to be statistically related to monthly returns in every country during the period from the beginning of 1981 until the month before the crash, albeit with a wildly varying magnitude of the responses across countries [30]. This correlation was found to swamp the influence of the institutional market characteristics. This signals the possible existence of a subtle but nonetheless influential worldwide cooperativity at times preceding crashes.

HISTORICAL CRASHES

In the financial world, risk, reward, and catastrophe come in irregular cycles witnessed by every generation. Greed, hubris, and systemic fluctuations have given us the tulip mania, the South Sea bubble, the land booms in the 1920s and 1980s, the U.S. stock market and great crash in 1929, and the October 1987 crash, to name just a few of the hundreds of ready examples [454].

THE TULIP MANIA

The years of tulip speculation fell within a period of great prosperity in the republic of the Netherlands. Between 1585 and 1650, Amsterdam became the chief commercial emporium, the center of the trade of the northwestern part of Europe, owing to the growing commercial activity in newly discovered America. The tulip as a cultivated flower was imported into western Europe from Turkey and it is first mentioned around 1554. The scarcity of tulips and their beautiful colors made them a must for members of the upper classes of society (see Figure 1.1).

During the build-up of the tulip market, the participants were not making money through the actual process of production. Tulips acted

FIG. 1.1. A variety of tulip (the Viceroy) whose bulb was one of the most expensive at the time of the tulip mania in Amsterdam, from *The Tulip Book* of P. Cos, including weights and prices from the years of speculative tulip mania (1637); Wageningen UR Library, Special Collections.

as the medium of speculation and their price determined the wealth of participants in the tulip business. It is not clear whether the build-up attracted new investment or new investment fueled the build-up, or both. What is known is that as the build-up continued, more and more people were roped into investing their hard-won earnings. The price of the tulip lost all correlation to its comparative value with other goods or services.

What we now call the "tulip mania" of the seventeenth century was the "sure thing" investment during the period from the mid-1500s to 1636. Before its devastating end in 1637, those who bought tulips rarely lost money. People became too confident that this "sure thing" would always make them money and, at the period's peak, the participants mortgaged their houses and businesses to trade tulips. The craze was so overwhelming that some tulip bulbs of a rare variety sold for the equivalent of a few tens of thousands of dollars. Before the crash, any suggestion that the price of tulips was irrational was dismissed by all the participants.

The conditions now generally associated with the first period of a boom were all present: an increasing currency, a new economy with novel colonial possibilities, and an increasingly prosperous country together had created the optimistic atmosphere in which booms are said to grow.

The crisis came unexpectedly. On February 4, 1637, the possibility of the tulips becoming definitely unsalable was mentioned for the first time. From then until the end of May 1637, all attempts at coordination among florists, bulbgrowers, and the Netherlands were met with failure. Bulbs worth tens of thousands of U.S. dollars (in present value) in early 1637 became valueless a few months later. This remarkable event is often discussed by present-day commentators, and parallels are drawn with modern speculation mania. The question is asked, Do the tulip market's build-up and its subsequent crash have any relevance for today's markets?

THE SOUTH SEA BUBBLE

The South Sea bubble is the name given to the enthusiatic speculative fervor that ended in the first great stock market crash in England, in 1720 [454]. The South Sea bubble is a fascinating story of mass hysteria, political corruption, and public upheaval. (See Figure 1.2.) It is really a collection of thousands of stories, tracing the personal fortunes of countless individuals who rode the wave of stock speculation for a furious six months in 1720. The "bubble year," as it is called, actually involves several individual bubbles, as all kinds of fraudulent joint-stock companies sought to take advantage of the mania for speculation. The following account borrows from "The Bubble Project" [60].

In 1711, the South Sea Company was given a monopoly of all trade to the South Sea ports. The real prize was the anticipated trade that would open up with the rich Spanish colonies in South America. In return for this monopoly, the South Sea Company would assume a portion of the national debt that England had incurred during the War of the Spanish Succession. When Britain and Spain officially went to war again in 1718, the immediate prospects for any benefits from trade to South America

FIG. 1.2. An emblematical print of the South Sea scene (etching and engraving), by the artist William Hogarth in 1722 (now located at The Charles Deering McCormick Library of Special Collections, Northwestern University). With this scene, Hogarth satirizes crowds consumed by political speculation on the verge of the stock market collapse of 1720. The "merry-go-round" was set in motion by the South Sea Company, who held a monopoly on trade between South America, the Pacific Islands, and England. The Company tempted vast numbers of middle-class investors to make quick money through absurd speculations. The wheel of fortune in the center of the print is broken, symbolizing the abandonment of values for quick money, while "Trade" lies starving to death. On the right, the original inscription on the London Fire Monument—erected in memory of the destruction of the City by the Great Fire in 1666—has been altered to read: "This monument was erected in memory of the destruction of the city by the South Sea in 1720." Reproduced by permission from McCormick Library of Special Collections, Northwestern University Library.

were nil. What mattered to speculators, however, were future prospects, and here it could always be argued that incredible prosperity lay ahead and would be realized when open hostilities came to an end.

The early 1700s was also a time of international finance. By 1719 the South Sea directors wished, in a sense, to imitate the manipulation of public credit that John Law had achieved in France with the Mississippi Company, which was given a monopoly of French trade to North America. Law had connived to drive the price of its stock up, and the South Sea directors hoped to do the same. In 1719 the South Sea directors made a proposal to assume the entire public debt of the British government. On April 12, 1720 this offer was accepted. The company immediately started to drive the price of the stock up through artificial means; these largely took the form of new subscriptions combined with the circulation of pro-trade-with-Spain stories designed to give the impression that the stock could only go higher. Not only did capital stay in England, but many Dutch investors bought South Sea stock, thus increasing the inflationary pressure.

South Sea stock rose steadily from January through the spring. As every apparent success would soon attract its imitators, all kinds of joint-stock companies suddenly appeared, hoping to cash in on the speculation mania. Some of these companies were legitimate, but the bulk were bogus schemes designed to take advantage of the credulity of the people. Several of the bubbles, both large and small, had some overseas trade or "New World" aspect. In addition to the South Sea and Mississippi ventures, there was a project for improving the Greenland fishery and another for importing walnut trees from Virginia. Raising capital by selling stock in these enterprises was apparently easy work. The projects mentioned so far all have a tangible specificity at least on paper, if not in practice; others were rather vague on details but big on promise. The most remarkable was "a company for carrying on an undertaking of great advantage, but nobody to know what it is." The prospectus stated that "the required capital was half a million, in five thousand shares of 100 pounds each, deposit 2 pounds per share. Each subscriber, paying his [or her] desposit, was entitled to 100 pounds per annum per share. How this immense profit was to be obtained, [the proposer] did not condescend to inform [the buyers] at that time" [60]. As T. J. Dunning [114] wrote:

> Capital eschews no profit, or very small profit.... With adequate profit, capital is very bold. A certain 1 percent will ensure its employment anywhere; 20 percent certain will produce eagerness; 50 percent, positive

audacity; 100 percent will make it ready to trample on all human laws; 300 percent and there is not a crime at which it will scruple, nor a risk it will not run, even to the chance of its owner being hanged.

Next morning, at nine o'clock, this great man opened an office in Cornhill. Crowds of people beset his door, and when he shut up at three o'clock, he found that no less than one thousand shares had been subscribed for, and the deposits paid. He was thus, in five hours, the winner of £2,000. He was philosophical enough to be contented with his venture, and set off the same evening for the Continent. He was never heard of again.

Such scams were bad for the speculation business and so, largely through the pressure of the South Sea directors, the so-called "Bubble Act" was passed on June 11, 1720 requiring all joint-stock companies to have a royal charter. For a moment, the confidence of the people was given an extra boost, and they responded accordingly. South Sea stock had been at £175 at the end of February, 380 at the end of March, and around 520 by May 29. It peaked at the end of June at over £1,000 (a psychological barrier in that four-digit number).

With credulity now stretched to the limit and rumors of more and more people (including the directors themselves) selling off, the bubble then burst according to a slow but steady deflation (not unlike the 60% drop of the Japanese Nikkei index after its all-time peak at the end of December 1989). By mid-August, the bankruptcy listings in the *London Gazette* reached an all-time high, an indication that many people had bought on credit or margin. Thousands of fortunes were lost, both large and small. The directors attempted to pump up more speculation. They failed. The full collapse came by the end of September, when the stock stood at £135. The crash remained in the consciousness of the Western world for the rest of the eighteenth century, not unlike our cultural memory of the 1929 Wall Street Crash.

THE GREAT CRASH OF OCTOBER 1929

The Roaring 20s—a time of growth and prosperity on Wall Street and Main Street—ended with the Great Crash of October 1929 (for the most thorough and authoritative account and analysis, see [152]). (See Figure 1.3.) The Great Depression that followed put 13 million Americans out of work. Two thousand investment firms went under, and the American banking industry underwent the biggest structural changes

FIG. 1.3. The front page of the October 30, 1929 *New York Times* exclaimed the massive loss on Wall Street. It worked hard to ease fear among panicked investors—without success, as history has shown.

of its history, as a new era of government regulation began. Roosevelt's New Deal politics would follow.

The October 1929 crash is a vivid illustration of several remarkable features often associated with crashes. First, stock market crashes are often unforeseen for most people, especially economists. "In a few months, I expect to see the stock market much higher than today." Those words were pronounced by Irving Fisher, America's distinguished and famous economist and professor of economics at Yale University, 14 days before Wall Street crashed on Black Tuesday, October 29, 1929.

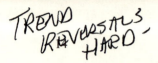

"A severe depression such as 1920–21 is outside the range of probability. We are not facing a protracted liquidation." This was the analysis offered days after the crash by the Harvard Economic Society to its subscribers. After continuous and erroneous optimistic forecasts, the society closed its doors in 1932. Thus, the two most renowned economic forecasting institutes in America at the time failed to predict that crash and depression were forthcoming and continued with their optimistic views, even as the Great Depression took hold of America. The reason is simple: the prediction of trend-reversals constitutes by far the most difficult challenge posed to forecasters and is very unreliable, especially within the linear framework of standard (auto-regressive) economic models.

A second general feature exemplified by the October 1929 event is that a financial collapse has never happened when things look bad. On the contrary, macroeconomic flows look good before crashes. Before every collapse, economists say the economy is in the best of all worlds. Everything looks rosy, stock markets go up and up, and macroeconomic flows (output, employment, etc.) appear to be improving further and further. This explains why a crash catches most people, especially economists, totally by surprise. The good times are invariably extrapolated linearly into the future. Is it not perceived as senseless by most people in a time of general euphoria to talk about crash and depression?

During the build-up phase of a bubble such as the one preceding the October 1929 crash, there is a growing interest in the public for the commodity in question, whether it consists of stocks, diamonds, or coins. That interest can be estimated through different indicators: an increase in the number of books published on the topic (see Figure 1.4) and in the subscriptions to specialized journals. Moreover, the well-known empirical rule according to which the volume of sales is growing during a bull market, as shown in Figure 1.5, finds a natural interpretation: sales increases in fact reveal and pinpoint the progress of the bubble's diffusion throughout society. These features have been recently reexamined for evidence of a bubble, a "fad" or "herding" behavior, by studying individual stock returns [455]. One story often advanced for the boom of 1928 and 1929 is that it was driven by the entry into the market of largely uninformed investors, who followed the fortunes of and invested in "favorite" stocks. The result of this behavior would be a tendency for the favorite stocks' prices to move together more than would be predicted by their shared fundamental economic values. The co-movement indeed increased significantly during the boom and was a signal characteristic of the tumultuous market of the early 1930s. These results are

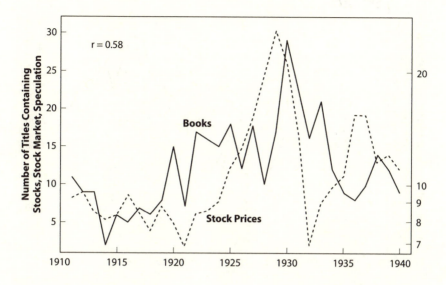

FIG. 1.4. Comparison between the number of yearly published books about stock market speculation and the level of stock prices (1911–1940). Solid line: Books at Harvard's library whose titles contain one of the words "stocks," "stock market," or "speculation". Broken line: Standard and Poor's index of common stocks. The curve of published books lags behind the price curve with a time-lag of about 1.5 years, which can be explained by the time needed for a book to get published. Source: The stock price index is taken from the Historical Abstract of the United States. Reproduced from [349].

thus consistent with the possibility that a fad or crowd psychology played a role in the rise of the market, its crash, and subsequent volatility [455].

The political mood before the October 1929 crash was also optimistic. In November 1928, Herbert Hoover was elected president of the United States in a landslide, and his election set off the greatest increase in stock buying to that date. Less than a year after the election, Wall Street crashed.

EXTREME EVENTS IN COMPLEX SYSTEMS

Financial markets are not the only systems with extreme events. Financial markets constitute one among many other systems exhibiting a complex organization and dynamics with similar behavior. Systems with a large number of mutually interacting parts, often open to their environment, self-organize their internal structure and their dynamics with novel and sometimes surprising macroscopic ("emergent") properties. The complex

 # SHARES TRADED ISOLATED ANALYSIS SYSTEM

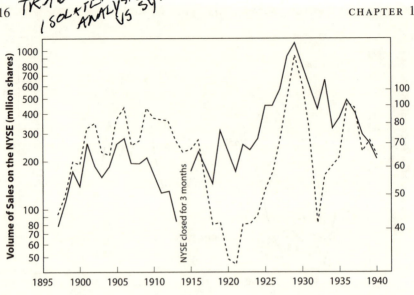

FIG. 1.5. Comparison between the number of shares traded on the NYSE and the level of stock prices (1897–1940). Solid line: Number of shares traded. Broken line: Deflated Standard and Poor's index of common stocks. Source: Historical Statistics of the United States. Reproduced from [349].

system approach, which involves "seeing" interconnections and relationships, that is, the whole picture as well as the component parts, is nowadays pervasive in modern control of engineering devices and business management. It also plays an increasing role in most of the scientific disciplines, including biology (biological networks, ecology, evolution, origin of life, immunology, neurobiology, molecular biology, etc.), geology (plate-tectonics, earthquakes and volcanoes, erosion and landscapes, climate and weather, environment, etc.), and the economic and social sciences (cognition, distributed learning, interacting agents, etc.). There is a growing recognition that progress in most of these disciplines, in many of the pressing issues for our future welfare as well as for the management of our everyday life, will need such a systemic complex system and multidisciplinary approach. This view tends to replace the previous "analytical" approach, consisting of decomposing a system in components, such that the detailed understanding of each component was believed to bring understanding of the functioning of the whole.

A central property of a complex system is the possible occurrence of coherent large-scale collective behaviors with a very rich structure, resulting from the repeated nonlinear interactions among its constituents: the whole turns out to be much more than the sum of its parts. It is widely believed that most complex systems are not amenable to mathematical, analytic descriptions and can be explored only by means of "numerical experiments." In the context of the mathematics of algorithmic complexity [73], many complex systems are said to be computationally irreducible; that is, the only way to decide about their evolution is to actually let them evolve in time. Accordingly, the "dynamical" future time evolution of complex systems would be inherently unpredictable. This unpredictability does not, however, prevent the application of the scientific method to the prediction of novel phenomena as exemplified by many famous cases (the prediction of the planet Neptune by Leverrier from calculations of perturbations in the orbit of Uranus, the prediction by Einstein of the deviation of light by the sun's gravitation field, the prediction of the helical structure of the DNA molecule by Watson and Crick based on earlier predictions by Pauling and Bragg, etc.). In contrast, it refers to the impossibility of satisfying the quest for the knowledge of what tomorrow will be made of, often filled by the vision of "prophets" who have historically inspired or terrified the masses.

The view that complex systems are unpredictable has recently been defended persuasively in concrete prediction applications, such as the socially important issue of earthquake prediction (see the contributions in [312]). In addition to the persistent failures at reaching a reliable earthquake predictive scheme, this view is rooted theoretically in the analogy between earthquakes and self-organized criticality [26]. In this "fractal" framework (see chapter 6), there is no characteristic scale, and the power-law distribution of earthquake sizes reflects the fact that the large earthquakes are nothing but small earthquakes that did not stop. They are thus unpredictable because their nucleation is not different from that of the multitude of small earthquakes, which obviously cannot all be predicted.

Does this really hold for all features of complex systems? Take our personal life. We are not really interested in knowing in advance at what time we will go to a given store or drive to a highway. We are much more interested in forecasting the major bifurcations ahead of us, involving the few important things, like health, love, and work, that count for our happiness. Similarly, predicting the detailed evolution of complex systems has no real value, and the fact that we are taught that it is out of reach from a fundamental point of view does not exclude the more interesting possibility of predicting phases of evolutions of complex systems that really count, like the extreme events.

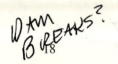

It turns out that most complex systems in natural and social sciences do exhibit rare and sudden transitions that occur over time intervals that are short compared to the characteristic time scales of their posterior evolution. Such extreme events express more than anything else the underlying "forces" usually hidden by almost perfect balance and thus provide the potential for a better scientific understanding of complex systems.

These crises have fundamental societal impacts and range from large natural catastrophes, such as earthquakes, volcanic eruptions, hurricanes and tornadoes, landslides, avalanches, lightning strikes, meteorite/asteroid impacts (see Figure 1.6), and catastrophic events of environmental degradation, to the failure of engineering structures, crashes in the stock market, social unrest leading to large-scale strikes and upheaval, economic drawdowns on national and global scales, regional power blackouts, traffic gridlock, and diseases and epidemics. It is essential to realize

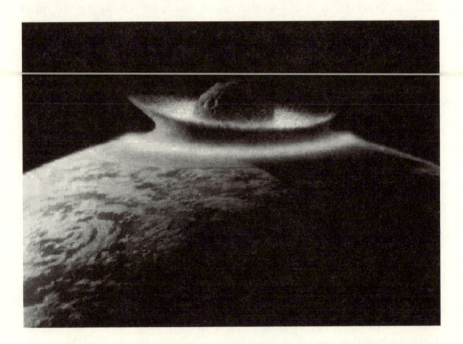

FIG. 1.6. One of the most fearsome possible catastrophic events, but one with very low probability of occurring. A collision with a meteorite with a diameter of 15 km with impact velocity of 14 km/s (releasing about the same energy, equal to 100 Megatons of equivalent TNT, as what is thought to be the dinosaur killer) occurs roughly once every 100 million years. A collision with a meteorite with a diameter of the order of 1,000 km as shown in this figure occurred only early in the solar system's history. (Creation of the space artist Don Davis.)

that the long-term behavior of these complex systems is often controlled in large part by these rare catastrophic events: the universe was probably born during an extreme explosion (the "big bang"); the nucleosynthesis of all important heavy atomic elements constituting our matter results from the colossal explosion of supernovae (stars more heavy than our sun whose internal nuclear combustion diverges at the end of their life); the largest earthquake in California, repeating about once every two centuries, accounts for a significant fraction of the total tectonic deformation; landscapes are more shaped by the "millenium" flood that moves large boulders than by the action of all other eroding agents; the largest volcanic eruptions lead to major topographic changes as well as severe climatic disruptions; according to some contemporary views, evolution is probably characterized by phases of quasi-stasis interrupted by episodic bursts of activity and destruction [168, 169]; financial crashes, which can destroy in an instant trillions of dollars, loom over and shape the psychological state of investors; political crises and revolutions shape the long-term geopolitical landscape; even our personal life is shaped in the long run by a few key decisions or happenings.

The outstanding scientific question is thus how such large-scale patterns of catastrophic nature might evolve from a series of interactions on the smallest and increasingly larger scales. In complex systems, it has been found that the organization of spatial and temporal correlations do not stem, in general, from a nucleation phase diffusing across the system. It results rather from a progressive and more global cooperative process occurring over the whole system by repetitive interactions. For instance, scientific and technical discoveries are often quasi-simultaneous in several laboratories in different parts of the world, signaling the global nature of the maturing process.

Standard models and simulations of scenarios of extreme events are subject to numerous sources of error, each of which may have a negative impact on the validity of the predictions [232]. Some of the uncertainties are under control in the modeling process; they usually involve trade-offs between a more faithful description and manageable calculations. Other sources of error are beyond control, as they are inherent in the modeling methodology of the specific disciplines. The two known strategies for modeling are both limited in this respect: analytical theoretical predictions are out of reach for most complex problems. Brute force numerical resolution of the equations (when they are known) or of scenarios is reliable in the "center of the distribution," that is, in the regime far from the extremes where good statistics can be accumulated. Crises are extreme events that occur rarely, albeit with extraordinary impact, and are thus completely undersampled and poorly constrained. Even the introduction of "teraflop" supercomputers does not qualitatively change this fundamental limitation.

Notwithstanding these limitations, I believe that the progress of science and of its multidisciplinary enterprises makes the time ripe for a full-fledged effort toward the prediction of complex systems. In particular, novel approaches are possible for modeling and predicting certain catastrophic events or "ruptures," that is, sudden transitions from a quiescent state to a crisis or catastrophic event [393]. Such ruptures involve interactions between structures at many different scales. In the present book, I apply these ideas to one of the most dramatic events in social sciences, financial crashes. The approach described in this book combines ideas and tools from mathematics, physics, engineering, and the social sciences to identify and classify possible universal structures that occur at different scales and to develop application-specific methodologies for using these structures for the prediction of the financial "crises." Of special interest will be the study of the premonitory processes before financial crashes or "bubble" corrections in the stock market.

For this purpose, I shall describe a new set of computational methods that are capable of searching and comparing patterns, simultaneously and iteratively, at multiple scales in hierarchical systems. I shall use these patterns to improve the understanding of the dynamical state before and after a financial crash and to enhance the statistical modeling of social hierarchical systems with the goal of developing reliable forecasting skills for these large-scale financial crashes.

IS PREDICTION POSSIBLE? A WORKING HYPOTHESIS

With the low of 3227 on April 17, 2000, identified as the end of the "crash," the Nasdaq Composite index lost in five weeks over 37% of its all-time high of 5133 reached on March 10, 2000. This crash has not been followed by a recovery, as occurred from the October 1987 crash. At the time of writing, the Nasdaq Composite index bottomed at 1395.8 on September 21, 2001, in a succession of descending waves. The Nasdaq Composite consists mainly of stock related to the so-called "New Economy," that is, the Internet, software, computer hardware, telecommunications, and similar sectors. A main characteristic of these companies is that their price–earning ratios (P/Es), and even more so their price–dividend ratios, often come in three digits. Some, such as VA LINUX, actually have a *negative* earning/share (of −1.68). Yet they are traded at around $40 per share, which is close to the price of a share of Ford in early March 2000. In constrast, so-called "Old Economy" companies, such as Ford, General Motors, and DaimlerChrysler, have P/E $\approx$ 10. The difference between Old Economy and New Economy stocks is thus the expectation of *future earnings* as discussed in [282] (see also [395] for a new view on speculative pricing): investors expect an enormous increase in, for example, the sale of Internet and computer-related products rather than of cars and are hence more willing to invest in Cisco rather than in Ford, notwithstanding the fact that the earning per share of the former is much smaller than for the latter. For a similar price per share (approximately $60 for Cisco and $55 for Ford), the earning per share in 1999 was $0.37 for Cisco compared with $6.00 for Ford. Close to its apex on April 14, 2000, Cisco had a total market capitalization of $395 billion compared with $63 billion for Ford. Cisco has since bottomed at about $11 in September 2001 and traded at around $20 at the end of 2001.

In the standard fundamental valuation formula, in which the expected return of a company is the sum of the dividend return and of the growth rate, New Economy companies are supposed to compensate for their lack of present earnings by a fantastic potential growth. In essence, this means that the bull market observed in the Nasdaq in 1997–2000 is fueled by expectations of increasing future earnings rather than economic fundamentals: the price-to-dividend ratio for a company such as Lucent Technologies (LU) with a capitalization of over $300 billion prior to its crash on January 5, 2000 (see Figure 1.7) is over 900, which means that you get a higher return on your checking account (!) unless the price of the stock increases. In contrast, an Old Economy company such as DaimlerChrysler gives a return that is more than 30 times higher. Nevertheless, the shares of Lucent Technologies rose by more than 40% during 1999, whereas the share of DaimlerChrysler declined by more than 40% in the same period. Recent crashes of IBM, LU, and Procter & Gamble (P&G), shown in Figures 1.7–1.9 correspond to a loss equivalent to the national budget of many countries! And this is usually attributed to a "business-as-usual" corporate statement of a slightly revised smaller-than-expected earnings!

These considerations suggest that the *expectation* of future earnings (and its perception by others), rather than present economic reality, is an important motivation for the average investor. The inflated price may be a speculative bubble if the growth expectations are unrealistic (which is, of course, easy to tell in hindsight but not obvious at all in the heat of the action!). As already alluded to, history provides many examples of

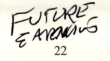
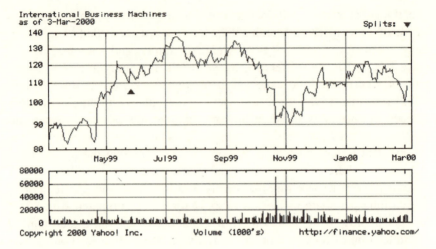

FIG. 1.7. Top panel: Time series of daily closes and volume of the IBM stock over a one-year period around the large drop of October 21, 1999. The time of the crash can be seen clearly as coinciding with the peak in volume (bottom panel). Taken from http://finance.yahoo.com/.

bubbles driven by unrealistic expectations of future earnings followed by crashes [454]. The same basic ingredients are found repeatedly: fueled by initially well-founded economic fundamentals, investors develop a self-fulfilling enthusiasm from an imitative process or crowd behavior that leads to the building of "castles in the air," to paraphrase Burton Malkiel [282]. Furthermore, the causes of the crashes on the U.S. markets in October 1929, October 1987, August 1998, and April 2000 belong to the same category, the difference being mainly in which sector the bubble was created. In 1929, it was utilities; in 1987, the bubble was supported by a general deregulation of the market, with many new private investors entering the market with very high expectations about the profit they would make; in 1998, it was an enormous expectation for the investment opportunities in Russia that collapsed; until early 2000, it was the extremely high expectations for the Internet, telecommunications, and similar sectors that fueled the bubble. The IPOs (initial public offerings) of many Internet and software companies have been followed by a mad frenzy, where the share price has soared during the first few hours of trading. An excellent example is VA LINUX SYSTEMS whose $30 IPO price increased a record 697% to close at $239.25 on its

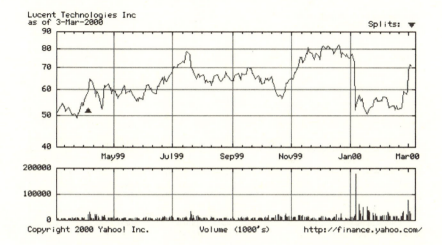

Fig. 1.8. Top panel: Time series of daily closes and volume of the Lucent Technology stock over a one-year period around the large drop of January 6, 2000. The time of the crash can be seen clearly as coinciding with the peak in volume (bottom panel). Taken from http://finance.yahoo.com/.

opening day December 9, 1999, only to decline to $28.94 on April 14, 2000.

Building on these insights, our hypothesis is that stock market crashes are caused by the slow build-up of long-range correlations leading to a global cooperative behavior of the market and eventually ending in a collapse in a short, critical time interval. The use of the word "critical" is not purely literary here: in mathematical terms, complex dynamical systems can go through so-called critical points, defined as the explosion to infinity of a normally well-behaved quantity. As a matter of fact, as far as nonlinear dynamical systems go, the existence of critical points is more the rule than the exception. Given the puzzling and violent nature of stock market crashes, it is worth investigating whether there could possibly be a link between stock market crashes and critical points.

- Our key assumption is that a crash may be caused by *local* self-reinforcing imitation between traders. This self-reinforcing imitation process leads to the blossoming of a bubble. If the tendency for traders to "imitate" their "friends" increases up to a certain point called the "critical" point, many traders may place the same order (sell) at the same time, thus causing a crash. The interplay between the progressive strengthening of imitation and the ubiquity of noise requires a probabilistic description: a crash is *not* a certain outcome of the bubble but

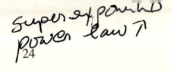

FIG. 1.9. Top panel: Time series of daily closes and volume of the Procter & Gamble stock over a one-year period ending after the large drop of March 7, 2000. The time of the crash can be seen clearly as coinciding with the peak in volume (bottom panel). Taken from http://finance.yahoo.com/.

can be characterized by its hazard rate, that is, the probability per unit time that the crash will happen in the next instant, provided it has not happened yet.

- Since the crash is not a certain deterministic outcome of the bubble, it remains rational for investors to remain in the market provided they are compensated by a higher rate of growth of the bubble for taking the risk of a crash, because there is a finite probability of "landing smoothly," that is, of attaining the end of the bubble without crash.

In a series of research articles performed in collaboration with several colleagues and mainly with Anders Johansen, we have shown extensive evidence that the build-up of bubbles manifests itself as an overall super-exponential power-law acceleration in the price decorated by log-periodic precursors, a concept related to fractals, as will become clear later (see chapter 6). In telling this story, this book will address the following questions: Why and how do these precursors occur? What do they mean? What do they imply with respect to prediction?

My colleagues and I claim that there is a degree of predictive skill associated with these patterns, which has already been used in practice and has been investigated by us as well as many others, academics and, most-of-all, practitioners. The evidence I discuss in what follows arises from many crashes, including

- the October 1929 Wall Street crash, the October 1987 World crash, the October 1987 Hong Kong crash, the August 1998 World crash, and the April 2000 Nasdaq crash;

- the 1985 foreign exchange event on the U.S. dollar and the correction of the U.S. dollar against the Canadian dollar and the Japanese Yen starting in August 1998;

- the bubble on the Russian market and its ensuing collapse in 1997–98;

- 22 significant bubbles followed by large crashes or by severe corrections in the Argentinian, Brazilian, Chilean, Mexican, Peruvian, Venezuelan, Hong-Kong, Indonesian, Korean, Malaysian, Philippine, and Thai stock markets.

In all these cases, it has been found that, with very few exceptions, log-periodic power-laws adequately describe speculative bubbles on the Western markets as well as on the emerging markets.

Notwithstanding the drastic differences in epochs and contexts, I shall show that these financial crashes share a common underlying background as well as structure. The rationale for this rather surprising result is probably rooted in the fact that humans are endowed with basically the same emotional and rational qualities in the twenty-first century as they were in the seventeenth century (or at any other epoch). Humans are still essentially driven by at least a modicum of greed and fear in their quest for well-being. The "universal" structures I am going to uncover in this book may be understood as the robust emergent properties of the market resulting from some characteristic "rules" of interaction between investors. These interactions can change in details due, for instance, to computers and electronic communications. They have not changed at a qualitative level. As we shall see, complex system theory allows us to account for this robustness.

CHAPTER 2

FUNDAMENTALS OF

FINANCIAL MARKETS

Notwithstanding the drama surrounding crashes, there is a growing body of scholarly work suggesting that they are part of the family of usual daily price variations; this view, which is rooted theoretically in some branches of the theory of complex systems, posits that there is no characteristic scale in stock market price fluctuations [287]. As a consequence, the very large price drops (crashes) are nothing but small drops that did not stop [26]. According to this view, since crashes belong to the same family as the rest of the returns we observe on normal days, they should be inherently unpredictable because their nucleation is not different from that of the multitude of small losses which obviously cannot be predicted at all.

In chapter 3, we examine in detail whether this really holds for the very largest crashes. In particular, we shall provide strong evidence that large crashes are in fact in a league of their own: they are "outliers." This realization will call for new explanations and hence may suggest a possibility of predictability. In order to reach this surprising conclusion, we first need to recall some basic facts about the distribution (also called the frequency) of price variations or of price returns and their respective correlation. To this end, we first present the standard view about price variations and returns on the stock market. A simple toy model will illustrate why arbitrage opportunities (the possibility to get a "free lunch") are usually washed out by the intelligent investment of informed traders, leading to the concept of the efficient stock market. We shall then test this concept in the next chapter, by studying the distribution of drawdowns, that is, runs of losses over several days, demonstrating that the largest drawdowns, the crashes (fast or slow), belong to a class of their own.

THE BASICS

PRICE TRAJECTORIES

Stock market prices show changes at all time scales. From the time scale of "ticks" to that of centuries, prices embroider their complex trajectories. A tick is the price increment from the last to the next trade, separated typically by a few seconds or less for major stocks in active markets. The minimum tick is the smallest increment for which stock prices can be quoted. Figure 2.1 shows monthly quotes of the Dow Jones Industrial Average (DJIA) from 1790 to 2000. The great crash of October 1929 followed by the great depression is the most striking pattern in this figure. In contrast, on this long time scale the crash of October 1987 is barely visible as a small glitch between the two vertical lines.

What is the Dow Jones Industrial Average? The DJIA is an index of 30 "blue-chip" U.S. stocks. It is the oldest continuing U.S. market index. It is called an "average" because it was originally computed by adding up stock prices and dividing by the number of stocks (the very first average price of industrial stocks, on May 26, 1896, was 40.94) and should ideally represent a correct measure of the state of the economy. The methodology remains the same today, but the divisor has been changed to preserve historical continuity. The editors of *The Wall Street Journal* select the components of the industrial average by taking a broad view of what "industrial" means. The most recent changes in the components of the DJIA occurred Monday, November 1, 1999, when Home Depot Inc., Intel Corp., Microsoft Corp., and SBC Communications replaced Union Carbide Corp. (in the DJIA since 1928), Goodyear Tire & Rubber Co. (in the DJIA since 1930), Sears, Roebuck & Co. (in the DJIA since 1924), and Chevron (in the DJIA since 1984). The previous change occurred in March 7, 1997, when Hewlett-Packard, Johnson & Johnson, Traveller's Group (Now Citigroup), and Wal-Mart Stores replaced Woolworth, Westinghouse Electric, Texaco and Bethlehem Steel. The components of the Dow Jones Averages are daily listed on page C3 of the Money and Investing section in *The Wall Street Journal*. See http://averages.DowJones.com/about.html. The Dow Jones index shown

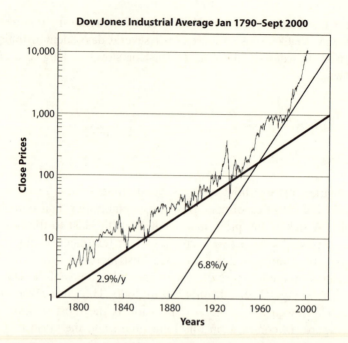

FIG. 2.1. Monthly quotes of the DJIA from September 2000 extrapolated back to January 1790. The vertical axis uses logarithmic scales such that multiplication by a fixed factor, for instance 10, corresponds to addition of a constant in this representation. Mathematically, this corresponds to a mapping from multiplication to addition and allows us to show on the same graph prices that have changed by factors of thousands (in the present case, from a value of about 3 in 1790 to a value above 10,000 in 2000). The thick (respectively, thin) straight line corresponds to the exponential growth of an initial wealth of $1 in 1780 (respectively, 1880) invested at the annual rate of return of ≈2.9% (respectively, 6.8%), which would have transformed into $1,000 (respectively, $10,000) in 2020.

in figure 2.1 is the true Dow Jones index back to 1896 extrapolated back to 1790 by The Foundation for the Study of Cycles [138].

The thick straight line in Figure 2.1 corresponds to the exponential growth of an initial wealth of $1 invested in 1780 at the annual rate of return of ≈2.9%, which will grow to $1,000 in 2020. The thin straight line corresponds to the exponential growth of an initial wealth of $1 invested in 1880 at the annual rate of return of 6.8%, which will grow to $10,000 in 2020. They both show the power of compounded interest! The comparison of these two lines is suggestive of an acceleration of the growth rate of return of the DJIA, which was on average about 3% per year 1780 until the 1930s and then shifted to an average of about 7%

per year. But even this description falls short of capturing adequately the behavior of the DJIA: the growth of the DJIA is even stronger than given by the thin straight line and seems to accelerate progressively upward (at the end of the book, chapter 10 will offer insights one can extract from this observation).

Figure 2.2 shows the daily close quotes of the DJIA from January 2, 1980 until December 31, 1987. This time period corresponds to a magnification of the interval bracketed by the two vertical lines in Figure 2.1. While Figure 2.2 shows only eight years of data compared to the 210 years of data of figure 2.1, the two figures are strikingly similar. Some caution must be exercised, however, as the scales used in the two figures are different (logarithmic scale for the ordinate of Figure 2.1 vs. linear scale for Figure 2.2). We shall perform a detailed comparison in chapters 7 and 10 of the information provided by these two kinds of plots.

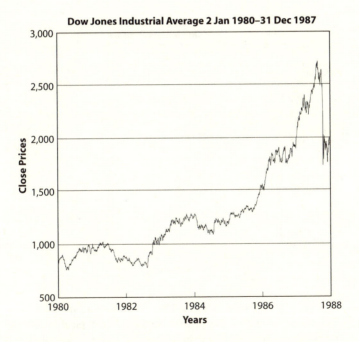

FIG. 2.2. Daily quotes of the Dow Jones Industrial Average from January 2, 1980 until December 31, 1987. This time period corresponds to a magnification of the interval bracketed by the two vertical lines in Figure 2.1.

RETURN TRAJECTORIES

Figures 2.3, 2.4, and 2.5 show three time series of returns, rather than the prices themselves, at three very different time scales: the time scale of minutes over a full day of trading, the time scale of days over eight years of trading, and the time scale of months over more than two centuries of trading. For comparison, Figure 2.6 is obtained by randomly tossing coins, that is, by choosing at random a positive or negative return with a probability given by the Gaussian bell curve with an average return amplitude (standard deviation) equal to 1%. Real returns exhibit much larger variability and clustering of variability compared to the artificial time series.

What are returns? If your wealth is 100 today, with an interest rate of 5% per year, it will transform into 105 after one year, since $(105 - 100)/100 = 5\%$. The one-year return is then equal to $(105 - 100)/100 = 5\%$; that is, it is equal to the interest rate. More generally, the return derived from an asset whose price changed from $p(t)$ at time t to $p(t + dt)$

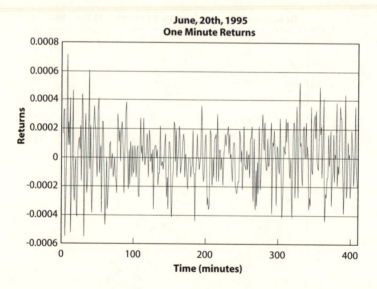

FIG. 2.3. Minute by minute returns of the S&P 500 index on June 20, 1995 showing the highly stochastic nature of the price dynamics. The typical amplitude of the return fluctuations is large at the beginning of the day, when traders place orders and discover the price dynamics (mood?) of the day. The fluctuations go through a low around noon and then increase again at the end of the day, when trading increases due to the action of strategies trading at the close.

Dow Jones Index Returns Jan. 2nd 1980–Dec.31st 1987

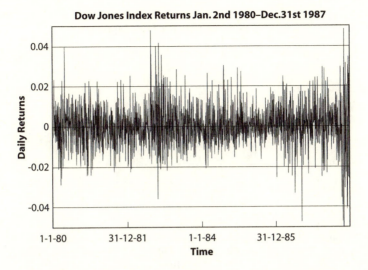

FIG. 2.4. Daily returns of the DJIA from January 2, 1980 until December 31, 1987. The running sum of these series gives approximately the price trajectory shown in Figure 2.2. Notice the large returns, both positive and negative, associated with the crash of October 1987. The largest negative daily return (the crash) reached -22.6% on October 19, 1987. The largest positive return (the rebound after the crash) reached $+9.7\%$ on October 21, 1987. Both are completely off-scale.

at time $t + dt$ is $(p(t + dt) - p(t))/p(t)$. Continuously compounding interest rates amounts to replacing $(p(t + dt) - p(t))/p(t)$ by the so-called logarithmic return $\ln[p(t + dt)/p(t)]$. In the previous example, $(p(t + dt) - p(t))/p(t) = 5\%$, compared to $\ln[p(t + dt)/p(t)] = \ln(105/100) = 4.88\%$. Notice that the two ways of calculating the return give approximately the same results (5% compared to 4.88%) but not exactly the same result: the logarithmic return is smaller since you need a smaller return to obtain the same total capital at the end of the investment period, if the generated interest is continuously reinvested rather than, say, reinvested annually. Indeed, the interest itself generates interest, which generates interest, and so forth.

It is striking how both randomness and patterns seem to coexist in these time series. Figures 2.3, 2.4, and 2.5 show the pervasive variability of prices at all time scales. These variations are the "pulsations" of the stock market, the result of investors' actions. They are fascinating with their spontaneous motion and they give an appearance of life, akin to the complexity of the world around us. They condition the future return of our investment. The price trajectories seen in Figures 2.1 and 2.2 as

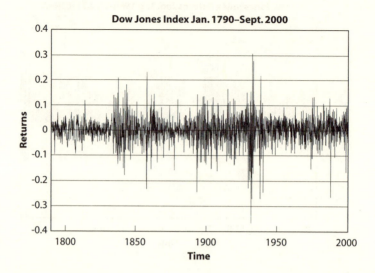

FIG. 2.5. Monthly returns of the DJIA from January 1790 until September 2000. The running sum of these series gives approximately the price trajectory shown in Figure 2.1. Notice the large returns, both positive and negative, associated with the crashes of October 1929 and of October 1987.

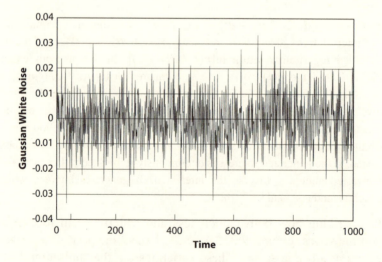

FIG. 2.6. Gaussian white noise time series with a standard deviation of 1% constructed using a random number generator. The running sum of these numbers define a random walk as defined in the text (see Figure 2.9).

well as the returns shown in Figures 2.3, 2.4, and 2.5 have both an aesthetic and an almost mystical appeal, with their delicate balance between randomness and apparent order. The many kinds of structures observed on stock price trajectories, such as trends, cycles, booms, and bursts, have been the object of extensive analysis by the scientists of the social and financial fields as well as by professional analysts and traders. The work of the latter category of analysts has led to a fantastic lexicon of these patterns with colorful names, such as "head and shoulder," "double-bottom," "hanging-man lines," "the morning star," "Elliott waves," and so on (see, for instance, [316]).

Investments in the stock market are based on a quite straightforward rule: if you expect the market to go up in the future, you should buy (this is referred to as being "long" in the market) and hold the stock until you expect the trend to change direction; if you expect the market to go down, you should stay out of it, sell if you can (this is referred to as being "short" of the market) by borrowing a stock and giving it back later by buying it at a smaller price in the future. It is difficult, to say the least, to predict future directions of stock market prices even if we are considering time scales of the order of decades, for which one could hope for a negligible influence of "noise." To illustrate this, even the widely cited "fact" that in the United States there has been no thirty-year period over which stocks underperformed bonds turns out to be incorrect for the period from 1831 to 1861 [378]. If one chooses ten- or twenty-years periods, the conclusions are much more murky and the evidence that stocks always outperform bonds over long time intervals does not exist [375]. The point in comparing stocks and bonds is that bonds are so-called fixed-income and ensure the capital (in denominated currency but not in real value if there is inflation) as well as a fixed return. Bonds thus provide a kind of anchor or benchmark against which to compare the highly volatile stocks.

RETURN DISTRIBUTIONS AND RETURN CORRELATION

To decide whether to buy or sell, it seems useful to try to understand the origin of the price changes, whether prices will go up or down, and when; more generally, what are the properties of price changes that can help us guess the future? Two characteristics among many have attracted attention: the distribution of price variations (or of price returns) and the correlation between successive price variations (or returns).

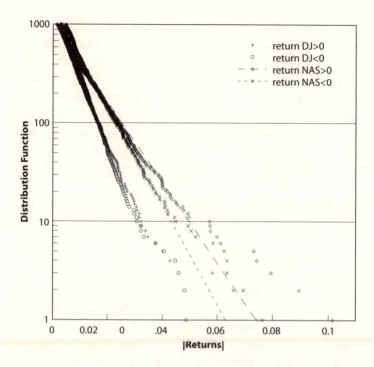

FIG. 2.7. Distribution of daily returns for the DJIA and the Nasdaq index for the period January 2, 1990 until September 29, 2000. The distributions shown here give, by definition, the number of times a return larger than or equal to a chosen value on the abscissa has been observed from January 2, 1990 till 29 September 2000. The distributions are thus a measure of relative frequency of the different observed returns. The lines corresponds to fits of the data by models discussed in the text.

Figure 2.7 shows the distribution of daily returns of the DJIA and of the Nasdaq index for the period January 2, 1990 until September 29, 2000. The ordinate gives the number of times a given return larger than a value read on the abscissa has been observed. For instance, we read on Figure 2.7 that five negative and five positive daily DJIA market returns larger than or equal to 4% have occurred. In comparison, fifteen negative and twenty positive returns larger than or equal to 4% have occurred for the Nasdaq index. The larger fluctuations of returns of the Nasdaq compared to the DJIA are also quantified by the so-called volatility, equal to 1.6% (respectively, 1.4%) for positive (respectively, negative) returns of the DJIA, and equal to 2.5% (respectively, 2.0%) for positive (respectively, negative) returns of the Nasdaq index. The lines shown in Figure 2.7 correspond to representing the data by a so-called exponential. The upward convexity of the trajectories defined by the symbols for the

Nasdaq qualifies a so-called stretched exponential model [253], which embodies the fact that the tail of the distribution is "fatter"; that is, there are larger risks of large drops (as well as ups) in the Nasdaq compared to the DJIA.

What is the Nasdaq composite index? In 1961, in an effort to improve overall regulation of the securities industry, The Congress of the United States asked the U.S. Securities and Exchange Commission (SEC) to conduct a special study of all securities markets. In 1963, the SEC released the completed study, in which it characterized the over-the-counter (OTC) securities market as fragmented and obscure. The SEC proposed a solution—automation—and charged The National Association of Securities Dealers, Inc. (NASD) with its implementation. In 1968, construction began on the automated OTC securities system, then known as the National Association of Securities Dealers Automated Quotation, or "NASDAQ" System. In 1971, Nasdaq celebrated its first official trading day on February 8. This was the first day of operation for the completed NASDAQ automated system, which displayed median quotes for more than 2,500 OTC securities. In 1990, Nasdaq formally changed its name to the Nasdaq Stock Market. In 1994, the Nasdaq Stock Market surpassed the New York Stock Exchange in annual share volume. In 1998, the merger between the NASD and the AMEX created The Nasdaq-AMEX Market Group.

Figure 2.8 shows the minute per minute time correlation function of the returns of the Standard & Poors 500 futures for a single day, June 20, 1995, whose time series is shown in Figure 2.3. The correlation function at time lag τ is nothing but a statistical measure of the strength with which the present price return resembles the price return at τ time steps in the past. In other words, it quantifies how the future can be predicted from the knowledge of a single measure of the past, as we show in the following technical inset. The sum of the correlation function over all possible time lags (from 1 to infinity) is simply proportional to the number of occurrences when future returns will be close to the present return for reasons other than pure chance. A correlation function that is zero for all nonzero time lags implies that returns are random, as in a fair dice game. A correlation of 1 corresponds to perfect correlation, which is found only for the return at a given time with itself. (We should remark, however, that a zero-correlation function does not rule out completely the possibility of predicting future prices to some degree, since other quantities constructed using at least three returns [corresponding to

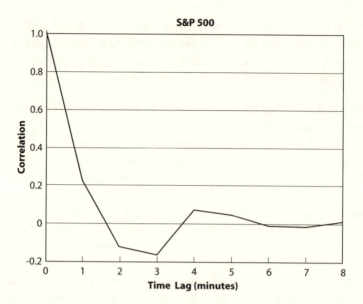

FIG. 2.8. Correlation function of the returns at the minute time scale of the Standard & Poors 500 futures for a single day, June 20, 1995, whose time series is shown in Figure 2.3. Note the fast decay to zero of the correlations over a few minutes with a few oscillations. This curve shows that there is a persistence of a price move lasting a little more than one minute. After two minutes, the price tends to reverse with a clear anticorrelation (negative correlation) corresponding to a kind of price reversal. Beyond, the correlation is indistinguishable from noise.

so-called "nonlinear" correlations] may better capture the price dynamics. However, such dependence is much harder to detect, establish, and use [see chapter 3].) As we see in Figure 2.8, the correlation function is nonzero only for very short time scales, typically of the order of a few minutes. This means that, beyond a few minutes, future price variations cannot be predicted by simple (linear) extrapolations of the past.

Trading strategy to exploit correlations. The reason why, in very liquid markets of equities and foreign exchanges, for instance, correlations of returns are extremely small is because any significant correlation would lead to an arbitrage opportunity that is rapidly exploited and thus washed out. Indeed, the fact that there are almost no correlations between price variations in liquid markets can be understood from the following simple calculation [50, 348]. Consider a return r that occurred at time t and a return r' that occurred at a later time t', where t and t' are multiples of some time unit (say 5 minutes). r and r' can each be decomposed into an average contribution and a varying part. We are interested in quantifying the correlation $C(t, t')$ between the uncertain varying part, which is defined as the average of the product of the varying part of r and of r' normalized by the variance (volatility) of the returns, so that $C(t, t' = t) = 1$ (perfect correlation between r and itself). A simple mathematical calculation shows that the best linear predictor m_t for the return at time t, knowing the past history $r_{t-1}, r_{t-2}, \ldots, r_i, \ldots$, is given by

$$m_t \equiv \frac{1}{B(t, t)} \sum_{i < t} B(i, t) r_i, \tag{1}$$

where each $B(i, t)$ is a factor that can be expressed in terms of the correlation coefficient $C(t', t)$ and is usually called the coefficient (i, t) of the inverse correlation matrix. This formula (1) expresses that each past return r_i impacts on the future return r_t in proportion to its value with a coefficient $B(i, t)/B(t, t)$ which is nonzero only if there is nonzero correlation between time i and time t. With this formula (1), you have the best linear predictor in the sense that it will minimize the errors in variance. Armed with this prediction, you have a powerful trading strategy: buy if $m_t > 0$ (expected future price increase) and sell if $m_t < 0$ (expected future price decrease).

Let us consider the limit where only $B(t, t)$ and $B(t, t-1)$ are nonzero and the natural waiting time between transactions is approximately equal to the correlation time taken as the time unit, again equal to five minutes in this exercise. The point is that you don't want to trade too much, otherwise you will have to pay for significant transaction costs. The average return over one correlation time that you will make using this strategy is of the order of the typical amplitude of the return over these five minutes, say 0.03% (to account for imperfections in the prediction skills, we take a somewhat more conservative measure than the scale of 0.04% over one minute used before). Over a day, this gives an average gain of 0.59%, which accrues to 435% per year when return is reinvested, or 150% without reinvestment! Such small correlations would lead to substantial profits if transaction costs and other friction phenomena like slippage did not exist (slippage refers to the fact that market orders are not always executed at the order price due to limited liquidity and finite human execution time). It is clear that a transaction cost as small as 0.03%, or $3 per $10,000 invested is enough to destroy the expected gain of this strategy. The conundrum is that you cannot trade at a slower rate in order to reduce the transaction costs because, if you do so, you lose your prediction skill based on correlations only present within a five minute time horizon. We can conclude that the residual correlations are those little enough not to be profitable by strategies such as those described above due to "imperfect" market conditions. In other words, the liquidity and efficiency of markets control the degree of correlation that is compatible with a near absence of arbitrage opportunity.

THE EFFICIENT MARKET HYPOTHESIS AND THE RANDOM WALK

Such observations have been made for a long time. A pillar of modern finance is the 1900 Ph.D. thesis dissertation of Louis Bachelier, in Paris, and his subsequent work, especially in 1906 and 1913 [25]. To account for the apparent erratic motion of stock market prices, he proposed that price trajectories are identical to random walks.

THE RANDOM WALK

The concept of a random walk is simple but rich for its many applications, not only in finance but also in physics and the description of natural phenomena. It is arguably one of the most important founding concepts in modern physics as well as in finance, as it underlies the theories of elementary particles, which are the building blocks of our universe, as well as those describing the complex organization of matter around us. In its most simple version, you toss a coin and walk one step up if heads and one step down if tails. Repeating the toss many times, where will you finally end up standing? The answer is multiple: on average, you remain at the same position since the average of one step down and one step up is equivalent to no move. However, it is clear that there are fluctuations around this zero average, which grow with the number of tosses. This is shown in Figure 2.9, where the trajectory of a synthetic random market price has been simulated by tossing "computer coins" to decide whether to make the price go up or go down. In this simulation, the steps or increments have random signs and have amplitudes distributed according to the so-called Gaussian distribution, the well-known bell curve.

To the eye, it is rather difficult to see the difference between the synthetic and typical price trajectories such as those in Figures 1.7–1.8, except at the time of the crash leading to jumps or when there is a strong market trend or acceleration as in Figures 2.1 and 2.2. This is bad news

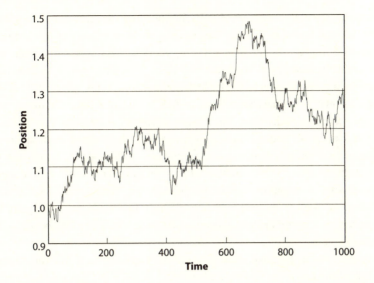

FIG. 2.9. Synthetic random market price (or position of the random walk) obtained by tossing "computer coins" to decide whether to make the price go up or down. In this simulation, the steps or increments have random signs and have amplitudes distributed according to the so-called Gaussian distribution with a 1% standard deviation. The same increments as in Figure 2.6 have been used: the synthetic price trajectory observed here is thus nothing but the running sum of the increments shown in Figure 2.6.

for investment targets: if the price variations are really like tossing coins at random, it seems impossible to know what the direction of the price will be between today and tomorrow, or between any two other times.

A qualifying scaling property of random walks. To get a more quantitative feeling for how well the random walk model can constitute a good model of stock market prices, consider Figures 2.3, 2.4, and 2.5 of return time series at three very different time scales (minute, day, and month). The most important prediction of the random walk model is that the square of the fluctuations of its position should increase in proportion to the time scale. This is equivalent to saying that the typical amplitude of its position is proportional to the square root of the time scale. This means that, for instance, if we look at returns over four minute intervals, the typical return amplitude should be twice (and not four times) that at the minute time scale. This result is subtle and profound: since a random walker has the same probability of making a positive or negative step, on average his position remains where he started. However, it is intuitive that, as he accumulates steps randomly, his position deviates from the exact average, and the longer the time, the larger the deviation of his position from the origin. Rather than cruising at a constant speed such that his position increases proportionally with time, a random walker describes an erratic motion in which the typical fluctuations of his position increase more slowly than linearly in time, in fact at the square root of time. This slow increase results from the many retracings of his steps upward and downward at all scales. Since steps have random ± signs, their square is always positive and thus the sum of squares of the steps is increasing in proportion to the number of steps, that is to time. Due to the randomness in the sign of steps, the square of the total displacement is equal to the sum of squares of the steps. Hence we have the result that the square of the typical amplitude of the fluctuations in a random walk increases in proportion to time.

Let us see if this prediction is borne out from the data. The underlying idea of this test is that a return at the daily scale is the sum of the returns over all the minutes constituting the day. Similarly, a monthly return is the sum of the daily returns over all the days of this given month. Since the returns are close to random steps, the previously discussed "square-root" law should apply. To test it, we observe in Figure 2.3 that the typical amplitude of the returns at the time scale of 1 minute is about 0.04% (this is the ordinate of the level of the majority of the values). In Figure 2.4, by the same estimate made by visual inspection, we estimate a typical amplitude of the return fluctuations of about 1%. Now, 1% divided by 0.04% is 25, which is quite close to the square root 20.25 of the number of minutes in a trading day (typically 410). Similarly, we estimate from Figure 2.5 that the typical amplitude of the return fluctuations at the monthly scale is about 5%. The ratio of the monthly value 5% by the daily value of 1% equal to 5 is not far from the square root of the number of trading days in a month, typically equal to 20–24. The random walk model thus explains quite well the way typical returns in the stock market change with time and with time scale. However, it does not explain the large fluctuations that are not "typical," as can be seen in Figures 2.4 and 2.5.

The concept that price variations are inherently unpredictable has been generalized and extended by the famous economist and Nobel prize winner Paul Samuelson [357, 358]. In a nutshell, Bachelier [25] and Samuelson and an army of economists after them have observed that even the best investors on average seem to find it hard *in the long run* to do better than the comprehensive common-stock averages, such as the Standard & Poors 500, or even better than a random selection among stocks of comparable variability. It thus seems as if relative price changes (properly adjusted for expected dividends paid out) are practically indistinguishable from random numbers, drawn from a coin-tossing computer or a roulette. The belief is that this randomness is achieved through the active participation of many investors seeking greater wealth. This crowd of investors actively analyze all the information at their disposal and form investment decisions based on them. As a consequence, Bachelier and Samuelson argued that any advantageous information that may lead to a profit opportunity is quickly eliminated by the feedback that their action has on the price. Their point is that the price variations in time are not independent of the actions of the traders; on the contrary, it results from them. If such feedback action occurs instantaneously, as in an idealized world of idealized "frictionless" markets and costless trading, then prices must always fully reflect all available information and no profits can be garnered from information-based trading (because such profits have already been captured). This fundamental concept introduced by Bachelier, now called "the efficient market hypothesis," has a strong counterintuitive and seemingly contradictory flavor to it: the more active and efficient the market, the more intelligent and hard working the investors; as a consequence the more random is the sequence of price changes generated by such a market. The most efficient market of all is one in which price changes are completely random and unpredictable.

There is an interesting analogy with the information coded in DNA, the molecular building block of our chromosomes. Here, our genetic information is encoded by the order in which the four constituent bases of DNA are positioned along a DNA strand, similarly to words using a four-letter alphabet. DNA is usually organized in so-called coding sections and noncoding sections. The coding sections contain the information on how to synthetize proteins and how to work all our biological machinery. Recent detailed analyses of the sequence of these letters have shown [444, 286, 14] that the noncoding parts of DNA seem to have long-range correlations while, in contrast, the coding regions seem to have short-range or no correlations. Notice the wonderful paradox: information leads to randomness, while lack of information leads to regularities. The reason for this is that a coding region must appear random since all bases contain useful, that is, different information. If there were some correlation, it would mean that it is possible to encode the information in fewer bases and the coding regions would not be optimal. In contrast, noncoding regions contain few or no information and can thus be highly correlated. Indeed, there is almost no information in a sequence like 1111111 ... but there may be a lot in 429976545782 .... This paradox, that a message with a lot of information should be uncorrelated while a message with no information is highly correlated, is at the basis of the notion of random sequences. A truly random sequence of numbers or of symbols is one that contains the maximum possible information; in other words, it is not possible to define a shorter algorithm that contains the same information [73]. The condition for this is that the sequence be completely uncorrelated so that each new term carries new information.

It is worthwhile to stop and consider in more detail this extraordinary concept, that the more intelligent and hard working the investors, the more random is the sequence of price changes generated by such a market. In particular, it embodies the fundamental difference between financial markets and the natural world. The latter is open to the scrutiny of the observer and the scientist has the possibility to construct explanations and theories that are independent of his or her actions. In contrast, in social and financial systems, the actors are both the observers and the observed, which thus create so-called feedback loops. The following simple parable is a useful illustration.

A PARABLE: HOW INFORMATION IS INCORPORATED IN PRICES, THUS DESTROYING POTENTIAL "FREE LUNCHES"

Let us assume that half the population of investors are informed today that the price will go up tomorrow from its present value p_0, naturally not with complete certainty, but still with a rather high probability of 75% (there is therefore a 25% probability that the price goes down tomorrow). The other half of the population is kept uninformed and we shall call them the "noise traders," after the famous description by Black [40] of the individuals who trade on what they think is information but is in fact merely noise. These noise traders will buy and sell on grounds that are unrelated to the movements of the market, although they believe the "information" they have is relevant. For noise traders, selling may be triggered by a need for cash for reasons completely unrelated to the market. We capture this behavior by tossing coins at random to decide the fraction y of noise traders who want to sell. Correspondingly, the fraction of noise traders who want to buy is $1 - y$. The important point is that noise traders are insensitive, by definition, to the present price or to the price offered for the transaction.

In contrast, the informed traders want to buy because they see an opportunity for profit with a high success rate—as high as 3 out of 4. In order to buy, they have to make a bid to a central agent, the "market maker." The role of the market maker is to compile all buy and sell offers and to adjust the price so that the maximum number of transactions can be satisfied. This is a form of balance between supply and demand.

However, informed traders will not buy at any price because they will use their special information to estimate what will be their expected gain. If the price at which they are offered to buy by the market maker is larger than their expectation for the price increase, they will not have an incentive to buy. We call $\langle \delta p_+ \rangle$ the expected gain conditioned on the realization of the tip (i.e., that the price will increase). The fraction of informed traders still willing to buy at a price x above the last quoted price p_0 is clearly a decreasing function of x. Two limits are simple to guess: for $x = 0$, all the informed traders want to buy at price p_0 because the expected gain is positive. In contrast, for x equal to $\langle \delta p_+ \rangle$ or larger, the offered buy price is larger than the price expected tomorrow on the basis of the prediction, and none of the informed traders wish to buy due to the unfavorable probability of a loss. In between, we will for simplicity assume a linear relationship fixing the fraction of informed traders willing to buy at the price $p_0 + x$, which interpolates smoothly between these two extremes, as shown in Figure 2.10.

The decision of the informed traders depends on the noise traders. We assume for simplicity that each seller (respectively, buyer) sells (buys) only one stock. Then two situations can occur.

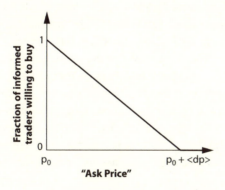

FIG. 2.10. Fraction of informed traders who are willing to buy as a function of the "ask price": if the ask price is the last quote p_0, all the informed traders want to bid for the stock because their expected return is positive. If the ask price is equal to or larger than the last quote plus the expected increase, informed traders are not interested in bidding for the stock. This dependence corresponds to so-called "risk-neutral" agents.

- If the fraction y of noise traders who sell is less than $1/2$, there is a severe undersupply of stocks: both the fraction $1 - y > 1/2$ of noise traders and all the informed traders want to buy. The selling noise traders cannot even supply enough stocks for their buying counterparts, not to mention to the aggressive informed traders. In this situation, the market maker increases the price up to the level at which informed traders turn down the buying offer. For the noise traders, the price does not make a difference since they have no information on what the future price will be. In this situation, where $y < 1/2$, the transaction price therefore is equal to the minimum price $p_0 + \langle \delta p_+ \rangle$ at which all informed traders turn down the buying option. There is no average profit from selling later at the expected future price $p_0 + \langle \delta p_+ \rangle$, since it equals the buying price! Note in contrast that, in the absence of informed traders, the profit opportunity would remain, as the buying price is unchanged at p_0. It is *the presence* of the informed traders that pushes the price up to the threshold where they do not wish to act. While the informed traders do not appear explicitly in this transaction, their bid to the market maker has pushed the price up, such that the profit opportunity has disappeared.

- The second situation occurs when the fraction y of noise traders who sell is larger than $1/2$. They can then supply all their buying counterparts as well as a fraction of the informed traders. The price of the transaction $p_0 + x$ is then set by the market maker such that the fraction of the informed traders willing to buy at this price is equal to the remaining available stock after the buying noise traders have been served. Counting all possible outcomes for y larger than $1/2$ (but of course smaller than 1), we see that the average of y, conditioned to be larger than $1/2$, is $3/4$, the middle point between $1/2$ and 1. Thus, the average transaction price is $1/2$ the expected conditional gain $\langle \delta p_+ \rangle$ ($x = \langle \delta p_+ \rangle / 2$), such that $1/2$ of the informed traders are still willing to buy. In this situation, the balance of supply and demand is upheld: the average fraction, $3/4$, of noise traders who sell balances exactly the other $1/4$ of buying noise traders and the $1/2$ of the informed traders.

What, then, is the expected gain for the informed traders? It is (the probability $3/4$ that the price increases) times (the average gain $\langle \delta p_+ \rangle$ − x) minus (the probability $1/4$ that the price decreases) times (the loss amplitude). This loss amplitude is x minus the expected amplitude of the price drop, conditioned on its drop. By symmetry of the distribution of price variations (very well verified in most stock markets), this is the same in amplitude as the expected conditional gain $\langle \delta p_+ \rangle$. In sum, the total expected gain is

$$(3/4) \times ((\langle \delta p_+ \rangle) - x) - (1/4)((\langle \delta p_+ \rangle) + x). \qquad (2)$$

Using the above result, $x = \langle \delta p_+ \rangle/2$, we find that this is in fact zero: the action of the noise traders and the response of the informed traders to them and to their information makes the buying price increase to a level $p_0 + x$ such that the expected gain vanishes!

Prices Are Unpredictable, or Are They?

This conclusion remains qualitatively robust against a change of the value of the parameters of this toy model or of the buying strategies developed by the informed traders. This simple model illustrates the following fundamental ideas.

1. Acting on advantageous information moves the price such that the a priori gain is decreased or even destroyed by the feedback of the action on the price. This makes concrete the concept that prices are made random by the intelligent and informed actions of investors, as put forward by Bachelier, Samuelson, and many others. In contrast, without informed traders, the profit opportunity remains, since the buying price is unchanged at p_0.

2. Noise traders are essential for the function of the stock market. They are known under many names: sometimes as speculators, or traders basing their strategies on technical indicators or on supposedly relevant economic information. All informed traders in our example agree that the best strategy is to buy. However, in the absence of noise traders, they would not find any counterpart, and there would be no trade: If everybody agrees on the price, why trade? No profit can be made. Thus the stock market needs the existence of some "noise," however small, which provides "liquidity." Then, the intelligent traders work hard and, according to this theory, will by their investments make the market totally and utterly noisy, with no remaining piece of intelligible signal.

3. The fact that the informed traders are unable on average to make a profit notwithstanding their large confidence in an upward move is not in contradiction with the notion that, if you alone had this information and were willing to be cautious and trade only a few stocks, you would on average be able to make a good profit. The reason is simply that

your small action would not have a significant impact on the market. In contrast, if you were bold enough to borrow a lot and buy a significant share of the market, you would move the price up, in a way similar to the informed traders who constitute half of the total population. Thus, the price dynamics becomes random only if there are sufficiently many informed traders to affect the dynamics by their active feedback.

General proof that properly anticipated prices are random. Samuelson has proved a general theorem showing that the concept that prices are unpredictable can actually be deduced rigorously [357] from a model that hypothesizes that a stock's present price p_t is set at the expected discounted value of its future dividends $d_t, d_{t+1}, d_{t+2}, \ldots$ (which are supposed to be random variables generated according to any general (but known) stochastic process):

$$p_t = d_t + \delta_1 d_{t+1} + \delta_1 \delta_2 d_{t+2} + \delta_1 \delta_2 \delta_3 d_{t+3} + \cdots , \qquad (3)$$

where the factors $\delta_i = 1 - r < 1$, which can fluctuate from one time period to the next, account for the depreciation of a future price calculated at present due to the nonzero consumption price index r. We see that $p_t = d_t + \delta_1 p_{t+1}$, and thus the expectation $E(p_{t+1})$ of p_{t+1} conditioned on the knowledge of the present price p_t is

$$E(p_{t+1}) = \frac{p_t - d_t}{\delta_1} . \qquad (4)$$

This shows that, barring the drift due to the inflation and the dividend, the price increment does not have a systematic component or memory of the past and is thus random. Therefore, even when the economy is not free to wander randomly, intelligent speculation is able to transform the observed stock-price changes into a random process.

At first glance, these ideas seem to be confirmed by the data. As shown in Figure 2.7, the distributions of positive and negative returns are almost identical: there is almost the same probability for a price increase or a decrease. In addition, Figure 2.8 has taught us that returns are essentially decorrelated beyond a few minutes in active and well-organized markets. As a consequence, successive returns cannot be predicted by linear extrapolations of the past.

However, as already noted, this does not exclude the possibility that there might be other kinds of dependence between price variations of a more subtle nature, which might remain either because they have not yet been detected or taken advantage of by traders or because they are not providing significant profit opportunities.

Asymmetry between positive and negative returns. The distribution of price variations may often exhibit a residual bias associated with the overall rate of return of the market. For instance, for a 10% annual return, this corresponds to an average daily drift of approximately $10\%/365 = 0.03\%$. This value is small compared to the typical scale of daily fluctuations of the order of 1% for most markets (and more for growth and emergent markets which present a larger volatility). Such a drift translates into a bias in the frequency of gains versus losses. For the DJIA from 1897 to 1997, over the 27,819 trading days, the market declined on 13,091 days and rose on 14,559 days. This translates into a 47.06% probability of a decline and a 52.34% probability of a stock market rise (the probabilities do not sum up to 1 because there were some days for which the price remained unchanged). In a similar fashion, the decline probability is 47.27% during the 1946–1997 DJIA period and 46.86% during 1897–1945 (about 0.5% lower). Preserving the same qualitative pattern, during the 1897–1997 DJIA period, the weekly decline (rise) probability is 43.98% (55.87%). For the Nasdaq from 1962 to 1995, the daily decline (rise) probability is 46.92% (52.52%). For the IBM stock from 1962–1996, the daily decline (rise) probability is 47.96% (48.25%).

RISK–RETURN TRADE-OFF

One of the central insights of modern financial economics is the necessity of some trade-off between risk and expected return, and although Samuelson's version of the efficient markets hypothesis places a restriction on expected returns, it does not account for risk in any way. In particular, if a security's expected price change is positive, it may be just the reward needed to attract investors to hold the asset and bear the associated risks. Indeed, if an investor is sufficiently risk averse, he might gladly pay to avoid holding a security that has unforecastable returns.

Lo and MacKinlay [464] discuss this issue in the following terms:

Grossman and Stiglitz [180] went even further. They argue that perfectly informationally, efficient markets are an impossibility, for if markets are perfectly efficient, the return on gathering information is nil, in which case there would be little reason to trade and markets would eventually collapse. Alternatively, the degree of market inefficiency determines the effort investors are willing to expend to gather and trade on information, hence a nondegenerate market equilibrium will arise only when there are sufficient profit opportunities, that is, inefficiencies, to compensate investors for the costs of trading and information-gathering. The profits earned by these industrious investors may be viewed as economic rents that accrue to those willing to engage in such activities. Who are the providers of these rents? Black [40] gave us a provocative answer: noise traders, individuals who trade on what they think is information but is in fact merely noise. More generally, at any time there are always investors who trade for reasons other than information (for example, those with unexpected liquidity needs), and these investors are willing to "pay up" for the privilege of executing their trades immediately.

CHAPTER 3

FINANCIAL CRASHES ARE "OUTLIERS"

In the spirit of Bacon in *Novum Organum* about 400 years ago, "Errors of Nature, Sports and Monsters correct the understanding in regard to ordinary things, and reveal general forms. For whoever knows the ways of Nature will more easily notice her deviations; and, on the other hand, whoever knows her deviations will more accurately describe her ways," we propose in this chapter that large market drops are "outliers" and that they reveal fundamental properties of the stock market.

WHAT ARE "ABNORMAL" RETURNS?

Stock markets can exhibit very large motions, such as rallies and crashes, as shown in Figures 2.4 and 2.5. Should we expect these extreme variations? Or should we consider them anomalous?

Abnormality is a relative notion, constrasted to what is considered "normal." Let us take an example. In the Bachelier-Samuelson financial world, in which returns are distributed according the Gaussian bell-shape distribution, all returns are scaled to a fundamental "ruler" called the standard deviation. Consider the daily time scale and the corresponding time series of returns of the Dow Jones index shown in Figure 2.4. As we indicated in chapter 2, the standard deviation is close to 1%. In this Gaussian world, it is easy to quantify the probability of observing a given

TABLE 3.1

X	Probability$_>$	One in N events	Calendar waiting time
1	0.317	3	3 days
2	0.045	22	1 month
3	0.0027	370	1.5 year
4	6.3×10^{-5}	15,787	63 years
5	5.7×10^{-7}	1.7×10^6	7 millenia
6	2.0×10^{-9}	5.1×10^8	2 million years
7	2.6×10^{-12}	3.9×10^{11}	1562 million years
8	1.2×10^{-15}	8.0×10^{14}	3 trillion years
9	2.3×10^{-19}	4.4×10^{18}	17,721 trillion years
10	1.5×10^{-23}	6.6×10^{22}	260 million trillion years

How probable is it to observe a return larger in amplitude (i.e., in absolute value) than some value equal to X times the standard deviation? The answer is given in this table for the Gaussian world. The left column gives the list of values of X from 1 to 10. The second column gives the probability that the absolute value of the return is found larger than X times the standard deviation. The third column translated this probability into the number of periods (days in our example) one would typically need to wait to witness such a return amplitude. The fourth column translates this waiting time into calendar time in units adapted to the value, using the conversion that one month contains approximately 20 trading days and one year contains about 250 trading days. For comparison, the age of the universe is believed to be (only) of the order of 10–15 billion years.

return amplitude, as shown in Table 3.1. We read that a daily return amplitude of more than 3% should be typically observed only once in 1.5 years. A daily return amplitude of more than 4% should be typically observed only once in 63 years, while a return amplitude of more than 5% should never be seen in our limited history.

Armed with this Table 3.1, it is now quite clear what is "normal" and what can be considered "abnormal" according to the Gaussian model. The drop of −22.6% on October 19, 1987 and the rebound of +9.7% on October 21, 1987 are abnormal: they should not occur according to the standard Gaussian model. They are essentially impossible. The fact that they occurred tells us that the market can deviate significantly from the norm. When it does, the "monster" events that the market creates are "outliers." In other words, they lie "out" and beyond what is possible for the rest of the population of returns.

In reality, the distributions of returns are not Gaussian, as shown in Figure 2.7. If they were, they would appear as inverted parabola in this semilogarithmic plot. The approximate linear dependence qualifies rather as a dependence not far from an exponential law. In this new improved representation, we can again calculate the probability of observing a return amplitude larger than, say, 10 standard deviations (10% in our example). The result is 0.000045, which corresponds to one event in 22,026 days, or in 88 years. The rebound of October 20, 1987 becomes less extraordinary. Still, the drop of 22.6% of October 19, 1987 would correspond to one event in 520 million years, which qualifies it as an "outlier."

Thus, according to the exponential model, a 10% return amplitude does not qualify as an "outlier" in a clear-cut and undisputable manner. In addition, we see that our discrimination between normal and abnormal returns depends on our choice for the frequency distribution. Qualifying what is the correct description of the frequency distribution, especially for large positive and negative returns, is a delicate problem that is still a hot domain for research. Due to the lack of certainty on the best choice for the frequency distribution, this approach does not seem the most adequate for characterizing anomalous events.

Up to now, we have only looked at the distribution or frequency of returns. However, the complex time series of returns have many other structures not captured by the frequency distribution. We have already discussed the additional diagnostic in terms of the correlation function shown in Figure 2.8. We now introduce another diagnostic that allows us to characterize abnormal market phases in a much more precise and nonparametric way, that is, without referring to a specific mathematical representation of the frequency distribution.

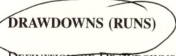

DRAWDOWNS (RUNS)

DEFINITION OF DRAWDOWNS

One measure going beyond the simple frequency statistics and the linear correlations is provided by the statistics of "drawdowns." A drawdown is defined as a persistent decrease in the price over consecutive days. A drawdown, as shown in Figure 3.1, is thus the cumulative loss from the last maximum to the next minimum of the price. Drawdowns are indicators that we care about: they measure directly the cumulative loss that an investment may suffer. They also quantify the worst-case scenario of an investor buying at the local high and selling at the next minimum. It is thus worthwhile to ask if there is

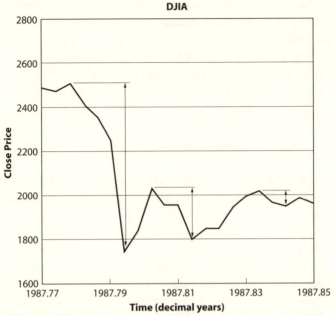

Fig. 3.1. Definition of drawdowns. Taking the example of the crash that occurred on October 19, 1987, this figure shows three drawdowns corresponding to cumulative losses from the last maximum to the next minimum of the price. The largest drawdown of a total loss of −30.7% is made of four successive daily drops: on October 14, 1987 (1987.786 in decimal years), the DJIA index is down by 3.8%; on October 15, the market is down 6.1%; on October 16, the market is down 10.4%. The weekend passes and the drop on Black Monday October 19, 1987 leads to a cumulative loss or drawdown of 30.7%. In terms of consecutive daily losses, this correspond to the series 3.8%, 2.4%, 4.6%, and 22.6% (note that returns are not exactly additive, since they are price variations normalized by the price, which itself varies).

any structure in the distribution of drawdowns absent in that of price variations.

Drawdowns embody a rather subtle dependence since they are constructed from runs of the same sign variations (see below). Their distribution thus capture the way successive drops can influence each other and construct in this way a persistent process. This persistence is not measured by the distribution of returns because, by its very definition, it forgets about the relative positions of the returns as they unravel themselves as a function of time by only counting their frequency. This is also not detected by the two-point correlation function, which measures an *average* linear dependence over the whole time series, while the dependence may only appear at special times, for instance for very large runs, as we shall demonstrate below, a feature that will be washed out by the global averaging procedure.

A nonlinear model with zero correlation but high predictability. To understand better how subtle dependences in successive price variations are measured by drawdowns, let us play the following game in which the price increments $\delta p(t)$ are constructed according to the following rule:

$$\delta p(t) = \epsilon(t) + \epsilon(t-1)\epsilon(t-2), \tag{5}$$

where $\epsilon(t)$ is a white noise process with zero mean and unit variance. For instance, $\epsilon(t)$ is either $+1$ or -1 with probability $1/2$. The definition (5) means that the price variation today is controlled by three random coin tosses, one for today, yesterday, and the preceeding day, such that a positive coin toss today as well as two identical coin tosses yesterday and the day before make the price move up. Reciprocally, a negative coin toss today as well as two different coin tosses yesterday and the day before make the price move down.

It is easy to check that the average $E(\delta p(t))$ as well as the two-point correlation $E(\delta p(t)\delta p(t'))$ for $t \neq t'$ are zero and $\delta p(t)$ is thus also a white noise process. Intuitively, this stems from the fact that an odd number of coin tosses ϵ enter into these diagnostics, whose average is zero $((1/2) \times (+1) + (1/2) \times (-1) = 0)$. However, the three-point correlation function $E(\delta p(t-2)\delta p(t-1)\delta p(t))$ is nonzero and equal to 1 and the expectation of $\delta p(t)$ given the knowledge of the *two* previous increments $\delta p(t-2)$ and $\delta p(t-1)$ is nonzero and equal to $E(\delta p(t)|\delta p(t-2), \delta p(t-1)) = \delta p(t-2)\delta p(t-1)$. This means that it is possible to predict the price variation today with better success than 50%, knowing the price variations of yesterday and the day before!

While the frequency distribution and the two-point correlation function are blind to this dependence structure, the distribution of drawdowns exhibits a specific diagnostic. To simplify the analysis and make the message very clear, let us again restrict to the case where $\epsilon(t)$ can only take two values ± 1. Then, $\delta p(t)$ can take only three values 0 and ± 2, with the correspondence

$$\epsilon(t-2), \epsilon(t-1), \epsilon(t) \quad \rightarrow \quad \delta p(t),$$
$$+++ \quad \rightarrow \quad +2,$$
$$++- \quad \rightarrow \quad 0,$$
$$+-+ \quad \rightarrow \quad 0,$$
$$+-- \quad \rightarrow \quad -2,$$
$$-++ \quad \rightarrow \quad 0,$$
$$-+- \quad \rightarrow \quad -2,$$
$$--+ \quad \rightarrow \quad +2,$$
$$--- \quad \rightarrow \quad 0,$$

where the left column gives the three consecutive values $\epsilon(t-2), \epsilon(t-1), \epsilon(t)$ and the right column is the corresponding price increment $\delta p(t)$. We see directly by this explicit construction that $\delta p(t)$ is a white noise process. However, there is a clear predictability and the distribution of drawdowns reflects it: there are no drawdowns of duration larger than two time steps. Indeed, the worst possible drawdown corresponds to the following sequence for ϵ: $--+--$. This corresponds to the sequence of price increments $+2, -2, -2$, which is either stopped by a $+2$ if the next ϵ is $+$ or by a sequence of 0s interrupted by a $+2$ at the first $\epsilon = +$. While the drawdowns of the process $\epsilon(t)$ can in principle be of infinite duration, the drawdowns of $p(t)$ cannot. This shows that the structure of the process $\delta p(t)$ defined by (5) has a dramatic signature in the distribution of drawdowns in $p(t)$. This illustrates that drawdowns, rather than daily or weekly returns or any other fixed time scale returns, are more adequate time-elastic measures of price moves.

DRAWDOWNS AND THE DETECTION OF "OUTLIERS"

To demonstrate further the new information contained in drawdowns and contrast it with the fixed time-scale returns, let us consider the hypothetical situation of a crash of 30% occurring over three days with three successive losses of exactly 10%. The crash is thus defined as the total

CORRELATION DAILY RETURNS

loss or drawdown of 30%. Rather than looking at drawdowns, let us now follow the common approach and examine the daily data, in particular the daily distribution of returns. The 30% drawdown is now seen as three daily losses of 10%. The essential point to realize is that the construction of the distribution of returns amounts to counting the number of days over which a given return has been observed. The crash will thus contribute to three days of 10% loss, *without* the information that the three losses occurred sequentially! To see what this loss of information entails, we consider a market in which a 10% daily loss occurs typically once every four years (this is not an unreasonable number for the Nasdaq composite index at present times of high volatility). Counting approximately 250 trading days per year, four years correspond to 1,000 trading days and one event in 1,000 days thus corresponds to a probability $1/1,000 = 0.001$ for a daily loss of 10%. The crash of 30% has been dissected as three events that are not very remarkable (each with a relatively short average recurrence time of four years). The plot thickens when we ask, What is, according to this description, the probability for three successive daily losses of 10%? Elementary probability tells us that it is the probability of one daily loss of 10% times the probability of one daily loss of 10% times the probability of one daily loss of 10%. The rule of products of probability holds if the three events are considered to be independent. This products gives $0.001 \times 0.001 \times 0.001 = 0.000,000,001 = 10^{-9}$. This corresponds to one event in 1 billion trading days! We should thus wait typically 4 millions years to witness such an event!

What has gone wrong? Simply, looking at daily returns and at their distributions has destroyed the information that the daily returns may be correlated, at special times! This crash is like a mammoth that has been dissected in pieces without memory of the connection between the parts, and we are left with what look like mouses (bear with the slight exaggeration)! Our estimation that three successive losses of 10% are utterly impossible relied on the incorrect hypothesis that these three events are independent. Independence between successive returns is remarkably well verified most of the time. However, it may be that large drops may not be independent. In other words, there may be "bursts of dependence," that is, "pockets of predictability."

It is clear that drawdowns will keep precisely the information relevant to identifying the possible burst of local dependence leading to possibly extraordinarily large cumulative losses.

EXPECTED DISTRIBUTION OF "NORMAL" DRAWDOWNS

Before returning to the data, we should ask ourselves what can be expected on the basis of the random walk hypothesis. If price variations are independent, positive (+) and negative (−) moves follows each other like the "heads" and "tails" of a fair coin toss. For symmetric distributions of price variations, starting from a positive, +, the probability to have one negative, −, is 1/2. The probability to have two negatives in a row is $1/2 \times 1/2 = 1/4$; the probability to have three negatives in a row is $1/2 \times 1/2 \times 1/2 = 1/8$, and so on. For each additional negative, we observe that the probability is divided by two. This defines the so-called exponential distribution, describing the fact that increasing a drawdown by one time unit makes it doubly less probable. This exponential law is also known as the Poisson law and describes processes without memory: for the sequence $+ - - - -$, the fact that four negatives have occurred in a row does not modify the probability for the new event, which remains 1/2 for both a positive and a negative. Such a memoryless process may seem counterintuitive (many people would rather bet on a tail after a sequence of ten heads than on another head; this is often refered to as the "gambler's fallacy") but it reflects accurately what we mean by complete randomness: in a fair coin toss, it can happen that ten heads in a row are drawn. The eleventh event still has the probability of 1/2 to be head. The absence of memory of such random processes can be stated as follows: given the past observation of n successive negatives, the probability for the next one is unchanged from the unconditional value 1/2 independently of the value of n. Any deviation from this exponential distribution of drawdowns will signal some correlation in the process and thus a potential for a prediction of future events.

Since, in the random memoryless model, there are half as many drawdowns of duration one time step longer, it is convenient to visualize the empirical distribution of drawdowns on the stock market on a logarithmic scale, where the expected exponential distribution of drawdowns becomes a straight line. This is a quite efficient method to test for the validity of the hypothesis: deviations from the straight line will signal some deviation from the exponential distribution and thus from the hypothesis of absence of memory.

The evidence presented below on the presence of "outliers" does not rely on the validity of this Poisson law. Actually, we have identified slight deviations from it already in the bulk of the distribution of drawdowns, suggesting a subtle departure from the hypothesis of independence between successive price returns. This leads us to a quite delicate point that escaped the attention of even some of our cleverest colleagues for some time and is still overlooked by many others. This subtle point is that the evidence for outliers and extreme events does not require and is not even synonymous in general with the existence of a break in the distribution of the drawdowns. Let us illustrate this pictorially and forcefully by borrowing from another domain of active scientific investigation, namely the search for an understanding of the complexity of eddies and vortices in turbulent fluid flows, such as in a mountain river or in atmospheric weather. Since solving the exact equations of these flows does not provide much insight as the results are forbidding, a useful line of attack has been to simplify the problem by studying simple toy models, such as so-called "shell" models of turbulence, that are believed to capture the essential ingredient of these flows, while being amenable to analysis. Such "shell" models replace the three-dimensional spatial domain by a series of uniform onion-like spherical layers with radii increasing as a geometrical series $1, 2, 4, 8, \ldots, 2^n$ and communicating with each other mostly with nearest neighbors.

As for financial returns, a quantity of great interest is the distribution of velocity variations between two instants at the same position or between two points simultaneously. Such a distribution for the square of the velocity variations is shown in Figure 3.2. Notice the approximate exponential drop-off represented by the straight line and the coexistence with larger fluctuations on the right for values above 4 up to 7 and beyond (which are not shown). Usually, such large fluctuations are not considered to be statistically significant and do not provide any specific insight. Here, it can be shown that these large fluctuations of the fluid velocity correspond to intensive peaks propagating coherently over several shell layers with a characteristic bell-like shape, approximately independent of their amplitude and duration (up to a rescaling of their size and duration). When extending the observations to much longer times so that the anomalous fluctuations beyond the value 4 in Figure 3.2 can be sampled much better, one gets the continuous curves (apart from some residual noise always present) shown in Figure 3.3. Here, each of the three curves corresponds to the measurement of a distribution in a given shell layer ($n = 11, 15,$ and 18).

In Figure 3.3, a standard transformation has been performed, that is, contracting or magnifying the abscissa and ordinate for each curve so that the three curves are collapsed on each other. If one succeeds in doing so, this means that, up to a definition of units, the three distributions are identical, which is very helpful for understanding the underlying

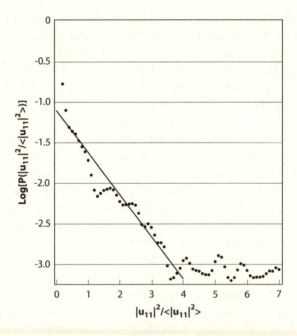

FIG. 3.2. Apparent probability distribution function of the square of the fluid velocity, normalized to its time average, in the eleventh shell of the toy model of hydrodynamic turbulence discussed in the text. The vertical axis is in logarithmic scale
such that the straight line, which helps the eye, qualifies as an apparent exponential
distribution. Note the appearance of extremely sparse and large bursts of velocities at
the extreme right above the extrapolation of the straight line. Reproduced from [252].

mechanism as well as for future use for risk assessement and control.
Naively, we would expect that the same physics apply in each shell layer
and that, as a consequence, the distributions should be the same, up to
a change of unit reflecting the different scale embodied by each layer.
Here, we observe that the three curves are indeed nicely collapsed, but
only for the small velocity fluctuations, while the large fluctuations are
described by very different heavy tails. Alternatively, when one tries to
collapse the curves in the region of the large velocity fluctuations, then
the portions of the curves close to the origin are not collapsed at all and
are very different. The remarkable conclusion is that the distributions
of velocity increment seem to be composed of two regions, a region of
so-called "normal scaling" and a domain of extreme events.

Here is the message that comes out of this discussion: the concept
of outliers and of extreme events does not rest on the requirement that
the distribution should not be smooth, as shown on the right side of

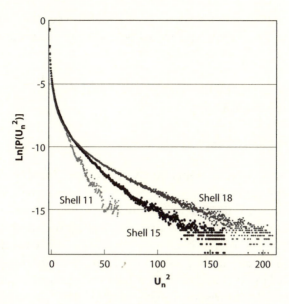

FIG. 3.3. Probability distribution function of the square of the velocity as in Figure 3.2 but for a much longer time series, so that the tail of the distributions for very large fluctuations is much better constrained. The hypothesis that there are no outliers is tested here by "collapsing" the distributions for the three shown layers. While this is a success for small fluctuations, the tails of the distributions for large events are very different, indicating that extreme fluctuations belong to a class of their own, and hence are outliers. The vertical axis is again in logarithmic scale. Reproduced from [252].

Figure 3.2. Noise and the very process of constructing the distribution will almost always smooth out the curves. What is found here [252] is that the distribution is made of two different populations, the body and the tail, which have different physics, different scaling, and different properties. This is a clear demonstration that this model of turbulence exhibits outliers in the sense that there is a well-defined population of very large and quite rare events that punctuate the dynamics and that cannot be seen as scaled-up versions of the small fluctuations. It is tempting to conjecture that the anomalous "scaling" properties of turbulence might be similarly controlled by the coexistence of normal innocuous velocity fluctuations and extreme concentrated events, possibly associated with specific vortex filaments or other coherent structures [371].

As a consequence, the fact that the distribution of small events might show some curvature or continuous behavior does not say anything against the outlier hypothesis. It is essential to keep this point in mind in looking at the evidence presented below for the drawdowns.

DRAWDOWN DISTRIBUTIONS OF STOCK MARKET INDICES

THE DOW JONES INDUSTRIAL AVERAGE

Figure 3.4 shows the distribution of drawdowns for the returns of the DJIA over this century.

The exponential distribution discussed in the previous section has been derived on the assumption that successive price variations are independent. There is a large body of evidence for the correctness of this assumption for most trading days [68]. However, consider, for instance, the fourteen largest drawdowns that have occurred in the DJIA in this century. Their characteristics are presented in Table 3.2. Only three lasted one or two days, whereas nine lasted four days or more. Let us examine in particular the largest drawdown. It started on October 14, 1987 (1987.786 in decimal years), lasted four days, and led to a total loss of −30.7%. This crash is thus a run of four consecutive losses: first day, the index is down by 3.8%; second day, by 6.1%; third day, by 10.4%; and

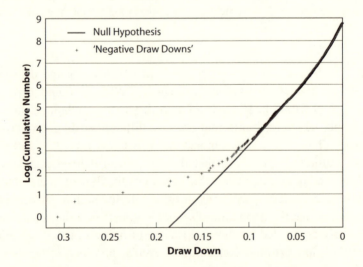

FIG. 3.4. Number of times a given level of drawdown has been observed in this century for the DJIA. Reproduced from [220].

Ex ponential curve (handwritten annotation)

TABLE 3.2
Characteristics of the 14 largest drawdowns of the DJIA in the twentieth century

Rank	Starting time	Index value	Duration (days)	Loss
1	87.786	2508.16	4	−30.7%
2	14.579	76.7	2	−28.8%
3	29.818	301.22	3	−23.6%
4	33.549	108.67	4	−18.6%
5	32.249	77.15	8	−18.5%
6	29.852	238.19	4	−16.6%
7	29.835	273.51	2	−16.6%
8	32.630	67.5	1	−14.8%
9	31.93	90.14	7	−14.3
10	32.694	76.54	3	−13.9%
11	74.719	674.05	11	−13.3%
12	30.444	239.69	4	−12.4%
13	31.735	109.86	5	−12.9
14	98.649	8602.65	4	−12.4%

The starting dates are given in decimal years. Reproduced from [220].

fourth day by 30.7%. In terms of consecutive losses, this corresponds to 3.8%, 2.4%, 4.6%, and then 22.6% on what is known as the Black Monday of October 1987.

The observation of large successive drops is suggestive of the existence of a transient correlation, as we already pointed out. For the Dow Jones, this reasoning can be adapted as follows. We use a simple functional form for the distribution of daily losses, namely an exponential distribution with decay rate 1/0.63% obtained by a fit to the distribution of drawdowns shown in Figure 3.4. The quality of the exponential model is confirmed by the direct calculation of the average loss amplitude equal to 0.67% and of its standard deviation equal to 0.61% (recall that an exact exponential would give the three values exactly equal: 1/decay = average = standard deviation). Using these numerical values, the probability for a drop equal to or larger than 3.8% is $\exp(-3.8/0.63) = 2.4 \cdot 10^{-3}$ (an event occurring about once every two years); the probability for a drop equal to or larger than 2.4% is $\exp(-2.4/0.63) = 2.2 \cdot 10^{-2}$ (an event occurring about once every two months); the probability for a drop equal to or larger than 4.6% is $\exp(-4.6/0.63) = 6.7 \cdot 10^{-4}$ (an event occurring about once every six years); the probability for a drop equal to or larger than 22.6% is $\exp(-22.6/0.63) = 2.6 \cdot 10^{-16}$ (an event occurring about once every 10^{14} years). All together, under the hypothesis that daily losses are uncorrelated from one day to the next, the sequence of four drops making the largest drawdown occurs with a probability 10^{-23}, that is, once in about 4 thousands of billions of billions of years. This exceedingly negligible value 10^{-23} suggests that the hypothesis of uncorrelated daily returns is to be rejected: drawdowns, especially the large ones, may exhibit intermittent correlations in the asset price time series.

THE NASDAQ COMPOSITE INDEX

In Figure 3.5, we see the rank ordering plot of drawdowns for the Nasdaq composite index, from its establishment in 1971 until April 18, 2000. The rank ordering plot, which is the same as the (complementary) cumulative distribution with axes interchanged, puts emphasis on the largest events. The four largest events are not situated on a continuation of the distribution of smaller events: the jump between rank 4 and 5 in relative value is larger than 33%, whereas the corresponding jump between rank 5 and 6 is less than 1%, and this remains true for higher ranks. This means that, for drawdowns less than 12.5%, we have a more or less "smooth" curve and then a larger than 33% gap to rank 3 and 4. The

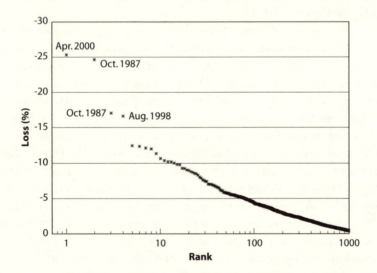

FIG. 3.5. Rank ordering of drawdowns in the Nasdaq composite since its establishment in 1971 until April 18, 2000. Rank 1 (Apr. 2000) is the largest drawdown, rank 2 (Oct. 1987, top) is the second largest, etc. Reproduced from [217].

four events are, according to rank, the crash of April 2000, the crash of October 1987, a larger than 17% "aftershock" related to the crash of October 1987, and a larger than 16% drop related to the "slow crash" of August 1998, which we shall discuss later, in chapter 7.

To further establish the statistical confidence with which we can conclude that the four largest events are outliers, we have reshuffled the daily returns 1,000 times and hence generated 1,000 synthetic data sets. This procedure means that the synthetic data sets will have exactly the same distribution of daily returns. However, higher order correlations and dependence that may be present in the largest drawdowns are destroyed by the reshuffling. This so-called "surrogate" data analysis of the distribution of drawdowns has the advantage of being *nonparametric*, that is, independent of the quality of fits with a model such as the exponential or any other model. We will now compare the distribution of drawdowns for both the real data and the synthetic data. With respect to the synthetic data, this can be done in two complementary ways.

In Figure 3.6, we see the distribution of drawdowns in the Nasdaq composite compared with the two lines constructed at the 99% confidence level for the entire *ensemble* of synthetic drawdowns, that is, by considering the individual drawdowns as independent: for any given drawdown, the upper (respectively, lower) confidence line is such that

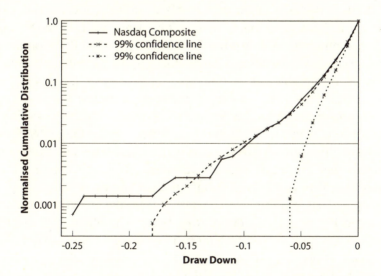

FIG. 3.6. Normalized cumulative distribution of drawdowns in the Nasdaq composite since its establishment in 1971 until April 18, 2000. The 99% confidence lines are estimated from the synthetic tests described in the text. Reproduced from [217].

five of the synthetic distributions are above (below) it; as a consequence, 990 synthetic times series out of the 1,000 are within the two confidence lines for any drawdown value, which defines the typical interval within which we expect to find the empirical distribution.

The most striking feature apparent in Figure 3.6 is that the distribution of the true data breaks away from the 99% confidence intervals at approximately 15%, showing that the four largest events are indeed "outliers." In other words, chance alone cannot reproduce these largest drawdowns. We are thus forced to explore the possibility that an amplification mechanism and dependence across daily returns might appear at special and rare times to create these outliers.

A more sophisticated analysis is to consider each synthetic data set *separately* and calculate the *conditional probability* of observing a given drawdown given some prior observation of drawdowns. This gives a more precise estimation of the statistical significance of the outliers, because the previously defined confidence lines neglect the correlations created by the ordering process which is explicit in the construction of a cumulative distribution.

Out of 10,000 synthetic data sets that were generated, we find that 776 had a single drawdown larger than 16.5%, 13 had two drawdowns larger than 16.5%, 1 had three drawdowns larger than 16.5%, and none had 4 (or more) drawdowns larger than 16.5% as in the real data. This means that, given the distribution of returns, by chance we have an 8% probability of observing a drawdown larger than 16.5%, a 0.1% probability of observing two drawdowns larger than 16.5%, and for all practical purposes, zero probability of observing three or more drawdowns larger than 16.5%. Hence, we can reject the hypothesis that the four largest drawdowns observed on the Nasdaq composite index could result from chance alone with a probability or confidence better than 99.99%, that is, essentially with certainty. As a consequence, we are led again to conclude that the largest market events are characterized by a stronger dependence than is observed during "normal" times.

This analysis confirms the conclusion from the analysis of the DJIA shown in Figure 3.4 that drawdowns larger than about 15% are to be considered as outliers with high probability. It is interesting that the same amplitude of approximately 15% is found for both markets considering the much larger daily volatility of the Nasdaq composite. This may result from the fact that, as we have shown, very large drawdowns are more controlled by transient correlations leading to runs of losses lasting a few days than by the amplitude of a single daily return.

The statistical analysis of the DJIA and the Nasdaq composite suggests that large crashes *are* special. In the following chapters, we shall show that there are other specific indications associated with these "outliers," such as precursory patterns decorating the speculative bubbles ending in crashes.

FURTHER TESTS

When one makes observations that deviate strikingly from existing belief (technically called the "null hypothesis"), it is important to keep a cool head and scrutinize all possible explanations. As Freeman Dyson eloquently expressed [116],

> The professional duty of a scientist confronted with a new and exciting theory is to try to prove it wrong. That is the way science works. That is the way science stays honest. Every new theory has to fight for its existence against intense and often bitter criticism. Most new theories turn out to be wrong, and the criticism is absolutely necessary to clear them away and make room for better theories. The rare theory which survives the criticism is strengthened and improved by it, and then becomes gradually incorporated into the growing body of scientific knowledge.

The powerful method of investigation underlying Dyson's verdict is the so-called scientific method. In a nutshell, it consists in the following steps: (1) we observe the data; (2) we invent a tentative description, called a hypothesis, that is consistent with what we have observed; (3) we use the hypothesis to make predictions; (4) we test those predictions by experiments or further observations and modify the hypothesis in light of our new results; (5) we repeat steps 3 and 4 until there are only a few or no discrepancies between theory and experiment and/or observation. When consistency is obtained, the hypothesis becomes a theory and provides a coherent set of propositions that explain a class of phenomena. A theory is then a framework within which observations are explained and predictions are made. In addition, scientists use what is known as "Occam's razor," also known as the law of parsimony, or the law of simplicity: "When you have two competing theories which make exactly the same predictions, the one that is simpler is preferable." There is a simple, practical reason for this principle: it makes life simpler for the prediction of the future, as fewer factors have to be determined or controlled.

More important is the fact that fewer assumptions and fewer parameters make the prediction of new phenomena more robust. Think, for instance, of the two competing explanations of Descartes and Newton for the regularities of planetary motions, such as those of Mercury, Venus, the Earth, Mars, Jupiter, and Uranus orbiting around the sun. According to Descartes, the motion of the planets could be explained by a complex system of vortices moving the Ether (the hypothetical matter filling space). In contrast, Newton proposed his famous universal inverse square distance law for the gravitational attraction between any two massive bodies. Both explanations are a priori valid and they can both explain the planetary motions. The difference lies in the fact that Descartes's explanation could not be extrapolated to predict new observations, while Newton's law led to the prediction of the existence of undetected planets, such as Neptune. The power of a model or a theory thus lies in its prediction of phenomena that have not served to construct it. Einstein put it this way: "A theory is more impressive the greater the simplicity of its premises, the more different the kinds of things it relates and the more extended its range of applicability."

Here is where we stand with respect to the scientific method:

1. We looked at financial data and found it apparently random.

2. We formed the hypothesis that the time evolution of stock market prices are random walks.

3. We used this hypothesis to make the prediction that the distribution of drawdowns should be exponential.

4. We tested this prediction by constructing this distribution for the DJIA and found an apparent discrepancy, especially with respect to the largest drawdowns.

Before rejecting our initial hypothesis and accepting the idea that stock market prices are not completely random, we must first verify that the observation is "statistically significant." In plain words, this means that the deviation from the exponential could be the result of the smallness of the data set or other factors not identified and unrelated to the data itself. The apparent deviation from an exponential distribution would thus not be genuine but an error, an artifact of our measurements, or simply accidental. In order to try to exclude these traps, we thus need tests that tell us if the observed deviation is significant and credible. Indeed, Occam's razor imposes that we should prefer the simpler hypothesis of randomness as long as the force of the evidence does not impose a change of our belief.

In order to see which one of the two descriptions (random or not random) is the most accurate, the following statistical analysis of market fluctuations is performed. First, we approximate the distribution of drawdowns for the DJIA up to 15% by an exponential and find a characteristic drawdown scale of 2%. This characteristic decay constant means that the probability of observing a drawdown larger than 2% is about 37%. Following the null hypothesis that the exponential description is correct and extrapolating this description to, for example, the three largest crashes on the U.S. market in this century (1914, 1929, and 1987), as indicated in Figure 3.4, yields a recurrence time of about fifty centuries for *each single* crash. In reality, the three crashes occurred in less than one century. This result is a first indication that the exponential model may not apply for the large crashes.

As an additional test, 10,000 so-called synthetic data sets, each covering a time span close to a century, hence adding up to about 1 million years, was generated using a standard statistical model used by the financial industry [46]. We use the model version GARCH(1,1) estimated from the true index with a student distribution with four degrees of freedom. This model includes both nonstationarity of volatilities (the amplitude of price variations) and the (fat tail) nature of the distribution of the price returns seen in Figure 2.7. Our analysis [209] shows that, in approximately 1 million years of heavy tail "GARCH-trading," with a reset every century, *never* did three crashes similar to the three largest observed in the true DJIA occur in a single "GARCH-century."

Another approach is to use the GARCH model with Student distribution of the noise with 4 degrees of freedom fitted to the DJIA to construct directly the distribution of drawdowns and compare with real data. From synthetic price time series generated by the GARCH model, the distribution of drawdowns is constructed by following exactly the same procedure as in the analysis of the real time series. Figure 3.7 shows two dotted lines defined such that 99% of the drawdowns of the synthetic GARCH with noise Student distribution are within the two lines: there is thus a 1% probability that a drawdown in a GARCH time series falls above the upper line or below the lower line. Notice that the distribution of drawdowns from the synthetic GARCH model is approximately exponential or slightly subexponential for drawdowns up to about 10% and fits well the empirical drawdown distribution shown as the symbol + in the DJIA. However, the three largest drawdowns are clearly above the upper line. We conclude that the GARCH dependencies cannot (fully) account for the dependencies observed in real data, in particular in the

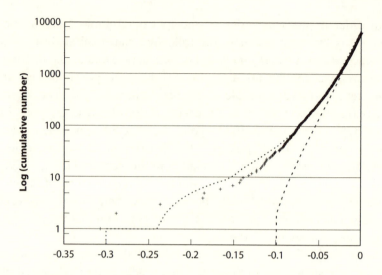

FIG. 3.7. The two dashed lines are defined such that 99% of the drawdowns of synthetic GARCH(1,1) with noise Student distribution with 4 degrees of freedom are within the two lines. The symbols + represent the cumulative distribution of the drawdowns for the DJIA. The ordinate is in logarithmic scale, while the abscissa shows the drawdowns; for instance, −0.30 corresponds to a drawdown of −30%. Reproduced from [399].

special dependence associated with very large drawdowns. This illustrates that one of the most used benchmark models in finance fails to match the data.

This novel piece of evidence, adding upon the previous rejection of the null hypothesis that reshuffled time series exhibit the same drawdowns as the real time series (see also below), strengthens the claim that large drawdowns are outliers.

Of course, these tests do not tell us what the correct model is. They only show that one of the standard models of the financial industry and of the academic world (which makes a reasonable null hypothesis of random markets) is utterly unable to account for the stylized facts associated with large financial crashes. It suggests that different mechanisms are responsible for large crashes. This conclusion justifies the special status that the media and the public in general attribute to financial crashes. If the largest drawdowns are outliers, we *must* consider the possibility that they may possess a higher degree of predictability than the smaller market movements.

This is the subject of the present book. The program in front of us is to build on this observation that large crashes are very special events in order to try understanding how and why, and then test for their potential predictability. Before proceeding, we summarize the evidence for the existence of outliers in other financial market securities. As outliers will be shown to be ubiquitous, this will force us to construct specific models for them.

THE PRESENCE OF OUTLIERS
IS A GENERAL PHENOMENON

The data sets that have been analyzed [220] comprise

1. major world financial indices: the Dow Jones, Standard & Poors, Nasdaq composite, TSE 300 Composite (Toronto, Canada), All Ordinaries (Sydney stock exchange, Australia), Strait Times (Singapore stock exchange), Hang Seng (Hong Kong stock exchange), Nikkei 225 (Tokyo stock exchange, Japan), FTSE 100 (London stock exchange, U.K.), CAC40 (Paris stock exchange, France), DAX (Frankfurt stock exchange, Germany), MIBTel (Milan stock exchange, Italy);

2. currencies: U.S. dollar versus German mark (UD$/DM), U.S. dollar versus Japanese yen (UD$/Yen), U.S. dollar versus Swiss franc (UD$/CHF);

3. gold;

4. the twenty largest companies in the U.S. market in terms of capitalization, as well as nine others taken randomly in the list of the fifty largest companies (Coca Cola, Qualcomm, Appl. Materials, Procter & Gamble, JDS Uniphase, General Motors, Am. Home. Prod., Medtronic, and Ford).

These different data sets do not have the same time span, largely due to different life spans, especially for some recent "new technology" companies. This selection of time series is far from exhaustive but is a reasonable sample for our purpose: as we shall see, with the exception of the index CAC40 (the "French exception"?), all time series exhibit clear outlier drawdowns. This suggests that outliers constitute a ubiquitous feature of stock markets, independently of their nature.

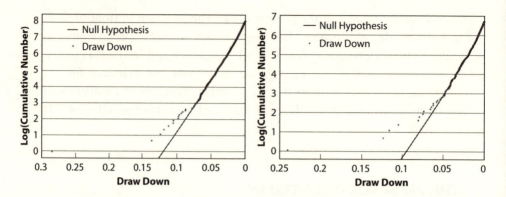

FIG. 3.8. Standard & Poor's (left) and TSE 300 composite (right). Note the isolated + at the bottom-left corner of each panel, indicating the largest drawdawn, clearly an "outlier." Its value on the vertical axis is 0 because only one such large event was observed and the logarithm of 1 is 0. Indeed, recall that this kind of cumulative distribution counts events from bottom to top, sorting them from the largest to the smallest when spanning from left to right. Reproduced from [220].

MAIN STOCK MARKET INDICES, CURRENCIES, AND GOLD

The set of Figures 3.8–3.14 tests whether the observations documented in the previous section for the U.S. markets is specific to it or is a general feature of stock market behavior. We have thus analyzed the main stock market indices of the remaining six G7 countries as well as those of Australia, Hong Kong, and Singapore and the other important U.S.

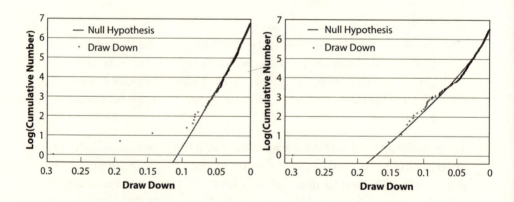

FIG. 3.9. All Ordinaries (Australian) (left) and Strait Times (Singapore) (right). Note again the isolated + at the bottom-left corner of each panel, indicating the largest drawdawn, clearly an outlier. Reproduced from [220].

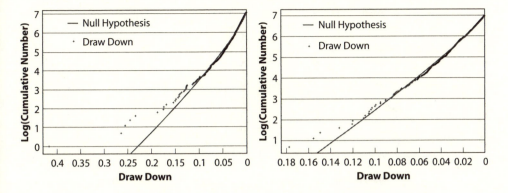

FIG. 3.10. Hang Seng (Hong Kong) (left) and Nikkei 225 (Japan) (right). Reproduced from [220].

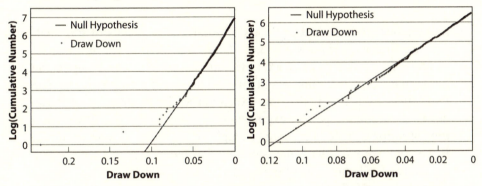

FIG. 3.11. FTSE 100 (United Kingdom) (left) and CAC 40 (France) (right). Reproduced from [220].

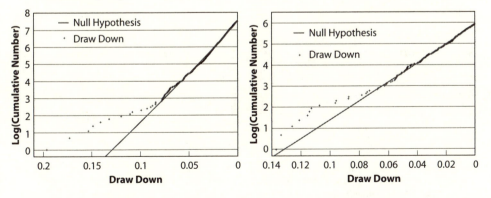

FIG. 3.12. DAX (Germany) (left) and MIBTel (Italy) (right). Reproduced from [220].

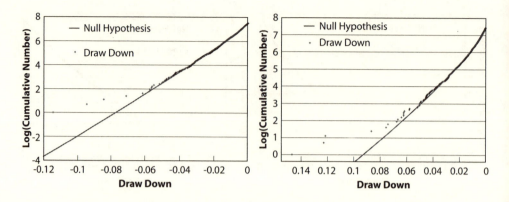

Fig. 3.13. U.S. dollar/DM currency (left) and U.S. dollar/Yen currency (right). Reproduced from [220].

index called the Standard & Poor's 500 index. The results of this analysis are shown in Figures 3.8–3.12. Quite remarkably, we find that all markets except the French market, with the Japanese market being on the borderline, show the same qualitative behavior exhibiting outliers. The Paris stock exchange is the only exception as the distribution of drawdowns is an almost perfect exponential. It may be that the observation time used for CAC40 is not large enough for an outlier to have occurred. If we compare with the Milan stock market index MIBTel, we see that the entire distribution except the single largest drawdown is also close to a pure exponential. The presence or absence of this outlier thus makes all the difference. In the case of the Japanese stock market, we note that it exhibited a general decline from 1990 to early 1999, which is more

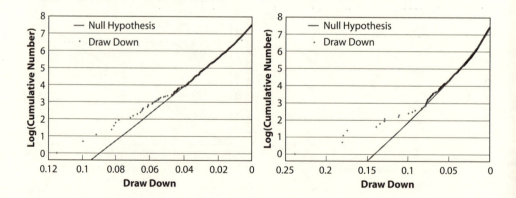

Fig. 3.14. U.S. dollar/CHF currency (left) and gold (right). Reproduced from [220].

than a third of the data set. The total decline was approximately 60% in amplitude. This may explain why the evidence is less striking than for the other indices.

Figures 3.13 and 3.14 show that similar behavior is observed also for currencies and for gold. Summarizing, the results of the analysis of different stock market indices, the exchange of the U.S. dollar against three different major currencies as well as the gold market are that outliers are ubiquitous features of major financial markets [220].

Largest U.S. Companies

Let us now extend this analysis to the very largest companies in the United States in terms of capitalization (market value) [220]. The ranking is that of *Forbes* at the beginning of the year 2000. The top twenty have been chosen, with, in addition, a random sample of other companies, namely number 25 (Coca Cola), number 30 (Qualcomm), number 35 (Appl. Materials), number 39 (JDS Uniphase), number 46 (Am. Home Prod.), and number 50 (Medtronic). Three more companies have been added in order to get longer time series as well as representatives of the automobile sector. These are Procter & Gamble (number 38), General Motors (number 43), and Ford (number 64). This represents an unbiased selection based on objective criteria. We show here only the distribution of drawdowns for the six first ranks and refer to [220] for access to the full data set.

From Figures 3.15, 3.16, and 3.17, we can see that the distributions of the five largest companies (Microsoft, Cisco, General Electric, Intel, and Exxon-Mobil) clearly exhibit the same features as those for the major financial markets. Of the remaining 23, for all but America Online and JDS Uniphase, we find clear outliers but also a variety of different tails of the distributions. It is interesting to note that the two companies, America Online and JDS Uniphase, whose distributions did not exhibit outliers are also the two companies with by far the largest number per year of drawdowns of amplitude above 15% (close to 4).

Drawups can be similarly defined as runs of positive returns beginning after a loss and stopping at a loss. The distributions of drawups also exhibit outliers but less strikingly than the distribution of drawdowns [220].

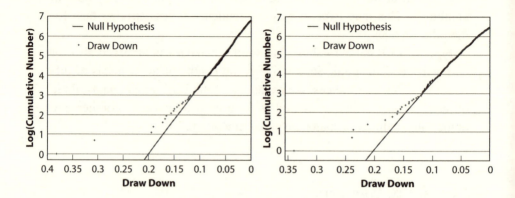

Fig. 3.15. Microsoft (left) and Cisco (right). Reproduced from [220].

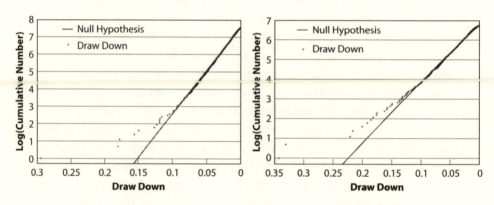

Fig. 3.16. General Electric (left) and Intel (right). Reproduced from [220].

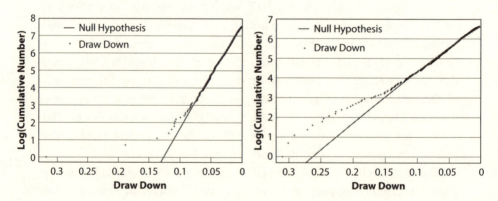

Fig. 3.17. Exxon-Mobil (left) and Oracle (right). Reproduced from [220].

SYNTHESIS

We have found the following facts [211, 217, 220].

1. Approximately 1% to 2% of the largest drawdowns are not at all explained by the exponential null hypothesis or its extension in terms of the stretched exponential [253]. Large drawdowns up to three times larger than expected from the null hypothesis are found to be ubiquitous occurrences of essentially all the times series that we have investigated, the only noticeable exception being the French index CAC40. We term these anomalous drawdowns "outliers."

2. About half of the time series show outliers for the drawups. The drawups are thus different statistically from the drawdowns and constitute a less conspicuous structure of financial markets.

3. For companies, large drawups of more than 15% occur approximately twice as often as large drawdowns of similar amplitudes.

4. The bulk (98%) of the drawdowns and drawups are very well fitted by the exponential null hypothesis (based on the assumption of independent price variations) or by a slight generalization called the stretched exponential model.

The most important result is the demonstration that the very largest drawdowns are outliers. This is true notwithstanding the fact that the very largest daily drops are *not* outliers, except for the exceptional daily drop on October 29, 1987. Therefore, the anomalously large amplitude of the drawdowns can only be explained by invoking the emergence of rare but sudden persistences of successive daily drops, with, in addition, correlated amplification of the drops. Why such successions of correlated daily moves occur is a very important question with consequences for portfolio management and systemic risk, to cite only two applications that we will investigate in the following chapters.

Systemic risks refer to the risk that a disruption (at a firm or bank, in a transfer system) causes widespread difficulties at other firms, or in other market segments. Systemic risk is the risk that such a failure could cause, at the extreme, a complete breakdown in a financial system due to the extensive linkages of today's markets. Such a risk of contagion arising from a disruption at a firm or in one market is known as systemic risk.

That systemic safety can be threatened by the failure of one small institution was vividly demonstrated in September 1998 when the U.S. Federal Reserve Bank organized a rescue of a hedge fund, Long-Term Capital

Management, because it feared the fund's collapse would set off havoc in the financial markets. LTCM had market exposures of over $200 billion, while its capital base was about $4.8 billion.

See, for instance, http://riskinstitute.ch/134720.htm for more information and a summary of countermeasures used to ensure systemic safety.

SYMMETRY-BREAKING ON CRASH AND RALLY DAYS

Lillo and Mantegna [267] have recently convincingly documented another clear indication that crash and rally days differ significantly from typical market days in their statistical properties. Specifically, they investigated the return distributions of an ensemble of stocks simultaneously traded on the New York Stock Exchange (NYSE) during market days of extreme crash or rally in the period from January 1987 to December 1998. The total number of assets n traded on the NYSE is rapidly increasing and it ranges from 1,128 in 1987 to 2,788 in 1998. The total number of data records treated in this analysis thus exceeds 6 million.

Figure 3.18 shows 200 distributions of returns, one for each of 200 trading days, where the ensemble of returns is constructed over the whole set of stocks traded on the NYSE. A sectional cut at a fixed trading day retrieves the kind of plot shown in Figure 2.7 (except for the absence of the folding back of the negative returns performed in Figure 2.7). Figure 3.18 clearly shows the anomalously large widths and fat tails on the day of the crash of October 19, 1987, as well as during other turbulent days.

Lillo and Mantegna [267] documented another remarkable behavior associated with crashes and rallies, namely that the distortion of the distributions of returns are not only strong in the tails describing large moves but also in their center. Specifically, they show that the overall shape of the distributions is modified on crash and rally days. To show this, the distributions of the nine trading days with the largest drops and of the nine trading days with the largest gains of the Standard & Poors 500 given in Table 3.3 are shown in Figures 3.19 and 3.20.

Figure 3.19 shows that on crash days the distribution of returns has a peak at a negative value and is skewed with an asymmetric and longer tail towards negative return. Not only are there more drops than gains among all assets, but the drops are more pronounced. The converse is true for rally days, as shown in Figure 3.20. Therefore, on crash and

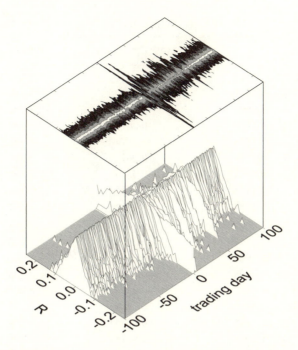

Fig. 3.18. Contour and surface plot of the ensemble return distribution in a 200-trading-days time interval centered at October 19, 1987 (corresponding to 0 in the abscissa). The probability density scale (z-axis) of the surface plot is logarithmic, so that a straight decay qualifies exponential distributions. The contour plot at the top is obtained for equidistant intervals of the logarithmic probability density. The brightest area of the contour plot corresponds to the most probable value. The symbol R stands for return. Reproduced from [267].

rally days, not only the scale but also the shape and symmetry properties of the distribution change.

The change of the shape and of the symmetry properties during the days of large absolute returns (crashes and rallies) suggests that, on extreme days, the behavior of the market cannot be statistically described in the same way as during "normal" periods.

IMPLICATIONS FOR SAFETY REGULATIONS OF STOCK MARKETS

The realization that large drawdowns and crashes in particular may result from a run of losses over several successive days is not without consequences for the regulation of stock markets. Following the market

TABLE 3.3

Date	S&P 500 return	Panel
19 10 1987	−0.2041	3.19a
26 10 1987	−0.0830	3.19b
27 10 1997	−0.0686	3.19c
31 08 1998	−0.0679	3.19d
08 01 1988	−0.0674	3.19e
13 10 1989	−0.0611	3.19f
16 10 1987	−0.0513	3.19g
14 04 1988	−0.0435	3.19h
30 11 1987	−0.0416	3.19i
21 10 1987	+0.0908	3.20a
20 10 1987	+0.0524	3.20b
28 10 1997	+0.0511	3.20c
08 09 1998	+0.0509	3.20d
29 10 1987	+0.0493	3.20e
15 10 1998	+0.0418	3.20f
01 09 1998	+0.0383	3.20g
17 01 1991	+0.0373	3.20h
04 01 1988	+0.0360	3.20i

List of the eighteen days of the investigated period (from January
1987 to December 1998) in which the S&P 500 index had the
greatest return in absolute value. The third column indicates the
corresponding panel of the ensemble return distribution shown in
Figures 3.19 and 3.20. Reproduced from [267].

crash of October 1987, in an attempt to head off future one-day stock
market tumbles of historic proportions, the Securities and Exchange
Commission and the three major U.S. stock exchanges agreed to install
so-called circuit breakers. Circuit breakers are designed to gradually
inhibit trading during market declines, first curbing NYSE program
trades and eventually halting all U.S. equity, options, and futures activity.
Similar circuit breakers are operating in the other world stock markets
with different specific definitions.

Circuit breaker values. Effective April 15, 1998, the SEC approved new
circuit breaker trigger levels for one-day declines in the DJIA of 10%,
20%, and 30%. The halt for a 10% decline will be one hour if triggered
before 2:00 p.m. Eastern Standard Time (EST). At or after 2:00 p.m. EST
but before 2:30 p.m. EST, the halt will be for one half-hour. At or after
2:30 p.m. EST, the market will not halt at the 10% level and will continue

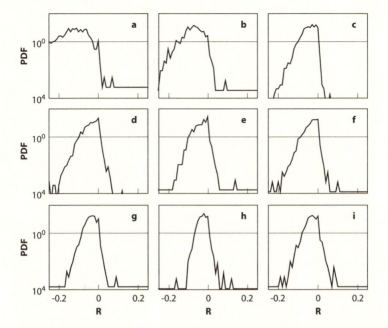

FIG. 3.19. Ensemble return distribution in days of S&P 500 index extreme negative return occurring in the investigated time period (listed in the first part of Table 3.3). The ordinate is in logarithmic scale. PDF stands for probability distribution function. Reproduced from [267].

trading. The halt for a 20% decline will be two hours if triggered before 1:00 p.m. EST. At or after 1:00 p.m. EST but before 2:00 p.m. EST, the halt will be for one hour. If the 20% trigger value is reached at or after 2:00 p.m. EST, trading will halt for the remainder of the day. If the market declines by 30%, at any time, trading will be halted for the remainder of the day. Previously, the circuit breakers were triggered when the DJIA declined 350 points (thirty-minute halt) and 550 points (one-hour halt) from the previous day's close. The circuit breakers are based on the average closing price of the Dow for the month preceding the start of each calendar quarter.

The argument is that the halt triggered by a circuit breaker will provide time for brokers and dealers to contact their clients when there are large price movements and to get new instructions or additional margin. They also limit credit risk and loss of financial confidence by providing a "time-out" to settle up and to ensure that everyone is solvent. This inactive period is of further use for investors to pause, evaluate, and inhibit panic. Finally, circuit breakers expose the illusion of market liq-

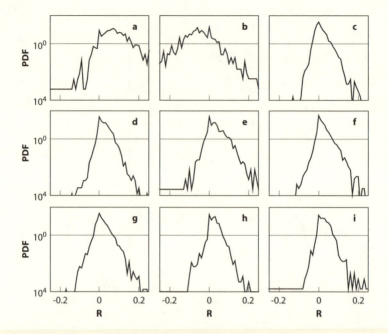

FIG. 3.20. Ensemble return distribution in days of greatest S&P 500 index positive return occurring in the investigated time period (listed in the second part of Table 3.3). The ordinate is in logarithmic scale. PDF stands for probability distribution function. Reproduced from [267].

uidity by spelling out the economic fact of life that markets have limited capacity to absorb massive unbalanced volumes. They thus force large investors, such as pension portfolio managers and mutual fund managers, to take even more account of the impact of their "size order," thus possibly cushioning large market movements.

However, others argue that a trading halt can increase risk by inducing trading in anticipation of a trading halt. Another disadvantage is that they prevent some traders from liquidating their positions, thus creating market distortion by preventing price discovery [188].

As shown in [30] for the October 1987 crash, countries that had stringent circuit breakers, such as France, Switzerland, and Israel, also had some of the largest cumulative losses. According to our finding that large drops are created by transient and rare dependent losses occurring over several days, circuit breakers should not be considered reliable crash killers.

CHAPTER 4

POSITIVE FEEDBACKS

Human behavior is a main factor in how markets
act. Indeed, sometimes markets act quickly, violently
with little warning. ... Ultimately, history tells us
that there will be a correction of some significant
dimension. I have no doubt that, human nature being
what it is, that it is going to happen again and again.
— Alan Greenspan, before the Committee on Banking
  and Financial Services, U.S. House of
  Representatives, July 24, 1998.

The previous chapter 3 documented convinc-
ingly that essentially all markets exhibit rare but anomalously large runs
of successive daily losses. How can we explain the existence of these
exceptionally large drawdown outliers?

Since it is the actions of investors whose buy and sell decisions move
prices up and down, any deviation from a random walk has ultimately to
be traced back to the behavior of investors. We are particularly interested
in mechanisms that may lead to positive feedbacks on prices, that is, to
the fact that, conditioned on the observation that the market has recently
moved up (respectively, down), this makes it more probable to keep it
moving up (respectively, down), so that a large cumulative move ensues.
The concept of "positive feedbacks" has a long history in economics
and is related to the idea of "increasing returns," which says that goods
become cheaper the more of them are produced (and the closely related

idea that some products, like fax machines, become more useful the more people use them). "Positive feedback" is the opposite of "negative feedback," a concept well known, for instance, in population dynamics: the larger the population of rabbits in a valley, the less grass there is per rabbit. If the population grows too much, the rabbits will eventually starve, slowing down their reproduction rate, which thus reduces their population at a later time. Thus negative feedback means that the higher the population, the slower the growth rate, leading to a spontaneous regulation of the population size; negative feedbacks thus tend to regulate growth towards an equilibrium. In contrast, positive feedback asserts that the higher the price or the price return in the recent past, the higher will be the price growth in the future. Positive feedbacks, when unchecked, can produce runaways until the deviation from equilibrium is so large that other effects can be abruptly triggered and lead to ruptures or crashes. Youssefmir, Huberman, and Hogg [460] have stressed the importance of positive feedback in a dynamical theory of asset price bubbles that exhibits the appearance of bubbles and their subsequent crashes. The positive feedback leads to speculative trends which may dominate over fundamental beliefs and which make the system increasingly susceptible to any exogenous shock, thus eventually precipitating a crash.

There are many mechanisms in the stock market and in the behavior of investors that may lead to positive feedbacks. Figure 4.1 provides a humorous account of trader folklore on the many influences and factors active in the stock market. Some of these influences lead to negative feedbacks, others to amplification.

We first sketch the evolution of economic thinking in relation to feedback and self-organization, then describe how positive feedback on prices can result from hedging of derivatives and from insurance portfolio strategies. We follow by turning to a general mechanism for positive feedback, which is now known as the "herd" or "crowd" effect, based on imitation processes. We present a simple model of the best investment strategy that an investor can develop based on interactions with and information taken from other investors. We show how the repetition of these interactions may lead to a remarkable cooperative phenomenon in which the market can suddenly "solidify" a global opinion, leading to large price variations.

FEEDBACKS AND SELF-ORGANIZATION IN ECONOMICS

The recognition of the importance of feedbacks to fathom the sheer complexity of economic systems has been at the root of economic thinking

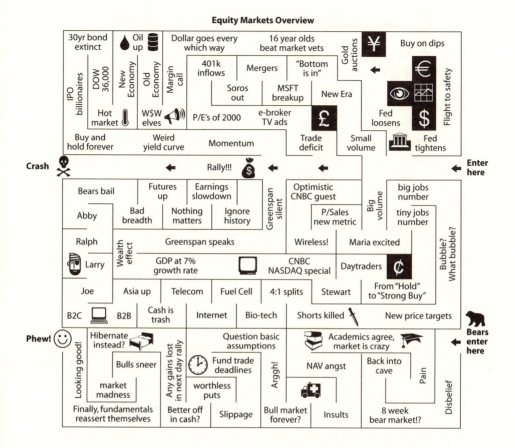

FIG. 4.1. Cartoon illustrating the many factors influencing traders, as well as the psychological and social nature of the investment universe (source: anonymous).

for a long time. Indeed, the general equilibrium theory is nothing but a formalization of the idea that "everything in the economy affects everything else" [244]. The historical root and best pictorial synthesis of this idea is found in the work of 18th-century Scotsman Adam Smith. Smith's masterpiece [384], *An Inquiry into the Nature and Causes of the Wealth of Nations*, introduced the then-radical notion that selfish, greedy individuals, if allowed to pursue their interests largely unchecked, would interact to produce a wealthier society as if guided by an "invisible hand." Smith never worked out a proof that this invisible hand existed. Not all subsequent economists agreed with his optimistic assessment. T. Malthus thought people would have too many children and overpopulate the world. Karl Marx thought capitalists would be so greedy they would bring down the system. But they all shared Smith's view of economics as the study of people trying to maximize their material well being. In 1954, K. Arrow and G. Debreu [16] published an article that in essence mathematically proved the existence of Adam Smith's invisible hand. This "general equilibrium" proof, which relies on a set of very restricted assumptions of an idealized world, has been a mainstay of graduate-level economics training ever since.

The most important tool in this analysis was game theory: the study of situations, like poker or chess games, in which players have to make their decisions based on guesses about what the other player is going to do next. Game theory was first adapted to economics in the 1940s by mathematician John von Neumann (the same von Neumann whose theoretical insights made the computer possible) and economist O. Morgenstern. Since then, the standard economics and social science model of a human agent is that it is like a general-purpose logic machine. All decision tasks, regardless of context, constitute optimization problems subject to external constraints whether from the physical environment or from the reaction functions of other agents. This central dogma is the core of economics courses taught in universities and is often found very difficult to "swallow" by students, many of whom give up, unable to learn it. This idealization both is convenient for the development of a coherent theoretical framework and has many rich consequences. However, it is a poor representation of reality, as most of us are actually not versed in economic optimization reasoning! The remarkable insight of Adam Smith is that this does not mean we shall fail to function effectively in social and economic exchanges in life. This is because people have natural intuitive mechanisms—mind modules that serve them well in daily interchanges—enabling them to "read" situations and the intentions and likely reactions of others without deep, tutored, cognitive analysis. This fact has been established by "experiments" performed by a large school of economics researchers (the bibliography of which contains 1500 entries [197]) in the fields of "experimental economics" [389].

These experimental approaches to economics, started in the mid-twentieth century, were developed to examine propositions implied by economic theories of markets. An untested theory is simply a hypothesis, and science seeks to expand our knowledge of things by a process of testing hypotheses. In contrast, much of traditional economic theory can be called, appropriately, "ecclesiastical theory"; it is accepted (or rejected) on the basis of authority, tradition, or opinion about assumptions, rather than on the basis of having survived a rigorous falsification process that can be replicated. Hundreds of experiments on artificial markets constructed and performed with students from economics classes and with professionals have shown the crucial importance of repeating interactions in the presence of unconscious decisions in order to lead to an apparent rationality in rule-governed problems [390]. In these so-called continuous double auction experiments, which attempt to mimick real market situations, subjects have private information on their own willingness-to-pay or willingness-to-accept schedules which bound the prices at which each can profitably trade. No subject has information on market supply and demand. After an experiment, upon interrogation, the participants deny that they could have maximized their monetary earnings or that their trading results could be predicted by a theory. Yet despite these conditions, the subjects tend to converge quickly over time to the competitive equilibrium. Thus "the most common responses to the market question were unorganized, unstable, chaotic, and confused. Students were both surprised and amazed at the conclusion of the experiment when the entrusted student opened a sealed envelope containing the correctly predicted equilibrium price and quantity" [157]. The fact that economic agents can achieve efficient outcomes that are not part of their intentions was the key principle formulated by Adam Smith [384], as we already stressed. Indeed, "in many experimental markets, poorly informed, error-prone, and uncomprehending human agents interact through the trading rules to produce social algorithms which demonstrably approximate the wealth maximizing outcomes traditionally thought to require complete information and cognitively rational actors" [391].

In much of the literature on experimental economics [101, 226, 143], the rational expectations model has been the main benchmark against which to check the informational efficiency of experimental markets. The research generally falls into two categories: information dissemination between fully informed agents ("insiders") and uninformed agents, and information aggregation among many partially informed agents. The former experiments investigate the common intuition that market prices reflect insider information, hence uninformed traders should be able to infer the true price from the market. The latter experiments explore the aggregation of diverse information by partially informed agents, a more challenging objective because none of the agents possesses full information (traders identify the state of the world with certainty only by pooling their private information through the process of trading). Experiments on markets with both insiders and uninformed traders [333, 334] show that equilibrium prices do reveal insider information after several trials of the experiments, suggesting that the markets disseminate information efficiently. The success of the rational expectations model can be attributed to the fact that traders learn about the equilibrium price and the state of the world simultaneously from market conditions [333].

However, these results are not always present if the following conditions are not fulfilled [334, 137]: identical preferences, common knowledge of the dividend structure, and complete contingent claims (i.e., existence of a full spectrum of derivative instruments allowing one to probe the expectation of future risks). These studies provide examples of the failure of the rational expectations model and suggest that information aggregation is a more complicated situation. In particular, it seems that market efficiency, defined as full information aggregation, depends on the "complexity" of the market, as measured by market parameters such as the number of stocks and the number of trading periods in the market [319]. For instance, overreaction of people to trades that are uninformative may create self-generated information "mirages," which may provide an explanation for the apparent excess volatility of asset prices [67]. Furthermore, there is evidence from market experiments about two types of judgment errors: errors in judging exogeneous events that affect the value of assets and errors in judging variables that are endogeneously created by market activity, such as prices in future trading periods. Notwithstanding ideal learning conditions, individual errors are not eliminated, but are, at best sometimes reduced [65]. Another idiosyncrasy of human beings highlighted by experiments is the so-called "disposition effect," corresponding to the tendency to sell assets that have gained value and to keep assets that have lost value [446]. Disposition effects can be explained by the idea that people value gains and losses relative to a reference point and have a tendency to seek risk when faced with possible losses but to avoid risk when a certain gain is possible. Another important psychological trait is that most people are overconfident about their own relative abilities and unreasonably optimistic about their futures. This has been shown to influence economic behavior, such as entry into competitive games or investment in stock markets[66].

It is in this context that the concept of the "emergence" of a macroscopic organization from the repeated action of simple rules at the microscopic level is particularly intriguing. The main question concerns the qualities of agents that are crucial to shape the properties of this emergence. This question is now at the center of an exciting and vigorous

HIERCHAL
LAWS

body of research aimed at understanding "complex systems" as a result of self-organization mechanisms [8]. Philip W. Anderson, a condensed-matter physicist and Nobel laureate in physics at Princeton University, contended in "More Is Different" [7] an essay published in 1972, that particle physics and indeed all reductionist approaches have only a limited ability to explain the world. Reality has a hierarchical structure, Anderson argued, with each level independent, to some degree, of the levels above and below. "At each stage, entirely new laws, concepts and generalizations are necessary, requiring inspiration and creativity to just as great a degree as in the previous one," Anderson noted. "Psychology is not applied biology, nor is biology applied chemistry."

This "emergence" principle does not imply, however, that the "market" will always be equivalent to an efficient and global optimization machine. Actually, empirical economics in particular has taught us that market forces may lead to plenty of imperfections, problems, and paradoxes, depending on many different ingredients that are indeed present in real-life situations.

1. Trading rules of market institutions seem to matter significantly in the realization of efficient markets. Inadequate methods of pricing may lead to a slow and inefficient convergence to the equilibrium price or event to a divergence from it.

2. Providing subjects with complete information, far from improving market competition, may tend to make it worse. Indeed, when people have complete information, they can identify more self-interested outcomes than competitive equilibria and use punishing strategies in an attempt to achieve them, which delays reaching equilibrium.

3. There is no assurance that a public announcement will yield common expectations among the players, since each person may still be uncertain about how others will use the information.

4. According to survey studies reported by Kahneman, Knetsch, and Thaler [227], people indicate that it is unfair for firms to raise prices and increase profits in response to certain changes in the environment that are not justified by an increase in costs. Thus, respondents report that it is "unfair" for firms to raise the price of snow shovels after a snowstorm or to raise the price of plywood after a hurricane. In these circumstances, economic theory predicts shortages, an increase in prices toward the new market clearing levels, and, eventually, an increase in output. In other words, the increase of price is the equilibrium solution associated with the new supply–demand relationship,

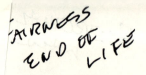

FAIRNESS
END OF LIFE

but this is considered unfair by people. How this perception impacts the real dynamics of the price and the behavior of firms and buyers to give rise to efficient or inefficient markets remains a subject of research.

5. Prices in experimental asset markets tend to bubble and then crash to their dividend value at the end of the asset's useful life [335]. The introduction of a futures market, that allows participants to obtain information on future share prices, is found to reduce the bubbles in experiments.

6. The experience of traders is paramount to the appearance of bubbles and crashes in these synthetic experimental markets. Providing full information on the future dividend flow, which should give full information on the equilibrium price of the corresponding asset, had little effect on the character of bubbles with inexperienced traders [335]. Repeating the market game several times, the bubbles tend to decrease in amplitude.

7. The phenomenon of "herding," discussed at length in the remainder of this chapter, can also be considered an example of market failure, as it leads to important deviations from "fundamental" or "equilibrium" prices.

This research has fertilized many novel approaches that are working out ways in which rational behavior could lead to less-than-optimal market outcomes. Another important step has been the introduction of so-called "information asymmetry," which describes situations in which different parties to a transaction possess different amounts of information. Such "asymmetric information," the fact that people are not equal with respect to the quality and quantity of information they use to make decisions, blossomed in the seventies as a way to explain the behavior of financial markets, which are indeed extremely susceptible to information difficulties.

The present situation is that economics has moved away from the dead certainties of the past into a much more interesting universe of research possibilities including, as we shall see, imperfection, bounded rationalities, behaviors, and even psychology. The mathematical models that had come to form the basis of academic economics are shifting from general equilibrium, in which everything would work out for the best, to multiple equilibriums and out-of-equilibrium, in which it might not. The resulting encompassing concept is that the economy and the stock market are self-organizing systems.

HEDGING DERIVATIVES, INSURANCE PORTFOLIOS, AND RATIONAL PANICS

Consider, for instance, a so-called call or buy option, which is a financial instrument issued by, say, a bank on an underlying stock such as IBM. An option gives the buyer the right, but not the obligation, to buy an IBM share in the future at a predefined price x_c (usually called the "strike"). It is clear that, if the IBM price goes up above this predefined price x_c, the option acquires a value equal to the difference between the IBM price and the predefined price x_c, since the owner of the option can always buy at x_c from the bank and sell immediately at market value, pocketing the difference. In order to be able to provide the IBM stock to the option holder, the bank has to buy the stock at the market value, if it has not taken the precautionary measure of holding some stock in reserve. This means that the bank has a potential maximum loss equal to the potential gain of the option holder. But the bank is not weaponless in this situation, as it can cover its risks against such a possibility by buying the stock in advance at a cheaper price, a procedure called "hedging." Such hedging strategy leads to positive feedback: if the price increases, the option issuer should buy more of the underlying stock to hedge its position and prepare to deliver to the option buyer. Buying the stock obviously provides a driving force for further increase of the price, hence the positive feedback. This is only one example among many cases associated with derivative products in financial markets.

A related phenomenon is the increase in market volatility of asset prices that have been observed and analyzed in recent years (see, for instance, Table 4.1 for a striking illustration) and its cause has often been attributed to the popularity of hedging strategies for derivative securities. It can indeed be shown that optimal hedging strategies (using improvements of the famous Black and Scholes methodology) not only provide a positive feedback on prices, they also increase the price volatility [381]. As Miller [298] noted, the view is widespread and is expressed almost daily in the financial press: stock market volatility has been rising in the last decade mainly due to the introduction of low-cost speculative vehicles such as stock index futures and options. It is, however, naive to attribute the increase in volatility only to this origin. As we shall see, there are many other causes, and disentangling them is difficult.

TABLE 4.1

Date	High − low	$Close(t) - close(t - 1)$
27 Oct 97	8%	−8%
28 Oct 97	12%	+6%
31 Aug 98	12%	−11%
1 Sept 98	6%	+8%
4 Apr 00	15%	−1%
12 Apr 00	9%	−8%
14 Apr 00	12%	−11%
17 Apr 00	12%	+9%
27 Apr 00	8%	+5%
23 May 00	9%	−7%
24 May 00	9%	+5%
13 Oct 00	8%	+8%

Daily highs minus lows larger than 5% for the Nasdaq composite index over the time period from 1991 to October 2000. Out of the twelve moves of more than 5% since 1991, none occurred before 1997 and eight have occurred in the time interval from April to October 2000! Notice that the variation of the close $close(t) - close(t - 1)$ from one day to the next day is not always a good signature of the excitement of the day, as can be seen for instance on April 4.

A second mechanism is provided by investment strategies with an "insurance portfolio." Indeed, the initial assessment of the origins of the October 1987 crash pointed to the then-popular hedging strategies deriving from portfolio insurance models. In a nutshell, such strategies consist of selling when price decreases below a threshold (stop loss) and in buying when price increases. It is clear that by increasing the volume of sell orders following a price decrease, this may lead to further price decreases, possibly cascading in a downward spiral. The 1988 Brady Commission appointed to investigate the cause of the 1987 crash has indeed named portfolio insurance as a major factor contributing to the downward pressure on stock prices that led to the crash of October 1987. Recent works, for instance, Barlevy and Veronesi [28], show that uninformed traders can behave as insurance portfolios and precipitate a price crash because, as price declines, they reasonably surmise that better informed traders could have received negative information which leads them to reduce their own demand for assets, driving the price of stocks even lower.

"HERD" BEHAVIOR AND "CROWD" EFFECT

BEHAVIORAL ECONOMICS

In debates and research on the social sciences, the sciences dealing with human societies, it is customary to oppose two approaches, the first striving for objectivism, the second being more interpretative.

- The first approach attempts to view "social facts" as "material things," looking for examples where human groups appear to behave as much as possible as inanimate matter, such as in crowds, queues, traffic jams, competition, attraction, perturbations, and markets.

- In contrast, the second approach attempts as much as possible to distinguish the behavior of social agents from that of inanimate matter. In this framework, it is believed that human endowments such as conscience, reflection, intention, morality, and history forbid the use and transfer of quantitative methods developed in the physical, material, and more generally natural sciences to the humanities.

In recent economic and finance research, there is a growing interest in marrying the two viewpoints, that is, in incorporating ideas from social sciences to account for the fact that markets reflect the thoughts, emotions, and actions of real people as opposed to the idealized economic investor who underlies the efficient market and random walk hypotheses. This was captured by the now-famous pronouncement of Keynes [235] that most investors' decisions "can only be taken as a result of animal spirits—of a spontaneous urge to action rather than inaction, and not the outcome of a weighed average of benefits multiplied by the quantitative probabilities" (see the section entitled "Is Prediction Possible?" in chapter 1 and the section entitled "Prices Are Unpredictable, or Are They?" in chapter 2). A real investor may intend to be rational and may try to optimize his or her actions, but that rationality tends to be hampered by cognitive biases, emotional quirks, and social influences. "Behavioral finance" [424, 372, 376, 163, 104] is a growing research field that uses psychology, sociology, and other behavioral theories to explain the behavior of investors and money managers. The behavior of financial markets is thought to result from varying attitudes toward risk, the heterogeneity in the framing of information, cognitive errors, self-control and lack thereof, regret in financial decision making, and the influence of mass psychology. Assumptions about the frailty of human rationality and the acceptance of such drives as fear and greed are underlying the recipes developed over decades by so-called technical analysts.

Prof. Thaler, now at the University of Chicago, was one of the earliest and strongest proponents of behavioral economics [424] and has made a career developing a taxonomy of anomalies that embarrass the standard view from neoclassical economics that markets are efficient and people are rational. According to accepted economic theory, for instance, a person is always better off with more rather than fewer choices. One day, Thaler noticed that a few of his supposedly rational colleagues who were over at his house were unable to stop themselves from gorging on some cashew nuts he had put out. Why, then, did Thaler's colleagues thank him for removing the tempting cashews from his living room? Another case-in-point was when a friend admitted to Thaler that, although he mowed his own lawn to save $10, he would never agree to cut the lawn next door in return for the same $10 or even more. According to the concept of "opportunity cost," foregoing a gain of $10 to mow a neighbor's lawn "costs" just as much as paying somebody else to mow your own. According to theory, you prefer either the extra time or the extra money—it cannot be both. Still another example reported in [272] is when Thaler and another friend decided to skip a basketball game in Rochester because of a swirling snowstorm. His friend remarked that if they had bought the tickets already, they would have gone. The problem refers to "sunk costs." Similarly, there is no sense going to the health club just because you have paid your dues. After all, the money is already paid: sunk. And yet, Thaler observed that we do, in general. People, in short, do not behave like rational economics would like them to. Even economics professors are not as rational as the people in their models. For instance, a bottle of wine that sells for $50 might seem far too expensive to buy for a casual dinner at home. But if you already owned that bottle of wine, having purchased it earlier for far less, you would be more likely to uncork it for the same meal. To an economist, this makes no sense, but Thaler culled that anecdote from Richard Rosett, a prominent neoclassicist [272]. The British economist K. Binmore once proclaimed at a seminar that people evolve toward rationality by learning from mistakes. Thaler retorted that people may learn how to shop for groceries sensibly because they do it every week, but the big decisions— marriage, career, retirement—do not come up very often. So Binmore's highbrow theories, he concluded, were good for "buying milk" [272]. In his doctoral thesis on the economic "worth" of a human life, Thaler proposed quantifying it by measuring the difference in pay between life-threatening jobs and safer lines of work. He came up with a figure of

$200 a year (in 1967 dollars) for each 1-in-1,000 chance of dying. When he asked friends about it, most insisted that they would not accept a 1-in-1,000 mortality risk for anything less than a million dollars. Paradoxically, the same friends said they would not be willing to forgo any income to eliminate the risks that their jobs already entailed. Thaler concluded that rather than rationally pricing mortality, people had a cognitive disconnect; they put a premium on new risks and casually discounted familiar ones [272]. In experiments designed to test his ideas, Thaler found that subjects would usually agree to pay more for a drink if they were told that the beer is being purchased from an exclusive hotel rather than from a rundown grocery. It strikes them as unfair to pay the same. This violates the law-of-one-price that one drink is worth the same as another, and it suggests that people care as much about being treated fairly as they do about the actual value of what they are paying for [227, 228]. An important discovery, extending the framing principle of Kahneman and Tversky, was "mental accounting" [423, 373]. "Framing" says that the positioning of choices prejudices the outcome, an issue that received a lot of publicity in the 2000 U.S. presidential election. "Mental accounting" says that people draw their own frames, and that where they place the boundaries subtly affects their decisions. For instance, most people sort their money into accounts like "current income" and "savings" and justify different expenditures from each [425]. Applied to the stock market, Thaler noticed that some behavioral patterns like "categorization" may provide arbitrage opportunities: for instance, when Lucent Technologies was riding high, people categorized it as a "good stock" and mentally coded news about it in a favorable way. Later, when Lucent had become a "bad stock," similar news was interpreted more gloomily. Another anomaly, called "hyperbolic discounting" [254, 255], refers to preference reversals: when people expect money but have not yet received it, they are capable of planning, quite rationally, how much of it to spend immediately and how much to save. This is in agreement with economics theory, which argues that for a modest incentive, people are willing to save and put off spending. But when the money actually arrives, willpower breaks down and the money is often spent right away. In other words, when sacrifices are distant, patience predominates: I want/plan/intend to start exercising next month. But next month, the designated sacrifice is often avoided. Such preferences, neglected by neoclassical economics, have important implications, in particular for investors' life-cycle savings decisions.

One of the most robust findings in the psychology of judgment is that people are overconfident (see the review [104] and references therein).

A significant manifestation in the context of herding is that people over-estimate the reliability of their knowledge and of their abilities: one famous finding is that 90% of the automobile drivers in Sweden consider themselves "above average" [417], while of course by definition (for a symmetric distribution) 50% are below average and 50% are above average! Most people also consider themselves above average in their ability to get along with others. Such overconfidence is enhanced in domains where people have self-declared expertise, holding their actual predictive ability comparable [190]. This seems to have important implications for understanding managers' decisions concerning corporate growth and external acquisition and why most funds are actively managed [104]. Overconfidence implies that managers all think they can pick winners.

HERDING

There is growing empirical evidence of the existence of herd or "crowd" behavior in speculative markets as carefully documented in the recent book of Shiller [375] and references therein. Herd behavior is often said to occur when many people take the same action, because some mimic the actions of others. The term "herd" obviously refers to similar behavior observed in animal groups. Other terms such as "flocks" or "schools" describe the collective coherent motion of large numbers of self-propelled organisms, such as migrating birds and gnus, lemmings and ants [426]. In recent years, physicists have shown that much of the observed herd behavior in animals can be understood from the action of simple laws of interactions between animals. With respect to humans, there is a long history of analogies between human groups and organized matter [64, 305]. More recently, extreme crowd motions such as in panic situations have been remarkably well quantified by models that treat the crowd as a collection of individuals interacting as a granular medium with friction, like the familiar sand of beaches [191].

Herding has been linked to many economic activities, such as investment recommendations [364, 171], price behavior of IPOs [450], fads and customs [39], earnings forecasts [427], corporate conservatism [463], and delegated portfolio management [290]. Researchers are investigating the incentives investment analysts face when deciding whether to herd and, in particular, whether economic conditions and agents' individual characteristics affect their likelihood of herding. Although herding behavior appears inefficient from a social standpoint, it can be rational from the perspective of managers who are concerned about their reputations in the labor market. Such behavior can be rational and may occur as an information cascade [450, 107, 39], a situation in which every subsequent actor, based on the observations of others, makes the same choice independent of his or her private signal. Herding among investment newsletters, for instance, is found to decrease with the precision of private information [171]: the less information you have, the stronger is your incentive to follow the consensus.

Research on herding in finance can be subdivided in the following non-mutually exclusive manner [107, 171].

1. **Informational cascades** occur when individuals choose to ignore or downplay their private information and instead jump on the bandwagon by mimicking the actions of individuals who acted previously. Informational cascades occur when the existing aggregate information becomes so overwhelming that an individual's single piece of private information is not strong enough to reverse the decision of the crowd. Therefore, the individual chooses to mimic the action of the crowd, rather than act on his private information. If this scenario holds for one individual, then it likely also holds for anyone acting after this person. This domino-like effect is often referred to as a cascade. The two crucial ingredients for an informational cascade to develop are: (i) sequential decisions with subsequent actors observing decisions (not information) of previous actors; and (ii) a limited action space.

2. **Reputational herding**, like cascades, takes place when an agent chooses to ignore his or her private information and mimic the action of another agent who has acted previously. However, reputational herding models have an additional layer of mimicking, resulting from positive reputational properties that can be obtained by acting as part of a group or choosing a certain project. Evidence has been found that a forecaster's age is positively related to the absolute first difference between his forecast and the group mean. This has been interpreted as evidence that as a forecaster ages, evaluators develop tighter prior beliefs about the forecaster's ability, and hence the forecaster has less incentive to herd with the group. On the other hand, the incentive for a second-mover to discard his private information and instead mimick the market leader increases with his initial reputation, as he strives to protect his current status and level of pay [171].

3. **Investigative herding** occurs when an analyst chooses to investigate a piece of information he or she believes others also will examine. The analyst would like to be the first to discover the information but can only

profit from an investment if other investors follow suit and push the price of the asset in the direction anticipated by the first analyst. Otherwise, the first analyst may be stuck holding an asset that he or she cannot profitably sell.

4. **Empirical herding** refers to observations by many researchers of "herding" without reference to a specific model or explanation. There is indeed evidence of herding and clustering among pension funds, mutual funds, and institutional investors when a disproportionate share of investors engage in buying, or at other times selling, the same stock. These works suggest that clustering can result from momentum-following, also called "positive feedback investment," for example, buying past winners or perhaps repeating the predominant buy or sell pattern from the previous period.

There are many reported cases of herding. One of the most dramatic and clearest in recent times is the observation by G. Huberman and T. Regev [204] of a contagious speculation associated with a nonevent in the following sense. A *Sunday New York Times* article on the potential development of a new cancer-curing drug caused the biotech company EntreMed's stock to rise from 12 at the Friday, May 1, 1998 close to open at 85 on Monday, May 4, close near 52 on the same day, and remain above 39 in the three following weeks. The enthusiasm spilled over to other biotechnology stocks. It turns out that the potential breakthrough in cancer research had already been reported in one of the leading scientific journals, *Nature*, and in various popular newspapers (including the *Times*) more than five months earlier. At that time, market reactions were essentially nil. Thus the enthusiastic public attention induced a long-term rise in share prices, even though no genuinely new information had been presented. The very prominent and exceptionally optimistic *Sunday New York Times* article of May 3, 1998 led to a rush on EntreMed's stock and other biotechnology companies' stocks, which is reminiscent of similar rushes leading to bubbles in historical times (see chapter 1). It is to be expected that information technology, the Internet, and biotechnology are among the leading new frontiers on which sensational stories will lead to enthusiasm, contagion, herding, and speculative bubbles.

EMPIRICAL EVIDENCE OF FINANCIAL ANALYSTS' HERDING

A recently published empirical work by Ivo Welch [451] shed new light on the important question of whether herding is more rational or "irrational." He considered the buy and sell recommendations of security analysts and asked whether previous recommendations as well as the prevailing consensus influence the recommendations of the following analyses. This is one of the rare studies where a scientific approach can be developed to gain insight into this delicate question. Welch studied more than 50,000 stock recommendations made between 1989 and 1994 by hundreds of U.S. security analysts from the Zacks database, which is a commercially compiled database of analysts'recommendation, used, for instance, by *The Wall Street Journal* to publish regular performance reviews of major brokerage houses. To formulate the problem in a langage suitable for a rigorous statistical analysis, the recommendations are divided into five classes: 1: "strong buy," 2: "buy," 3: "hold," 4: "sell," 5: "strong sell." From this numerical coding of the recommendation, Welch started by constructing Table 4.2 or "transition matrix," in which an entry denoted $N_{i \to j}$ represents the number of recommendations j, given that the previous recommendation was i. Thus, for example, $N_{1 \to 4} = 92$ is the number of recommendations "sell" following the previous recommendation "strong buy"; $N_{4 \to 3} = 1,826$ is the number of recommendations "hold" following the previous recommendation "sell," and so on. As can be seen from the table, the transition matrix is highly irregular: the numbers of recommendations vary strongly from one recommendation to another. The total number of recommendations (of any direction) starting from a previous "strong buy" is 14,682, compared to only 1,584 recommendations starting from a previous "strong sell." It is thus clear that there is a rather strong bias toward "buy" and "strong buy": the total number of such recommendations is 25,784 compared to only 4,951 "sell" and "strong sell" recommendations, that is, more than five times more "buy" and "strong buy" recommendations than "sell" and "strong sell" recommendations.

To test for herding, Welch first defined the global consensus as $T_0 = \sum_{j=1}^{5} j \ \text{total}(j)/N = [1 \times \text{total}(1) + 2 \times \text{total}(2) + 3 \times \text{total}(3) + 4 \times \text{total}(4) + 5 \times \text{total}(5)]/N$, which gives a value close to 2.5, where $\text{total}(j)$ is the total number of recommendation of type j following any previous recommendation as defined in Table 4.2. Since the value 2.5 is less than 3, which would be the expected result in the absence of bias, this confirms the bias toward "buy" positions corresponding to smaller coding numbers (1 and 2). The second step is to extract the subset of recommendations on a given day t and recalculate the transition matrix for this day. The entries will be smaller, but what is important are the proportions (i.e., normalized by $\text{total}(i)$), which will probably be different from those shown in Table 4.2. To quantify how different, one again

TABLE 4.2

From ↓ (i)	to → (j)	1	2	3	4	5	total(i)
1 : Strong buy		8,190	2,234	4,012	92	154	14,682
2 : Buy		2,323	4,539	3,918	262	60	11,102
3 : Hold		3,622	3,510	13,043	1,816	749	22,740
4 : Sell		115	279	1,826	772	375	3,367
5 : Strong sell		115	39	678	345	407	1,584
	Total(j)	14,365	10,601	23,477	3,287	1,745	53,475

The "transition matrix" giving the number of recommendations j, given that the previous recommendation was i, where the numbers i and j are taken from five values defined by classifying the recommendations into five classes: 1: strong buy, 2: buy, 3: hold, 4: sell, 5: strong sell. The total number of recommendations used in the construction of this table is $N = 53,475$. Reproduced from [451].

computes the consensus $T(t)$ for this day t. If $T(t) = T_0$, this day is like any other day and there is no special difference from the point of view of the analysts. More interesting are the days when $T(t)$ is significantly different from T_0. The question is, then, What is the origin of this difference? The answer is given by calculating how this difference depends on different factors, such as the recommendations made the previous day or the prevailing consensus. Welch introduced for this a "herding" parameter measuring the tendency to herd, that is, when recommendations are influenced by the prevailing consensus. The first result is that analysts do indeed bias their recommendations towards the prevailing consensus. He then measures the probability of making one of the five recommendations when herding is absent and compares it to that when herding is present: a "hold" recommendation, for instance, occurs 42% of the time when herding is absent and 47% when it is present. While this impact appears small, any statistically significant change in behavior indicates herding, given that analysts rarely agree on a stock pick when acting in isolation, and in a sense it is their job to disagree.

What is the cause of this herding? If all analysts receive new information about a stock at the same time and interpret it in the same way, rational herding could ensue. Alternatively, analysts could simply be mimicking their colleagues blindly, even when no new fundamental information is released, leading to "irrational" herding. In order to distinguish these two hypotheses, Welch measured the propensity to follow a consensus when the herd proves to be correct. The idea is that if herding is rationally based on fundamental information, it should lead to better recommendations, on average, than when it is irrationally based on mimicking behavior. The data shows that "analysts are more inclined to follow the prevailing consensus when it later on turns out to be wrong." Since there does not seem to be any informational advantage to consensus herding, one can conclude that it is of the irrational kind. It also constitutes evidence that analysts follow the prevailing consensus based on limited information, if any.

However, as is often the case in this difficult subject, there are alternative explanations. The fact that the prevailing consensus among analysts turns out to be wrong can also be interpreted as the fact that investors, who are not the same population as analysts, do not follow the recommendations of the latter! This situation is then similar to a natural system having its own dynamics, which are independent of the existence of observers or analysts trying to forecast, its dynamics being created by the aggregate investment actions of the investors.

Another important fact outlined by the research of Welch is that the strength of herding is different in bull and bear markets. Analysts tend to follow the consensus more strongly (1) in up-markets and (2) following recent revisions in down-markets. Behavior (1) tends to create "bubbles": price inflations deconnected from fundamental values. Behavior (2) suggests that revision from an optimistic to a pessimistic outlook can be amplified by herding, a mechanism that can amplify losses and may lead to brutal drops and crashes.

FORCES OF IMITATION

IT IS OPTIMAL TO IMITATE WHEN LACKING INFORMATION

All the traders in the world are organized into a network of family, friends, colleagues, contacts, and others who are sources of opinion, and influence each other *locally* through this network [48]. We call "neighbors" of agent Anne on this worldwide graph the set of people in direct contact with Anne. Other sources of influence also involve newspapers, Web sites, TV stations, and similar media. Specifically, if Anne is directly connected with k "neighbors" in the worldwide graph of connections, then there are only two forces that influence Anne's opinion: (a) the opinions of these k people together with the influence of the media; and (b) an idiosyncratic signal that she alone receives (or generates; see Figure 4.2). According to the concept of herding and imitation, the assumption is that agents tend to *imitate* the opinions of their

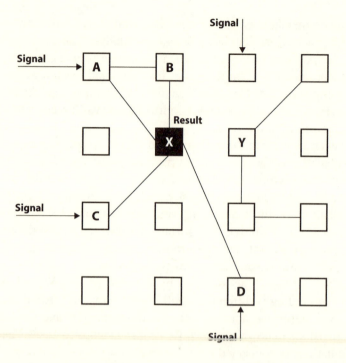

FIG. 4.2. A message path running through a block of agents. The signals are the idiosyncratic noise received at the previous time, which then combines with the state of each agent. Each agent sends a signal to neighbors. A given agent then makes a decision based on the signal of her neighbors and her own private information (reproduced from [383]).

"neighbors," not contradict them. It is easy to see that force (a) will tend to create order, while force (b) will tend to create disorder, or in other words, heterogeneity. The main story here is the fight between order and disorder, and the question we are now going to investigate is, What behavior can result from this fight? Can the system go through unstable regimes, such as crashes? Are crashes predictable? We show that the science of self-organizing systems (sometimes also referred to as "complex systems") bears very significantly on these questions: the stock market and the web of traders' connections can be understood in large part from the science of critical phenomena (in a sense that we are going to examine in some depth later in this chapter and in chapter 5), from which important consequences can be derived.

    To make progress, we formalize the problem a bit and consider a network of investors: each one can be named by an integer $i = 1, \ldots, I$, and

$N(i)$ denotes the set of the agents who are directly connected to agent i according to the worldwide graph of acquaintances. If we isolate one trader, Anne, $N(\text{Anne})$ is the number of traders in direct contact with her, who can exchange direct information with her and exert a direct influence on her. For simplicity, we assume that any investor such as Anne can be in only one of several possible states. In the simplest version, we can consider only two possible states: $s_{\text{Anne}} = -1$ or $s_{\text{Anne}} = +1$. We could interpret these states as "buy" and "sell," "bullish" and "bearish," "optimistic" and "pessimistic." Now, the section entitled "Explanation of the Imitation Strategy" shows that, based only on the information of the actions $s_j(t-1)$ performed yesterday (at time $t-1$) by her $N(\text{Anne})$ "neighbors," Anne maximizes her return by having taken yesterday the decision $s_{\text{Anne}}(t-1)$ given by the sign of the sum of the actions of all her "neighbors." In other words, the optimal decision of Anne, based on the local polling of her "neighbors," who she hopes represents a sufficiently faithful representation of the market mood, is to imitate the majority of her neighbors. This is, of course, open to some possible deviations when she decides to follow her own idiosyncratic "intuition" rather than being influenced by her "neighbors." Such an idiosyncratic move can be captured in this model by a stochastic component independent of the decisions of the neighbors or of any other agent. Intuitively, the reason why it is generally optimal for Anne to follow the opinion of the majority is simply because prices move in that direction, forced by the law of supply and demand. Later in this chapter and in chapter 5, we shall show that this apparently innocuous evolution law produces remarkable self-organizing patterns.

Explanation of the imitation strategy. Consider N traders in a network, whose links represent the communication channels through which the traders exchange information. The graph describes the chain of intermediate acquaintances between any two people in the world. We denote by $N(i)$ the number of traders directly connected to a given trader i on the graph. The traders buy or sell one asset at price $p(t)$ which evolves as a function of time assumed to be discrete and measured in units of the time step Δt. In the simplest version of the model, each agent can either buy or sell only one unit of the asset. This is quantified by the buy state $s_i = +1$ or the sell state $s_i = -1$. Each agent can trade at time $t-1$ at the price $p(t-1)$ based on all previous information, including that at $t-1$. The asset price variation is taken simply proportional to the aggregate sum $\sum_{i=1}^{N} s_i(t-1)$ of all traders' actions: indeed, if this sum is zero, there are as many buyers as there are sellers and the price does not change since there is a perfect balance between supply and demand. If, on the other hand, the sum is positive, there are more buy orders than sell orders and the price has to increase to balance the supply and the demand, as the asset is too rare to satisfy all the demand. There are many other influences impacting the price change from one day to the next, and this can usually be accounted for in a simple way by adding a stochastic component to the price variation. This term alone would give the usual log-normal random walk process [92], while the balance between supply and demand together with imitation leads to some organization, as we show below.

At time $t - 1$, just when the price $p(t - 1)$ has been announced, the trader i defines her strategy $s_i(t - 1)$ that she will hold from $t - 1$ to t, thus realizing the profit (or loss) equal to the price difference $(p(t) - p(t - 1))$ times her position $s_i(t - 1)$. To define her optimal strategy $s_i(t - 1)$, the trader should calculate her expected profit P_E, given the past information and her position, and then choose $s_i(t - 1)$ such that P_E is maximum. Since the price moves with the general opinion $\sum_{i=1}^{N} s_i(t - 1)$, the best strategy is to buy if it is positive and sell if it is negative. The difficulty is that a given trader cannot poll the positions s_j that will take all other traders, which will determine the price drift according to the balance between supply and demand. The next best thing that trader i can do is to poll her $N(i)$ "neighbors" and construct her prediction for the price drift from this information. The trader needs additional information, namely the a priori probability P_+ and P_- for each trader to buy or sell. The probabilities P_+ and P_- are the only information that she can use for all the traders that she does not poll directly. From this, she can form her expectation of the price change. The simplest case corresponds to a market without drift where $P_+ = P_- = 1/2$.

Based on the previously stated rule that the price variation is proportional to the sum of actions of traders, the best guess of trader i is that the future price change will be proportional to the sum of the actions of her neighbors who she has been able to poll, hoping that this provides a sufficiently reliable sample of the total population. Traders are indeed constantly sharing information, calling each other to "take the temperature," effectively polling each other before taking actions. It is then clear that the strategy that maximizes her expected profit is such that her position is of the sign given by the sum of the actions of all her "neighbors." This is exactly the meaning of the following expression:

$$s_i(t - 1) = \text{sign}\left(K \sum_{j \in N_i} s_j + \varepsilon_i \right) \qquad (6)$$

such that this position $s_i(t-1)$ gives her the maximum payoff based on her best prediction of the price variation $p(t) - p(t-1)$ from yesterday to today. The function sign(x) is defined by being equal to $+1$ (to -1) for positive (negative) argument x, K is a positive constant of proportionality between the price change and the aggregate buy/sell orders. It is inversely proportional to the "market depth": the larger the market, the smaller is the relative impact of a given unbalance between buy and sell orders, hence the smaller is the price change. ε_i is a noise and $N(i)$ is the number of neighbors with whom trader i interacts significantly. In simple terms, this law (6) states that the best investment decision for a given trader is to take that of the majority of her neighbors, up to some uncertainty (noise), capturing the possibility that the majority of her neighbors might give an incorrect prediction of the behavior of the total market.

Expression (6) can be thought of as a mathematical formulation of Keynes's beauty contest. Keynes [235] argued that not only are stock prices determined by the firm's fundamental value, but, in addition, mass psychology and investors' expectations influence financial markets significantly. It was his opinion that professional investors prefer to devote their energy, not to estimating fundamental values but rather, to analyzing how the crowd of investors is likely to behave in the future. As a result, he said, most persons are largely concerned not with making superior long-term forecasts of the probable yield of an investment over its whole life, but with foreseeing changes in the conventional basis of valuation a short time ahead of the general public. Keynes used his famous beauty contest as a parable for stock markets. In order to predict the winner of a beauty contest, the ability to recognize objective beauty is not nearly as important as the ability to predict others' recognition of beauty. In Keynes's view, the optimal strategy is not to pick those faces the player thinks are the prettiest, but those the other players are likely to think the average opinion will be, or those the other players will think the others will think the average opinion will be, or even further along this iterative loop. Expression (6) precisely captures this concept: the opinion s_i at time t of an agent i is a function of all the opinions of the other "neighboring" agents at the previous time $t-1$, which themselves depend on the opinion of the agent i at time $t-2$, and so on. In the stationary equilibrium situation in which all agents finally form an opinion after many such iterative feedbacks have had time to develop, the solution of (6) is precisely the one taking into account all the opinions in a completely self-consistent way compatible with the infinitely iterative loop.

MIMETIC CONTAGION AND THE URN MODELS

Orléan [323]–[328] has captured the paradox of combining rational and imitative behavior under the name "mimetic rationality" (*rationalité mimétique*). He has developed models of mimetic contagion of investors in the stock markets that are based on irreversible processes of opinion forming. In the simplest version, called the Urn model, which has a long history in the mathematical literature dating from Polya [269], let us assume that, at some time, there are M white balls and N black balls in an urn. Then, we draw one ball at random from the urn. Here, "random" means that any ball has the same probability $1/(M + N)$ to be chosen. Then, we return the winner as well as another additional ball of the same color to the set of balls from which it was drawn. Thus, after this experiment, if white is the winner, there will be $M + 1$ white balls in the white set and N black balls in the black set. On the other hand, if a black was chosen, there would be M white balls in the white set and $N + 1$ black balls in the black set. We repeat this experiment on and on. This simple model describes the process in which a newcomer (the added ball) mimicks in his action (his color) one of the existing investors. This irreversible process of aggregation is clearly based on imitation, but it also has a strong stochastic component.

Consider the initial fair state $M = N = 1$ at time $t = 0$. At the next time step $t = 1$, after application of the rules of the game, the urn contains either $M = 2$ white balls and $N = 1$ black balls with probability $1/2$ or $M = 1$ white balls and $N = 2$ black balls with probability $1/2$. At the next time step $t = 2$, the urn contains one of three possible populations: (1) $M = 3$ white balls and $N = 1$ black balls with probability $(1/2) \times (2/3) = 1/3$. (2) $M = 2$ white balls and $N = 2$ black balls with probability $(1/2) \times (1/3) + (1/2) \times (1/3) = 1/3$. There are indeed two paths to achieve this final state, and we have thus to sum over them to obtain the correct probability. (3) $M = 1$ white balls and $N = 3$ black balls with probability $(1/2) \times (2/3) = 1/3$. It is easy but becomes more and more cumbersome to continue counting the different possibilities and their associated probabilities as time goes on. A typical trajectory of the fraction f_w of white and f_b of black balls in the urn may be as follows. Time ($t = 0$, $f_w = 1/2$, $f_b = 1/2$); ($t = 1$, $f_w = 1/3$, $f_b = 2/3$); ($t = 3$, $f_w = 1/4$, $f_b = 3/4$); ($t = 4$, $f_w = 2/5$, $f_b = 3/5$), ... In the limit where the game is repeated a large number of times, one obtains a truly remarkable result [269], whose two sides are enticingly paradoxical: on one hand, the fractions $M/(M + N)$ of white balls and $N/(M + N)$ of black balls eventually converge towards well-defined numbers f_W and $f_B = 1 - f_W$, which *do not fluctuate* anymore; on the other hand, f_W and thus $f_B = 1 - f_W$ can take any arbitrary value between 0 and 1 with equal uniform probability. This means that, restarting the game several times, the final fraction of white and black balls will be different, with no relationship between one play and the next! This irreversible model describes an imitation process that can lead to a continuum of states; in other words, many different possible states coexist and compete. Phrased in the context of imitation between agents that successively enter the market and imitate at random one of the already active investor, a bull or bear market may emerge completely at random as the volume of investors progressively grows. What controls the long-term value of f_W and $f_B = 1 - f_W$ is the initial fluctuation of the random drawing process: if, for instance, a white ball is drawn four times in a row, this gives a probability 4/5 to continue drawing a white ball at the next time step, compared to only 1/5 for a black ball. If at the tenth time step, there are 11 white and 1 black balls, the probability of reinforcing the dominance of white balls is 11/12 compared to a probability of only 1/12 to get a black ball. This progressive freezing of the probabilities and its feedback on the fraction of the two populations is the underlying mechanism. We thus see that the fractions of the two populations and their corresponding probabilities become progressively frozen, simply by the law of large numbers.

The urn model can be generalized by changing the rules of addition of the new balls; that is, how many new investors come into play, how do they do so, and how do they imitate the existing players so as to include more complex nonlinear behaviors [20, 19, 325].

This class of models also offers a mechanism for curious facts in economics and history. Two well-cited examples are the dominance of the VHS over the Betamax standard in the video industry and the blossoming of concentrations of high-tech companies such as Silicon Valley in California. In both cases, it is argued that some slight advantage due to chance or other factors, such as a few more buys and movies favoring the VHS standard, has progressively been amplified and frozen by the urn mechanism. Similarly, if two valleys are competing in order to attract high-tech companies, the one that initially has a few more companies than the other will be more attractive to new start-ups, as they will get a slighty more active business environment. Again, this slight initial advantage may be amplified and lead to a major advantage in the end. The urn mechanism also provides a natural framework for reanalyzing historical facts, in particular the often tortuous paths of human societies.

Accordingly, the urn mechanism may cast some doubts on the view often constructed in retrospect that history is following a deterministic trajectory. In contrast, the Urn process suggests that some major historical facts may have resulted from progressive freezing of stochastic events that accumulated to finally put the balance on one side.

This class of models provides an alternative to the "influence" model summarized by the expression (6), putting more emphasis on the irreversibility of the decision processes. In contrast, the imitation model (6) is more in tune with a kind of "equilibrium," allowing changes of opinion for any of the investors. Notwithstanding these differences, the important message is that apparently anomalous bubble phases of the market are robust consequences of the imitative behavior of agents.

IMITATION FROM EVOLUTIONARY PSYCHOLOGY

Beyond the rationale to imitate discussed before, justification for imitative tendencies can be found in evolutionary psychology [93]. The point is that humans are rarely at their best when they use rational reasoning. It can indeed be demonstrated that "rational" decision-making methods (i.e., the usual methods drawn from logic, mathematics, and probability theory) are incapable of solving the natural adaptive problems our ancestors had to solve reliably in order to survive and reproduce. Because biological evolution is a slow process, and the modern world has emerged in an evolutionary eye-blink, our present abilities are inherited from the past and remain functionally specialized to solving the particular problems facing the hunter-gatherers of the past. This poor performance on most natural problems is the primary reason why problem-solving specializations were favored by natural selection over general-purpose problem solvers. Despite widespread claims to the contrary, the human mind is not worse than rational, but may often be better than rational! On evolutionarily recurrent computational tasks, such as object recognition, grammar acquisition, or speech comprehension, the human mind exhibits impressive skills of a quality often comparable to or better than the best artificial problem-solving systems that decades of research have produced.

General-purpose systems are constrained to apply the same problem-solving methods to every problem and make no special assumption about the problem to be solved. Specialized problem solvers are not handicapped by these limitations. From this perspective, the human mind is powerful and intelligent primarily because it comes equipped with a large array of what one might call "reasoning instincts." Although instincts are often thought of as the polar opposite of reasoning, a growing body of evidence indicates that humans have many reasoning, learning, and preference circuits that are complexly specialized for solving the specific adaptive problems our hominid ancestors regularly encountered. These circuits are developed without conscious effort and are applied without any awareness of their underlying logic. In other words, these reasoning, learning, and preference circuits have all the hallmarks of what people usually think of as "instincts." They make certain kinds of inferences just as easy and natural to humans as spinning a web is to a spider or building a dam is to a beaver. For example, humans do not seem to have available on-line circuits that perform many logic operations. On the other hand, experimental evidence indicates that humans have evolved circuits dedicated to a more specialized task of equal or greater complexity: detecting cheaters in situations of exchange. Equally important, humans have specialized circuits for understanding threats, as well as recognizing bluffs and double-crosses. Such skills allowed the emergence of coercive coalitions, governments, and other social arrangements, and probably the stock market. The large risks of failure involved in hunting game and gathering food led hunter-gatherers to cooperate in small tribes and share food in order to smooth out the otherwise wildly fluctuating feast-or-famine cycles that prevailed for individuals and families. In more modern contexts, upon stress under sufficiently large risks and uncertainties, humans may switch on some of these adaptive sharing programs.

Experiments show that a lucky event can lead to overconfidence [100]. In the experiments of Darke and Freedman [100], some subjects experienced a lucky event, whereas others did not. All subjects then completed an unrelated decision task, rated their confidence, and placed a bet. After the lucky event, those who believed in luck (i.e., thought of luck as a stable, personal attribute) were more confident and bet more. Subjects who did not believe in luck (i.e., thought luck was random) were less confident and bet less. Studies have also compared decisions made alone to decisions made following interactions with others [189]. Results show that, while interaction did not increase decision accuracy or metaknowledge, subjects frequently showed stable or increasing confidence when they interacted with others, even with those who disagreed with them [189, 361, 382, 346, 347]. A possible interpretation is that the interaction serves the role of rationalizing the subjects' decisions rather than that of collecting valuable information. There is also a herding effect. In the same spirit, exposing to others the rationale behind decisions has been shown to markedly increase subjects' confidence that their choices were appropriate [377]. This is reminiscent of a well-known fact established in education studies that writing enhances comprehension. It has also been demonstrated that feedback concerning the appropriateness of confidence judgments improves calibration and resolution skills [369]. The effect is significantly stronger in men compared to women, as men often exhibit stronger confidence in situations in which they are wrong [291].

More to the point, psychological experiments [10] have been conducted in which subjects are shown real stock prices from the past and asked to forecast subsequent changes while performing trades consistent with these forecasts and, by so doing, accumulating wealth. These subjects, of course, were asked to trade only based on past prices and were not exposed to external "fundamental" news. It was found that subjects track the past average when the stock prices are stable, thus trading against price fluctuations when they arise. However, as prices began to show consistent trends, they began to switch to a trend-chasing strategy, buying more when prices increase and selling when prices decrease. Perhaps even more compelling evidence of the presence of trend-chasing strategies is the wide prevalence of "technical analysis" that tries to spot trends and trend reversals by using technical indicators associated with past price movements [53].

RUMORS

Many on Wall Street think that rumors move stocks (see Figure 4.3). The old Wall Street saying, "buy on the rumor, sell on the news," is alive and well, as can be seen from numerous sources in the media and the Internet. Rumors can drive herding behavior strongly.

Rumors are most easily documented for extraordinary events. Here are a few remarkable examples. The Y2K bug is one of the most famous recent rumors during which misinformation was rampant. Rumors, assertions, predictions, demagoguery, bluster, cover-up, and denial abounded, such that, for the layman, it was almost impossible to sort fact from fiction. Another example is the completely false rumor concerning the U.S. Postal Service that was being circulated on Internet e-mails. The e-mail message claimed that a "Congressman Schnell" has introduced "Bill 602P" to allow the federal government to impose a ¢5 surcharge on each e-mail message delivered over the Internet. The money would be collected by Internet service providers and then turned over to the Postal Service. No such proposed legislation exists. In fact, no "Congressman

KAL
BALTIMORE SUN
Baltimore
USA

FIG. 4.3. Cartoon of the impact of rumors in stock market behavior taken from the front page of *The Economist*, November 1–7, 1997, commenting on the turmoil following the 7% loss of October 27, 1997 on the DJIA. Creation of KAL.

Schnell" exists. And the U.S. Postal Service denied having any authority to surcharge e-mail messages sent over the Internet [430].

Large-scale rumors have also developed on the scale of nations [259]. Hideo Ibe, previous president of the Research Institute for Policies on Aging, declared in a press release on February 14, 1996: "It has been brought to my attention that Deng Xiaoping has said: Since Japanese do not have enough children, we could send them fifty million Chinese." This statement seemed strange given that Japan had 340 inhabitants per square kilometer while China had only 100, and also inprobable in view of the strong control exerted by the immigration service of Japan.

Had Deng Xiaoping pronounced this sentence, or was it expected from Japanese public opinion? To determine the truth, the source of the information should be checked, which implies checking all Chinese newspapers, radio, and TV recordings during the months and perhaps the few years preceding this announcement. This would be a difficult task that could well fail, as occurred in the case of an alleged declaration to the *Washington Post* by Algerian president Houari Boumediene: "One day, millions of men and women will leave the meridonial and poor parts of the world to erupt in the relatively accessible regions of the north hemisphere in search of their survival." Cited by famous French demographers and amplified by important media managers, the declaration, which fed a fear of invasion, has never been documented, notwithstanding a careful investigation by the *Washington Post* over several years.

Circulation of such rumors calls for epidemiological studies such as the one performed by Edgar Morin to investigate the rumor that spread through Orléans, France, that young women were disappearing from fashion shops owned by Jews. Morin showed how all social layers participated in the diffusion of this rumor. On the other hand, in the two previous examples, the contagion was maintained, justified, and probably even created by elites, either scientists or people in charge of the media. These rumors do not circulate in all directions, but essentially from the top to the bottom of society. The rather sophisticated presentations, the apparently serious references that seem to justify their origins, and their distinguished proponents provide food for amplifications serving diverse interests and psychological biases in all layers of society.

Notwithstanding the probable confusion it may bring to the mind of readers, it seems appropriate to mention here a recent book by P. M. Garber that reexamined the tulip mania and the Law and South Sea bubbles described in chapter 1 with a fresh and close look at the historical record [153]. His main conclusion is that the fabled elements ritually invoked as underlying speculative bubbles with herding and irrational behavior are just not true. Instead, he defends the view that these events have a possible explanation in terms of fundamental valuation. The interesting part is that Garber views the tulip mania "myth" as originating from a rumor that was progressively strengthened by successive authors using it for their own agenda, such as to support moralistic attacks against "excessive speculation" and, in modern times, to plead for government regulation: "the tulipmania episode ... is simply a rhetorical device used to put forward an argument that ... the existence of tulipmania proves that markets are crazy. A curious disturbance in a particular modern market can then be attributed to crazy behavior, so perhaps the market needs to be more severely regulated" [153, p. 11.], While Garber's book has been hailed by a series of financial economists with high reputations, economist C. P. Kindleberger pointed out some of the work's shortcoming and concludes [237]: "The debate between those who believe markets are always rational and efficient, resting on fundamentals, and historians who call attention to a series of financial crises going back to at least 1550 is likely to continue. Parsimony calls for making a choice for or against financial crises; complexity permits one to say that markets are mostly reliable but occasionally get caught up in untoward activities."

THE SURVIVAL OF THE FITTEST IDEA

The drive of humans to share ideas and behaviors can be tracked back to a more fundamental level, according to the theory of "memes" introduced by Richard Dawkins [102, 42]. A meme is to thinking what a gene is to evolution. A meme is defined as any idea, behavior, or skill. Like a gene, it can replicate by transferrring from one person to another by imitation: stories, fashions, inventions, recipes, songs, ways of plowing a field or throwing a baseball or making a sculpture. Like a gene, it competes with other memes, as ideas and behavior compete in a culture and between cultures. The memes come to us from all the speakers who are vocal wherever we happen to grow up: parents, siblings, friends, neighbors, teachers, preachers, bosses, coworkers, and everyone involved in producing things like textbooks, novels, comic books, movies, television shows, newspapers, magazines, Internet sites, and so on. All these people are constantly repeating to each other (and of course to their children, their students, their employees, and so on) the memes they have received during their lifetime. All these voices taken together constitute the voice of Mother Culture [339]. According to the meme theory, "just as the design of our bodies can be understood only in terms of natural selection, so the design of our minds can be understood in terms of memetic selection" [42]. For instance, Blackmore [42] showed that once our distant ancestors acquired the crucial ability to imitate, a second kind of natural selection began, a survival of the fittest among competing ideas and behaviors. Ideas that proved most adaptive—making tools, for example, or using language—survived and flourished, replicating themselves in as many minds as possible. These memes then passed themselves on from generation to generation by helping to ensure that the genes of those who acquired them also survived and reproduced. Applying this theory to many aspects of human life, this offers new perspectives for why we live in cities, why we talk so much, why we can't stop thinking, why we behave altruistically, how we choose our mates, and much more. According to Blackmore, "When we look at religions" or other nonscientific beliefs such as astrology,

> from a meme's eye view, we can understand why they have been so successful. These religious memes did not set out with an intention to succeed. They were just behaviors, ideas and stories that were copied from one person to another in the long history of human attempts to understand the world. They were successful because they happened to come together into mutually supportive gangs that included all the right tricks to keep them safely stored in millions of brains, books and buildings, and repeatedly passed on to more. They evoked strong emotions and strange experiences. They provided myths to answer real questions and the myths were protected by untestability, threats, and promises. They created and then reduced fear to create compliance, and they used the beauty, truth and altruism tricks to help their spread. [42, p. 192]

In a similar vein, it is tempting to interpret within the same theory some behaviors observed on stock markets, for instance, the use of technical analysis (for a large collection of free technical analysis materials, see http://decisionpoint.com/) for which a genuine "culture" is striving, even if technical analysis has not been really established from a firm scientific point of view (see, however, [53, 36, 6]).

GAMBLING SPIRITS

Investing in the stock market is a kind of lottery or gambling to many investors, at least if one follows some of the popular press, which coined the expression "casino stock market." The gambling spirit, usually exerted in lotteries and in casinos, has become a prominent state of mind in many states of the United States of America and may be an important psychological factor at work in the stock market as well. Gambling is more than taking risks. There is, of course, risk in gambling, but gambling is something more. The word "gambling" is related to the word "game" and comes from an old English word *gammon*. Gambling is thus associated with the idea of a game. Gambling is a game. It is not a game based on skill or on reason; it is a game based on sheer chance.

Gambling is an appeal to sheer chance: random luck without skill or one's personal involvement [277]. Gambling is an activity in which a person risks something of value to forces of chance completely beyond his or her control, or any rational expectation, in hopes of winning something of greater value, usually more money.

The lottery has become a major American fantasy. Estimates of the total amount wagered are difficult to obtain, but about $500 billion are wagered every year legally in America, and estimates run as high as $1 trillion total when illegal gambling is added in. The best statistics indicate that there are about 10 million compulsive gamblers in the United States, more than the number of alcoholics. It is interesting to realize that gambling also played a prominent role in early American history. In 1612, the British government ran a lottery to assist the new settlement at Jamestown, Virginia. In 1776, the First Continental Congress of the United States sold lottery tickets to finance the American Revolution. President Washington himself bought the first lottery ticket to build the new capital, called Federal City—now known as Washington, D.C. The United States was founded on a lottery, the revolution was financed by a lottery, and the capital city was financed by a lottery.

From 1790 to 1860, 24 of the 36 states sponsored government-run lotteries. Many schools, universities, colleges, and hundreds of churches conducted their own lotteries to raise funds for their own buildings. Through this period of early American history and involvement with lotteries and government-sponsored gambling, because of the increasing corruption of the gambling, by 1894 it had disappeared from America. By 1894, there was no more government-sponsored gambling—it ended in corruption and in a financial fiasco. Public gambling at any level was stopped completely. Between 1894 and 1964, there was no government-sponsored gambling in America. In 1964, it was reintroduced by the state of New Hampshire, which became the first state to offer a lottery, and now there are 37 states that have government-sponsored lotteries, and Washington D.C. makes 38 entities. There are over 500 casinos across the nation.

In 1974, thus 10 years later, a poll indicated that 61% of Americans gambled, wagering $47.4 billion annually. In 1989, 71% were wagering $246 billion. In 1992, $330 billion was being wagered. By 1995, studies indicate that 95% of Americans gamble, 82% play the lottery, 75% play slot machines, 50% bet on dogs and horses, 44% on cards, 34% on bingo, 26% on sporting events, 74% frequented casinos, and 89% approved of gambling. One cannot help but compare this growth of enthusiasm for gambling with the bullish stock market and the remarkable growth of the number of households owning stocks in the last decades.

Gambling expenditures each year exceed the amount spent on films, books, amusements, music, and entertainment combined. People spend more money gambling than they do buying tickets to all national athletic events put together (baseball, football, and everything else). In 1993, people spent $400 billion legally, $482 billion in 1994, and well over $500 billion in 1999! Five billion is spent every year just in the slot machines in Nevada alone! Ninety-two million households visit the casinos, and 10% of all money earned by people in America is thrown away in gambling!

It is difficult to assess how much this gambling spirit is active in the minds of individual investors. If it is, even to a small degree, it is relevant to our discussion since it makes investors prone to imitation and herding because they invest on little information. It may also explain the anomalously large volatility of prices [374] and their potential instabilities.

"ANTI-IMITATION" AND SELF-ORGANIZATION

Why It May Pay to Be in the Minority

In a practical implementation of a trading strategy, it is not sufficient to know or guess the overall direction of the market. There are additional subtleties governing how the trader is going to enter (buy or sell) the market. For instance, Anne will want to be slightly ahead of the herd to buy at a better price, before the price is pushed up for the bullish consensus. Symmetrically, she will want to exit the market a bit before the crowd, that is, before a trend reversal. In other words, she would like to be a little bit contrarian by buying when the majority is still selling and by selling when the majority is still buying, slightly before a change of opinion of the majority of her "neighbors." This means that she will not always want to follow the herd, at least at short time scales. At this level, Anne cannot rely on the polling of her "neighbors" because she knows that they, as well as the rest of the crowd, will have similar ideas to try to out guess each other on when to enter the market. More generally, Anne would ideally like to be in the minority when entering the market, in the majority while holding her position, and again in the minority when closing her position.

This leads to another class of behaviors, very different from those based on imitation and herding. Here, the problem for Anne is to use past information to make her decision to buy the market when she believes that the majority of the others will not yet do it. She thus has to be in the minority. Profiting from being in the minority leads to interesting paradoxes. Rather diabolically, if all traders use the same set of rules, they will end up doing the same thing at the same time and cannot therefore be in the minority. This leads to a wonderful paradox: contrary to imitative behavior that gets reinforced when everybody does it, to be in the minority implies striving to be different and, thus, cannot result from using the same rules for all. By adaptation, Anne and her colleagues will thus learn and be forced to differentiate their enter strategies based on past successes and failures.

El-Farol's Bar Problem

This issue has recently been formalized in the framework of so-called "minority games." A minority game is a repeated game where N players have to choose one out of two alternatives (say A and B) at each time step. Those who happen to be in the minority win. Although being rather simple at first glance, this game is subtle in the sense that, as we have already said, if all players analyze the situation in the same way, they all will choose the same alternative and lose. Moreover, there is a frustration since not all the players can win at the same time. Minority games are abstractions of the famous El-Farol's bar problem [17]. In that model, 100 people decide independently each week whether to go to a bar that offers entertainment on a certain night. Space is limited, and the evening is only enjoyable if the bar is not too crowded—specifically, if fewer than 60% of the possible 100 are present. There is no way to tell the numbers coming for sure in advance, therefore a person goes, that is, deems it worth going, if she expects fewer than 60 to show up; she stays home if she expects more than 60 to go. Choices are unaffected by previous visits; there is no collusion or prior communication among the people; and the only information available is the numbers who came in past weeks. What is the dynamics of the numbers attending from week to week?

To answer this, Arthur [17] assumed that the 100 persons can each individually form several predictors or hypotheses in the form of functions that map the past d weeks' attendance figures into next week's. Such predictors are the analog of technical trading recipes that investors use to help form their decisions. For example, following the example of Arthur, recent attendance numbers might be

44 78 56 15 23 67 84 34 45 76 40 56 22 35.

Particular hypotheses or predictors to predict next week's number might be [17]

- the same as last week's, giving 35 at the prediction for the attendence of next week,

- a mirror image around 50 of last week's, giving 65,

- a (rounded) average of the last four weeks, giving 49,

- the trend in the last eight weeks, bounded by 0 and 100, giving 29,

- the same as two weeks ago (two-period cycle detector), giving 22,

- the same as five weeks ago (five-period cycle detector), giving 76,

- etc.

Arthur assumes that each person possesses and keeps track of an individualized set of k such focal predictors. She decides to go or stay according to the currently most accurate predictor in her set. Once decisions are made, each agent learns the new attendance figure and updates the accuracies of her monitored predictors. In this bar problem, the set of hypotheses currently most credible and acted upon by the person determines the attendance. But the attendance history determines the set of active hypotheses. This is an analog to an important mechanism at work in stock markets: the use of predictors and their impact on attendance is indeed similar to the use of "technical indicators" used by technical analysts to forecast the market.

Using artificial persons who choose at random k (6 or 12 or 23, say) different predictors among several dozen focal predictors replicated many times, a computer simulation allows us to investigate what happens. Each artificial person then possesses k predictors or hypotheses she can draw upon, and at each time step, she chooses the one that has performed best in the past (even if it has not been used). This deterministic dynamics gives the bar attendance shown in Figure 4.4. The remarkable result is that the predictors self-organize into an equilibrium pattern in which the most accurate predictors, on average, are forecasting 40% of the time above 60, and 60% of the time below 60. While the population of best predictors splits into this 60/40 average ratio, it keeps changing

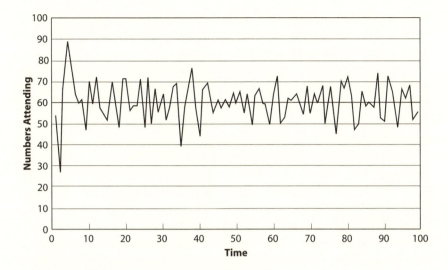

FIG. 4.4. Bar attendance in El Farol's bar problem posed by B. Arthur as a paradigm for "minority games." Reproduced from [17].

in membership forever. These results appear throughout the experiments robust to changes in types of predictors created and in numbers assigned [17]. The pattern shown in Figure 4.4 is reminiscent of the patterns of price variations observed for a typical stock (see chapter 2). This suggests a mechanism for the "noisy" structure of price variations and returns whose origin may be rooted in the fact that investors cannot all win at the same time and have to choose different strategies if they want to win.

MINORITY GAMES

Many variants of this minority game have been introduced which generalize the phenomenon and capture an essential feature of systems where agents compete for limited resources. In minority games, artificial agents with partial information and bounded rationality base their decision only on the knowledge of the M (for memory) last winning alternatives, called histories. Take all the histories and fix a choice (A or B) for each of them: you get a strategy, which is like a theory of the world. Each strategy has an intrinsic value, called virtual value, which is the total number of times the strategy has predicted the right alternative, A or B. At the beginning of the game, every player gets a limited set of S strategies. She uses them inductively; that is, she uses the strategy with the highest virtual value (ties are broken by coin tossing). It must be emphasized that a player does not know anything about the others; all her information come from the virtual values of the strategies.

The more striking properties of the minority game (MG) are: (1) it is a model that addresses the interaction between agents and information; (2) the agents are able to cooperate (but without direct exchanges); (3) the agents minimize the available information; (4) there is a critical transition between a symmetric phase with no information available to agents and an asymmetric phase with available information to agents. The control parameter is the ratio $\alpha = P/N$ of the number P of the different possible states of fundamental information divided by the number N of agents. When α is less than α_c, where α_c is a special value of the order of 1, the market is efficient and there is no information that can be used for prediction. In contrast, for α larger than α_c, a new agent could profit from the existence of predictive structure in the dynamics: there are not enough agents to exploit and remove all information. We recover here the insight already discussed in the section titled "A Parable," in chapter 2.

An intuitive and qualitative understanding of minority games can be obtained by using the insight obtained from expression (6) in the section titled "Explanation of the Imitation Strategy" for the imitative strategy. Indeed, in (6), a positive coefficient K quantifies the force of imitation. Contrarian behavior corresponds to the case where K is negative. In the analogy with spins of magnetic materials, imitation ($K > 0$) leads to the ferromagnetic phase (magnet) or global cooperative behavior that we describe in the following section, titled "Cooperative Behaviors Resulting from Imitation." Contrarian behavior ($K < 0$) corresponds to the so-called "antiferromagnetic" interaction. In the physics of material sciences, anti-ferromagnetic interactions are known to lead to weird behavior and often complex phases resulting from the frustration induced by not being able to satisfy all pairs of interacting elements simultaneously. This problem has the same qualitative paradoxical properties that we have described for the minority games.

IMITATION VERSUS CONTRARIAN BEHAVIOR

Real markets result from agents' behaviors, which are neither fully imitative nor fully anti-imitative, in contrast with the claims of presently available reductionist models and theories. A better representation of real markets requires a combination of the two. Indeed, one should distinguish the "buy" and "sell" actions from the "holding" period.

1. The price of an asset at any given time is fundamentally determined from the balance between supply and demand: more "buy" than "sell" orders will drive the price up and vice versa. If Anne wants to buy (sell), she wants to be in the minority such that the price tends to decrease (increase) and she thus gets a better *instantaneous* bargain. The "buy" and "sell" actions are optimized when Anne is able to be in the minority.

2. Once she is invested in the market, she gains if her investment agrees with the opinion of the majority: if she bought (sold), she would gain in a book-to-market measure only if the price goes up (down). The gain in the "holding" period is thus optimized when Anne belongs to the majority.

To fix these ideas, let us assume that the time it takes for a transaction to be concluded is Δt, equal to, say, one minute (most of the time, not-too-large transactions can be performed much faster through the Internet). The first minority optimization thus concerns this short time interval and amounts to minimizing the possible difference between an order price and its concrete implementation: Anne gives a "buy" order at 100 but the transaction is concluded at 101 because many others are buying, driving the price up during the short time interval between her order and its concrete implementation. She thus pays more than what she intended. This is what she wants to avoid by being in the minority, that is, buying before the crowd of buyers. In contrast to what happens at this short time scale, the holding period can last much longer, say $n\Delta t$. The relative impact of the contrarian behavior on the imitation forces is thus of the order of $1/n$, the ratio of the time to enter in position to the holding time. For "intraday" traders who are very active, this ratio may not be small at all. The large amount of works on minority games [77, 78, 76, 75] suggests that changing one's strategy often may be profitable in that situation. It also suggests that only when the information complexifies or when the number of traders decreases will the traders be able to make consistent profits. In contrast, the buy-and-hold strategies profit as long as the information remains simple, such as when a trend remains strong. The problem then boils down to exit/reverse before or at the reversal of the trend.

The difficulty however, as everyone who has tried to invest in the stock market will know, is that trends and trend reversals occur at all time scales. Figure 4.5 illustrates this observation by a construction based on the insertion of a succession of trends and trend reversals at all scales. This geometric construction, which improves and generalizes the random

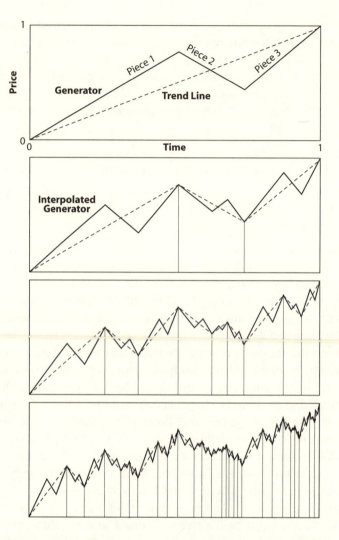

FIG. 4.5. Simple chart that inserts price changes from time 0 to a later time 1 in successive steps to illustrate the concept of trends occurring at all time scales. The intervals are chosen arbitrarily and may represent a minute, an hour, a day, or a year. The process begins with a trend from the bottom-left corner (0,0) to the right-up corner (1,1). Next, a broken line called a generator is used to create the up-and-down pattern piece 1–piece 2–piece 3. Then, each of the three pieces are themselves replaced by three smaller pieces obtained by a suitable scale reduction of the initial generator (the interpolated generator is inverted for each descending piece). Repeating these steps reproduces the shape of the generator, or price curve, but at compressed scales. Both the horizontal axis (time scale) and the vertical axis (price scale) are squeezed to fit the horizontal and vertical boundaries of each piece of the generator. Reproduced from [285] Courtesy of Laurie Grace.

walk model, reproduces quite closely the structure of price trajectories shown in chapter 2. These scale-invariant patterns are made of building blocks of up-and-down trends that can be observed and reproduce themselves at all scales and almost everywhere. These patterns belong to the geometry of fractals [284], a rough or fragmented geometric shape that can be subdivided into parts, each of which is (at least approximately) a reduced-size copy of the whole. The concept of fractals, introduced by Mandelbrot, captures the rough, broken, and irregular characteristics of many phenomena in nature, present at all scales. We shall come back to this construction, shown in Figure 4.5, and its implications in chapter 6.

COOPERATIVE BEHAVIORS RESULTING FROM IMITATION

We borrow and adapt the following tale on the slime mold from Steven Johnson [223] and Evelyn Fox Keller [233]. The slime mold (Dictyostelium discoideum) is a reddish orange mass of cells that can be found, among other places, coating rotting wood in damp sections of forests. Most of the time, the slime mold's motions are barely perceptible, except when the weather conditions grow wetter and cooler, when suddenly it "decides" to "walk away." Indeed, the slime mold spends much of its life as thousands of distinct single-celled units, each moving separately from its other comrades. Under the right conditions, those myriad cells will coalesce into a single, larger organism, which then begins its leisurely crawl across the forest floor, consuming rotting leaves and wood as it moves about.

When the environment is less hospitable, the slime mold acts as a single organism: when the mold enjoys a large food supply, "it" becomes a "they." The slime mold oscillates between being a single creature and a swarm. How do all these cells manage to work so well together? Slime cells have been shown to emit a common substance called acrasin (also known as cyclic AMP), through which they exchange information. For many years, scientists believed that the aggregation process was coordinated by specialized slime-mold cells, known as "pacemaker" cells. According to this theory, each pacemaker cell sends out a chemical signal, telling other slime-mold cells to gather around it, resulting in a cluster.

However, while scientists agreed that waves of cyclic AMP do indeed flow through the slime-mold community before aggregation, all the cells in the community are effectively interchangeable. None of them possess any distinguishing characteristics that might elevate them to pacemaker status. In the late 1960s, Evelyn Fox Keller and Lee Segel developed a mathematical model [234] (now called the Keller–Segel model in chemo-taxis) of how slime cells could self-organize into a coherent organism by continuous release and exchange of cyclic AMP. The model only assumes that every individual cell follows the same set of simple rules, involving the emission and sensing of chemicals. Altering the amount of cyclic AMP each cell releases individually as a function of the amount of cyclic AMP present in the environment, each cell can follow trails of the pheromone that they encounter as they wander through their envi-ronment. When the slime cells pump out enough cyclic AMP, clusters of cells start to form spontaneously. Cells can then better follow the trails created by other cells, creating a positive feedback loop that encourages more cells to join the cluster.

Slime mold aggregation is now recognized as a classic case study in bottom-up behavior and self-organization, similar in a sense to that occurring in stock markets. Spontaneous pattern formation has been and is still a very active domain of study, allowing us to understand, for instance, the origins of the patterns on the furs of zebras and leopards [409, 410]. The general concept works similarly in many distinct fields: pattern and evolving organization result from the com-petition between at least one disordering and one ordering force. In the case of the slime-mold, the disordering force is the spontaneous tendency of cells to wander on their own. The ordering force stems from the interactions mediated through the release and reaction of cells to cyclic AMP. The relative strength of these two forces decides whether the slime-mold cells self-organize into a single unit or live their own distinct lives. A similar fight between ordering and disordering forces between financial agents will be described in chapter 5. The concept that cooperative behavior leads to the emergence of self-organization into novel patterns is at the core of the take-home message of this book. The force derived from self-organization is nicely illustrated in the cartoon of Figure 4.6.

The Ising Model of Cooperative Behavior

The imitative behavior discussed in the section titled "It Is Optimal to Imitate When Lacking Information" in the present chapter and captured by the expression (6) on page 102 belongs to a very general class of

FIG. 4.6. Illustration of the concept that cooperative behavior is a strong force for self-organization. Created by and courtesy of B. A. Huberman.

so-called stochastic dynamical models developed to describe interacting elements, particles, and agents in a large variety of contexts, in particular physics and biology [265, 266]. The tendency or force towards imitation is governed by the parameter K, which can be called the "coupling strength"; the tendency towards idiosyncratic (or noisy) behavior is governed by the amplitude σ of the noise term. Thus the value of K relative to σ determines the outcome of the battle between order and disorder, and eventually the structure of the market prices. More generally, the coupling strength K could be heterogeneous across pairs of neighbors, and it would not substantially affect the properties of the model. Some of the K_{ij}'s could even be negative, as long as the average of all K_{ij}'s was strictly positive.

The expression (6) on page 102 only describes the state of an agent at a given time. In the next instant, new ε_i's are realized, new influences propagate themselves to neighbors, and agents can change their decision according to Figure 4.2. The system is thus constantly changing and reorganizing, as shown in Figure 4.7. The model does *not* assume instantaneous opinion interactions between neighbors. In real markets, opinions indeed tend not to be instantaneous, but are formed over a period of time by a process involving family, friends, colleagues, newspapers, web sites, TV stations, and so on. Decisions about the trading

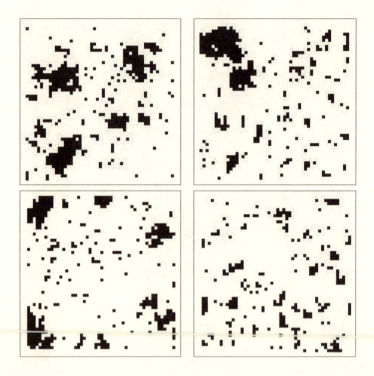

FIG. 4.7. Four snapshots at four successive times of the state of a planar system of 64×64 agents put on a regular square lattice. Each agent placed within a small square interacts with her four nearest neighbors according to the imitative rule (6) of page 102. White (respectively, black) squares correspond to "bull" (respectively, "bear"). The four cases shown here correspond to the existence of a majority of buy orders, as white is the predominant color.

activity of a given agent may occur when the consensus from all these sources reaches a trigger level. This is precisely this feature of a threshold reached by a consensus that expression (6) captures: the consensus is quantified by the sum over the $N(i)$ agents connected to agent i, and the threshold is provided by the sign function. The delay in the formation of the opinion of a given trader as a function of other traders' opinions is captured by the progressive spreading of information during successive updating steps (see, for instance, [265, 266]).

The simplest possible network is a two-dimensional grid in the Euclidean plane. Each agent has four nearest neighbors: one to the North, the South, the East, and the West. The tendency K towards imitation is balanced by the tendency σ towards idiosyncratic behavior.

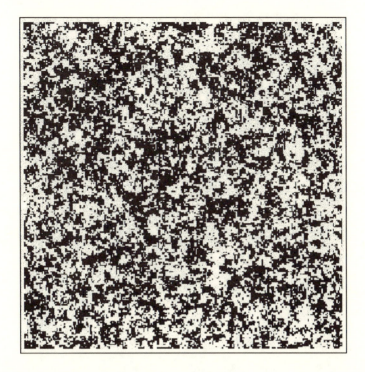

FIG. 4.8. $K < K_c$: Buy (white squares) and sell (black squares) configuration in a two-dimensional Manhattan-like planar network of 256×256 agents interacting with their four nearest neighbors. There are approximately the same number of white and black sells; that is, the market has no consensus. The size of the largest local clusters quantifies the correlation length, that is, the distance over which the local imitations between neighbors propagate before being significantly distorted by the "noise" in the transmission process resulting from the idiosyncratic signals of each agent.

In the context of the alignment of atomic spins to create magnetization (magnets), this model is identical to the so-called two-dimensional Ising model, which has been solved explicitly by Onsager [321]. Only its formulation is different from what is usually found in textbooks [164], as we emphasize a dynamical viewpoint.

In the Ising model, there exists a critical point K_c that determines the properties of the system. When $K < K_c$ (see Figure 4.8), disorder reigns: the sensitivity to a small global influence is small, the clusters of agents who are in agreement remain of small size, and imitation only propagates between close neighbors. In this case, the susceptibility χ of the system

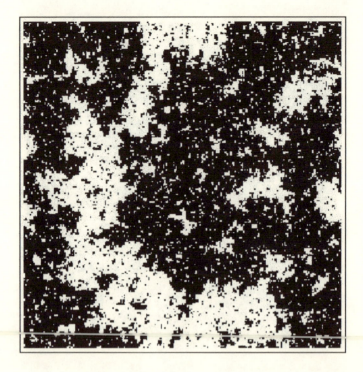

FIG. 4.9. Same as Figure 4.8 for K close to K_c. There are still approximately the same number of white and black sells; that is, the market has no consensus. However, the size of the largest local clusters has grown to become comparable to the total system size. In addition, holes and clusters of all sizes can be observed. The "scale-invariance" or "fractal"-looking structure is the hallmark of a "critical state" for which the correlation length and the susceptibility become infinite (or simply bounded by the size of the system).

to external news is small, as many clusters of different opinions react incoherently, thus more or less cancelling out their responses.

When the imitation strength K increases and gets close to K_c (see Figure 4.9), order starts to appear: the system becomes extremely sensitive to a small global perturbation, agents who agree with each other form large clusters, and imitation propagates over long distances. In the natural sciences, these are the characteristics of so-called *critical* phenomena. Formally, in this case the susceptibility χ of the system goes to infinity. The hallmark of criticality is the *power law*, and indeed the susceptibility goes to infinity according to a power law $\chi \approx A(K_c - K)^{-\gamma}$, where A is a positive constant and $\gamma > 0$ is called the *critical exponent* of the susceptibility (equal to 7/4 for the two-dimensional Ising model). This

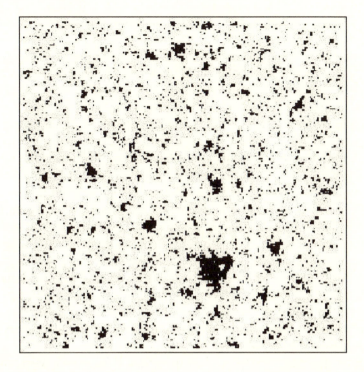

Fig. 4.10. Same as Figure 4.8 for $K > K_c$. The imitation is so strong that the network of agents spontaneously breaks the symmetry between the two decisions and one of them predominates. Here, we show the case where the "buy" state has been selected. Interestingly, the collapse into one of the two states is essentially random and results from the combined effect of a slight initial bias and of fluctuations during the imitation process. Only small and isolated islands of "bears" remain in an ocean of buyers. This state would correspond to a bubble: a strong bullish market.

kind of critical behavior is found in many other models of interacting elements [265, 266] (see also [310] for applications to finance, among others). The large susceptibility means that the system is unstable: a small external perturbation may lead to a large collective reaction of the traders who may drastically revise their decision, which may abruptly produce a sudden unbalance between supply and demand, thus triggering a crash or a rally. This specific mechanism will be shown to lead to crashes in the model described in chapter 5.

For even stronger imitation strength $K > K_c$, the imitation is so strong that the idiosynchratic signals become negligible and the traders self-organize into strong imitative behavior, as shown in Figure 4.10. The selection of one of the two possible states is determined from small and

subtle initial biases as well as from the fluctuations during the evolutionary dynamics.

These behaviors apply more generically to other network topologies.
Indeed, the stock market constitutes an ensemble of interacting investors
who differ in size by many orders of magnitude ranging from individuals to gigantic professional investors, such as pension funds. Furthermore, structures at even higher levels, such as currency influence
spheres (U.S.$, DM, Yen, ...), exist and with the current globalization
and deregulation of the market one may argue that structures on the
largest possible scale, that is, the world economy, are beginning to form.
This observation and the network of connections between traders show
that the two-dimensional lattice representation used in the Figures 4.7,
4.8, 4.9, and 4.10 is too naive. A better representation of the structure
of the financial markets is that of hierarchical systems with "traders" on
all levels of the market. Of course, this does not imply that any strict
hierarchical structure of the stock market exists, but there are numerous
examples of qualitatively hierarchical structures in society. In fact, one
may say that horizontal organizations of individuals are rather rare. This
means that the plane network used in our previous discussion may very
well represent a gross oversimplification.

One of the best examples of a hierarchy is found in the army. At
the lowest level of a military force is a single soldier. Ten soldiers produce a squad. Three squads produce a regiment; three regiments produce
a brigade; three brigades give a division; three divisions give a corps.
An army might have several corps and a country might have several
armies. In hierarchical networks, information can flow from the top down
and from bottom up, as shown in Figure 4.11. Notwithstanding the large
variety of topological structures, the qualitative conclusion of the existence of a critical transition between a mostly disordered state and an
ordered one, separated by a critical point, survives by-and-large for most
possible choices of the network of interacting investors, including for
hierarchical networks.

Even though the predictions of these models are quite detailed, they
are very robust to model misspecification. We indeed claim that models
that combine the following features would display the same characteristics, in particular apparent coordinate buying and selling periods, leading
eventually to several financial crashes. These features are:

1. a system of traders who are influenced by their "neighbors";

2. local imitation propagating spontaneously into global cooperation;

3. global cooperation among noise traders causing collective behavior;

4. prices related to the properties of this system;

5. system parameters evolving slowly through time.

As we shall show in the following chapters, a crash is most likely when the locally imitative system goes through a *critical* point.

In physics, critical points are widely considered to be one of the most interesting properties of complex systems. A system goes critical when local influences propagate over long distances and the average state of the system becomes exquisitely sensitive to a small perturbation; that is, different parts of the system become highly correlated. Another characteristic is that critical systems are self-similar across scales: in Figure 4.9, at the critical point, an ocean of traders who are mostly bearish may have within it several continents of traders who are mostly bullish, each of which in turns surrounds seas of bearish traders with islands of bullish traders; the progression continues all the way down to the smallest possible scale: a single trader [458]. Intuitively speaking, critical self-similarity is why local imitation cascades through the scales into global coordination.

Critical points are described in mathematical parlance as singularities associated with bifurcation and catastrophe theory. Catastrophe theory studies and classifies phenomena characterized by sudden shifts in behavior arising from small changes in circumstances. Catastrophes are bifurcations between different equilibria, or fixed point attractors of dynamical systems. Due to their restricted nature, catastrophes can be classified

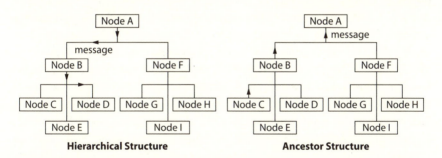

FIG. 4.11. In a hierarchical structure, the messages can move from the top of the hierarchy to the bottom (left panel) or from the bottom to the top (right panel), as in the ancestor structure. The difference between the two is that, in the hierarchical structure, the nodes have to make a decision (as to which node to pass the message on to) before they pass the message on, while in the ancestor structure there is no need to make such a decision because there is only the single choice available (reproduced from [383]).

based on how many control parameters are being simultaneously varied. For example, if there are two controls, then one finds the most common type, called a "cusp" catastrophe. Catastrophe theory has been applied to a number of different phenomena, such as the stability of ships at sea and their capsizing and bridge collapse. It has also been used to describe situations in which agents with similar characteristics and objectives and facing identical or similar environments make choices that are considerably different. The use of catastrophe theory relies on the desire to model many of the situations that lead to sudden changes in decisions on the part of policy makers and individuals, polarity of opinion, and group conflict [385, 47]. In essence, this book attempts to provide mechanisms for the spontaneous occurrence of bifurcations and "catastrophes" in the behavior of investors and of financial markets.

COMPLEX EVOLUTIONARY ADAPTIVE SYSTEMS OF BOUNDEDLY RATIONAL AGENTS

The previous Ising model is the simplest possible description of cooperative behaviors resulting from repetitive interactions between agents. Many other models have recently been developed in order to capture more realistic properties of people and of their economic interactions. These multiagent models, often explored by computer simulations, support the hypothesis that the observed characteristics of financial prices described in chapter 2, such as non-Gaussian "fat" tails of distributions of returns, mostly unpredictable returns, clustered and excess volatility, may result endogenously from the interaction between agents. This relatively new school of research, championed in particular by the Santa Fe Institute in New Mexico [8, 18] and being developed now in many other institutions worldwide, views markets as complex evolutionary adaptive systems populated by boundedly rational agents interacting with each other. El-Farol's bar problem and the minority games discussed previously are examples of this general class of models. We now briefly review some representative works to illustrate the variety and power but also the limitations of these approaches. These agent-based models owe a great intellectual debt to the work of Herbert Simon [379], whose notion of "bounded rationality," based on his contributions at the intersection of economics, psychology, and computer science, is the foundation on which much of the recent behavioral economics literature is built. The principal concern of this school of research applied to economic modeling [2] is to understand

why certain global regularities have been observed to evolve and persist
in decentralized market economies despite the absence of top-down
planning and control such as trade networks, socially accepted monies,
market protocols, business cycles, and the common adoption of technological innovations. The challenge is to demonstrate constructively
how these global regularities might arise from the bottom up, through
the repeated local interactions of autonomous agents. A second concern
of researchers is to use this framework as computational laboratories
within which alternative socioeconomic structures can be studied and
tested with regard to their effects on individual behavior and social
welfare.

Typical of the Sante Fe school, Palmer et al. [329, 21, 258] modelled traders as so-called "genetic algorithms," which are computer software creatures mimicking the adaptative and evolving biological genes
that compete for survival and replication. These intelligent algorithms
make predictions about the future, and buy and sell stock as indicated
by their expectations of future risk and return. With certain characteristics, these computer agents are found to be able to collectively learn to
create a homogeneous rational expectations equilibrium, that is, to discover dynamically the economic equilibrium imagined by pure theoretical economists. In this highly competitive artificial world, a trader-gene
taking some "vacation" loses his "shirt" when returning back in the stock
market arena, because he is no longer adapted to the new structures that
were developed by the market in his absence! Farmer [123] has simplified this approach using the analogy between financial markets and an
ecology of strategies. In a variety of examples, he shows how diversity
emerges automatically as new strategies exploit the inefficiencies of old
strategies.

The Laboratory for Financial Engineering at the Massachusetts Institute of Technology [251, 341] is another noteworthy example of such
pursuits. The artificial market project in particular focuses on the dynamics arising from interactions between human and artificial agents in a
stochastic market environment in which agents learn from their interactions, using recently developed techniques in large-scale simulations,
approximate dynamic programming, computational learning, and tapping
insights in and resources from mathematics, statistics, physics, psychology, and computer science. This laboratory recently constructed an artificial market, designed to match those in experimental-market settings
with human subjects, to model complex interactions among artificially
intelligent (AI) traders endowed with varying degrees of learning capa-
bilities [79]. The use of AI agents with simple heuristic trading rules and

learning algorithms shows that adding trend-follower traders to a population of empirical fundamentalists has an adverse impact on market performance, and the trend-follower traders do poorly overall. However, this effect diminishes over time as the market becomes more effcient. In numerical experiments in which "scalper" traders, who simply trade on patterns in past prices, are added to a population of fundamentalists, the "scalpers" are relatively successful free riders, not only matching the performance of fundamentalists in the long run, but outperforming them in the short run.

Brock and Hommes and coworkers [54, 58, 55, 56, 57, 200, 257] have developed models of financial markets seen as "adaptive belief" systems of boundedly rational agents using different, competing trading strategies. The terms "rational" and "adaptive" refer to the fact that agents tend to follow strategies that have performed well, according to realized profits or accumulated wealth, in the recent past; the adjective "boundedly" refers to the fact that they can only use one among a set of relatively simple strategies. Price changes are explained by a combination of economic fundamentals and "market psychology," that is, by the interplay between several coexisting heterogeneous classes of trading strategies. Most of the systems considered by Brock and Hommes and their coworkers have specialized to the case of a small number of competing strategies leading to dynamical trajectories of prices governed by so-called low-dimensional strange attractors, exemplifying the importance of chaos, of the simultaneous importance of different attractors, and of the existence of local bifurcations of steady states in these models. This theoretical approach explains why simple technical trading rules may survive evolutionary competition in a heterogeneous world where prices and beliefs coevolve over time. These evolutionary models account for stylized facts of real markets, such as the fat tails and volatility clustering described in chapter 2.

Several works have modelled the epidemics of opinion and speculative bubbles in financial markets from an adaptive agent point of view [238, 273, 274, 275, 276]. The main mechanism for bubbles is that above average returns are reflected in a generally more optimistic attitude that fosters the disposition to overtake others' bullish beliefs and vice versa. The adaptive nature of agents is reflected in the alternatives available to agents to choose between several classes of strategies, for instance, to invest according to fundamental economic valuation or by using technical analysis of past price trajectories. Other relevant works put more emphasis on the heterogeneity and threshold nature of decision making, which lead in general to irregular cycles [421, 460, 262, 360, 263, 154].

These approaches are to be constrasted with the efficient market hypothesis that assumes that the movement of financial prices is an immediate and unbiased reflection of incoming news about future earning prospects. Under the efficient market hypothesis, the deviations from the random walk observed empirically would simply reflect similar deviations in extraneous signals feeding the market. The simulations performed on computers allow us to test this hypothesis in artificial stock markets. Notwithstanding the fact that the news arrival processes are constructed as random walk processes, non-random-walk price characteristics emerge spontaneously as a result of the nonlinear and imitative interactions between investors. This shows that one does not need to assume a complex information flow to account for the complexity of price structures: the self-organization of the market dynamics is sufficient to create it endogenously.

In conclusion, we see that there is a plethora of models that account approximately for the usual main stylized facts observed in stock markets (fat tail of the distribution of returns, absence of correlation between returns, long-range dependence between successive return amplitudes, and volatility clustering). However, these models do not predict the characteristic bubble structures discussed in this book (see chapters 6–10). In the next chapter, we therefore turn to models aimed specifically at capturing these important patterns.

CHAPTER 5

MODELING FINANCIAL

BUBBLES AND MARKET

CRASHES

The purpose of models is not to fit the data but to sharpen the questions.
— S. Karlin, 11th R. A. Fisher Memorial Lecture, Royal Society, April 20, 1983.

WHAT IS A MODEL?

Knowledge is encoded in models. Models are synthetic sets of rules, pictures, and algorithms providing us with useful representations of the world of our perceptions and of their patterns. As argued by philosophers and shown by scientists, we do not have access to "reality," only to some of its manifestations, whose regularities are used to determine rules, which when widely applicable become "laws of nature." These laws are constantly tested in the scientific march, and they evolve, develop and transmute as the frontier of knowledge recedes further away.

Like a novel, a model may be convincing—it may ring true if it is consistent with our experience of the natural world. But just as we may wonder how much the characters in a novel are drawn from real life and how much is artifice, we might ask the same of a model: how much is based on observation and measurement of accessible phenomena, how much is based on informed judgment, and how much is convenience? Verification and validation of numerical models of natural systems is impossible. The only propositions that can be verified, that is, proved true, are those concerning closed systems, based on pure mathematics and logic. Natural systems are open: our knowledge of them is always partial, approximate, at best. [322]

Models are usually formulated with mathematics. Mathematics is nothing but a language, with its own grammar and syntax—arguably the simplest, clearest, and most concise language of all. It allows us to articulate efficiently and guide our trains of thought. It gives us logical deductions, flowing from the premises that we imagine to their forceful consequences. Learning and using mathematics is like striving to master Kung-Fu, both a technique and a way of life that enhances your skills and awareness. As with Kung-Fu, mathematics may be frightening or incomprehensible to many. As with any foreign language or combat technique, you have to learn it and practice it to be fluent and comfortable with it. The two models presented in what follows are also based on mathematics, and their rigorous treatment requires its use. Here, however, we shall strive to remove all the unnecessary technicalities and present only the main concepts with illustrations and pictures.

STRATEGY FOR MODEL CONSTRUCTION IN FINANCE

BASIC PRINCIPLES

The consistent modeling of financial markets remains an open and challenging problem. A simple, economically plausible mathematical approach to market modeling is needed which captures the essence of reality. The existing approaches to financial market modeling are quite diverse, and the literature is rather extensive. Significant progress in our understanding of financial markets was acquired, for instance, by Markowitz with the mean-variance portfolio theory [288], the capital asset pricing model of Sharpe [370] and its elaboration by Lintner, Merton's [293] and Black and Scholes's option pricing and hedging theory [41], Ross's arbitrage pricing theory [353], and Cox, Ingersoll, and Ross's theory of interest rates [95], to cite a few of the major advances.

Economic models differ from models in the physical sciences in that economic agents are supposed to anticipate the future. Each one's decision depends on the decisions of others (strategic interdependence) and on expectations about the future. This is illustrated by the following pictorial analogy [113]. Suppose that in the middle ages, before Copernicus and Galileo, the Earth really was stationary at the center of the universe, and only began moving later on. Imagine that during the nineteenth century, when everyone believed classical physics to be true, it really was true, and quantum phenomena were nonexistent. These are not philosophical musings, but an attempt to portray how physics might look if it actually behaved like the financial markets. Indeed, the financial world is such that any insight is almost immediately used to trade for a profit. As the insight spreads among traders, the "universe" changes accordingly. As G. Soros has pointed out, market players are "actors observing their own deeds." As E. Derman, head of quantitative strategies at Goldman Sachs, puts it, in physics you are playing against God, who does not change his mind very often. In finance, you are playing against God's creatures, whose feelings are ephemeral, at best unstable, and the news on which they are based keeps streaming in. Value clearly derives from human beings, while mass, electric charge and electromagnetism apparently do not. This has led to suggestions that a fruitful framework for studying finance and economics is to use evolutionary models inspired from biology and genetics, to which we alluded in chapter 4.

Perhaps the most profound synthesis of physical sciences came from the realization that everything could be understood from "conservation laws" and symmetry principles. For instance, Newton's law that the acceleration, that is, the rate of change of velocity of a body of mass m, is proportional to the total force applied to it divided by m, follows from the conservation of momentum in free space (the law of inertia associated with Galilean invariance). Another example is that the fundamental equations of motion of so-called "strings," formulated to describe the fundamental particles such as quarks and electrons, derive from global symmetry principles and dualities between descriptions at long-range and short-range scales. Are there similar principles that can guide the determination of the equations of motion of the more down-to-earth financial markets?

THE PRINCIPLE OF ABSENCE OF ARBITRAGE OPPORTUNITY

One such organizing principle is the condition of absence of arbitrage opportunity, which we have already visited in chapter 2. Recall that no-arbitrage, also known as the Law of One Price, states that two assets with identical attributes should sell for the same price, and so should the same asset trading in two different markets. If the prices differ, a profitable opportunity arises to sell the asset where it is overpriced and to buy it where it is underpriced. The basic idea is that, if there are arbitrage opportunities, they cannot live long or must be quite subtle, otherwise traders would act on them and arbitrage them away. The no-arbitrage condition is an idealization of a self-consistent dynamical state of the market resulting from the incessant actions of the traders (arbitragers). It is not the out-of-fashion equilibrium approximation sometimes described; rather, it embodies a very subtle cooperative organization of the market. We take this condition as the first-order approximation of reality. We shall see that it provides strong constraints on the structure of the model and allows us to draw interesting and surprising predictions. The idea to impose the no-arbitrage condition is in fact the prerequisite of most models developed in the academic finance community. Modigliani and Miller [302, 299], for instance, have indeed emphasized the critical role played by arbitrage in determining the value of securities.

It is important here to stress again that the no-arbitrage condition together with rational expectations is not a mechanism. It does not explain its own origin. It is a principle describing the emergent large-scale organization of market participants. It does not tell us what its underlying specific mechanisms are. Assuming the validity of the no-arbitrage condition together with rational expectations amounts to postulating that a fraction of the population of traders behave in such a way that prices tend to reflect available information and that risk is adequately and approximately fairly remunerated. In order to understand the specific manners with which this is attained would require a level of modeling not yet available at present and whose achievement is at the heart of a very active domain of research that we only glimpsed in chapter 4.

As we pointed out in chapter 2, the existence of transaction costs and other imperfections of the market should not be used as an excuse for disregarding the no-arbitrage condition but rather should be constructively invoked to study its impacts on the models. In other words, these market imperfections are considered as second-order effects.

EXISTENCE OF RATIONAL AGENTS

Mainstream finance and economic modeling add a second overarching organizing principle, namely that investors and economic agents are rational. Contrary to an oft-quoted perception in the popular press and in certain circles of the stock market as populated by irrational herds (see chapter 4), a significant fraction of the traders most of the time do exhibit a rational behavior in which they try to optimize their strategies based on the available information. One may refer to this as "bounded rationality" since not only is the available information in general incomplete, but stock market traders also have limited abilities with respect to analyzing the available information. In addition, investors are uncertain about the characteristics and preferences of other investors in the market. This means that the process of decision making is essentially a "noisy process" and, as a consequence, a probabilistic approach in stock market modeling is unavoidable since there are no certainties. Clearly, a noise-free stock market with all information available occupied by fully rational traders of infinite analysis abilities would have a very small trading volume, if any.

The assumption of perfectly rational, maximizing behavior won out until recently in the art of modeling, not because it often reflects reality, but because it was useful. It enabled economists to build mathematical models of behavior and to give their discipline a rigorous, scientific air. This process started in the mid-1800s, evolving by the end of the century into the approach known today as neoclassical economics. And while twentieth-century critics like the University of Chicago's T. Veblen and Harvard's J. K. Galbraith argued that people are also motivated by altruism, envy, panic, and other emotions, they failed to come up with a way to fit these emotions into the models that economists had grown accustomed to—and thus had little impact, until recently. As we showed in chapter 4, the field is being enriched with revisitations and extensions of these approaches based on novel research encompassing the sciences of human behavior, psychology, and social interactions and organization.

This long list of irrational or anomalous behavior shown by human beings in certain specific systematic ways should not confuse us: the relevant task for understanding stock markets is not so much to focus on these irrationalities but rather to study how they aggregate in the complex, long-lasting, repetitive, and subtle environment of the market. This extension requires us to put aside the description of the individual in favor of the search for emerging collective behaviors. The market may have many special features that protect it from aggregating the irrationalities of individuals into prices. In other instances, the aggregation may stigmatize this irrationality in what we shall refer to as "speculative bubbles."

Market rationality should thus be understood in the sense that asset prices are set as if all investors are rational [354]. Clearly, markets can be rational even if not all investors are actually rational, as discussed extensively in chapter 4. The "minority game" described in chapter 4 taught us in particular that the market becomes rational if there are sufficiently many heterogeneous agents acting on limited information. This is consistent with the view of M. Rubinstein from the University of California at Berkeley, who argued that the most important trait of investor irrationality, to the extent that it affects prices, is particularly likely to be manifest through overconfidence, which in turn is likely to make the market "hyperrational" [354]. Indeed, overconfidence leads investors to believe they can beat the market, causes them to spend too much time on research, and causes many to trade too quickly on the basis of their information without recovering in benefits what they pay in trading costs. Thus, overconfidence leads to extensive analysis of the scarce available information and its incorporation into stock prices, which is consistent with the conclusions of the "minority games."

Therefore, the machinery behind market rationality is that each investor, using the market to serve his or her own self-interest, unwittingly makes prices reflect that investor's information and analysis. It is as if the market were a huge, relatively low-cost continuous polling mechanism that records the updated votes of millions of investors in continuously changing current prices. In light of this mechanism, for a single investor (in the absence of inside information) to believe that prices are significantly in error is almost always folly [354]. Let us quote Rubinstein:

> Remember the chestnut about the professor and his student. On one of their walks, the student spies a $100 bill lying in the open on the ground. The professor assures the student that the bill cannot be there because if it were, someone would already have picked it up. To this attempt to illustrate the stupidity of believing in rational markets, my colleague Jonathan Berk asks: How many times have you found such a hundred dollar bill? He implies, of course, that such a discovery is so rare that the professor is right in a deeper sense: It does not pay to go out looking for money lying around.

"RATIONAL BUBBLES" AND GOLDSTONE MODES OF THE PRICE "PARITY SYMMETRY" BREAKING

Blanchard [43] and Blanchard and Watson [45] originally introduced the model of rational expectations (RE) bubbles to account for the possibility, often discussed in the empirical literature and by practitioners, that observed prices may deviate significantly and over extended time intervals from fundamental prices. While allowing for deviations from fundamental prices, rational bubbles keep a fundamental anchor point of economic modeling, namely that bubbles must obey the condition of rational expectations and of no-arbitrage opportunities. Indeed, for fluid assets, dynamic investment strategies rarely perform better than simple buy-and-hold strategies [282]; in other words, the market is not far from being efficient and few arbitrage opportunities exist as a result of the constant search for gains by sophisticated investors. The conditions of rational expectations and of no-arbitrage are useful approximations. The rationality of both expectations and behavior does not imply that the price of an asset is equal to its fundamental value. In other words, there can be rational deviations of the price from this value, called "rational bubbles." A rational bubble can arise when the actual market price depends positively on its own expected rate of change, as sometimes occurs in asset markets, which is the mechanism underlying the models of [43] and [45].

Price Parity Symmetry

Recall that pricing of an asset under rational expectations theory is based on the two following hypotheses: the rationality of the agents and the "no-free lunch" condition. In addition, the "firm-foundation" theory asserts that a stock has an intrinsic value determined by careful analysis of present conditions and future prospects. Developed by S. Eliot Guild [183] and John B. Williams [457], it is based on the concept of discounting future dividend incomes. In the words of Burton G. Malkiel [282], discounting refers to the following concept:

> Rather than seeing how much money you will have next year (say $1.05 if you put $1 in a saving bank at 5% interest), you look at money expected in the future and see how much less it is currently worth (thus next year's $1 is worth today only about 95 ¢, which would be invested at 5% to produce $1 at that time).

The discounting process thus captures the usual concept that something tomorrow is less valuable than today: a given wealth tomorrow has a little less value than the same wealth today, as we have to wait to use it. In practice, the intrinsic value approach is a quite reasonable idea that is, however, confronted with slippery estimations: the investor has to estimate future dividends, their long-term growth rates as well as the time horizon over which the growth rate will be maintained. Notwithstanding these problems, this approach has been promoted by Irving Fisher [134] and Graham and Dodd [170] so that generations of Wall Street security analysts have been using some kind of "firm-foundation" valuation to pick their stocks.

Therefore, under the rational expectation condition, the best estimation at time t of the price p_{t+1} of an asset at time $t+1$ viewed from time t is given by the expectation of p_{t+1} given the knowledge of all available information accumulated up to time t. The "no-free-lunch" condition then imposes that the expected returns of all assets are equal to the return r of the risk-free asset, such as a return on CD bank accounts. From this condition, one obtains the "fundamental" price today as equal to the sum of the price tomorrow discounted by a discount factor acting from today to tomorrow and of the dividend served today. The dividend is added to express the fact that the expected price tomorrow has to be decreased by the dividend since the value before giving the dividend incorporates it into the pricing. The standard "forward" or "fundamental" value p_t^f at time t is thus the sum over all future dividends discounted to the present t. According to this rule, if interest rates are 4%, a promise to pay (dividend) $4 per year forever is worth $100, but a promise to pay $4 this year, $4.12 next year, and $4.24 the year after (the payout increases each year at the same rate as GDP, say 3%) should be worth $400—100 times the current payment.

It turns out that this fundamental price is not the full solution of this valuation problem. It is easy to show that the most general solution is the sum of the fundamental solution plus an arbitrary "bubble" component X_t. This bubble component has to obey the single no-free-lunch condition; that is, its value today is equal to its expected value tomorrow discounted by the discount factor. In the bubble component, there is no dividend! It is important to note that the speculative bubbles appear as a natural consequence of the fundamental "firm-foundation" valuation formula, that is, as a consequence of the no-free-lunch condition and of the rationality of the agents. Thus, the concept of bubbles is not an addition to the theory but is entirely embedded in it.

It is interesting to pause a bit to ponder this result and deepen our understanding by developing an analogy with another deep result from particle and condensed-matter physics. The novel insight [403] is that the arbitrary bubble component X_t of an asset price plays a role analogous to the so-called "Goldstone mode" in nuclear, particle, and condensed-matter physics [59, 62]. Goldstone modes are the zero-energy infinite-wavelength mode fluctuations that attempt to restore broken symmetry.

For instance, consider a "Bloch" wall between two large magnetic domains of opposite magnetization within a magnet, for instance, selected by opposite magnetic fields at boundaries far away. The broken symmetry is the fact that the two domains separated by the wall have opposite magnetization. A full symmetry would be that both domains have the same magnetization or both have magnetization with equal probability.

It turns out that, at nonzero temperature, "capillary" waves propagating along the wall are excited by thermal fluctuations. The limit of very long-wavelength capillary modes corresponds to arbitrary translations of the wall, an embodiment of the concept of Goldstone modes, which tend to restore the translational symmetry broken by the presence of the "Bloch" wall.

What could be the symmetry-breaking acting in asset pricing? The answer may be surprising. It is the so-called "parity symmetry" between positive and negative prices [395],

$$p \to -p \quad \text{parity symmetry,} \tag{7}$$

where both positive and negative prices quantify our liking or disliking of the commodity. Indeed, it makes perfect sense to think of *negative* prices. We are ready to pay a (positive) price for a commodity that we need or like. However, we will not pay a positive price to get something we dislike or which disturbs us, such as garbage, waste, a broken and useless car, chemical and industrial hazards, and so on. Consider a chunk of waste. We will be ready to buy it for a negative price; in other words, we are ready to take the unwanted commodity if it comes with cash. This exchange of waste for income is the basis for the industry of waste management. Nuclear waste from some countries, such as Japan, are shipped to La Hague reprocessing complex in France, which is ready to store the unwanted wastes for income. The Japanese are thus paying a price to get rid of their waste, that is, La Hague is paying a negative price to get the nuclear waste commodity! As a matter of fact, this exchange of wastes is at the basis of a huge business for the present and future management of industrial and nuclear waste that counts in the hundreds of billions of dollars. A less obvious example is the case of electricity companies in California, for instance, which sell surplus electricity in exceptional cases for negative prices; it is expensive for them to shut down a power plant and to restart it again [452]. My German colleague, Prof. D. Stauffer, humorously points out that the page charges some authors pay to journals to get rid of their manuscripts are an example of

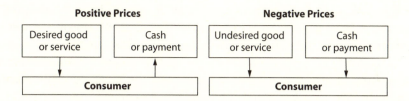

FIG. 5.1. Graphic showing that the sign of price is defined by the relative direction of the flow of cash or payment compared to the flow of goods or services; a positive price corresponds to the more commonly experienced situation where the cash or payment flow is with a direction opposite to the flow of goods or services; a negative price corresponds to the reverse situation where the cash or payment flow has the same direction as the flow of goods or services. Reproduced from [395].

negative prices. Actually, this is not correct, but this example illustrates the subtlety of the concept: authors pay to get published, not to get rid of their paper but to buy fame; that is, cash leaves the authors but fame comes to them (hopefully), hence the positivity of the price in this case. In sum, we pay a positive price for something we like and a negative price for something we would rather be spared of; that is, we pay a positive price to get rid of it or we need a remuneration to accept this unwanted commodity. This concept is illustrated in Figure 5.1.

In the economy, what makes a share of a company desirable? Answer: Its earnings, which provide dividends, and its potential appreciation, which gives rise to capital gains. As a consequence, in the absence of dividends and of speculation, the price of share must be nil. The earnings leading to dividends d thus act as a symmetry-breaking "field," since a positive d makes the share desirable and thus develops a positive price. This is, as we have seen, at the basis of the "firm-foundation" fundamental pricing of assets. It is clear that a negative dividend, a premium that must be paid regularly to own the share, leads to a negative price, that is, to the desire to get rid of that stock if it does not provide other benefits. For a share of a company that is providing neither utility nor a waste, there is no intrinsic value for it if it does not give you more buying power for something you desire. Hence, its price is $p = 0$ for a vanishing dividend $d = 0$. In this case, we can allow for both positive and negative price fluctuations, but there is a priori nothing that breaks the symmetry (7).

We stress that the price symmetry (7) is distinct from the gain/loss symmetry of stock holders, before the advent of limited liability companies in the middle of the nineteenth century. With the present limited liability of stock holders, owning a stock is akin to holding an option: gain is accrued from dividend and capital gains; on the downside, losses are limited at the buying price of the stock. This asymmetry, which is a relatively recent phenomenon and led to the full development of capitalism, is also conceptually distinct from the breaking of the parity symmetry (7) of prices induced by a positive dividend.

It is now clear that there are no restrictions on the nature of the bubble X_t added to the fundamental price p_t^f, except for the no-free-lunch condition. The bubble is thus playing the role of the Goldstone modes, restoring the broken parity symmetry: the bubble price can wander up or down and, in the limit where it becomes very large in absolute value, dominate over the fundamental price, restoring the independence of the price with respect to dividend. Moreover, as in condensed-matter physics, where the Goldstone mode appears spontaneously since it has no energy cost, the rational bubble itself can appear spontaneously with no dividend. A similar point of view has been advocated in [27] to explain the dynamics of money.

Speculation as Spontaneous Symmetry Breaking.
When the dividends are not constant and grow with time, the fundamental price is larger since it must incorporate the additional expected value of the future cash flow. There is thus a competition between the increasing growth of the dividends far in the expected future resulting from the expected growth of the company and the decreasing impact of dividends further in the future due to the effect of the discount factor (for instance, inflation). The increasing growth of dividends tends to increase the fundamental price. The decreasing impact of dividends further in the future tends to decrease the fundamental price. In the example in which the Interest rate is 4% and the growth rate of dividend is 3%, and if there were no risks, stocks would be worth 100 times the current cash flow to stockholders. But a stock is not riskless, and the future dividend flow is only a hope, not a promise. Thus, investors require a "risk premium" to compensate them for the risk. This amounts to reducing the dividend growth rate to a so-called risk-adjusted growth rate r_d'.

Now, when this risk-adjusted growth rate r_d' becomes equal to or larger than the discount rate r, the fundamental valuation formula becomes meaningless, as it predicts an infinite price: the effect of discounting the future dividends is perfectly balanced by the dividend growth rate and, with an infinite time horizon, the price is just the sum of all future presently adjusted dividends. In the economic literature, this regime is known as the growth stock paradox [44]. This valuation problem was posed in 1938 by Von Neumann [442], who demonstrated that, in an economy with balanced growth, the growth rate is always identical to the interest rate and thus equal to the discount rate. Zajdenweber [461] later pointed out that the value of a share is, as a consequence, always infinite since it is based on an infinite sum of nondecreasing future dividends (this reasoning neglects the finiteness of human life and therefore the finiteness of the utility of an asset for a given investor). The intuition is that when r'_d becomes equal to (and this is all the more true when it is larger than) r, the price of money is not enough to stabilize the economy: it becomes favorable to borrow money to buy shares and earn an effective rate of return, which is positive for all values of the dividend. This is exactly what happened on the U.S. market in the rally preceeding the October 1929 crash [152]. Note that a negative $r - r'_d$ is similar to a negative interest rate r in the absence of growth and risks: it leads to an arbitrage opportunity since you can borrow \$1 now, keep it under your mattress, and give back $\$1 \times (1 - |r|)$ at a later time, pocketing $100|r|$ cents in the process.

The existence of the parity symmetry of the price and the breakdown of the fundamental pricing formula when the risk-adjusted growth rate r'_d of the dividend becomes equal to or larger than the discount rate r suggests a novel interpretation of speculative regimes and of bubble formations: the price can become nonzero or develop an important component decoupled from the dividend flow by a mathematical mechanism known as "spontaneous symmetry breaking."

Spontaneous symmetry breaking is one of the most important concepts in modern science as it underpins our present understanding of the universe, of its interactions, and of matter—nothing less! Its basic principle can be illustrated by a very simple dynamical system whose stationary solutions are represented in Figure 5.2 as a function of a control parameter $\mu = -(r - r'_d)$. This dynamical system possesses a priori the parity symmetry (7), since both the prices p and $-p$ are solutions of the same equation. A solution respecting this symmetry obeys the symmetry condition $p = -p$ whose unique solution $p = 0$ is called the symmetry-conserving solution. There is a critical value μ_c such that for $\mu < \mu_c$, p is attracted to zero and the asymptotic solution $p(t \to +\infty)$ is zero, which, as we said, is the only solution respecting the parity symmetry. However, a solution of the dynamical evolution may not always respect the parity symmetry of its equation. This occurs for $\mu > \mu_c$ for which the dynamical system possesses two distinct solutions, each of them being related to the other by the action of the parity transformation $p \to -p$: the set of solutions respects the parity symmetry as an ensemble but each

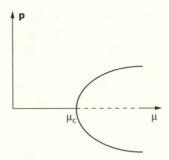

FIG. 5.2. Bifurcation diagram, near the threshold μ_c, of a "supercritical" bifurcation. The "order parameter" that is, the price p bifurcates from the symmetrical state zero to a nonzero value $\pm p_s(\mu)$ represented by the two branches, as the control parameter crosses the critical value μ_c. The parity symmetry preserving value $p = 0$, shown as the dashed line, becomes unstable for $\mu > \mu_c$. Reproduced from [395].

solution separately does not respect this symmetry. This phenomenon is called "spontaneous symmetry breaking." More generally, the concept of spontaneous symmetry breaking describes the situation in which a solution has a lower symmetry than its equation. The so-called "super-critical bifurcation" diagram near the threshold $\mu = \mu_c$, representing the transition from a symmetric solution $p = 0$ to a spontaneous symmetry-breaking solution is shown in Figure 5.2. Spontaneous symmetry breaking refers to the fact that the dynamical system will choose only one of the two branches, as its evolution is unique (you cannot be at two places at the same time) and will thus have a lower symmetry as a consequence.

The concept of spontaneous symmetry breaking takes its full meaning in the presence of a small external perturbation or "field" H. In the spontaneous symmetry-breaking regime $\mu > \mu_c$, p jumps from one branch to the other when the perturbation H goes from positive to negative, as illustrated in Figure 5.3: any infinitesimal field is enough to flip the price p abruptly from one of its two symmetry-broken solutions to the other. It cannot be stressed sufficiently how important this concept of spontaneous symmetry breaking is. For instance, it is invoked for unifying fundamental interactions: weak, strong, and electromagnetic interactions are now understood as the result of a more fundamental spontaneous symmetry-broken interaction [448]. In another sweeping application, particles and matter in this universe seem to be the spontaneous symmetry-broken phases of a fundamental vacuum state [448], similar to the nonvanishing price emerging in the spontaneous

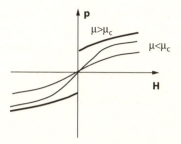

FIG. 5.3. "Order parameter" or price p as a function of the external field for different values of the control parameter μ. The two thin lines correspond to two different values of $\mu < \mu_c$. The thick line is the spontaneous symmetry broken phase occurring for $\mu > \mu_c$. Reproduced from [395].

symmetry-breaking phase $\mu > \mu_c$ out of the symmetry-conserved "vacuum" solution $p = 0$. Critical phase transitions are also understood as spontaneous symmetry-breaking phenomena [164].

In the context of the asset valuation problem, we propose [395] that, when the risk-adjusted growth rate r'_d of the dividend becomes equal to or larger than the discount rate r, assets acquire a spontaneous valuation as a result of this spontaneous symmetry-breaking mechanism. When $r - r'_d$ becomes negative, money is not a desirable commodity. You lose money by keeping it. Other commodities become valuable in comparison with money, hence the spontaneous price valuation in the absence of a dividend. We thus propose that, for $r - r'_d < 0$, the price becomes spontaneously positive (or possibly negative depending on initial conditions or external constraints), and this spontaneous valuation is nothing but the appearance of a *speculation* regime or bubble: investors do not look at or care for dividends; the increase of price is self-fulfilling.

According to this theory, the regime $r < r'_d$ is a self-sustained growth regime where prices become unrelated to earnings and dividends: prices can go up independently of the dividends due to the spontaneous symmetry breaking, where a company's shares spontaneously acquire value without any earnings. This situation is similar to the spontaneous magnetization of iron at sufficiently low temperature, which acquires a spontaneous magnetization under zero magnetic field. This regime could be relevant to understanding periods of bubbles such as in the so-called New Economy, where price increases result in high price-over-dividend ratios with debatable economic rationalization.

The self-sustained growth regime $r < r'_d$, where the expected growth rate of the dividends is larger than the discount rate, accounts for a number of stylized facts observed during speculative bubbles:

- The sentiment is broadly shared that the "run" will last indefinitely.

- There is a large increase in the price-over-dividend ratio;

- So-called "growth companies" are present: each speculative move has had its growth companies: in 1857, the railways; in 1929, the utilities (electricity production); in the 1960s, the office equipment companies (e.g., IBM) and the rubber companies (car makers); today, we have the Internet, software companies, banks, and investment companies. These companies have a fast growth rate (usually larger than 30% per year) and investors thus expect a large growth rate, r_d, for their earnings.

- Speculative phases are often stopped by successive increases of the discount rate; this occurred in 1929 (increase from 3.25% up to 6%), in 1969, and in 1990 in Japan (increase from 2.5% to 6%).

- The high sensitivity of valuation close to the critical point $r - r'_d = 0$ and the spontaneous speculative valuation below it suggest that crashes and rallies can also be interpreted as reassessments of expected risk-adjusted returns and their growth rates.

This leads to the following avenue for future research: new technologies, such as Internet, wireless communication, and wind power, should be compared to old technologies, such as cars, shipping, and mining. We expect that stocks in the new technology class have high prices and low earnings and thus high price-over-dividend and price-over-earnings ratios, while stocks in the old technology class have lower prices and higher earnings and then lower price-over-dividend and price-over-earnings ratios. This is indeed what is observed. If one goes back in time, present "old technology" was new technology and a similar pattern of high price-over-dividend and price-over-earnings ratios should be seen. This has indeed been documented, for instance during the 1929 and 1962 bubbles.

BASIC INGREDIENTS OF THE TWO MODELS

We now describe two models, which provide two extreme views of the relationship between returns and risks associated with crashes. These models use the no-arbitrage condition to link stock market returns during bubbles and the risk associated with potential crashes. Bounded rationality is used to obtain a simple specification of price dynamics. These two models recognize as essential the coexistence of and interplay between two distinct populations of traders: the "noise" traders on one hand and the "rational" traders on the other hand.

In the first "risk-driven" model, by their imitative and cooperative behavior, the exhuberant noise traders may make the market more and more unstable at certain times, as they can sometimes change opinion abruptly on a large scale. As the risk of a crash looms stronger, rational traders are enticed to stay invested only because of the higher accelerating returns, which provide an adequate compensation for the increasing risks. The fundamental point in this model is that a crash is not certain and there is a finite chance that the bubble ends and lands smoothly, thus making it rational for traders to stay invested in the market and to profit from (risky) gains.

The second "price-driven" model, discussed in this chapter, is also based on the interplay between two distinct and complementary groups of traders. The first population of noise traders drives the price volatility up in an accelerating but stochastic spiral by their collective behavior, allowing the emergence of price bubbles. The rational investors then recognize that such a bubble is unsustainable and identify the existence of an associated risk for a crash or of a severe correction that may drive the price back to its fundamental value. This behavior, embodied by the condition of no-arbitrage, leads to the following consequence: anomalous sky-rocketing prices imply an increasing crash hazard rate, defined as the probability that a crash will occur the next day, conditioned on the fact that it has not yet happened. This increasing risk of a crash is the unavoidable dark side of the market gains. Again, crashes are stochastic events quantified by this hazard rate, which diverges when the market valuation blows up. In this model, the long-term stationary behavior of the market is a succession of normal random-walk phases, with interpersed bubble phases ending in crashes bringing the market back closer to fundamental valuation, like a springy young dog running along with his mistress and receiving bolts that bring him back each time he reaches the end of the rope. The remarkable property of this model is that a crash may never happen if prices remain reasonable. This is because the crash hazard rate is a strongly nonlinear amplifying function of the price level. The probability of a crash is therefore very low at modest price deviations from the fundamental value but becomes larger and larger as the price increases. Even if the market price blows up, it is always possible that the price will reverse smoothly without a crash, a scenario that, however, becomes less and less probable the higher the price is.

THE RISK-DRIVEN MODEL

SUMMARY OF THE MAIN PROPERTIES OF THE MODEL

The rational expectation model of bubbles and crashes discussed below is an extension [221, 209, 212] of the Blanchard model [43] and of the Blanchard and Watson model [45]. It finds justifications in microscopic models of investor behaviors, developed to formalize herd behavior or mutual mimetic contagion in speculative markets [273]. In such a class of models, the emergence of bubbles is explained as a self-organizing process of "infection" among traders, leading to equilibrium prices that deviate from fundamental values. Assuming that the speculators' readiness to follow the crowd may depend on an economic variable, such as actual returns, above-average returns are reflected in a generally more optimistic attitude that fosters the disposition to overtake others' bullish beliefs, and vice versa. This economic influence makes bubbles transient phenomena and leads to repeated fluctuations around fundamental values.

Here, we stress the salient features that will be useful for the analysis of the market data sets presented in chapters 7–10. Our model has two main components.

- Its key assumption is that a crash may be caused by *local* self-reinforcing imitation between traders. This self-reinforcing imitation process leads to the blossoming of a bubble. If the tendency for traders to "imitate" their "friends" increases up to a certain point called the "critical" point, many traders may place the same order (sell) at the same time, thus causing a crash. The interplay between the progressive strengthening of imitation and the ubiquity of noise requires a stochastic description: a crash is not certain but can be characterized by its hazard rate $h(t)$, that is, the probability per unit time that the crash will happen in the next instant provided it has not happened yet.

- Since the crash is not a certain deterministic outcome of the bubble, it remains rational for traders to remain invested provided they are compensated by a higher rate of growth of the bubble for taking the risk of a crash, because there is a finite probability of "landing smoothly," that is, of attaining the end of the bubble without crash. In this model, the ability to predict the critical date is perfectly consistent with the behavior of the rational agents: they all know this date, the crash may happen anyway, and they are unable to make any abnormal risk-adjusted profits by using this information.

The model distinguishes between the end of the bubble and the time of the crash: the rational expectation constraint has the specific implication that the date of the crash must have some degree of randomness. The theoretical death of the bubble is not the time of the crash, because the crash could happen at any time before, even though this is not very likely. The death of the bubble is the most probable time for the crash.

The model does not impose any constraint on the amplitude of the crash. If we assume that it is proportional to the current price level, then the natural variable is the logarithm of the price. If, instead, we assume that the crash amplitude is a finite fraction of the gain observed during the bubble, then the natural variable is the price itself [212]. The standard economic proxy is the logarithm of the price and not the price itself, since only relative variations should play a role. However, different price dynamics give both possibilities.

In the construction of a model, it is convenient to retain only the essential aspects of reality and simplify by forgetting all the gory details that are immaterial for the purpose of the model and that would blur the demonstration. We thus neglect or incorporate dividends in the price, we neglect the risk-free interest rate such as the interest you get on a CD bank account (which can easily be reincorporated by a simple modification of the argument), and we assume that investors are neutral with respect to risks (again, this can be easily relaxed with some complication of the model without changing the main conclusions) and that all have the same information. Then, the no-arbitrage condition together with rational expectations are simply equivalent to the statement that the average of the price tomorrow based on all present knowledge and all information revealed until the present is equal to the price today. In other words, the average of the total price variation is zero. The same principle is used when it is sometimes claimed that the best forecast for the weather tomorrow is the weather today. This principle is a message of complete randomness or, equivalently, of complete absence of knowledge of the future. This condition is illustrated geometrically in Figure 5.4 and corresponds to imposing that the average over all scenarios, shown as the dark circle, be at the same price level as the empty circle representing the price at the present time.

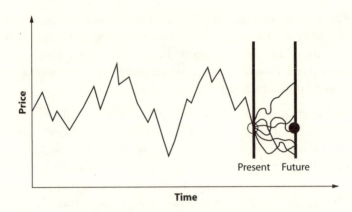

FIG. 5.4. A price trajectory ending at the present, at the position of the open circle. The six trajectories from present to future delineated by the vertical lines constitute six possible scenarios. Averaging over all possible scenarios, given the present price, gives a price shown as the dark circle.

THE CRASH HAZARD RATE DRIVES THE MARKET PRICE

For each period, for instance a day, the model assumes that two components, and only two, compete to determine the price increment from one day to the next: (1) a daily market return that may change and fluctuate from day to day; (2) the possibility that a crash will occur.

In this framework, the no-arbitrage condition together with rational expectations tell us that the price variation due to the market return should compensate exactly the average loss due to the possibility of a crash. The average loss is performed by considering all possible scenarios, most of them having no crash and thus no loss. Only those scenarios that lead to a crash yield a loss. We can group all scenarios that give a crash and count them. Their proportion among all possible scenarios is nothing but the hazard rate previously defined, that is, the probability that a crash occurs knowing that it has not yet happened. Then, the average loss is simply equal to the market drop due to a crash times the probability that such a crash will occur on this day, since all other scenarios that do not give a crash do not contribute to a loss. For instance, suppose that, on a given day, a crash of 30% has a probability of 0.01 (a chance of one in one hundred) to occur and a probability of 0.99 not to happen. Then, the loss averaged over all possible scenerios is $30\% \times 0.01 = 0.3\%$. The no-arbitrage condition together with rational expectations hold true, under the condition that the market remunerates investors by a return of 0.3%. In this presentation of the argument, we have assumed, to simplify the discussion, that all crashes have the same amplitude. The results are essentially the same when one takes into account the variability of crash sizes. We would then need to perform an additional average over all possible crash amplitudes.

This line of reasoning provides us with the following important result: the market return from today to tomorrow is proportional to the crash hazard rate. As we announced, we have derived that the higher the risk of a crash, the larger is the price return. In essence, investors must be compensated by a higher return in order to be induced to hold an asset that might crash. This is the only effect that we wish to capture in this part of the model. This effect is fairly standard, and it was pointed out earlier in a closely related model of bubbles and crashes under rational expectations by Blanchard [43]. It may go against the naive preconception that price is adversely affected by the probability of the crash, but this result is the only one consistent with rational expectations.

Let us stress an interesting subtlety that this reasoning allows us to unearth. The no-arbitrage condition together with rational expectations imposes that the total average return at any time is exactly zero. The zero average return embodies the unrealized risks of a looming crash. This return is not what investors actually experience but would correspond to the average gain that a pool of many investors would get by aggregating their portfolios when living over many repetitions of history, some with a crash and most without a crash. In contrast, knowing that the crash has not yet occurred, the return is not zero and may indeed exhibit all features of a speculative bubble with inflating prices. We cannot stress enough that there is no contradiction between the two ways of quantifying market returns. Some might question the validity of the averaging procedure over all possible scenarios. The point is that, in the absence of advanced knowledge of the future, its best predictor is the average of all possible scenarios. This market price reflects the equilibrium between the greed of buyers who hope the bubble will inflate and the fear of sellers that it may crash. A bubble that goes up is just one that could have crashed but did not.

The situation can perhaps be clarified further with the following analog example. Suppose you are given the possibility to play a casino game with a rotating wheel with 100 numbers, such that you lose $30 if the number comes out as 1 and you gain x otherwise. What is the minimum value of the gain x that can make this a game fair and entice you to play? The simplest idea is to request that you should obtain at least a nonnegative gain, on average, over many repetitions of the game. This average is $x \times 99 - \$30 \times 1$ divided by the total number 100 of outcomes of the casino wheel. We thus see that the minimum value of x that makes the average gain positive is $30/99, which is close to $0.3. A minimum gain of $0.3 for any of the numbers 2 to 100 is thus required to make the gain at least fair from your point of view (and profitable on average if x is larger). Thus, as long as the number 1 does not come up, each game remunerates you with a gain of $0.3, which thus gives the impression of an anomalous bias in your favor. Indeed, since the number 1 has only one chance in one hundred to come out, the typical number of games one needs to play to encounter it once is 100. One may thus be attracted to this game and reason that it is safe to play the game for a while, say $n < 100$ times, and thus accumulate a profit equal to n times $0.3. As in the stock market, the gambler needs to decide when to stop (exit) and be happy with her gains. Otherwise, she will eventually get the number 1 and suddenly lose the gain of 100 games. This example illustrates how a return can be large, *conditioned* on the fact that the crash has not occurred. This return actually compensates for the risk that the number 1 may come up at any time.

Now, suppose that you knew in advance that the number 1 was not going to come out in the next game. It is clear that you would play the game even if the gain x is smaller than $0.3 as long as it remains positive. It is the absence of knowledge of the future that requires a remuneration for taking risks precisely associated with the lack of knowledge of the future. If we knew the specific future exactly, risk would vanish (which does not mean that bad news would disappear).

To be complete, we should add that most people would not play this game if the gain x for the numbers 2 to 100 were only $0.3 because they are "risk averse": this means that most people do not like to gain zero on average while facing the possibility of losing at some times. Most people need a positive bias above $0.3 to play such a game. This subject of risk aversion and its consequences for economic modeling is an important subject of its own, which refers to a large body of scholarly work dating back at least from the founding book [443] of Von Neumann and Morgenstern, which introduced the concept of a utility function to address this problem specifically. Risk aversion is a central feature of economic theory, and it is generally thought to be stable within a reasonable range, associated with slow-moving secular trends like changes in education, social structures, and technology. For our purpose here, it suffices to say that the market return may be larger than the minimum value imposed by the no-arbitrage condition together with the rational expectations discussed above. The important message is thus the existence of this minimum. Risk aversion is easily incorporated into our model, for instance by saying that the probability of a crash in the next instant is perceived by traders as being some factor F times bigger than it objectively is. This amounts to multiplying our hazard rate by this same factor F. This makes no substantive difference to our conclusion as long as F is bounded away from zero and infinity (a very weak restriction indeed).

IMITATION AND HERDING DRIVE THE CRASH HAZARD RATE

The crash hazard rate quantifies the probability that a large group of agents place sell orders simultaneously and create enough of an imbalance in the order book for market makers to be unable to absorb the other side without lowering prices substantially. Most of the time, market agents disagree with one another and submit roughly as many buy orders as sell orders (these are all the times when a crash *does not* happen). The key question is, By what mechanism did they suddenly manage to organize a coordinated sell-off?

As discussed in the last section of chapter 4, titled "Cooperative Behavior Resulting from Imitation," all the traders in the world are organized into a network (of family, friends, colleagues, etc.) and they influence each other *locally* through this network. For instance, an active trader is constantly on the phone exchanging information and opinions with a set of selected colleagues. In addition, there are indirect interactions mediated, for instance, by the media and the Internet. Our working hypothesis is that agents tend to *imitate* the opinions of their connections according to the mechanism detailed in the section titled "It Is Optimal to Imitate," in chapter 4. The interaction between connections will tend to create order, while personal idiosynchrasis will tend to create disorder. Disorder represents the notions of heterogeneity or diversity as opposed to uniformity.

The main story here is a fight between order and disorder. As far as asset prices are concerned, a crash happens when order wins (a majority has the same opinion: selling), and normal times are when disorder wins (buyers and sellers disagree with each other and roughly balance each other out). This mechanism does not require an overarching coordination, since macro-level coordination can arise from micro-level imitation and it relies on a realistic model of how agents form opinions by constant interactions.

Many models of interaction and imitation between traders have been developed. We have described some of them in chapter 4. To make a long story short, the upshot is that the fight between order and disorder often leads to a regime where order may win. When this occurs, the bubble ends. Models that contain the imitation mechanism undergo this transition in a "critical" manner: the sensitivity of the market reaction to news or external influences increases in an accelerated manner on the approach to this transition. This was shown in chapter 4 in the set of Figures 4.8–4.10 representing the configurations of buyers and sellers in a simple space of investors arranged on a square Manhattan-like lattice. When the imitation strength K gets close to a special critical value K_c (whose specific value is not important and depends on details of the models), very large groups of investors share the same opinion and may act in a coordinate manner. This leads to a remarkable and very specific precursory "power law" signature, which we now explain.

Let us assume that the imitation strength K changes smoothly with time, as will be shown later in Figure 5.7, as a result, for instance, of the varying confidence level of investors, the economic outlook, and similar factors. The simplest assumption, which does not change the nature of the argument, is that K is proportional to time. Initially, K is small and only small clusters of investors self-organize, as shown in Figure 4.8. As K increases, the typical size of the clusters increases as shown in Figure 4.9. These kinds of systems exhibiting cooperative behavior are characterized by a broad distribution of cluster sizes s (the size of the black islands, for instance) up to a maximum s^*, which itself increases in an accelerating fashion up to the critical value K_c as shown in Figure 5.5. As explained in chapter 4, right at $K = K_c$, the geography of clusters of a given kind becomes self-similar with a continuous hierarchy of sizes from the smallest (the individual investor) to the largest (the total system). Within this phenomenology, the probability for a crash to occur is constructed as follows.

First, a crash corresponds to a coordinated sell-off of a large number of investors. In our simple model, this will happen as soon as a single cluster of connected investors, which is sufficiently large to set the market off-balance, decides to sell off. Recall indeed that "clusters" are defined by the condition that all investors in the same cluster move in concert. When a very large cluster of investors sells, this creates a sudden unbalance, which triggers an abrupt drop of the price, and hence a crash. To be concrete, we assume that a crash occurs when the size (number of investors) s of the active cluster is larger than some minimum value s_m. The specific value s_m is not important, only the fact that s_m is much larger than 1, so that a crash can only occur as a result of a cooperative action of many traders who destabilize the market. At this

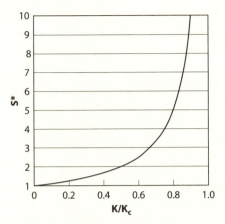

FIG. 5.5. Power law acceleration of the size s^* (in arbitrary units) of the typical largest cluster as a function of the imitation strength K. As K approaches K_c, s^* diverges. This divergence embodies the observation that infinitely large clusters form at the critical point K_c. In practice, s^* is bounded by the system size.

stage, we do not specify the amplitude of the crash, only its triggering as an instability. In general, investors change opinion and send market orders only rarely. Therefore, we should expect only one or few large clusters to be simultaneously active and able to trigger a crash.

For a crash to occur, we thus need to find at least one cluster of size larger than s_m and to verify that this cluster is indeed actively selling off. Since these two events are independent, the total probability for a crash to occur is thus the product of the probability of finding such a cluster of size larger than the threshold s_m by the probability that such a cluster begins to sell off collectively. The probability n_s of finding a cluster of size s is a well-known characteristic of critical phenomena [164, 414]: it is a power law distribution truncated at a maximum s^*; this maximum increases without bound (except for the total system size) on the approach to the critical value K_c of the imitation strength, as we see in Figure 5.5.

If the decision to sell off by an investor belonging to a given cluster of size s was independent of the decisions of all the other investors in the same cluster, then the probability per unit time that such a cluster of size s would become active would be simply proportional to the number s of investors in that cluster. However, by the very definition of a cluster, investors belonging to a given cluster do interact with each other. Therefore, the decision of an investor to sell off is probably quite strongly coupled with those of the other investors in the same cluster. Hence, the

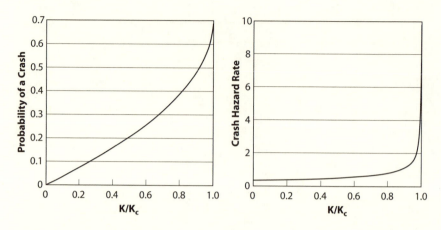

FIG. 5.6. Left panel: Probability for a crash to occur. In this example, the probability reaches its maximum equal to 0.7 at the critical point $K = K_c$ with an infinite slope. Right panel: Crash hazard rate. The crash hazard rate is proportional to the slope of the probability shown in the left panel and goes to infinity at $K = K_c$. Equivalently, the area under the curve of the hazard rate of the right panel up to a given K/K_c is proportional to the probability shown in the left panel for this same value $K = K_c$.

probability per unit time that a specific cluster of s investors becomes active is a function of the number s of investors belonging to that cluster and of all the interactions between these investors. Clearly, the maximum number of interactions within a cluster is $s \times (s - 1)/2$; that is, for large s, it becomes proportional to the square of the number of investors in that cluster. This occurs when each of the s investors speaks to each of his or her $s - 1$ colleagues. The factor $1/2$ accounts for the fact that if investor Anne speaks to investor Paul, then in general Paul also speaks to Anne, and their two-ways interactions must be counted only once. Of course, one can imagine more complex situations in which Paul listens to Anne but Anne does not reciprocate, but this does not change the results. Notwithstanding these complications, one sees that the probability $h(t)\Delta t$ per unit time Δt that a specific cluster of s investors becomes active must be a function growing with the cluster size s faster than s but probably slower than the maximum number of interactions (proportional to s^2). A simple parameterization is to take $h(t)\Delta t$ proportional to the cluster size s elevated to some power α larger than 1 but smaller than 2. This exponent α captures the collective organization within a cluster of size s due to the multiple interactions between its investors. It is deeply related to the concept of fractal dimensions, explained in chapter 6.

The probability for a crash to occur, which is the same as the probability of finding at least one active cluster of size larger than the minimum destabilizing size s_m, is therefore the sum over all sizes s larger than s_m of all the products of probabilities n_s to find a cluster of a specific size s by their probability per unit time to become active (itself proportional to s^α, as we have argued). With mild technical conditions, it can then be shown that the crash hazard rate exhibits a power law acceleration as shown in Figure 5.6. Intuitively, this behavior stems from the interplay between the existence of larger and larger clusters as the interaction parameter K approached its critical value K_c and from the nonlinear accelerating probability per unit time for a cluster to become active as its typical size s^* grows with the approach of K to K_c. In sum, the risk of a crash per unit time, knowing that the crash has not yet occurred, increases dramatically when the interaction between investors becomes strong enough that the network of interactions between traders self-organizes into a hierarchy containing a few large, spontaneously formed groups acting collectively.

If the hazard rate exhibits this behavior, the previous section convinced us that the return must exhibit the same behavior in order for the no-arbitrage condition together with rational expectations to hold true. We find here our first prediction of a specific pattern of the approach to a crash: returns increase faster and faster; that is, they accelerate with time. Since prices are formed by summing returns, the typical trajectory of a price as a function of time, which is expected on the approach to a critical point, is parallel to the dependence of the probability of a crash shown in the left panel of Figure 5.6.

We stress that K_c is not the value of the imitation strength at which the crash occurs, because the crash could happen for any value before K_c, though this is not very likely. K_c is the most probable value of the imitation strength for which the crash occurs. To translate these results as a function of time, it is natural to expect that the imitation strength K is changing slowly with time as a result of several factors influencing the tendency of investors to herd. A typical trajectory $K(t)$ of the imitation strength as a function of time t is shown in Figure 5.7. The critical time t_c is defined as the time at which the critical imitation strength K_c is reached for the first time starting from some initial value. t_c is not the time of the crash, it is the end of the bubble. It is the most probable time of the crash because the hazard rate is largest at that time. Due to its probabilistic nature, the crash can occur at any other time, with the likelihood changing with time following the crash hazard rate. In a given time history, the evolution of K as a function of time follows a trajectory like that shown in Figure 5.7. For each value of K, we read on

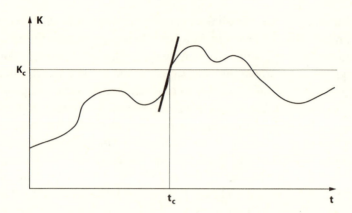

FIG. 5.7. A typical evolution of the imitation strength $K(t)$ as a function of time t showing its smooth and slow variation. As time goes on, K may approach and even cross the critical value K_c at a critical time t_c at which very large clusters of investors are created spontaneously and may trigger a crash. Around t_c, the dependence of $K(t)$ is approximately linear, as shown by the thick linear segment tangent to the curve.

the right panel of Figure 5.6 the corresponding value of the crash hazard rate. Since K may go up and down, so does the crash hazard rate.

As shown in the left panel of Figure 5.6, there is a residual finite probability (0.3 in this example) of attaining the critical time t_c without a crash. This residual probability is crucial for the coherence of the story, because otherwise the whole model would unravel since rational agents would anticipate the crash with certainty.

Intuitive explanation of the creation of a finite-time singularity at t_c.
The faster-than-exponential growth of the return and of the crash hazard rate correspond to nonconstant growth rates, which increase with the return and with the hazard rate. The following reasoning allows us to understand intuitively the origin of the appearance of an infinite slope or infinite value in a finite time at t_c, called a finite-time singularity.

Suppose, for instance, that the growth rate of the hazard rate doubles when the hazard rate doubles. For simplicity, we consider discrete-time intervals as follows. Starting with a hazard rate of 1 per unit time, we assume it grows at a constant rate of 1% per day until it doubles. We estimate the doubling time as proportional to the inverse of the growth rate, that is, approximately $1/1\% = 1/0.01 = 100$ days. There is a multiplicative correction term equal to $\ln 2 = 0.69$ such that the doubling time is $\ln 2/1\% = 69$ days. But we drop this proportionality factor $\ln 2 = 0.69$ for the sake of pedagogy and simplicity. Including it just multiplies all time intervals below by 0.69 without changing the conclusions.

When the hazard rate turns 2, we assume that the growth rate doubles to 2% and stays fixed until the hazard rate doubles again to reach 4. This new doubling time is only approximately $1/0.02 = 50$ days at this 2% growth rate. When the hazard rate reaches 4, its growth rate is doubled to 4%. The doubling time of the hazard rate is therefore approximately halved to 25 days, and the scenario continues with a doubling of the growth rate every time the hazard rate doubles. Since the doubling time is approximately halved at each step, we have the following sequence: (time = 0, hazard rate = 1, growth rate = 1%), (time = 100, hazard rate = 2, growth rate = 2%), (time = 150, hazard rate = 4, growth rate = 4%), (time = 175, hazard rate = 8, growth rate = 8%), and so on. We observe that the time interval needed for the hazard rate to double is shrinking very rapidly by a factor of 2 at each step. In the same way that

$$\frac{1}{2} + \frac{1}{4} + \frac{1}{8} + \frac{1}{16} + \cdots = 1,$$

which was immortalized by the ancient Greeks as Zeno's paradox, the infinite sequence of doubling thus takes a finite time and the hazard rate reaches infinity at a finite "critical time" approximately equal to $100 + 50 + 25 + \cdots = 200$ (a rigorous mathematical treatment requires a continuous-time formulation, which does not change the qualitative content of the example). A spontaneous singularity has been created by the increasing growth rate! This process is quite general and applies as soon as the growth rate possesses the property of being multiplied by some factor larger than 1 when the hazard rate or any other observable is multiplied by some constant larger than 1. We shall revisit this example in chapter 10 when we analyze the world demography, major financial indices, and the World Gross Economic product over several centuries to look ahead and attempt to predict what is coming next.

To sum up, we have constructed a model in which the stock market price is driven by the risk of a crash, quantified by its hazard rate. In turn, imitation and herding forces drive the crash hazard rate. When the imitation strength becomes close to a critical value, the crash hazard rate diverges with a characteristic power law behavior. This leads to a specific power law acceleration of the market price, providing our first predictive precursory pattern anticipating a crash. The imitation between agents leading to an accelerating crash hazard rate may result, for instance, from a progressive shift in the belief of investors about market liquidity, without invoking asymmetric information, and independently of the price behavior and its deviation from its fundamental value [132].

THE PRICE-DRIVEN MODEL

The price-driven model inverts the logic of the previous risk-driven model: here, again as a result of the action of rational investors, the price is driving the crash hazard rate rather than the reverse. The price itself is driven up by the imitation and herding behavior of the "noisy" investors.

As before, a stochastic description is required to capture the interplay between the progressive strengthening of imitation controlled by the connections and interactions between traders and the ubiquity of idiosyncratic behavior as well as the influence of many other factors that are impossible to model in detail. As a consequence, the price dynamics are stochastic and the occurrence of a crash is not certain but can be characterized by its hazard rate $h(t)$, defined as the probability per unit time that the crash will happen in the next instant if it has not happened yet.

IMITATION AND HERDING DRIVE THE MARKET PRICE

Hsieh has stressed that the evidence documented in chapter 2 of an absence of correlation of price changes and a strong persistence of volatility (i.e., the amplitude of the price variations), when taken together, cannot be explained by any linear model [201, 202]. Recall that a linear model is a description in which the consequence or output is proportional to the cause. Nonlinearity generalizes tremendously the quite special "linear" behavior by allowing the output to depend on the cause in a more complicated way. Nonlinearity is an ingredient of chaos, a theory of complex systems that have been studied intensely in the last few decades as a possible origin of complexity. Chaos has been widely popularized and has even been advocated by some as a useful description of stock markets. This, however, remains too simplistic, as chaos theory relies on the assumption that only a few major variables interact nonlinearly and create complicated trajectories. In reality, the stock market needs many variables to obtain a reasonably accurate description. In technical jargon, the stock market has many degrees of freedom, while chaos theory requires only a few. The existence of many degrees of freedom is precisely the ingredient used by the models of collective behavior that exhibit critical points described in the previous section and in chapter 4. Here, we retain only the more general observation that effects are not proportional to causes, that is, that the world and the stock market are nonlinear systems.

A well-known joke among scientists in this field is to compare "nonlinearity" with a "non-elephant": all creatures, except the elephants, are non-elephant; similary, all systems and phenomena are nonlinear, except the very special subsystems that are linear. Notwithstanding the fact that we are educated at school in a "linear" framework of thoughts, this ill-prepares us for the intrinsic nonlinearity of the universe, be it physical, biological, psychological, or social. Nonlinearity is at the origin of the most profound difficulties in disentangling the causes of a given observation: since effects are not in general proportional to causes, two causes do not add up their impacts. Indeed, the output resulting from the presence of two causes acting simultaneously is not the sum of the outputs obtained in the presence of each cause in the absence of the other one.

It is customary among modelers of financial markets to represent the price variation over an elementary time period as resulting from two contributions: a certain instantaneous return and a random return. The first constribution embodies the remuneration due to estimated risks as well as the effect of imitation and herding. The second contribution embodies the noise component of the price dynamics with an amplitude called the volatility. The volatility can also present a systematic component controlled by imitation as well as many other factors. If the first contribution is absent and the volatility is constant, the second term alone creates the random walk trajectories described in chapter 2. Reinserting the ubiquitous property of nonlinear dependence of the volatility and of the certain instantaneous return on past values of the volatility and the returns provides a rich universe of possible trajectories. Here, I am interested in the many possible mechanisms leading to a nonlinear positive feedback of prices on themselves. For instance, imperfect information and risk shifting from investors to lending banks may lead investors to bid up asset prices far above what they would be willing to pay if they were fully exposed to all potential losses [3]. We shall return to an intuitive description of other mechanisms in chapters 7 and 8.

THE PRICE RETURN DRIVES THE CRASH HAZARD RATE

Earlier in this chapter, we showed that the no-arbitrage condition together with the rational expectations imposes that the price variations from one day to the next should compensate exactly for the average loss due to the possibility of a crash. We now view this balance in the reverse logic: noisy investors look at the market price going up, they speak to each other, develop herding, buy more and more of the stock, thus pushing prices further up. As the price variation speeds up, the no-arbitrage condition, together with rational expectations, then implies that there must be an underlying risk, not yet revealed in the price dynamics, which justifies this apparent free ride and free lunch. The fundamental logic here is that the no-arbitrage condition, together with rational expectations, automatically implies a dramatic increase of a risk looming ahead each time the price appreciates significantly, such as in a speculative frenzy or in a bubble. This is the conclusion that rational traders will reach. This phenomenon can be summarized by the following proverb applied to an accelerating bullish market: "It's too good to be true."

In the goal of capturing the phenomenon of speculative bubbles, we focus on the class of models with positive feedbacks, as discussed in chapter 4. In the present context, this means that the instantaneous return as well as the volatility become larger and larger when past prices and/or past returns and/or past volatilities become large. As explained in the technical insert entitled "Intuitive Explanation of the Creation of a Finite-Time Singularity at t_c" earlier in this chapter, such positive feedbacks with increasing growth rate may lead to singularities in a finite time. Here, this means that, unchecked, the price would blow up without bounds. However, two effects compete to tamper with this divergence. First, the stochastic component impacting the price variations makes the price much more erratic, and the convergence to the critical time becomes a random, uncertain event. This is represented in Figure 5.8, illustrating the variability of the price trajectory preceding the singularity of $B(t)$.

Figure 5.8 shows a typical trajectory of the bubble component of the price generated by the nonlinear positive feedback model [396], starting from some initial value up to the time just before the price starts to blow up. The simplest version of this model consists in a bubble price $B(t)$ being essentially a power of the inverse of a random walk $W(t)$ in the following sense. Starting from $B(0) = W(0) = 0$ at the origin of time, when the random walk approaches some value W_c, here

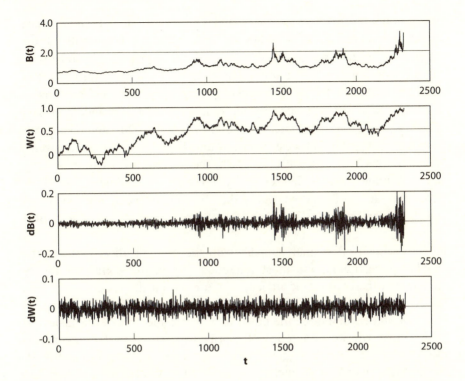

FIG. 5.8. Top panel: Realization of a bubble price $B(t)$ as a function of time constructed from the "singular inverse random walk." This corresponds to a specific realization of the random numbers used in generating the random walks $W(t)$ represented in the second panel. The top panel is obtained by taking a power of the inverse of a constant W_c, here taken equal to 1 minus the random walk shown in the second panel. In this case, when the random walk approaches 1, the bubble diverges. Notice the similarity between the trajectories shown in the top ($B(t)$) and second ($W(t)$) panels as long as the random walk $W(t)$ does not approach the value $W_c = 1$ too much. It is free to wander, but when it approaches 1, the bubble price $B(t)$ shows much greater sensitivity and eventually diverges when $W(t)$ reaches 1. Before this happens, $B(t)$ can exhibit local peaks, that is, local bubbles, which come back smoothly. This corresponds to realizations of when the random walk approaches W_c without touching it and then spontaneously recedes away from it. The third (respectively, fourth) panel shows the time series of the increments $dB(t) = B(t) - B(t-1)$ of the bubble (respectively, $dW(t) = W(t) - W(t-1)$ of the random walk). Notice the intermittent bursts of strong volatility in the bubble compared to the featureless constant level of fluctuations of the random walk (reproduced from [396]).

taken equal to 1, $B(t)$ increases and vice versa. In particular, when $W(t)$ approaches 1, $B(t)$ blows up and reaches a singularity at the time t_c when the random walk crosses 1. This process generalizes in the random domain the finite-time singularities described earlier in this chapter, such that the monotonously increasing process culminating at a critical time t_c is replaced by the random walk that wanders up and down before eventually reaching the critical level. This nonlinear positive feedback bubble process $B(t)$ can thus be called a "singular inverse random walk." In absence of a crash, the process $B(t)$ can exist only up to a finite time: with probability 1 (i.e., with certainty), we know from the study of random walks that $W(t)$ will eventually reach any level, in particular the value $W_c = 1$ in our example, at which $B(t)$ diverges.

The second effect that tampers with the possible divergence of the bubble price, by far the most important one in the regime of highly overpriced markets, is the impact of the price on the crash hazard rate discussed above: as the price blows up due to imitation, herding, speculation, and randomness, the crash hazard rate increases even faster, so that a crash will occur and drive the price back closer to its fundamental value. The crashes are triggered in a random way governed by the crash hazard rate, which is an increasing function of the bubble price. In the present formulation, the higher the bubble price, the higher is the probability of a crash. In this model, a crash is similar to a purge administered to a patient.

Determination of the crash hazard rate. Concretely, a simulation using a computer program proceeds as follows. First, we choose a discretization of the time in steps on size δt. Then, knowing the value of the random walk $W(t - \delta t)$ and the price $B(t - \delta t)$ at the previous time $t - \delta t$, we construct $W(t)$ by adding an increment taken from the centered Gaussian distribution with variance δt. From this, we construct the price $B(t)$ by taking the inverse of $(W_c - W(t))^\alpha$, where α is a positive exponent defined in the model. We then read off from the no-arbitrage condition together with the rational expectations what the probability $h(t)\,\delta t$ is for a crash to occur during the next time step, where $h(t)$ is the crash hazard rate. We compare this probability with a random number *ran* uniformly drawn in the interval $[0, 1]$ and trigger a crash if $ran \le h(t)\,\delta t$. In this case, the price $B(t)$ is changed into $B(t)(1 - \kappa)$, where κ is drawn from a prechosen distribution. For instance, the crash drop κ can be fixed to, say, 20%. It is straightforward to generalize to an arbitrary distribution of jumps. After the crash, the dynamics proceeds incrementally as before, starting from this new value for time t after a proper translation of $W(t)$ to ensure continuity of prices. If $ran > h(t)\,\delta t$, no crash occurs and the dynamics can be iterated another time step.

This model thus proposes two scenarios for the end of a bubble: either a spontaneous deflation or a crash. These two mechanisms are natural features of the model and have not been artificially added. These two scenarios are indeed observed in real markets, as will be described in chapters 7–9.

This model has an interesting and far-reaching consequence in terms of the repetition and organization of crashes in time. Indeed, we see that each time the random walk approaches the chosen constant W_c, the bubble price blows up and, according to the no-arbitrage condition together with rational expectations, this implies that the market enters "dangerous waters" with a crash looming ahead. The random walk model provides a very specific prediction of the waiting times between successive approaches to the critical value W_c, that is, between successive bubbles. The distribution of these waiting times is found to be a very broad power law distribution [394], so broad that the average waiting time is mathematically infinite. In practice, this leads to two interrelated phenomena: clustering (bubbles tend to follow bubbles at short times) and long-term memory (there are very long waiting times between bubbles once a bubble has deflated for a sufficiently long time). In particular, amusing paradoxes follow, such as "the longer since the last bubble, the longer the waiting time till the next" [402]. Anecdotally, this property of random walks also explains the overwhelming despair of frustrated drivers on densely packed highways that neighboring lanes always go faster than their lane because they often do not notice catching up to a car that was previously adjacent to them: assuming that we can model the differential motion of lanes in a global traffic flow by a random walk, this impression is a direct consequence of the divergence of the expected return time of a random walk! To summarize, the "singular inverse random walk" bubble model predicts very large intermittent fluctuations in the recurrence time of speculative bubbles.

An additional layer of refinement can easily be added. Indeed, following [184], which introduced so-called Markov switching techniques for the analysis of price returns, many scholarly works have documented the empirical evidence of regime shifts in financial data sets [432, 175, 63, 431, 363, 24, 80, 110]. For instance, Schaller and Van Norden [363] have proposed a Markov regime-switching model of speculative behavior whose key feature is similar to ours, namely overvaluation of the price above the fundamental price increases the probability and expected size of a stock market crash.

This evidence, taken together with the fact that bubbles are not expected to permeate the dynamics of the price all the time, suggests the following natural extension of the model. In the simplest and most parsimonious extension, we can assume that only two regimes can occur: bubble and normal. The bubble regime follows the previous model definition and is punctuated by crashes occuring with the hazard rate governed by the price level. The normal regime can be, for instance, a standard random walk market model with constant small drift and volatility. The regime switches are assumed to be completely random. This dynamical and very simple model recovers essentially all the stylized facts of empirical prices, that is, no correlation of returns, long-range correlation of volatilities, a fat tail on return distributions, apparent fractality and multifractality, and sharp peak–flat trough pattern of price peaks. In addition, the model predicts and we confirm by empirical data analysis that times of bubbles are associated with nonstationary increasing volatility correlations. This will be further elaborated in our empirical chapters 7–10. The apparent long-range correlation of volatility is proposed to result from random switching between normal and bubble regimes. In addition, and perhaps most importantly, the visual appearance of price trajectories is very reminiscent of real ones, as shown in Figure 5.9. The remarkably simple formulation of the price-driven "singular inverse random walk" bubble model is able to reproduce convincingly the salient properties and appearance of real price trajectories, with their randomness, bubbles, and crashes.

RISK-DRIVEN VERSUS PRICE-DRIVEN MODELS

Together, the risk-driven model and the price-driven model presented in this chapter describe a system of two populations of traders, the "rational" and the "noisy" traders. Occasional imitative and herding behaviors of the noisy traders may cause global cooperation among traders, causing a crash. The rational traders provide a direct link between the crash risks and the bubble price dynamics.

In the risk-driven model, the crash hazard rate determined from herding drives the bubble price. In the price-driven model, imitation and herding induce positive feedbacks on the price, which itself creates an increasing risk for a looming yet unrealized financial crash.

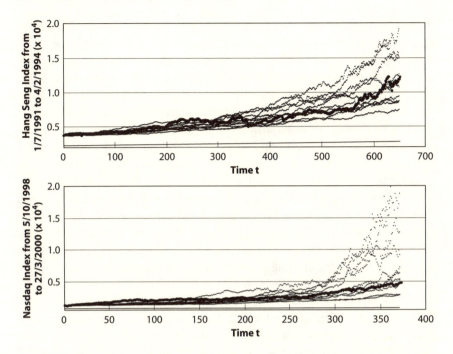

FIG. 5.9. Top panel: The Hang Seng index (thick line) from July 1, 1991 to February 4, 1994 (denoted "bubble II" in Figure 7.8 and analyzed in Figure 7.10) as well as ten realizations of the "singular inverse random walk" bubble model generated by the nonlinear positive feedback model [396]. Each realization corresponds to an arbitrary random walk whose drift and variance have been adjusted so as to best fit the distribution of the Heng Seng index returns. Bottom panel: The Nasdaq composite index bubble (thick line) from October 5, 1998 to March 27, 2000 analyzed in Figure 7.22 as well as ten realizations of the "singular inverse random walk" bubble model generated by the nonlinear positive feedback model [396]. Each realization corresponds to an arbitrary random walk whose drift and variance have been adjusted so as to best fit the distribution of the Nasdaq index returns. Reproduced from [396].

We believe that both models capture a part of reality. Studying them independently is the standard strategy of dividing-to-conquer the complexity of the world. The price-driven model appears as perhaps the most natural and straightforward, as it captures the intuition that skyrocketing prices are unsustainable and announce endogenously a significant correction or a crash. The risk-driven model captures a very subtle self-organization of stock markets, related to the ubiquitous balance between risk and returns. Both models embody the notion that the market anticipates the crash in a subtle, self-organized, and cooperative fashion, hence releasing precursory "fingerprints" observable in stock market prices. In other words, this implies that market prices contain information on impending crashes. The next chapter 6 explores the origin and nature of these precursory patterns and prepares the road for a full-fledged analysis of real stock market crashes and their precursors.

Chapter 6 also provides a description of price dynamics incorporating the interplay between trend-followers (who replace the noisy traders considered here) and value-investors (who replace the rational traders envisioned here). Recognizing the importance of their nonlinear (close to threshold-like) behavior leads to regimes similar to but richer than those described until now. This approach pertains to a body of literature taking a middle ground between fully rational and irrational behavior [239]: stock prices can rationally change as information is released and revealed through the trading process itself. As the market conditions do not allow the complete aggregation of individuals' information in a fully revealing rational expectation equilibrium, prices may deviate substantially from their fundamental value. Lack of common knowledge about traders' preferences or beliefs has been shown to create crashes in models (see [239] and references therein). The mechanism is that some external news may provide the trigger that reveals internal news (among traders) through the trading process.

CHAPTER 6

HIERARCHIES, COMPLEX

FRACTAL DIMENSIONS,

AND LOG-PERIODICITY

The previous chapter 5 put forward the concept that a critical point in the time domain, or equivalently a finite-time singularity, underlies stock market crashes. A crash is not the critical or singular point itself, but its triggering rate is strongly influenced by the proximity of the critical point: the closer to the critical time, the more probable is the crash. We have seen that the hallmark of critical behavior is a power law acceleration of the price, of its volatility, or of the crash hazard rate, as the critical time t_c is approached. The purpose of the present chapter is to extend this analysis and suggest that additional important ingredients and patterns beyond the simple power law acceleration should be expected. An important motivation is that a power law acceleration is notoriously difficult to detect and to qualify in practice in the presence of the ubiquitous noise and irregularities of the trajectories of stock market prices.

As we already emphasized, the stock market is made of actors that differ in size by many orders of magnitudes, ranging from individuals to gigantic professional investors such as pension funds. Structures at even higher levels, such as currency influence spheres (U.S.$, Euro, Yen, . . .), exist and with the current globalization and deregulation of the market one may argue that structures on the largest possible scale—that of the world economy—are beginning to form. This means that the structure of the financial markets has features that resemble that of hierarchical systems with "agents" on all levels of the market. Of course, this does not imply that any strict hierarchical structure of the stock market exists. However, critical phenomena induced by imitation forces in these conditions may often exhibit a rather nonintuitive phenomenon, called "log-periodicity," in which, for instance, the probability or the hazard rate are not monotonously accelerating as shown in Figure 5.6 but are decorated by oscillations with frequencies accelerating as the critical time is approached. In the present chapter, we explore this novel phenomenon and explain its possible origins. The main message is that these oscillatory structures provide a complementary signature of impending criticality which is more robust with respect to noise. These patterns will turn out to be instrumental in the analysis performed on past crashes and in the prediction of future crashes presented in chapters 7–10.

In this chapter, we first show how models of cooperative behaviors resulting from imitation between agents organized within a hierarchical structure exhibit the announced critical phenomena decorated with "log-periodicity." Log-periodicity turns out to be a direct and general signature of the existence of a preferred scaling factor of similarity (which is then called discrete scale invariance), corresponding to the magnifying factor linking one level of the hierarchy to the next. We then formalize this idea a bit and show how a remarkable technique, called the "renormalization group," capitalizes on the existence of multiscale self-similar properties of critical phenomena to derive a fundamental and concise description of these patterns. We provide several graphical examples, including the generalized Weierstrass function, a fractal model of stock market price trajectories that is continuous but exhibits jerky structures at all scales of magnification.

Even more interesting and surprising is the discovery that log-periodicity and discrete scale invariance in critical phenomena may emerge spontaneously from a purely dynamical origin, without a pre-existing hierarchy. To show this, we discuss a simple model exhibiting a finite-time singularity due to a positive feedback induced by trend-following investment strategies. Without any additional ingredients, it does not introduce a significant novelty compared to the models presented in chapter 5. The novel idea is to add the impact of fundamental analysts who tend to restore the price back to its fundamental value. When this restoring force is a nonlinear function of the difference between the bubble price and the fundamental value, the dynamics of the price exhibits a competition between power law acceleration culminating in a finite-time singularity, as shown in chapter 5, and accelerating log-periodic oscillations decorating this power law acceleration. The interplay between these two patterns is shown to be robust as a function of model specification. Intuitively, the strategies based on fundamental analysis introduce a restoring "force" on the price, which constantly overshoots the target, that is, the fundamental price. In the presence of trend-following strategies, which provide a positive feedback, the overshots tend to accelerate and follow the acceleration of the price, leading to ever accelerating oscillations.

CRITICAL PHENOMENA BY IMITATION ON HIERARCHICAL NETWORKS

THE UNDERLYING HIERARCHICAL STRUCTURE OF SOCIAL NETWORKS

Investors are organized into social/professional networks, defined as a collection of people, each of whom is acquainted with some subset of the others. Social networks have been studied intensively because they embody patterns of human interactions and because their structure controls the spread of information (and of diseases), as we showed in chapters 4 and 5.

Stanley Milgram [297] conducted one of the first empirical studies of the structure of social networks. He asked test subjects, chosen at random from a Nebraska telephone directory, to get a letter to a target subject in Boston, a stockbroker friend of Milgram's. The instructions were that the letters were to be sent to their addressee (the stockbroker) by passing them from person to person, but that they could be passed only to someone whom the passer knew on a first-name basis. Since it was not likely that the initial recipients of the letters were on a first-name basis with a Boston stockbroker, their best strategy was to pass their letter to someone whom they felt was nearer to the stockbroker in some sense, either social or geographical—perhaps someone they knew in the financial industry, or a friend in Massachusetts.

A moderate number of Milgram's letters did eventually reach their destination, and Milgram discovered that the average number of steps taken to get there was only about six, a result which has since passed into folklore and was immortalized by John Guare in the title of his 1990 play *Six Degrees of Separation* [182]. Milgram's result is usually taken as evidence of the "small world hypothesis" [445] that most pairs of people in a population can be connected by only a short chain of intermediate acquaintances, even when the size of the population is very large. This result has been shown to apply to essentially all social networks that have been investigated, including affiliation networks such as clubs, teams, or organizations. Examples include women and the social events they attend, company CEOs and the clubs they frequent, company directors and the boards of directors on which they sit, and movie actors and the movies in which they appear. Recently, M. E. J. Newman has studied the affiliation networks of scientists in which a link between two scientists is established by their coauthorship of one or more scientific papers [313, 314]. This network may represent a good proxy for professional networks such as traders and, to a lesser degree, investors. The idea is that most pairs of people who have written a scientific paper together are genuinely acquainted with one another, as they are supposed to have conducted together the research reported in the paper.

The idea of networks of coauthorship is not new. Most practicing mathematicians are familiar with the definition of the Erdös number [178]. Paul Erdös (1913–1996), the widely traveled and incredibly prolific Hungarian mathematician, wrote at least 1,400 mathematical research papers in many different areas, many in collaboration with others. His Erdös number is 0 by definition. Erdös's coauthors have Erdös number 1. There are 507 people with Erdös number 1. People other than Erdös who have written a joint paper with someone with Erdös number 1 but not with Erdös have Erdös number 2 and so on. There are currently 5,897 people with Erdös number 2. If there is no chain of coauthorships connecting someone with Erdös, then that person's Erdös number is said to be infinite. The present author has Erdös number 3; that is, I have published with a colleague who has published with another colleague who has written a paper with Erdös. There is a mathematical conjecture that the graph of mathematicians organized around the vertex defined by Erdös himself and connected to him contains almost all present-day publishing mathematicians and has a not very large diameter; that is, the largest finite Erdös number is 15, while the average value is about 4.7 [179, 33].

The explanation of the "small world" effect is illustrated in Figure 6.1, which shows all the collaborators of the author of [313, 314] and all the collaborators of those collaborators, that is, all his first and second neighbors in the collaboration network of scientists. As the figure shows, M. E. J. Newman has 26 first neighbors and 623 second neighbors. As the increase in numbers of neighbors with distance continues at this impressive rate, it takes only a few steps to reach a size comparable to the whole population of scientists, hence the "small-world" effect.

FIG. 6.1. The point in the center of the figure represents the author of two articles [313, 314] studying the network of scientists, the first ring his collaborators, and the second ring their collaborators. Collaborative ties between members of the same ring, of which there are many, have been omitted from the figure for clarity. Courtesy of M. E. J. Newman [313, 314]. A similar construction holds for most scientists, including the author of this book. However, being older than the author of [313, 314], the present author has fifty-five (instead of twenty-six) nearest neighbor collaborators in the first ring, and many more in the second ring, counting only his collaborators from 1996 to 2000. The corresponding figure would not be as aesthetically pleasing at the present one, being too crowded to appeal to the eye.

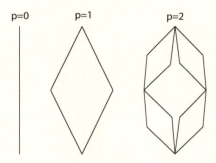

FIG. 6.2. First three steps of the iterative construction of the hierarchical diamond lattice. p refers to the index of the iteration.

Indeed, in most networks, the average distance between any pair of vertices (scientists or traders in our example below) is proportional to the logarithm of the number of vertices. Recall that the logarithm of a number is nothing but the exponent in the exponential representation of that number; that is, it is roughly equal to the number of digits minus one (the logarithm of 1,000 in base 10 is 3 because $1,000 = 10^3$). The logarithm is thus a very slowly varying function, since multiplying the number by 10 corresponds to adding 1 to its logarithm. A hierarchical network provides a simple justification of this point. Let us therefore consider a simplified hierarchical structure, called the diamond hierarchy, whose construction is represented in Figure 6.2. Let us start with a pair of investors who are linked to each other ($p = 0$). Let us replace this link by a diamond, where the two original traders occupy two diametrically opposed vertices, and where the two other vertices are occupied by two new traders ($p = 1$). This diamond contains four links. For each one of these four links, let us replace it by a diamond in exactly the same way ($p = 2$). Iterating the operation a large number of times gives the hierarchical diamond lattice. After p iterations, we have $N = \frac{2}{3}(2 + 4^p)$ traders and $L = 4^p$ links between them. Since N and L are essentially proportional to 4^p for large p, reciprocally the order p of the iteration is proportional to the logarithm of the number of traders and of the number of links between them. The logarithm of a number N is thus nothing but a quantity proportional to the exponent of the power of a given reference number (here 4), providing a representation of the number N.

Most traders have only two neighbors, a few traders (the original ones) have 2^p neighbors, and the others are in between. Note that the least-connected agents have 2^{p-1} times fewer neighbors than the most-connected ones, who themselves have approximately 2^p fewer neighbors than there are agents in total. Averaging over all traders, we retrieve the result that the average distance between any pair of traders is proportional to the index p of iteration, that is, to the logarithm of the number of vertices.

Such a hierarchical network may be a more realistic model of the complicated network of communications between financial agents than the grid in the Euclidean plane used in chapters 4 and 5 with Figures 4.7–4.10.

CRITICAL BEHAVIOR IN HIERARCHICAL NETWORKS

Consider a network of agents positioned at the nodes of the hierarchical diamond lattice shown in Figure 6.2 and interacting with their nearest neighbors through the links in a noisy imitative fashion according to expression (6) on page 102. We recall that this expression (6) embodies the competition between the ordering effect of imitation and the disordering forces of idiosyncratic signals modeled as random noise. This network as well as different extensions turns out to be exactly solvable [106, 9]. The extensions of the network shown in Figure 6.2 comprise networks constructed by substituting any link of a given generation by a set of q branches, each containing a series of r bonds. The construction of Figure 6.2 corresponds to $q = r = 2$.

The basic properties obtained for these networks are similar to the ones described in the risk-driven model of chapter 5 using the grid in the Euclidean plane shown in Figures 4.7–4.10. There exists a critical point K_c for the imitation strength. As shown in the left panel of Figure 6.3, the probability $P(K)$ for a crash to occur goes to a constant $P(K_c)$ (=0.7 in this example), by accelerating upward, reaching an infinite acceleration right at the critical point $K = K_c$. Recall that the mechanism underlying this behavior stems from the existence of larger and larger clusters of traders as K approaches K_c and from the larger and larger probability for the collective activation of a very large cluster, thus triggering the coordinated sell-off of the group. The novel pattern shown in the left panel of Figure 6.3 compared to that of Figure 5.6 is the existence of an oscillation decorating the overall acceleration. Notice that these oscillations also accelerate, as can be seen from the fact that the distances between successive crossings with the dashed line become smaller and smaller as K_c is approached. To visualize the nature of these oscillations, the left panel of Figure 6.4 shows the difference $P(K_c) - P(K)$ of the accelerating part of the probability, again as a function of the reduced distance

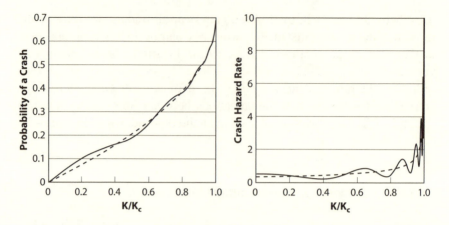

FIG. 6.3. Left panel: Probability for a crash to occur in the hierarchical diamond network. In this example, the probability reaches its maximum, equal to 0.7, at the critical point $K = K_c$ with an infinite slope after accelerating with log-periodic oscillations. The dashed line is the same as in the left panel of Figure 5.6 obtained for the Euclidean lattice. Right panel: Crash hazard rate for the hierarchical diamond network. The dashed line is the same as in the right panel of Figure 5.6, obtained for the Euclidean lattice. The crash hazard rate is proportional to the slope of the probability shown in the left panel.

$(K_c - K)/K_c$ to the critical point K_c. This novel representation uses a logarithmic scale both for the abscissa and for the ordinate, such that a power law acceleration is seen as the straight dashed line. Decorating this, we see periodic oscillations. Since these oscillations are periodic in the logarithm of the variable $(K_c - K)/K_c$, we refer to them as "log-periodic." The strength of these log-periodic oscillations depends on the nature of the interactions between traders within the hierarchical lattice and on the choice of the observable. When one utilizes these models for other purposes, such as in models of magnetic materials for which the traders on the nodes are replaced by tiny magnets, called spins, the relevant physical observables such as the energy or the magnetization usually exhibit log-periodic oscillations with quite tiny amplitudes. For the sake of pedagogy, we have thus artificially enhanced their amplitude compared to what they would be in the physical problem, in order to obtain a clearer visual appearance. However, this enhancement is not really artificial in the financial context. It can be justified by the fact that financial crashes are not characterized by the same observables as physical quantities. As explained in chapter 1, market crashes are more like ruptures, which are sensitive to extreme fluctuations in the distribution

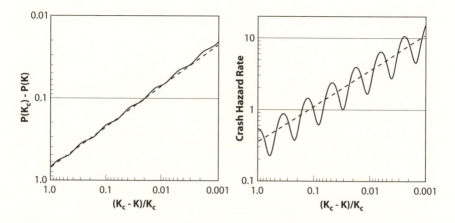

FIG. 6.4. Left panel: Logarithm scale of the difference $P(K_c) - P(K)$ of the accelerating part of the probability shown in the left panel of Figure 6.3 as a function of the reduced distance $(K_c - K)/K_c$, also in logarithmic scale. The grid on the two axis are inverted to obtain the correct visual impression that the closer we get to K_c, the larger is the probability. Right panel: Logarithmic scale of the crash hazard rate shown in the right panel of Figure 6.3 as function of the reduced distance $(K_c - K)/K_c$, also in logarithmic scale. The dashed line corresponds to the pure power law acceleration obtained for the Euclidean lattice and shown on the right panel of Figure 5.6. The grid on the horizontal axis has been inverted to obtain the correct visual impression that the closer we get to K_c, the larger is the crash hazard rate.

of clusters of imitative traders. The log-periodic signals can be much stronger when the largest fluctuations are emphasized. This is illustrated in Figure 6.5 in another context, corresponding to a model of chaotic and turbulent dynamics [462]. The log-periodicity is clearly seen as regular steps for the values of the parameter $m = 3$ and 4, whose increasing value corresponds to putting more and more emphasis on the largest fluctuations. This figure illustrates that log-periodicity may not be detectable in some observables, while being a strong feature of others for the same system.

The diverging acceleration of the crash probability shown in Figure 6.3 again implies that the crash hazard rate, which is nothing but the rate of change of the probability of a crash as a function of time, increases without bounds as K goes to K_c. The novel feature is the existence of the log-periodic oscillations. They are accelerating as the critical point is approached, while their arches are represented as equidistant in the double-logarithmic representation of the right panel

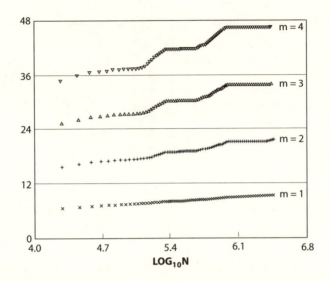

FIG. 6.5. The ordinate is a measure of the average amplitude of fluctuations in the dynamical evolution in a simple model of hydrodynamic turbulence, weighted more and more towards large amplitudes as m increases. The abscissa is the time window in which the measures are calculated. This figure illustrates that log-periodicity may not be detectable in some observables (here, for $m = 1$), while being a strong feature of others (for $m = 3$ and 4). Reproduced from [462].

of Figure 6.4. The oscillations are more pronounced for the hazard rate than for the (cumulative) probability of the crash, because constructing a rate (derivative quantity) enhances local features. This implies that the risk of a crash per unit time, knowing that the crash has not yet occurred, increases dramatically when the interaction between investors becomes strong enough, but this acceleration is interrupted by and mixed with an accelerating sequence of quiescient phases (the decreasing parts of the log-periodic oscillations) in which the risk decreases.

If the hazard rate exhibits this behavior, we have seen in chapter 5 that the return must, as a consequence, possess the same qualitative properties in order for the no-arbitrage condition together with rational expectations to hold true. We obtain our second prediction of a specific pattern of the approach to a crash: returns increase faster and faster in an intermittent fashion; that is, they alternatively accelerate and decelerate with time, with a pattern converging to the critical point. Since prices are formed by summing returns, the typical trajectory of a price as a function of time, which is expected on the approach to a critical point, is parallel to the dependence of the probability of a crash shown in the left panel of Figure 6.3.

A HIERARCHICAL MODEL OF FINANCIAL BUBBLES

It is useful to illustrate further the impact of a hierarchical structure of imitative behavior between traders on observable signatures in the stock market. We thus assume the hierarchical organization shown in Figure 6.6 such that a trader influences only a limited number of traders at the same level of the hierarchy and below. Due to a cascade effect, the decisions of the lower levels in turn influence the higher levels. For instance, the position of a bank within a country will be highly sensitive to the position of the currency block as a whole and to that of its country and of other banks from which it can get information. On the other hand, the position of the currency block will be an aggregate of that of the constituting countries.

The model formalizes the hierarchical organization and refers to the individual traders as traders of order 0. According to the hierarchical organization, these traders are organized in groups of m traders and we consider each such group as a single "trader" of order 1. These groups (or "traders") of order 1 are also organized in groups of m to form a group of order 2 and so forth. In this way, a hierarchical organization is obtained, where a group of order n is made of m^n individual traders. For simplicity, but without loss of generality, we take $m = 2$. The analysis

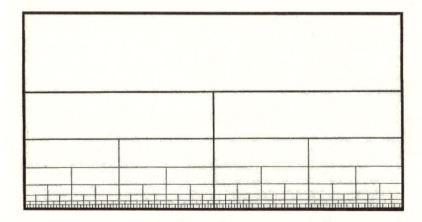

FIG. 6.6. Schematic representation of a simple dichotomous hierarchical structure of influences between the traders. Reproduced from [398].

for other values of m is the same and only detailed numerical values are modified.

At time 0, all individual traders of the zeroth level of the hierarchy are assumed to start gathering and processing information to form a decision on whether or when to enter the market. The traders are thought to be heterogeneous in the sense that the time they need to perform their analysis of the situation is different for each of them and hence each trader has a characteristic time to form his decision and enter the market. The behavior of the traders thus differs with respect to the timing of their action [437]. Assume that the trader i has a preferred time t_i to buy the stock (assumed to be unique in this toy-market model) and that the t_i's are distributed according to some distribution, say a Poisson (exponential) distribution. Trader i's time to buy t_i should not be confused with his reaction time once his decision is made. The latter is almost instantaneous, as it is to the trader's benefit that his order be executed efficiently. In contrast, the time to buy t_i reflects the need for the trader to accumulate data, to carry out his analysis, and to be convinced that he has to enter the market. In a sense, this is the time that he needs for strengthening his confidence that his decision is correct. Establishing this confidence can be a long learning process, also rooted in different psychologies and past experiences. The characteristic time scales t_i are expected to range from minutes (or less) to years. These are the time scales for new information to be gathered and analyzed.

One trader's move in the market can be interpreted by another trader as relevant additional information due to the uncertainty he faces. To be specific, consider the hierarchical organization with $m = 2$ shown in Figure 6.6. Suppose that, at the zeroth level, one of the two traders of a group reaches the end of his time-to-buy period and enters the market. The rule of the model is that the other trader of the group, and only him, has the privilege of incorporating this information. In principle, a trader would probably benefit from a survey of other traders' actions. However, getting the information on the different levels of the hierarchy is not easy and may not be possible for all. Furthermore, this would have a cost, which introduces a severe limitation. Our simplifying assumption thus corresponds to the limit of a cost-effective minimal information strategy. After the analysis of this information, the second trader in general is influenced positively towards the decision of entering the market. The model specifies that the remaining waiting time is reduced by a fixed "influence" factor β less than 1. This is basically an imitation rule and is devised in order to model the highly nonlinear (threshold-like) behavior of traders, with positive and negative feedback patterns, as discussed in chapter 4. If β is close to 1, then the interaction is weak and a trader does not significantly modify his strategy after receiving the information on the action of his neighboring trader. On the contrary, in the limit $\beta \to 0$, the second trader almost instantaneously enters the market on the knowledge of the action of the first trader; this is the regime where traders are strongly influenced by the other traders in the same group and will amplify the actions of the other traders by their own decision. A strong "crowd" effect is expected in this regime.

The model assumes that the imitation process works at all levels of the hierarchy. When two "traders" of order m belonging to the same group have finally bought the stock, this information is transferred to the next level in the hierarchy. Since the two traders of order m have bought, the trader of order $m + 1$, defined as their sum, has also bought, and this information is reported to the other trader of order $m + 1$ of the pair. This will then change the time-to-buy of this "trader" of order $m + 1$. As a consequence, the remaining waiting time of the two traders of this neighboring group of order $m + 1$ is also multiplied by β at this next level of the hierarchy. This process may continue to increasingly high levels and lead to a complex superposition of actions and influences starting at the lowest level of the hierarchy and progressively overlapping as more groups get linked at higher levels. This cascade process of information is illustrated geometrically in Figure 6.7.

The price of the stock is strongly influenced by the behavior of the traders in a nontrivial way. This drastically simplified description does not provide a specific formula for the price. Instead, the model uses the very weak assumption that the price is a nondecreasing function of the total number of buy positions taken by the traders up to time t. In other words, the demand curve is positive. The idea is simply that demand has a direct influence on the price and tends to appreciate it. Another important simplification is that the traders are only interested in buying the stock, an assumption which, taken at face value, would obviously be in contradiction with the balance between sellers and buyers: to be able to buy, some traders must sell! The model assumes, in fact, that the sellers are necessarily a homogeneous group that remains fixed and neutral throughout the period in which the progressive cooperative activity between the buyers develops. The problem thus reduces to determining quantitatively the temporal behavior of the total number of buy positions.

This model allows for a rigorous definition of a crash. Indeed, in the limit of an infinite number of traders (and therefore of hierarchical levels), the existence of a crash occurring at some time t_c is defined by the fact that at times much before t_c the number of buyers remains small

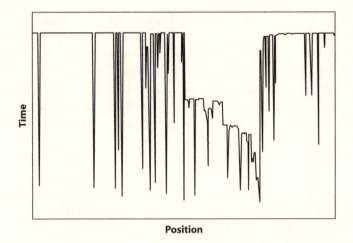

Position

FIG. 6.7. Spatiotemporal evolution of the system. The abscissa represents 512 traders who are linked hierarchically, as shown in Figure 6.6. The ordinate is time, which flows from bottom to top. Those buyers who have entered the markets are represented by the wells. The widening of the wells depicts the progressive "invasion" among neighboring agents of a buy order spreading from an agent. Notice the cascade of doubling that can be observed at many different scales and along many different branches. There are many competing cascades starting from different traders and at different times, which lead to the noisy structure observed in Figure 6.8. Reproduced from [398].

and their mutual influences are small. As time goes on, these quantities accelerate progressively until t_c, at which a finite fraction of the traders have made buy orders and already entered the position, thus saturating the market with no more buyer to be found. The model describes the preparation phase, called a bubble, ending in a crash, which is not specifically modeled itself.

Figure 6.8 shows the number of traders who have made buy orders as a function of time. The left panel corresponds to one specific realization of the initial population of traders' waiting times at the zeroth order. The right panel shows five realizations with different initial configurations of waiting times, in a double logarithmic scale, such that a power law acceleration of the form shown in Figures 6.3 and 6.4 is represented as a straight line. One can indeed observe a characteristic power law acceleration, which is decorated by log-periodic structures at many different scales as the critical time is approached. It turns out to be possible to explicitly solve this model and demonstrate rigorously the existence of these log-periodic structures decorating the average power law [398].

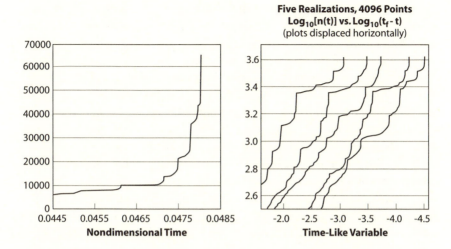

FIG. 6.8. Left panel: Number of traders who have made buy orders as a function of time. Notice the power law acceleration and the log-periodic structure of step-like jumps decorating this acceleration. Right panel: Same as the left panel in a double logarithmic representation of the number of traders who have entered the market as a function of the distance to the critical time. Five different trajectories are shown, each one corresponding to a different but statistically equivalent initial condition, reflecting the variability of the real world. The approximate linear dependence decorated by large and complicated log-periodic structures qualifies as a power law, as discussed in the text. Reproduced from [398].

The log-frequencies of the log-periodic oscillations are determined by the "influence" factor β, which quantifies the change of the remaining waiting time of a trader observing the action of his companions and of traders at the higher levels of the hierarchy.

Note the strength of the log-periodic oscillations seen in Figure 6.8. This can be traced back to the fundamental threshold nature of the cascade of traders' influences. As we have indicated with Figure 6.5, observables that put an emphasis on extreme and abrupt behavior will enhance the effect of log-periodicity. To make the argument even clearer, let us mention that this model can be mapped exactly onto a model of material failure according to a cascade of abrupt ruptures [355].

The acceleration of the number of traders buying the market in the inflating bubble captures the oft-quoted observation that bubbles are times when the "greater fool theory" applies. In financial circles, this refers to buyers of stocks buying confidently irrespective of the dividends or other underlying fundamental factors, expecting to sell to someone else at an even higher price in some future. As an illustration, it has been reported [142] that Henry Ford was taking the elevator to his penthouse one day in 1929, and the operator said, "Mr. Ford, a friend of mine who knows a lot about stocks recommended that I buy shares in X, Y, and Z. You are a person with a lot of money. You should seize this opportunity." Ford thanked him, and as soon as he got into his penthouse, he called his broker, and told him to sell everything. He explained afterwards: "If the elevator operator recommends buying, you should have sold long ago." More generally, this refers to the following cascade [309]: New demographic, technological, or economic developments prompt spontaneous innovation in financial markets and the first wave of investors and innovators become wealthy. Then, imitators arrive and overdo the new techniques. In the ensuing crises, latecomers lose big before regulators and academics put out the fires.

ORIGIN OF LOG-PERIODICITY IN HIERARCHICAL SYSTEMS

Discrete Scale Invariance

What is the origin of the novel log-periodic oscillations decorating the overall acceleration of the probability of a crash, of the crash hazard rate, and of the returns and price trajectories themselves, documented in the previous section?

The answer turns out to be quite simple: hierarchical networks such as the diamond lattice shown in Figure 6.2 or the tree lattice shown in Figure 6.6 possess a fundamental symmetry property, called "discrete scale invariance." A symmetry refers to the property of a geometrical figure, a system, or an observable to remain invariant under a specific transformation, such as a translation, rotation, inversion, or dilation. For instance, regular tilings paving floors are endowed with discrete translational symmetries, because they are invariant with respect to discrete translations of a multiple of one motif, since the same motif is repeated periodically. Symmetries are aesthetically pleasing as in tiling, carpets, furnitures, diamond stones, and antique churches. Nature seems to have organized its laws around a core set of fundamental symmetries, such as the symmetry under translation, under rotation, under a change between two frames moving at different constant velocities (called Galilean invariance), as well as under a set of more esoteric symmetries called gauge symmetries (which refer to other internal variables describing fundamental particles). All the phenomena, matter, and energy of our universe seem to emerge as slight deviations (resulting from spontaneous symmetry breaking) from these fundamental symmetries [448]. Thus, we cannot emphasize enough the overarching importance of symmetries in helping us understanding the organization and complexity of the world.

The diamond and tree lattices of Figures 6.2 and 6.6 also enjoy a symmetry, called the symmetry of "scale invariance": in the limit where both geometrical constructions are extrapolated up to an infinite number of iterations, replacing a diamond by a single link and vice versa does not change the diamond network. Similarly, replacing a branch by two subbranches and vice versa does not change the tree lattice of Figure 6.6. In other words, the hierarchical diamond and tree networks have the property of reproducing themselves exactly on different magnifications. Such a property has been coined "fractal" by Mandelbrot [284], who recognized, based on the pioneering work of Richardson [343], that many natural and social phenomena are endowed, at least approximately, with the scale invariance symmetry. Many of us have met fractals through their beautiful, delicately complex pictures, which are usually computer generated. Modern Hollywood movies use landscapes, mountain ranges, cloud structures, and other artificial constructions that are computer generated according to recipes devised to obtain fractal geometries. It turns out that many of the natural structures of the world are approximately fractal [29, 126, 88, 31, 292, 394] and that our aesthetic sense resonates with fractal forms.

In most simple fractal constructions and textbook examples, the scale invariance property does not hold for arbitrary magnification. This is also true for the two hierarchical lattices of Figures 6.2 and 6.6. For the diamond lattice, only magnifications that multiply the number of links by a factor of 4, or more generally by any power of 4, leave the network invariant. In the tree lattice, only magnifications that multiply the number of branches for a factor of 2, or more generally by any power of 2, leave the tree invariant. These special magnification factors 4 and 2, respectively, are the direct consequence of the construction scheme of the two hierarchical networks. Such systems, which are self-similar only under magnifications by arbitrary integer powers 4^n or 2^n or any other fixed factor λ^n, where $n = \cdots - 3, -2, -1, 0, 1, 2, 3, \ldots$ is an integer number, are said to enjoy the symmetry of discrete scale invariance [392]. Discrete scale invariance is a weaker symmetry than the general scale invariance: it is the latter restricted to special discrete choices of magnification factors, here integer powers of 4 or of 2.

FRACTAL DIMENSIONS

During the third century before the Christian epoch, Euclid and his students introduced the concept of "dimension," an exponent that can take positive integer values equal to the number of independent directions. The dimension d, for instance, is used as an exponent linking the volume V to the length L: $V = L^d$, where V is the generalized volume of a generalized cube of side length L. For a real cube in our three-dimensional space, $d = 3$ and the volume is the cube $L^3 = L \times L \times L$ of a side L. For a square, $d = 2$, and its surface is the square $L^2 = L \times L$ of its side. For a segment, $d = 1$, its length $L^1 = L$ is equal to its length L. A line has a dimension 1, a plane has a dimension 2, and a volume has a dimension 3. The surface of a sphere also has a dimension 2, since any point on it can be located with two coordinates, the latitude and longitude. Another way of realizing that the surface of a sphere has a dimension 2 is that its area is proportional to the square of its radius.

In the second half of the nineteenth century and in the first quarter of the twentieth century, mathematicians imagined geometrical figures that are endowed with dimensions that can take fractional values, for instance, $d = 1.56$ or $d = 2.5$ or any other number. The remarkable discovery was the understanding that this generalization of the notion of a dimension from integers to real numbers reflects the conceptual jump from translational invariance to continuous scale invariance. A line and a plane are unchanged when viewed from different points translated from one to another, a property called translational invariance. Objects with fractional dimensions turn out to possess the property of scale invariance. To capture this novel concept, we already mentioned that the word "fractal" was coined by Mandelbrot [284], from the Latin root *fractus* to capture the rough, broken, and irregular characteristics of the objects presenting at least approximately the property of scale invariance. This roughness can be present at all scales, which distinguishes fractals from Euclidean shapes. Mandelbrot worked actively to demonstrate that this concept is not just a mathematical curiosity but has strong relevance to the real world. The remarkable fact is that this generalization, from integer dimensions to fractional dimensions, has a profound and intuitive interpretation: noninteger dimensions describe irregular sets consisting of parts similar to the whole.

There are many examples of (approximate) fractals in nature, such as the distribution of galaxies at large scales, certain mountain ranges, fault networks and earthquake locations, rocks, lightning bolts, snowflakes,

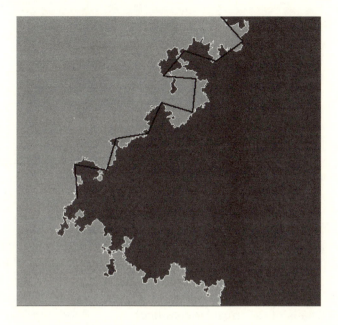

FIG. 6.9. Synthetic fractal coastline (courtesy of P. Trunfio).

river networks, coastlines, patterns of climate change, clouds, ferns and trees, mammalian blood vessels, and so on.

In his pioneering paper [283], Mandelbrot revisited and extended the investigation launched by Richardson [343] concerning the regularity between the length of national boundaries and scale size. He dramatically summarized the problem by the question written in the title of his article [283], "How Long Is the Coast of Britain?" This question is at the core of the introduction of fractal geometry. Figure 6.9 shows a synthetically generated coastline that has a corrugated structure reminiscent of the coastline of Brittany in France.

Such a coastline is irregular, and therefore a measure with a straight ruler, as in Figure 6.10, provides only an estimate. The estimated length $L(\epsilon)$ equals the length of the ruler ϵ multiplied by the number $N(\epsilon)$ of such rulers needed to cover the measured object. In Figure 6.10, the length of the coastline is measured twice with two rulers of length ϵ_1 and ϵ_2, where the length of the second ruler is approximately half that of the first one: $\epsilon_2 = \epsilon_1/2$. It is clear that the estimate of the length $L(\epsilon_2)$ using the smaller ruler ϵ_2 is significantly larger than the length $L(\epsilon_1)$ using the larger ruler ϵ_1. For very corrugated coastlines exhibiting roughness at all length scales, as the ruler becomes very small, the length grows without

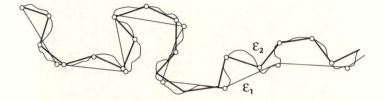

FIG. 6.10. Implementation of the ruler method consisting in covering the rough line by segments of fixed size. As the ruler length decreases, finer details are captured, and the total length of the line increases. Courtesy of G. Ouillon.

bound. The concept of (intrinsic) length begins to make little sense and has to be replaced by the notion of (relative) length measured at two resolutions. To the question, "What is the length of the coast of Britain?" the wise one should thus reply either "it is a function of the ruler" or "infinity" (obtained for an infinitely small ruler capable of detecting the smallest details of the irregular coastline).

The fractal dimension d quantifies precisely how the relative length $L(\epsilon)$ changes with the ruler length ϵ (which we also call "resolution" as details smaller than ϵ are not seen by definition). By construction, $L(\epsilon)$ is proportional to ϵ to the power $1 - d$: $L(\epsilon) \sim \epsilon^{1-d}$. The fact that $1 - d$ and not d appears in this expression comes from the definition of the fractal dimension in terms of the number of elements identified at a given resolution: for a resolution ϵ, one typically sees $M(\epsilon) = L(\epsilon)/\epsilon$ elements. The number of elements resolved with a ruler ϵ is inversely proportional to ϵ to the power d. For Great Britain, $d = 1.24$, which is a fractional value. In constrast, the coastline of South Africa is very smooth, virtually an arc of a circle, and $d = 1$. In general, the "rougher" the line, the larger the fractal dimension, that is, the closer is the line to filling a plane (of dimension 2). When $d = 1$, the length $L(\epsilon) \sim \epsilon^{1-d}$ becomes independent of the resolution ϵ since $\epsilon^0 = 1$: only when the fractal dimension is equal to the topological dimension can the measure be independent of the scale of the ruler. This is the situation with which we are most familiar from our school lessons on Euclidean geometry. However, as this discussion shows, this constitutes an exceptionally special case: the general situation is when any measure performed on an object depends on the scale at which the measure is performed.

Let us apply this definition of a fractal dimension to the two hierarchical networks of Figures 6.2 and 6.6. For the diamond lattice of

Figure 6.2, let us assume that the ratio of the length of the four bonds replacing one link to the length of the link is r, equal to, say, 2/3. Then, each time the resolution is magnified by a factor $1/r = 3/2$, four new links are observable. In other words, the number of links is multiplied by 4 when the resolution is enhanced by 3/2. By the definition of the fractal dimension, 3/2 raised to the power d must give 4. This implies that $d = \ln 4/\ln 3/2 = 3.42$. This object thus has a dimension larger than that of our familiar space. The fact that a high-dimensional object can be represented in a (two-dimensional) plane is not a problem; it just means that the hierarchical construction will cross itself many many times and, in the present case where the dimension is smaller than 4, only by unfolding it in a space of at least four dimensions shall we avoid crossings and overlaps. Notice that the fractal dimension increases when r increases, that is, when the ratio of the size of each of the four "daughter" links to the "mother" link increases (while still being less than 1). This simply reflects the fact that the fractal object fills more and more space.

The same calculation can be repeated for the tree lattice of Figure 6.6. Let us assume that the length of the vertical segments separating each branching shrinks by the same factor $r = 2/3$. Now, each time the resolution increases by the factor $1/r = 3/2$, twice as many branches can be detected. The number of branches thus doubles when the resolution is enhanced by 3/2. By the definition of the fractal dimension, 3/2 raised to the power d must give 2. This implies that $d = \ln 2/\ln 3/2 = 1.71$. This hierarchical network of dimension 1.71 is thus intermediate in some sense between a line and a plane. Notice again that the fractal dimension increases when r increases, that is, when the four links become not much shorter than the initial bond.

Scale invariance and scaling law. The concept of (continuous) scale invariance means reproducing oneself on different time or space scales. More precisely, an observable $\mathcal{O}$ which depends on a "control" parameter x is scale invariant under the arbitrary change $x \rightarrow \lambda x$, if there is a number $\mu(\lambda)$ such that

$$\mathcal{O}(x) = \mu \mathcal{O}(\lambda x). \tag{8}$$

Expression (8) defines a so-called homogeneous function and is encountered in the theory of critical phenomena of liquid-gas and magnet phase transitions, in hydrodynamic turbulence, and many other systems [112]. Its solution is simply a power law $\mathcal{O}(x) = x^\alpha$, where the exponent α

(which plays the same role as the fractal dimension d discussed before) is given by

$$\alpha = -\frac{\ln \mu}{\ln \lambda}. \tag{9}$$

This solution can be verified directly by insertion in expression (8). Power laws are the hallmark of scale invariance, as the ratio $\frac{\mathcal{O}(\lambda x)}{\mathcal{O}(x)} = \lambda^\alpha$ does not depend on x; that is, the relative values of the observable at two different scales only depend on the *ratio* of the two scales. This is the fundamental property that associates power laws to scale invariance, self-similarity, and criticality.

ORGANIZATION SCALE BY SCALE: THE RENORMALIZATION GROUP

Principle and Illustration of the Renormalization Group.
The expression (8) describes the system precisely standing at the critical point at which the scale invariance symmetry is exact. For concrete applications, we would like to have a fuller description of the properties of the system in the vicinity of the critical point, and not just right at the critical point. The obvious reason is that precursors of the critical point may be deciphered before reaching it. The question is to determine how much of expression (8) remains valid and how much of it must be modified. In other words, how much of the exact scale invariance symmetry is conserved when not standing right at the critical point.

The answer to this question is provided by a calculation technique called the "renormalization group," whose invention is mainly attributed to K. Wilson, who received the Nobel prize for physics in 1982 for it, but its maturation owes a lot to other physicists such as B. Widom, M. Gellman, L. Kadanoff, A. Migdal, M. Fisher, and others. The renormalization group has been invented to tackle critical phenomena which, as we have stressed, already correspond to a class of behaviors characterized by structures on many different scales [458] and by power law dependences of measurable quantities on the control parameters. It is a very general mathematical tool, which allows one to decompose the problem of finding the "macroscopic" behavior of a large number of interacting parts into a succession of simpler problems with a decreasing number of interacting parts, whose effective properties vary with the scale of observation. The renormalization group thus follows the proverb "divide to conquer" by organizing the description of a system scale-by-scale. It is particularly adapted to critical phenomena and to systems close to being scale invariant. The renormalization group translates into mathematical language the concept that the overall behavior of a system is the aggregation of an ensemble of arbitrarily defined subsystems, with each subsystem defined by the aggregation of sub-subsystems, and so on.

It works in three stages. To illustrate it, let us consider a population of agents, each of whom has one out of two possible opinions (bull or bear, yes or no, vote for A or vote for B, etc.). The renormalization group then works as follows.

1. The first step is to group neighboring elements into small groups. For instance, in a two-dimensional square lattice, we can group agents in clusters of size equal to nine agents corresponding to squares of side 3 by 3.

2. The second step is to replace the cacophony of opinions within each group of nine agents by a single representative opinion, resulting from a chosen majority rule. Doing this "decimation" procedure obviously lowers the complexity of the problem since there are nine times fewer opinions to keep track of.

3. The last step is to scale down or shrink the superlattice of squares of size 3 by 3 to make them of the same size as the initial lattice. Doing this, each cluster is now equivalent to an effective agent endowed with an opinion representing an average of the opinions of the nine constitutive agents.

One loop involving the three steps applied to a given system transforms it into a new system that looks quite similar but is different in one important aspect: the distribution and spatial organization of the opinions have been modified as shown in Figures 6.11, 6.12, and 6.13.

Three situations can occur that are illustrated in Figures 6.11, 6.12, and 6.13. Let us discuss them in the context of the model of imitative behavior presented in chapter 4 and summarized by the evolution equation (6) on page 102. Let us recall that, in this model, agents tend to imitate each other according to an inclination strength K that quantifies the relative force of imitation compared to idiosynchratic judgment. A large K leads to strong organization where most of the agents share the same opinion. A small K corresponds to a population that is split in half between the two opinions such that the spatial organization of agents is disorganized. In between, we have shown in chapter 4 that there exists a critical value K_c separating these two extreme regimes at which

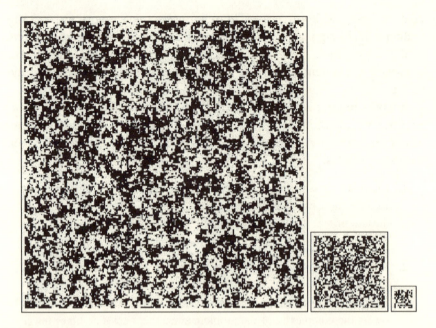

Fig. 6.11. This figure illustrates the effect of renormalization for $K < K_c$ of the Ising model (6) on page 102, which corresponds to the disordered regime. The two discording opinions are encoded in white and black. Starting from a square lattice with some given configuration of opinions on the left, two successive applications of the renormalization group are shown in the right panels. Repeated applications of the renormalization group change the structure of the lattice with more and more disorganization. All the shorter range correlations, quantified by the typical sizes of the black and white domains, are progressively removed by the renormalization process and the system becomes less and less ordered, corresponding to an effective decrease in the imitation strength K. Eventually, upon many iteration of the renormalization group, the distribution of black and white squares becomes completely random. The system is driven away from criticality by the renormalization. The renormalization group thus qualifies this regime as disordered under change of scales.

the system is critical, that is, scale invariant. The renormalization group makes these statements precise, as shown in Figures 6.11, 6.12, and 6.13.

Except for the special critical value K_c, application of the renormalization group drives the system away from the critical value. It is possible to use this "flow" in the space of systems to calculate precisely the critical exponents characterizing the divergence of observables when approaching the critical points. Critical exponents play the role of control functions of this flow; that is, they describe the speed of separation from the critical point.

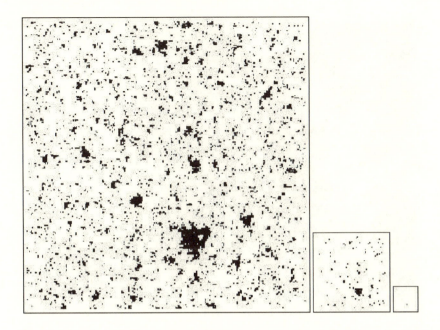

Fig. 6.12. This figure illustrates the effect of renormalization for $K > K_c$ of the Ising model (6) on page 102, which corresponds to the ordered regime in which one opinion (white) dominates (the two discording opinions are encoded in white and black). Starting from a square lattice with some given configuration of opinions, two successive applications of the renormalization group are shown in the right panels. We observe a progressive change of the structure of the lattice with more and more organization (one color, i.e., opinion, dominates more and more). All the shorter range correlations are removed by the renormalization process and the system becomes more and more ordered, corresponding to an effective increase in the imitation strength K. The system is driven away from criticality by the renormalization. The renormalization group thus qualifies this regime as ordered under change of scales.

The Fractal Weierstrass Function: A Singular Time-Dependent Solution of the Renormalization Group.

Right at the critical point, scale invariance holds exactly. It is only broken at either the smallest scale, if there is a minimum unit scale, and/or the largest scale corresponding to the finite system size. In between these two limiting scales, the system is fractal.

When not exactly at the critical point, the same description holds true, but only up to a scale, called the correlation length, which now plays the same role as did the finite size of the system at the critical point. Figure 4.8 showed us that the correlation length is the size of largest

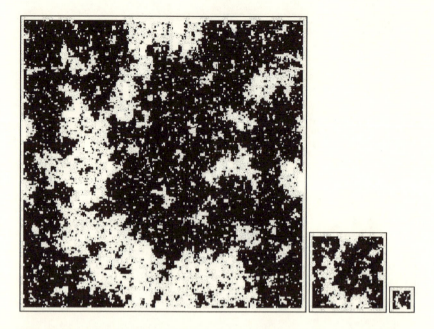

Fig. 6.13. This figure illustrates the effect of renormalization for $K = K_c$ of the Ising model (6) on page 102, which corresponds to the critical point. The two discording opinions are encoded in white and black. Repeated applications of the renormalization group leave the structure of the lattice invariant statistically. All the shorter range correlations are removed by the renormalization process; nevertheless, the system keeps the same balance between order and disorder and the effective imitation strength remains unchanged and fixed at the critical value K_c. The system is kept fixed at criticality by the renormalization. The renormalization group thus qualifies this regime as critical, which is characterized by the symmetry of scale invariance. In other words, the system of clusters of opinions is fractal.

clusters, that is, the distance over which the local imitations between neighbors propagate before being significantly distorted by the "noise" in the transmission process resulting from the idiosynchratic signals of each agent. This means that the mathematical expression (8) on page 191 expressing exact scale invariance is no longer exactly true and must be slightly modified. The renormalization group provides the answer and shows that a new term must be added to the right-hand side of expression (8). This new term captures the effect of the degrees-of-freedom leftover in the coarse-graining procedure of the renormalization group when going from one scale to the next larger one.

With the choice of this new term equal to the simple cosine function $\cos x$, corresponding to regular oscillations, the solution of the

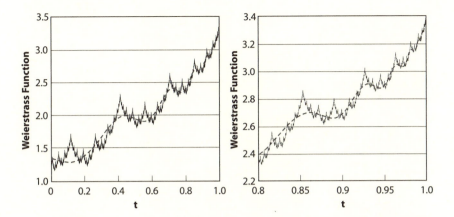

FIG. 6.14. The Weierstrass function defined as the solution of the renormalization group equation obtained from the exact self-similar critical expression (8) on page 191 by adding a simple cosine embodying the effect of the degrees of freedom at small scales on the next larger scale. The Weierstrass function exhibits the property of self-similarity as demonstrated by comparing a magnified portion in the right panel to the left panel. There is an infinitely ramified set of structures accumulating as the critical time $t_c = 1$ is approached. This self-similarity is captured by a fractal dimension equal to 1.5. The power law singularity at $t_c = 1$ is described by an exponent $\alpha = 1/2$. The slowly oscillating dashed line, which captures the large scale structure of the Weierstrass function, is a simple power law $3.4 - (t_c - t)^{1/2}$ with critical exponent $1/2$ decorated by a log-periodic oscillation $\cos(2\pi \ln(t_c - t)/\ln 2)$ showing that the dominating discrete scale factor is $\lambda = 2$ in this example. The repetition of spiky structures thus occurs in a regular geometrical log-periodic manner with a main log-periodicity given by $\lambda = 2$ in the present example. A mathematical transformation (called the Mellin transform) furthermore shows that there is an infinite hierarchy of harmonics of this major log-periodicity with all integer powers of $\lambda = 2$, which are responsible for the delicately corrugated structure at all scales.

renormalization group equation turns out to be a famous function, called the Weierstrass function [447] (see [117] for an English translation). This function, shown in Figure 6.14, has the remarkable property of being continuous but nowhere differentiable. Intuitively, continuity means that there are no holes. Nondifferentiability means that we cannot define a local tangent slope; that is, the curve is rough at all length scales. The Weierstrass curve is critical at $t_c = 1$ in the example shown in Figure 6.15. In addition, it is characterized by a self-similar hierarchy of log-periodic structures accumulating at the critical time $t_c = 1$.

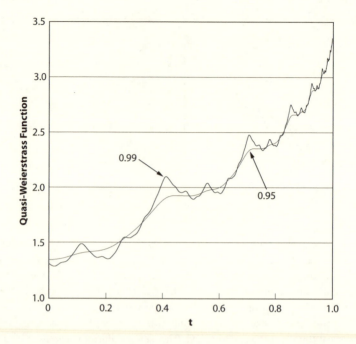

FIG. 6.15. Same as Figure 6.14 but for the replacement of the cosine function by an exponentially attenuated cosine function whose decay rate is equal to 1 minus the number indicated by the arrows. This "quasi-Weierstrass" function is no longer exactly fractal, as it becomes smooth at small scales. Note that the log-periodicity is conserved at large scales but is destroyed at the smaller scales.

COMPLEX FRACTAL DIMENSIONS AND LOG-PERIODICITY

We are now in position to make intuitive sense of the description of discrete scale invariance presented earlier in the chapter. As we said previously, discrete scale invariance is nothing but a weaker kind of scale invariance according to which the system or the observable obeys scale invariance as defined above only for specific choices of the magnification or resolution factor λ, which form in general an infinite but countable set of values $\lambda_1, \lambda_2, \ldots$ that can be written as integer powers $\lambda_n = \lambda^n$. λ is the fundamental scaling ratio.

It is obvious that the two hierarchical networks of Figures 6.2 and 6.6 obey discrete scale invariance but not (continuous) scale invariance. Indeed, by construction, the diamond lattice is recovered exactly only under a discrete set of successive magnifications replacing each link by four links, each of the four links by four new links, and so on. In the same vein, the dichotomous tree is invariant only under a discrete set of magnifications under which each branch is doubled in a discrete hierarchy. Indeed, all regular constructions of fractals are endowed with the discrete scale invariance symmetry. Other famous examples are the Cantor set, the Sierpinsky gasket, and the Koch snowflake, among many others [284].

We have seen that the hallmark of scale invariance is the existence of power laws reflecting the absence of preferred scales. The exponents of these power laws define the fractal dimensions. The signature of discrete scale invariance turns out to be the existence of log-periodic oscillations decorating the power laws. As we shall see, these log-periodic structures can be represented mathematically by the fact that the exponents α, or equivalently the dimensions d, are not only noninteger but become complex numbers.

We have seen that continuous scale invariance gives rise to noninteger (real) fractal dimensions. We now claim that discrete scale invariance is characterized by complex fractal dimensions. Before backing up this claim, let us reflect a bit on this wonderful example of the incredible adequacy of mathematics for describing natural phenomena: the search for a more "aesthetically" pleasing generality and consistency in mathematics turns out to capture the generalization of a deep concept. E. P. Wigner, a Nobel prize winner in physics for his work on symmetries of nuclear physics and quantum mechanics, put it this way [456]: "The enormous usefulness of mathematics in the natural sciences is something bordering on the mysterious. . . . The miracle of the appropriateness of the language of mathematics for the formulation of the laws of physics is a wonderful gift, which we neither understand nor deserve."

Complex numbers form the most general set of numbers obeying the standard rules of addition/subtraction and multiplication/division. They contain in particular the integers numbers $0, 1, 2, 3, \ldots$ and the real numbers, such as any number with an integer and decimal part like $876.34878278\ldots$. Fractions of two integers like $13/8$ are special real numbers called rational because they are characterized by either a finite decimal part ($13/8 = 1.625$) or an infinite but periodic decimal part, for instance, $13/11 = 1.181818181818\ldots$, where the motif 18 is repeated ad infinitum. Most of the real numbers allowing engineers to perform calculations of length, weight, force, resistance, and so on, are characterized in principle by an infinite nonrepetitive decimal part. The set of all real numbers can be represented as a continuous line, each point on the line in exact correspondence with a single real number. The real numbers

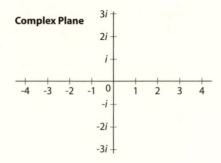

FIG. 6.16. Complex plane: The horizontal line represents the real numbers, which include in particular the integers $-3, -2, -2, 0, 1, 2, 3, \ldots$. The vertical line represents the purely imaginary numbers, products of i by arbitrary real numbers. The rest of the plane is the set of nonreal complex numbers. The terms "complex" and "imaginary" are suggestive of the fact that these numbers lie above the real numbers and are observed as projections or "shadows" on the real axis.

are thus the marks pinpointing the position along the line, as shown in Figures 6.16 and 6.17.

Any complex number is equivalent to a pair of real numbers. The first member of the pair is called the real part of the complex number. The second member of the pair is called the imaginary part. If this second member is 0, the complex number reduces to a pure real number. While a real number can be viewed as a point on a line, a complex number is nothing but a representation of a point in the plane, as shown in Figure 6.16, such that the pair of numbers constituting the complex number corresponds to the two coordinates or projections, respectively, onto the horizontal and vertical axes. "Imaginary" numbers are proportional to their fundamental representative denoted "i", which is such that its square $i^2 = i \times i$ is equal to -1. To the nonexpert, this property may seem unnatural, almost like a magical trick, but mathematicians like to define objects that have the most general properties and that are still consistent with the previous rules, here the standard rules of addition/subtraction and multiplication/division. The property $i^2 = -1$ turns out to be natural when interpreted as an operation in the plane, rather than only along the line of real numbers. While the multiplication by a real number corresponds to a shrinkage or a dilation along the real line, in contrast, a multiplication by i corresponds to a rotation by a rectangular angle (equal to 90 degrees or $\pi/2$ radians) in the plane. A multiplication by an arbitrary complex number is thus the combination

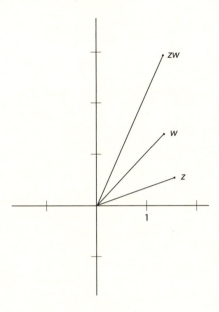

FIG. 6.17. Geometrical representation of the multiplication of a complex number z by another complex number w: the multiplication is equivalent to the combination of a stretching operation and of rotation.

of two transformations, a contraction or dilation as for a real number and a rotation (of an angle not necessarily equal to 90 degrees).

It turns out that introducing numbers like i does not lead to any inconsistency and all the standard calculations apply. More than a pure creation of imagination, complex numbers have found a fantastically large role for understanding properties of telecommunications by electromagnetic and acoustic waves, which we use daily in our modern civilization, because they conveniently encode the dual information of a wave, namely its amplitude (the loudness) and its frequency and phase (pitch). Complex numbers are also essential elements to formulating in a simple way one of the most fundamental theories of particles, quantum mechanics, for instance in the famous Schrödinger equation. The nonintuitive novel phenomena captured by quantum mechanics, such as the superposition principle made famous with Schrödinger's cat, which is both alive and dead as long as no one observes it, result technically from the fact that quantum mechanics is a theory of complex numbers; or, to be technically more specific, quantum mechanics is a theory of their immediate (noncommutative) generalization, called the quaternions.

We can now attempt to explain intuitively how a complex fractal dimension may lead to log-periodic oscillations, as claimed above. First,

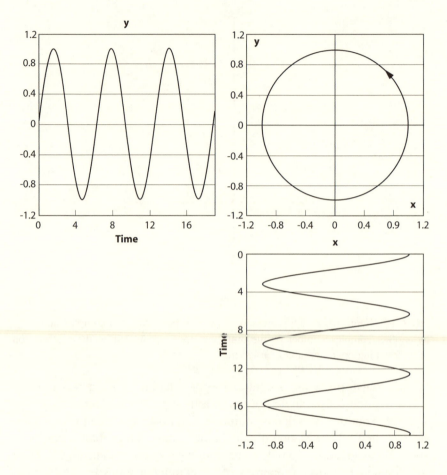

FIG. 6.18. Illustration of the fact that a circular motion in the x–y plane corresponds to oscillatory motions along each of the coordinates x and y, respectively.

recall the general result illustrated by Figure 6.17 that multiplication by a complex number correspond to the combination of a contraction/dilation and a rotation in the plane. For our purpose, let us forget the contraction/dilation and focus only on the rotation. Now consider a point rotating around a center as in Figure 6.18. For instance, consider the tip of the second-hand of a watch making a full circle in exactly one minute. The direction of rotation is not important for our discussion. This perfect periodic circular motion can actually be seen as the combination of two simultaneous and ordered oscillatory motions going back and forth between two extreme positions. The first motion is horizontal and goes from 9:00 to 3:00; the second motion is vertical and spans the interval from 6:00 to 12:00. Seen only as a projection along the horizontal axis, the circular motion of the tip of the second-hand is transformed into an oscillation similar to that shown in Figure 6.18. Seen as a projection along the vertical axis, the circular motion of the tip of the second-hand is transformed into another oscillation similar to that shown in Figure 6.18. This is a general result: any circular or locally curved motion can be transformed into a combination of oscillatory motions along straight lines.

Coming back to the complex fractal dimensions, we need in addition to recall the intuitive meaning of an exponent. As the notations $L^3 = L \times L \times L$ and $L^2 = L \times L$ used previously suggest, the exponents 3 and 2 used here indicate that L is multiplied with itself 3 and 2 times, respectively. The beauty of mathematics is often in generalizing such obvious notions to enlarge their use and meaning considerably. Here, the generalization from integer exponents to real exponents, for instance in $L^{1.5}$, means that L is multiplied with itself somehow 1.5 times! This curious statement can actually be made rigorous and makes perfect sense. Similarly, we can take the power of a complex number with a real exponent: the result is shown in Figure 6.19. Stretching the imagination even more, we can also take the power of L with a complex exponent. Since, as we just said, taking L to some power corresponds to multiplying it with itself a certain number of times, here we have to multiply L with itself a "complex number of times." Since complex numbers are pairs of num-

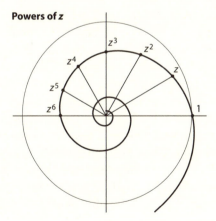

FIG. 6.19. Geometrical representation of successive $n = 1, 2, 3, \ldots$ powers of a complex number z for z inside the circle of radius 1. Varying the exponent n continuously as a real number gives the continuous spiraling curve. Courtesy of David E. Joyce, Clark University.

bers, the way to make sense of this curious statement is to decompose
the action of the complex exponent into two transformations, as in case
of multiplication. Focusing on the rotational component of the multiplication of complex numbers, we can guess (correctly) that the complex
exponent of L will also correspond to a rotation. Now comes the last step
of the reasoning: since we observe real numbers, such as stock market
prices, this corresponds to seeing only the projection on the real line of
the complex set of operations. As we said and showed with Figure 6.18,
a rotation is projected on a line as an oscillation. Therefore, constructing L^d, where d is a complex number, corresponds to performing an
oscillatory kind of multiplication, which turns out to be the log-periodic
oscillations.

In order to understand the log-periodic structure, we need to recall
the basic property of the logarithm function, used in many of the figures
in this book, namely that the logarithm transforms multiplications
into translations and thus powers into additions. As we have said and
used several times, the logarithms (in base 10) of $10, 100, 1,000, \ldots$,
noted $\log 10, \log 100, \log 1,000, \ldots$ are, respectively, $1, 2, 3, \ldots$. In
other words, they correspond to the exponent of the powers of 10:
$10 = 10^1, 100 = 10^2, 1,000 = 10^3, \ldots$. Therefore, an "oscillatory kind
of multiplication," induced by taking the power of a number with a complex exponent, should be seen as a regular oscillation in the logarithm
of the number, hence the log-periodicity.

We illustrate this surprising phenomenon in Figures 6.20 and 6.21,
which show a measure of the fractal dimensions in the presence of discrete scale invariance of the fractal objects. Specifically, we consider
so-called Cantor sets, which are among the simplest geometrical fractal
constructions. Figure 6.22 shows the first five iterations of the construction of the so-called triadic Cantor set. At the zeroth level, the construction of the Cantor set begins with the unit interval, that is, all points
on the line between 0 and 1. This unit interval is depicted by the filled
bar at the top of the figure. The first level is obtained from the zeroth
level by deleting all points that lie in the middle third, that is, all points
between 1/3 and 2/3. The second level is obtained from the first level
by deleting the middle third of each remaining interval at the first level,
that is, all points from 1/9 to 2/9 and 7/9 to 8/9. In general, the next
level is obtained from the previous level by deleting the middle third
of all intervals obtained from the previous level. This algorithm can be
encoded by the following symbolic rule: $1 \rightarrow 101$ and $0 \rightarrow 000$. This
process continues ad infinitum, and the result is a collection of points
that are tenuously cut out from the unit interval. At the nth level, the

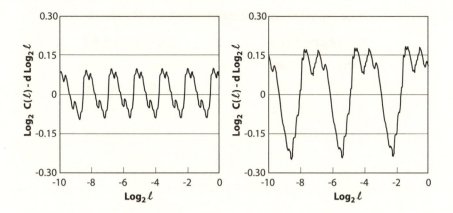

FIG. 6.20. Oscillatory residuals of the fractal dimensions obtained from the slope of the curve shown in Figure 6.22 for (a) the triadic Cantor set constructed with the iterative rule $1 \to 101$ and (b) the Cantor set constructed with the iterative rule $1 \to 101010001$. Both Cantor sets have the same real fractal dimension. They differ via the imaginary part of their fractal dimensions, which is reflected in the different log-periodic structures shown in the two panels. Reproduced from [387].

set consists of $N_n = 2^n$ segments, each of which has length $\ell_n = 1/3^n$, so that the total length (i.e., measure in a mathematical sense) over all segments of the Cantor set is $(2/3)^n$. This result is characteristic of a fractal set: as n goes to infinity, the number of details (here the segments) grows exponentially to infinity, while the total length goes to zero also

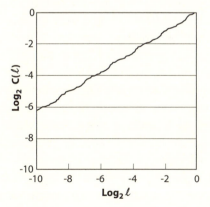

FIG. 6.21. Measure of the fractal dimension of the triadic Cantor set by the correlation method. The figure plots the logarithm of the correlation integral as a function of the logarithm of the separation. Reproduced from [387].

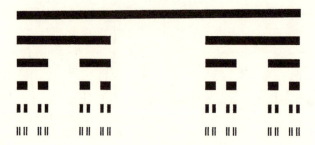

FIG. 6.22. The initial unit interval and the first five iterations of the construction of the so-called triadic Cantor set are shown from top to bottom.

exponentially fast. In the limit of an infinite number of recursions, we find the Cantor set made of an infinite number of dots of zero size. Since there are twice as many segments each time the resolution increases by a factor 3 the fractal dimension d of this triadic Cantor set is such that 2 to the power d should be equal to 3, hence $d = \ln 2/\ln 3 = 0.6309\ldots$. The Cantor set, which is an infinite dust of points, is more than a point (of dimension 0) but less than a line.

The difference between a measure of the fractal dimension of this triadic Cantor set and the theoretical value $0.6309\ldots$ is shown in the left panel of Figure 6.20 as a function of the (logarithm) of the resolution scale ℓ. Rather than a constant value 0 which should be obtained if the fractal dimension was exactly $d = \ln 2/\ln 3 = 0.6309\ldots$, we observe instead a complex oscillatory structure around the expected 0. The naive result $d = \ln 2/\ln 3 = 0.6309\ldots$ correctly embodies a part of the information on the Cantor set structure, but only a part, as it turns out. As we explained, these log-periodic (i.e., periodic in the logarithm of the scale ℓ) oscillations reflect the fundamental symmetry of discrete scale invariance of the triadic Cantor set. The fundamental period seen in the graph is $\ln 3$, corresponding to the preferred scaling factor 3 of the discretely self-similar construction of the Cantor set. It is obvious to see that, by construction, the triadic Cantor set is geometrically identical to itself *only* under magnification by factors $\lambda_p = 3^p$, which are arbitrary integer powers of 3. If you take another magnification factor, say 1.5, you will not be able to superimpose the magnified part on the initial Cantor set. We must thus conclude that the triadic Cantor set does not possess the property of continuous scale invariance but only that of discrete scale invariance under the fundamental scaling ratio 3. It is this property that is captured by the log-periodic oscillations.

Note that the oscillations are more complex than just a single smooth sinusoidal structure. Actually, this reflects the presence of all the other scaling ratios $3^2 = 9, 3^3 = 27, \ldots$ under which the Cantor set is invariant. The delicate structure observed in the left panel of Figure 6.20 is the result of the superposition of all the pure log-periodic oscillations, one for each of the admissible scaling factors. This is similar to a chord, composed by combining a set of pure tunes with different loudnesses.

The right panel of Figure 6.20 gives the same information as the left panel for another Cantor set obtained under a slightly different construction rule: the unit interval is divided into nine intervals of length $1/9$ and only the first, third, fifth, and last are kept. This is then iterated on each of the four remaining intervals. This construction is encoded symbolically into the rule $1 \rightarrow 101010001$. Notice that, each time the resolution is increased by a factor 9, four new segments appear. Hence the fractal dimension d of this new Cantor set should be such that 9 raised to the power d is equal to 4, hence $d = \ln 4/\ln 9 = 2\ln 2/2\ln 3 = \ln 2/\ln 3 = 0.6309\ldots$. This new Cantor set has the same real fractal dimension as the triadic Cantor set, but its structure is very different. The log-periodic oscillations seen in the right panel of Figure 6.20 make this point clear and show how they can embody important information on the construction rule beyond the simple self-similar properties captured by the real fractal dimension.

Figure 6.21 illustrates the dependence of a measure of the fractal structure of the triadic Cantor set as a function of the resolution scale. This measure is called a correlation and counts the number of pairs of points on the Cantor set separated by less than the resolution. In this double logarithmic representation, the slope should be equal to the real fractal dimension $d = \ln 2/\ln 3 = 0.6309\ldots$, as the correlation function grows according to the power d of the resolution. Here we again see the log-periodic oscillations decorating an average linear trend with the correct average slope. These log-periodic structures reflect the discrete scale invariance of the Cantor set.

To summarize, we have shown that the signature of discrete scale invariance is the presence of a power law with a *complex* exponent, which manifests itself in data by log-periodic oscillations providing corrections to the simple power law scaling. In addition to the existence of a single preferred scaling ratio and its associated log-periodicity discussed up to now, there can be several preferred ratios corresponding to several log-periodicities that are superimposed. This can lead to a richer behavior such as log-quasi-periodicity [400].

As a last illustration, the Weierstrass function shown in Figure 6.14 has a real fractal dimension equal to 1.5. As it exhibits a strong discrete scale invariance with preferred scaling ratio (the scale ratio of the successive spiky structures) equal to 2, it is endowed with an infinite number of complex fractal dimensions given by $1.5 + i2\pi n/\ln 2 = 1.5 + i9.06n$, where n takes any possible integer value. As the integer n increases to larger and larger values, the corresponding complex dimensions describe smaller and smaller discrete scale invariant patterns.

As we have seen, going from integer dimensions to real dimensions (with fractional parts) corresponds to a generalization of the translational symmetry to the scaling symmetry. It may come as a surprise to observe that further generalizing the concept of dimension to the set of complex numbers is, in contrast, reducing the scale symmetry into a subgroup, the discrete scale symmetry. This results from the fact that the imaginary part of the complex dimension is actually introducing an additional constraint that the symmetry must obey.

IMPORTANCE AND USEFULNESS OF DISCRETE SCALE INVARIANCE

Existence of Relevant Length Scales.
Suppose that a given analysis of some data shows log-periodic structures. What can we get out of it? First, as we have seen, the period in log-scale of the log-periodicity is directly related to the existence of a preferred scaling ratio. Thus, log-periodicity must immediately be seen and interpreted as the existence of a set of preferred characteristic scales forming altogether a geometrical series $\ldots, \lambda^{-p}, \lambda^{-p+1}, \ldots, \lambda, \lambda^2, \ldots, \lambda^n, \ldots$ Log-periodic structures in the data thus indicate that the system and/or the underlying physical mechanisms have characteristic length scales. This is extremely interesting, as it provides important constraints on the underlying mechanism. Indeed, simple power law behaviors are found everywhere, as seen from the explosion of the concepts of fractals, criticality, and self-organized criticality [26]. For instance, the power law distribution of earthquake energies known as the Gutenberg–Richter law can be obtained by many different mechanisms and described by a variety of models and is thus extremely limited in constraining the underlying physics (one fact, many competing explanations). Its usefulness as a modeling constraint is even doubtful, in contradiction with the common belief held by many scientists on the importance of this power law. In contrast, the presence of log-periodic features would teach us that

important physical structures, hidden in the fully scale invariant description, existed.

Let us mention a remarkable application of log-periodicity used by bats and dolphins. It turns out that the amplitude of the ultrasound signals sent by animal sonars for echolocation, such as by bats and dolphins, is remarkably well described by a mathematical function called the Altes wavelet [5]. Having little real-time high-performance computer processing in their brain, these animals compensate for this limitation by using a very special waveform for their ultrasound signals that turns out to be the optimal shape with respect to distortion under Doppler shifts (the pitch of a sound depends on the relative velocity between the listener and emitter; for instance, an approaching car is heard at a higher frequency (pitch) than a receeding one). The Altes wavelet, which has a log-periodic structure with a local frequency varying hyperbolically, also has the remarkable property of minimizing the time-scale uncertainty, in the same sense that the Gaussian law minimizes the time-frequency uncertainty. It also has the nice property that differentiating it corresponds to dilating it by a fixed factor. Such a typical waveform is shown in Figure 6.23.

Prediction.

It is important to stress the practical consequence of log-periodic structures. For prediction purposes, it is more constrained and thus reliable to fit a part of an oscillating data than a simple power law, which can be quite degenerate especially in the presence of noise. This is well known, for instance, in electronics and in signal processing in the presence of a controlled oscillatory wave carrier, on which one can "lock in" to extract a tiny signal from a large noise. This property that log-periodicity provides more reliable fits to data has been used and is vigorously investigated in several applied domains, such as rupture prediction [13, 12, 210, 215] and earthquakes [405, 355, 222], and will be discussed in depth in its application to financial crashes in its following chapters.

We shall show that log-periodicity is very useful from an empirical point of view in analyzing financial data because such oscillations are much more strikingly visible in actual data than a simple power law: as we said, a fit can lock in on the oscillations which contain information about the critical date t_c. If they are present, they can be used to predict the critical time t_c simply by extrapolating frequency acceleration. Since the probability of the crash is highest near the critical time, this can be an interesting forecasting exercise. Note, however, that for rational traders in the models of chapter 5, such forecasting is useless because they already

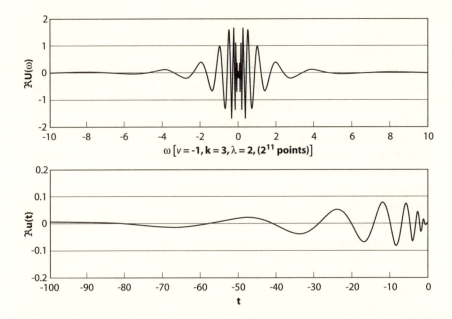

FIG. 6.23. Typical waveform of an Altes wavelet, a mathematical function exhibiting log-periodic symmetry, used by bats and dolphins to optimize their ultrasonic signals. The upper panel shows the Fourier transform as a function of angular frequency of the Altes wavelet represented in the lower panel as a function of time. Recall that the Fourier transform of a signal is nothing but the quantification of the sinusoidal components constituting the signal. Notice that both the Altes wavelet and its Fourier transform exhibit log-periodic oscillations.

know the crash hazard rate $h(t)$ at every point in time (including at t_c), and they have already reflected this information in prices through the rational expectation condition!

SCENARIOS LEADING TO DISCRETE SCALE INVARIANCE AND LOG-PERIODICITY

After the rather abstract description of discrete scale invariance given above, let us briefly discuss the mechanisms that may be found at its origin. It turns out that there is not a unique cause but several mechanisms that may lead to discrete scale invariance. Since discrete scale invariance is a partial breaking of a continuous symmetry, this is hardly surprising, as there are many ways to break a symmetry. Some mechanisms have already been unravelled, while others are still under investigation.

For a list of mechanisms, we refer to [392]. Discrete scale invariance is found in particular in chaotic systems, especially in the way they transit from order to chaos and respond to external perturbations. Discrete scale invariance is also a profound property of numbers and of the arithmetic system, symbolized by the so-called Newcomb–Benford law of first digits [195]. Before turning to a general dynamical system description of spontaneously generated log-periodic singularities in financial time series, we review the fascinating Newcomb–Benford law of first digits and its profound link with log-periodicity. Our motivation is that reducing a problem to number theory is like stripping it down to its sheer fundamentals.

NEWCOMB–BENFORD LAW OF FIRST DIGITS
AND THE ARITHMETIC SYSTEM

In this section and in the next one, we discuss two remarkable occurrences of log-periodicity which, by their breadth and generality, suggest that discrete scale invariance may be a very important organizing principle.

Maybe the simplest example of log-periodicity occurs in the frequencies of first digits in natural numbers, which provides a mechanism for the Newcomb–Benford law. Newcomb in 1881 and Benford in 1938 [38] noticed that the pages of much-used tables of logarithms show evidence of a selective use of the natural numbers. The pages containing the logarithms of the low numbers 1 and 2 were more stained and worn out than those of the higher numbers 8 and 9. Benford compiled more than 20,000 first digits taken from widely different sources, including river areas, population, constants of physics, newspapers, addresses, molecular weights, death rates, and so on, and showed that the frequency $p(n)$ with which the digit n appears is given by

$$p(n) = \log_{10} \frac{n+1}{n} \qquad \text{for } n = 1, \dots, 9. \qquad (10)$$

This gives $p(1) = 0.301$, $p(2) = 0.176$, $p(3) = 0.125$, $p(4) = 0.0969$, $p(5) = 0.0792$, $p(6) = 0.0669$, $p(7) = 0.0580$, $p(8) = 0.0512$, $p(9) = 0.0458$. The number 1 thus appears in the first position more than six times more frequently than the number 9! These frequencies $p(n)$ mean that out of 100 numbers drawn at random in a representative population of numbers, approximately 30 should start with 1 as the first digit, about

18 should start with 2 as the first digit, about 12 should start with 3 as the first digit, about 10 should start with 4 as the first digit, about 8 should start with 5 as the first digit, about 7 should start with 6 as the first digit, about 6 should start with 7 as the first digit, about 5 should start with 8 as the first digit, and about 4 should start with 9 as the first digit.

To explain this law, Benford constructed the running frequency $F_n(R)$ of the first digits $n = 1$ to 9 of natural numbers from 1 to R. In other words, for instance, $F_1(R) = N_1(R)/R$ is the ratio of the number $N_1(R)$ of occurrences of natural numbers between 1 and R with first digit 1 divided by the total number R. We thus have

1. $R = 19$, $N_1 = 11$, and $F_1 = 11/19 = 0.5789$, while for $R = 99$, $N_1 = 11$, and $F_1 = 11/99 = 1/9 = 0.1111$;

2. $R = 199$, $N_1 = 111$, and $F_1 = 111/199 = 0.5578$, while for $R = 999$, $N_1 = 111$ and $F_1 = 111/999 = 1/9 = 0.1111$;

3. $R = 1,999$, $N_1 = 1,111$, and $F_1 = 1,111/1999 = 0.5557$, while for $R = 9,999$, $N_1 = 1,111$ and $F_1 = 1,111/9,999 = 1/9 = 0.1111$;

and so on. We thus see that $F_1(R)$ grows monotonically from $1/9 = 0.1111$ at $R = 10^r - 1$ to ≈ 0.5555 at $2 \cdot 10^r - 1$. Then, $F_1(R)$ decays monotonically from this maximum down to $1/9 = 0.1111$, reached again at $R = 10^{r+1} - 1$. Notice that $F_1(R)$ is always larger than or equal to $1/9$. It is thus clear that $F_1(R)$ does not have a limit as R goes to infinity but endlessly oscillates as a log-periodic function of R, for large R, with log-period $\log_{10} 10$, that is, preferred scaling ratio 10 (see Figure 4 in [38]). This result of course generalizes to arbitrary counting systems, say in base b. Then, the scaling ratio controlling the log-periodicity is b. The log-periodicity is expressing simply the hierarchical rule of the numbering system. Thus log-periodicity is at the very root of our arithmetic system!

Generalization and statistical mechanism of the Newcomb–Benford law. A similar analysis can be performed for each of the digits. Let us discuss here $n = 9$ and its frequency $F_9(R)$:

1. $R = 89$, $N_9 = 1$, and $F_9 = 1/89 = 0.0112$, while for $R = 99$, $N_1 = 11$ and $F_9 = 11/99 = 1/9 = 0.1111$;

2. $R = 899$, $N_9 = 11$, and $F_9 = 11/899 = 0.0122$ while for $R = 999$, $N_1 = 111$ and $F_9 = 111/999 = 1/9 = 0.1111$;

3. $R = 8999$, $N_9 = 111$ and $F_9 = 111/8999 = 0.0123$ while for $R = 9999$, $N_1 = 1111$ and $F_9 = 1111/9999 = 1/9 = 0.1111$;

and so on. We thus see that $F_9(R)$ decreases monotonically from $1/9 = 0.1111$ at $R = 10^r - 1$ to ≈ 0.01234 at $10^{r+1} - 10^r - 1$. Then, $F_9(R)$ increases monotonically from this minimum up to $1/9 = 0.1111$, reached again at $R = 10^{r+1} - 1$. It is thus clear that $F_9(R)$ tends again to a (different) log-periodic function of R, for large R, again with log-period $\log_{10} 10$, that is, preferred scaling ratio 10. Notice that, in contrast to $F_1(R)$, $F_9(R)$ is always smaller than or equal to $1/9$. For the other digits, $n = 2, \ldots, 8$, the corresponding $F_n(R)$'s oscillate log-periodically by crossing the value $1/9$.

Averaging these frequencies $F_n(R)$ over a log-period (i.e., a factor of 10) can then be shown [38] to lead to the Newcomb–Benford law (10). This provides one possible mechanism. It turns out that there are other mechanisms and that, more deeply, the Newcomb–Benford law can be seen to be the only law that is invariant with respect to a change of scale, that is, to an arbitrary multiplication of all numbers by a common factor. Hill established in 1995 [194] that a probability measure is scale invariant if and only if the probability measure of the set of all intervals $[1, t) \times 10^n$ for all n integers is $\log_{10} t$, for any t in $[1, 10)$. Benford's law is then easily seen to result from this theorem since the probability of having a given first digit d corresponds to the difference $\log_{10}(d + 1) - \log_{10} d$ of the probability measure, thus giving expression (10). Notice that this does not provide a *mechanism* for Benford's law but rather relates it to a symmetry principle.

In [196], Hill gives a statistical mechanism: if distributions are selected at random and random samples are then taken from each of these distributions, the significant digits of the combined sample will converge to the logarithmic Benford distribution.

THE LOG-PERIODIC LAW OF THE EVOLUTION OF LIFE?

The founding concept of evolution was introduced by Darwin and Wallace in a paper presented in 1858 to the Linnean Society of London entitled "On the Tendency of Species to Form Varieties by Natural Selection." According to this now well-established theory, new biological species are created by direct mutation and selection from existing species. The complexity of the universe of vegetals and animals in particular can then be seen to be a beautiful "tree of life," as shown in Figure 6.24, whose branching or bifurcation structure reflects the cascades of jumps between species in the history of life. The evolu-

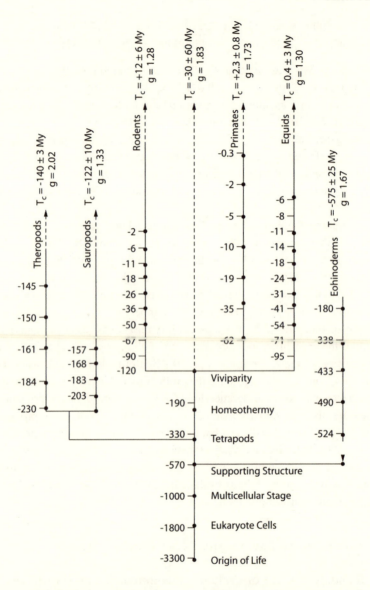

FIG. 6.24. The dates (in millions of years, denoted by the symbol "My") with respect to the origin of time taken to be the present (hence the negative dates that refer to the past), of major evolutionary events of seven lineages (common evolution from life origin to viviparity, theropod and sauropod dinosaurs, rodents, equidae, primates including hominidae, and echinoderms) are plotted as black points. The scale of the time axis is such that the black dots should be equidistant in the logarithm of the distance in time from the epoch of a dot to a critical time T_c which lies beyond the end of the sequence. The dates indicated close to each dot correspond to the exact numerical values predicted by the log-periodic model, computed from the

tionary view of biological species allows one to construct a taxonomy represented by this "tree of life," organized from trunk to the smallest leaves, from the superkingdoms (Archaea, Bacteria, Eukaryota, Viroids, Viruses), kingdoms, phyla, subphyla, orders, suborders, families, genus, and finally the species. These different levels correspond to the main nodes of bifurcations, such that, going from the species to the genus, then to the families, and so on, up to the superkingdoms, is similar to going backward in time and identifying the creation of new species in successive steps. For instance, the domestic cat has the following lineage: Eukaryota, Metazoa, Chordata, Craniata, Vertebrata, Euteleostomi, Mammalia, Eutheria, Carnivora, Fissipedia, Felidae, Felis domesticus (see http://www.ncbi.nlm.nih.gov/Taxonomy/tax.html/).

There is much evidence that evolution is characterized by phases of quasi-statis, where species remain stable for a long time, interrupted by episodic bursts of activity, with destruction of species and creation of new ones [168, 169]. There are thus rather precise dates for speciation events, and one can therefore define the length of branches between nodes in the "tree of life," which represent time intervals between such major evolutionary events. Can this tree be described by a mathematical structure, at least at a statistical level? Remarkably, Nottale, Chaline, and Grou [74, 317, 318] have recently suggested that a self-similar log-periodic law seems to characterize the tree of life. True or false, this example provides a simple and fascinating application of log-periodicity.

Recall that log-periodicity in the present context is synonymous with the existence of periodicity of some observable in the logarithm $\ln |T_c - T|$ of the time T to some critical time T_c. Periodicity of some observable in the variable $\ln |T_c - T|$ implies the existence of a hierarchy of characteristic time scales $T_0 < T_1 < \cdots < T_n < T_{n+1} < \cdots$, corresponding, for instance, to the periodic maxima of the observable as a function of time, given by

$$T_n = T_c - (T_c - T_0)g^{-n}, \tag{11}$$

where g is the preferred scaling factor of the underlying discrete scale invariance (which has also been denoted λ above). This formula (11)

FIG. 6.24 *continued*. best fit to each time series. Perfect log-periodicity is qualified by equidistant black points. The adjusted critical time T_c and scale ratio g are indicated for each lineage after the arrows. In the case of the echinoderms, the log-periodicity is inverted; that is, T_c is in the past and the characteristic times T_n are more and more spaced as time flows from past to future. Reproduced from [318].

turns out to fit the dates of the major evolutionary events shown in Figure 6.24 well.

Notice that the spacings $T_{n+1} - T_n$ between successive values of T_n approach zero as n becomes large and T_n converges to the critical time T_c. From three successive observed values of T_n, say T_n, T_{n+1}, and T_{n+2}, the critical time T_c can be determined by the formula

$$T_c = \frac{T_{n+1}^2 - T_{n+2}T_n}{2T_{n+1} - T_n - T_{n+2}}. \tag{12}$$

This relation is invariant with respect to an arbitrary translation in time. In addition, the next time T_{n+3} is predicted from the preceding T_n by

$$T_{n+3} = \frac{T_{n+1}^2 + T_{n+2}^2 - T_n T_{n+2} - T_{n+1}T_{n+2}}{T_{n+1} - T_n}. \tag{13}$$

These formulas are reproduced in chapter 9 as (23) and (24) in the section titled "A Hierarchy of Prediction Schemes."

Nottale, Chaline, and Grou [74, 317, 318] have found that the fossil equine of North America, the primates, the rodents, and other lineages have followed an evolution path punctuated by major events that follow the geometrical time series (11). The critical time T_c is roughly the present for the equines, in agreement with the known extinction of this species in North America 10,000 years ago (but this could be a coincidence, as North American horses went extinct when humans put foot on the continent and hunted them down). The critical time T_c is approximately 2 million years in the future for the primates and about 12 million years in the future for the rodents. T_c is the end (respectively, beginning) of the evolutionary process for an accelerating (respectively, decelerating) lineage. For an accelerating lineage, the critical time T_c may tentatively be interpreted as the end of the evolutionary ability of this lineage, not necessarily as a pre-set extinction age of the group.

There are, of course, many methological issues as well as fundamental biological problems associated with this proposed log-periodic law (11). It is far from impossible that this regularity could be an artifact of the data (which has many deficiencies) and of the method of analysis. In particular, the further back one goes in trying to reconstruct the past, the coarser and sparser the information becomes. It is possible that this uneven sampling may create an apparent log-periodicity in the manner discussed in [203], but several tests seem to exclude this possibility. If the "log-periodic law of the evolution of life" given by (11) turns out to be genuine, this would then call for a profound explanation. In any case, it provides a vivid example of the power of the discrete scale invariance symmetry to organize complex data in a more transparent way, maybe guiding us towards a possible deeper understanding.

NONLINEAR TREND-FOLLOWING VERSUS NONLINEAR FUNDAMENTAL ANALYSIS DYNAMICS

This section presents an alternative understanding of the emergence of critical points (finite-time singularities) decorated by accelerating oscillations, which complements the previous description. It is based on a "dynamical system" description in which these characteristics emerge dynamically. The main ingredient is the coexistence of two classes of investors, the "fundamentalists," or "value-investors," and the trend-followers (often called chartists, technical analysts, or noise traders in the jargon of academic finance). The second essential ingredient is to recognize that both classes of investors behave in a "nonlinear" way. These two ingredients produce a finite-time singularity with accelerating oscillations. The power law singularity results from the nonlinear accelerating growth rate due to trend-following. The oscillations, which are approximately log-periodic with remarkable scaling properties, result from the nonlinear restoring force exerted on price by value-investors, which tends to bring it back to its fundamental value. As a function of the degree of non-linearity of the growth rate and of the restoring term, a rich variety of behavior can be observed. We shall see that the dynamical behavior is traced back fundamentally to the self-similar spiral structure of the dynamics in a (price, price variation) space representation, unfolding around a central fixed point [205].

The price variation of an asset on the stock market is controlled by supply and demand, in other words by the net order size Ω equal to the number of buy orders minus the number of sell orders. It is clear that the price increases (respectively, decreases) if Ω is positive (respectively, negative). If the ratio of the price $\tilde{p}$ at which the orders are executed over the previous quoted price p is solely a function of the net order size Ω and assuming that it is not possible to make profits by repeatedly trading through a closed circuit (i.e., by buying and selling with final net position equal to zero), one can show that the difference in the logarithm of the price between tomorrow and today is directly proportional to the net order size Ω [123]. The net order size Ω resulting from the action of all traders is continuously readjusting with time so as to reflect the information flow in the market and the evolution of the traders' opinions and moods. Various derivations have related the price variation or the variation of the logarithm of the price to factors that control the net order size itself [123, 49, 330]. Three basic ingredients are thought to be important in determining the price dynamics: trend following, reversal to the estimated fundamental value, and risk aversion.

TREND FOLLOWING: POSITIVE NONLINEAR FEEDBACK AND FINITE-TIME SINGULARITY

Trend following (in various elaborated forms) was (and probably still is) one of the major strategies used by so-called technical analysts (see [6] for a review and references therein). In its simplest form, trend following amounts to taking the net order size Ω as proportional to the past trend, that is, to the difference between the logarithm of the price today and the logarithm of the price yesterday. Trend-following strategies thus exert a positive feedback on prices, since previous price increases (decreases) lead to buy (sell) orders, thus enhancing the previous trend. Taken alone, this implies that the difference in the logarithm of the price between tomorrow and today is proportional to the logarithm of the price between today and yesterday. This simple relationship expresses the existence of a constant growth rate, leading to an exponential growth of the logarithm of the price. This means that the price increases as the exponential of the exponential of time.

This linear relationship between past price variation and net order size is usually chosen by modelers. Here, we depart from this convention and consider it more realistic to assume that the net order size may grow faster than the previous price change; that is, that they are nonlinearly related. Indeed, a small price change from time $t - 1$ to time t may not be perceived as a significant and strong market signal. Since many of the investment strategies are nonlinear, it is natural to consider an average trend-following order size which increases in an accelerated manner as the price change increases in amplitude. Usually, trend-followers increase the size of their order faster than just proportionally to the last trend. This is reminiscent of the argument [6] that traders' psychology is sensitive to a change of trend ("acceleration" or "deceleration"), not simply to the trend ("velocity"). The fact that trend-following strategies have an impact on price proportional to the price change over the previous period raised to some power $m > 1$ means that trend-following strategies are not linear when averaged over all of them: they tend to underreact for small price changes and over-react for large ones. Note that the value

$m = 1$ retrieves the linear case. Figure 6.25 explains the concept of a nonlinear response.

When the sum of all trend-following behaviors is expressed in a nonlinear form so that the net order size Ω is proportional to a power of the difference between the logarithm of the price today and the logarithm of the price yesterday with an exponent larger than 1, by the same reasoning as in the technical inset entitled "Intuitive explanation of the creation of a finite-time singularity at t_c" in chapter 5, the price exhibits a finite-time

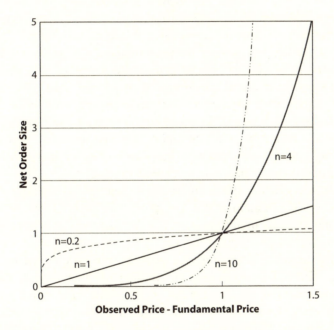

FIG. 6.25. We illustrate the different response of a system (the net order size shown on the ordinate) as a function of a stimulus (the distance between market price and the fundamental price shown in the abscissa) for different nonlinear dependences quantified by the parameter n: response = stimulus^n. For $n = 1$, the response is proportional to the stimulus, as shown with the straight continuous line: this is the linear description. For $n > 1$, for instance, $n = 4$, the response is very small for small stimulii but starts to shoot up when the stimulus increases above some characteristic value here normalized to 1, as shown with the curved continuous line. This is the case discussed here. The dotted-dashed line corresponds to a stronger nonlinearity with exponent $n = 10$, showing even more strongly the almost threshold-like nature of the response of the system. The thin dashed line illustrates the opposite nonlinear situation with a parameter $n < 1$ for which the response accelerates fast for small stimulii but saturates at large stimulii.

singularity. This effect is just a rephrasing of the phenomenon already described by the price-driven model discussed in that chapter.

REVERSAL TO THE FUNDAMENTAL VALUE: NEGATIVE NONLINEAR FEEDBACK

Fundamental value trading is based on an estimation of the financial value of the company based on objective economic and accounting criteria such as assets, earnings, and growth potential. The fundamental analyst thus establishes her estimation for the "correct" fundamental value of a given firm and then compares it with the price quoted in the stock market. If the latter is smaller than the fundamental price, this is a buy opportunity as the analyst expects that the stock market will soon realize that the stock is underpriced compared to its real value. The ensuing wave of preferential buy orders will drive the price up until the fundamental value is reached. In these circumstances, the buy decision is based on the belief that you are among the first to realize that the corresponding stock is underpriced. The reverse is expected to occur if the market price is larger than the fundamental value.

However, in practice, there are severe difficulties in obtaining a precise estimation of the fundamental value, as it is not clear how to value some of the important intangible assets of a company such as the quality of its managers, its position in its market niche, and so on. In addition, predicting future earnings and their growth is an inexact science, to say the least. This has a very important consequence that we now discuss.

An important feature of our model is the nonlinear dependence of the net order size Ω as a function of the difference between the logarithm of the price and the logarithm of the fundamental value. The nonlinearity allows one to capture the following effect. In principle, as we said above, the fundamental value p_0 is determined by the discounted expected future dividends and is thus dependent upon the forecast of their growth rate and of the riskless interest rate, both variables being very difficult to predict. The fundamental value is thus extremely difficult to quantify with high precision and is often estimated within relatively large bounds [282, 85, 260, 69]: all of the methods determining intrinsic value rely on assumptions that can turn out to be far off the mark. For instance, several academic studies have disputed the premise that a portfolio of sound, cheaply bought stocks will, over time, outperform a portfolio selected by any other method (see, for instance, [256]). As a consequence, a trader trying to track fundamental value has no incentive to react when she feels that the deviation is small since this deviation is more or less within the uncertainty of her estimations. Only when the departure of price from fundamental value becomes relatively large will the trader act. The strongly nonlinear dependence of the net order size Ω as proportional to the amplitude of the difference between the logarithm of the price and the logarithm of the fundamental value raised to a power n larger than 1 precisely accounts for this effect, as shown in Figure 6.25: for an exponent n larger than 1, Δ^n remains small for $\Delta < 1$ and shoots up rapidly only when it becomes larger than 1, approximating a threshold behavior of all or nothing.

Such a nonlinear sensitivity is not just a theoretical construction; it has been recently documented in the context of the sensitivity of the money demand to interest rate. Using a survey of roughly 2,700 households, Mulligan and Sala-i-Martin [311] estimated the interest elasticity of money demand (the sensitivity or log-derivative of money demand to interest rate) to be very small at low interest rates. This is due to the fact that few people decide to invest in interest-producing assets when rates are low, due to "shopping" costs. In constrast, for large interest rates or for those who own a significant bank account, the interest elasticity of money demand is significant. This is a clear-cut example of a threshold-like behavior characterized by a very nonlinear response. This can be captured by $e \equiv d \ln M / d \ln r = (r/r_{\text{infl}})^m$ with $m > 1$ such that the elasticity e of money demand M is negligible when the interest r is not significantly larger than the inflation rate r_{infl}, and becomes large otherwise.

From the fact that a low (large) price is driven upwards (downwards) towards the fundamental value, we see that the class of investment strategies based on fundamental valuation lead to a reversal of the price. This reversal force can be linear, that is, the corresponding net order size Ω is proportional to the difference between the logarithm of the price and the logarithm of the fundamental value. In the case $n = 1$, since the difference in the logarithm of the price between tomorrow and today is directly proportional to the net order size Ω, this implies that the difference in the logarithm of the price between tomorrow and today is proportional to the difference between the logarithm of the price today and the logarithm of the fundamental value. The relationship is an exact analog to the equation of an oscillator such as a pendulum: starting from a position away from its equilibrium immobile position, it undergoes endless oscillations around this equilibrium point, as shown by the thick line trajectory in Figure 6.26. Similarly, with this term alone the price oscillates endlessly around the fundamental value. The reason for the oscillations is that there is an inertia

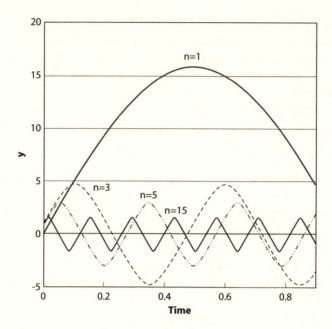

FIG. 6.26. Time dependence of the logarithm of the price normalized by the fundamental price resulting from the interplay between the reversal "force" created by fundamental value investing and the "inertia" stemming from the fact that the decision to invest from today to tomorrow is based on information from yesterday to today. Four different values of the exponent $n = 1, 3, 5$, and 15 are shown. Compared to the linear case $n = 1$ whose solution is a pure sine $y_1^{(n=1)}(t) = \frac{50}{\sqrt{10}} \sin(\sqrt{10}\,t)$, increasing the nonlinear exponent n has three effects: (i) decrease of the amplitude; (ii) increase of the frequency; and (iii) production of a saw-tooth profile with increasingly sharper corners as n increases. Reproduced from [205].

in the reversal force which does not vanish sufficiently rapidly and leads to overshooting. This overshooting then triggers a price motion in the opposite direction which itself overshoots and so on. When the fundamental reversal term is nonlinear, the oscillations persist but change shape. Their main properties is that their frequency (reciprocal of their period, which is the time interval between two successive maxima) becomes dependent on the amplitude of the deviation between market price and fundamental value. This property is very important because, if there are other effects or perturbations that tend to modify this amplitude, the frequency will be modified accordingly. This nonlinear frequency dependence upon the amplitude provides a mechanism for accelerating frequencies when the amplitude shoots up.

SOME CHARACTERISTICS OF THE PRICE DYNAMICS
OF THE NONLINEAR DYNAMICAL MODEL

Let us now put all the ingredients together:

- "inertia" resulting from the fact that a decision today to invest will bear its fruit in the future while it is based on past analysis;

- nonlinear trend following which, together with "inertia," creates a finite-time singularity in the amplitude of the deviation between market price and fundamental price;

- nonlinear fundamental value investing which, together with "inertia," produces nonlinear oscillations dependent on the amplitude of the deviation between market price and fundamental price.

Figure 6.27 shows the time evolution of the logarithm of the market price normalized by the fundamental value, which we shall refer to as

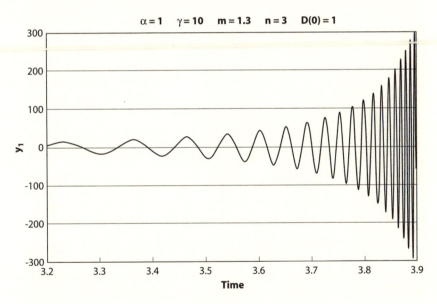

FIG. 6.27. Solution of the dynamical equation incorporating "inertia," nonlinear trend-following, and nonlinear fundamental value investing for the parameters $m = 1.3$, $n = 3$. The envelope of the "reduced price" $y_1(t)$ grows faster than exponentially and approximately as $(t_c - t)^{-1.5}$, where $t_c \approx 4$. A negative value of the reduced price y_1 just means that the observed price is below the fundamental value. This stems from the definition of reduced price as the logarithm of the ratio between observed price and fundamental value. Reproduced from [205].

the "reduced price" for the choice ($m = 1.3, n = 3$) of the exponents controlling, respectively, the nonlinear trend following (or elasticity) and the fundamental reversal (or sharpness of the threshold response) terms. Two main features are apparent. First, the reduced price diverges on the approach of the critical time t_c as $(t_c - t)^{-\beta}$. Note that the specific value of the critical time is dictated by initial conditions. Second, this acceleration is decorated by accelerating oscillations. As we mentioned in the previous section, the acceleration of the oscillations results from their nonlinear dependence upon the accelerating amplitude.

Figure 6.28 shows the same data as in Figure 6.27, but using scales such that a pure power law behavior qualifies as a straight line: the logarithm of the reduced price is plotted as a function of the logarithm of the distance from the critical time. We observe that the envelop is indeed well qualified by the power law shown as the straight dashed line. In addition, the oscillations are approximately equidistant in this representation, which, as we showed several times in the previous sections,

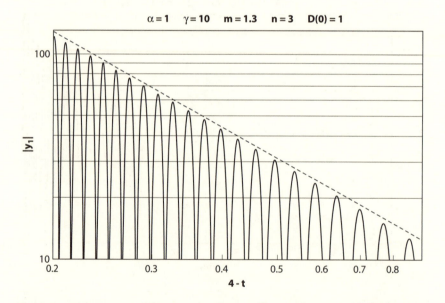

FIG. 6.28. Same data as in Figure 6.27: The absolute value $|y_1(t)|$ of the "reduced price" is shown as a function of $t_c - t$, where $t_c = 4$ in double logarithmic coordinates, such that a linear envelope qualifies the power law divergence $(t_c - t)^{-1.5}$. The slope of the dashed line is -1.5. Notice also that the oscillations are approximately equidistant in the variable $\ln(t_c - t)$, resembling log-periodic behavior of accelerating oscillations on the approach to the singularity. Reproduced from [205].

qualify as an approximate log-periodicity. The dynamics involving "inertia," nonlinear trend following, and nonlinear fundamental reversal behaviors is thus able to create a quasi-log-periodic behavior of accelerating oscillations on the approach to a finite-time singularity.

Figure 6.29 shows the reduced price for a larger value of the trend-following exponent $m = 2.5$. In this case, the reduced price goes to a constant at t_c with an infinite slope (the singularity is thus on its derivative, or "velocity"). We can also observe accelerating oscillations, somewhat reminiscent of log-periodicity. The novel feature is that the oscillations are only transient, leaving place to a pure final accelerating trend in the final approach to the critical time t_c.

Figure 6.18 has taught us that an oscillatory motion can be seen as the projection of a rotation occurring in a plane on one axis. We now extend this logic and show with Figure 6.30 that an oscillation with varying frequency and amplitude as in Figures 6.27 and 6.29 is nothing but the projection on one axis of a spiraling structure in the plane. Actually, Figure 6.30 shows more than that: in the plane of the

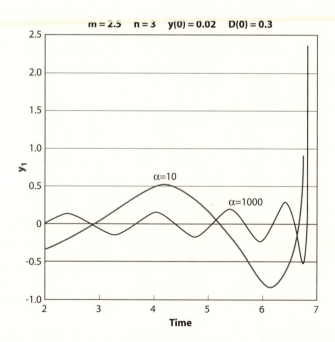

FIG. 6.29. "Reduced price" as a function of time for a trend-following exponent $m = 2.5$ with $n = 3$, with two amplitudes $\gamma = 10$ and $\gamma = 1,000$ of the fundamental reversal term. Reproduced from [205].

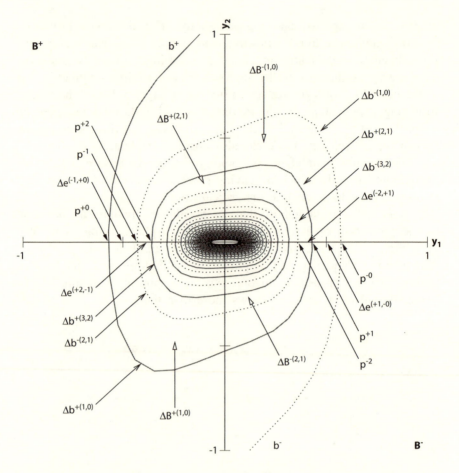

FIG. 6.30. Geometrical spiral showing two special trajectories (the continuous and dashed lines) in the "reduced price"–"velocity" plane (y_1, y_2) that exactly connect the origin $y_1 = 0$, $y_2 = 0$ to infinity. This spiraling structure, which exhibits scaling or fractal properties, is at the origin of the accelerating oscillations decorating the power law behavior close to the finite-time singularity. The different segments of curves and domains pointed out by the arrows are mapped from one to another throughout the dynamics of the model. Reproduced from [205].

reduced price y_1 and its "velocity" y_2, it shows two special trajectories that connect exactly the origin $y_1 = 0$, $y_2 = 0$ to infinity. From general mathematical theorems of dynamical systems, one can then show that any trajectory starting close to the origin will never be able to cross any of these two orbits. As a consequence, any real trajectory will be guided within the spiraling channel, winding around the central point 0 many times before exiting towards the finite-time singularies. The approximately log-periodic oscillations result from the oscillatory structure of the fundamental reversal term associated with the acceleration driven by the trend-following term. The conjunction of the two leads to the beautiful spiral, governing a hierarchical organization of the spiralling trajectories around the origin in the price-velocity space [205].

CHAPTER 7

AUTOPSY OF MAJOR
CRASHES: UNIVERSAL
EXPONENTS AND
LOG-PERIODICITY

THE CRASH OF OCTOBER 1987

As discussed in chapter 1, the crash of October 1987 and its Black Monday on October 19 remains one of the most striking drops ever seen in stock markets, both by its overwhelming amplitude and its encompassing sweep over most markets worldwide. It was preceded by a remarkably strong "bull" regime epitomized by the following quote from *The Wall Street Journal* on August 26, 1987, the day after the 1987 market peak: "In a market like this, every story is a positive one. Any news is good news. It's pretty much taken for granted now that the market is going to go up." Investors were thus largely unaware of the forthcoming risk happenings [174]. This surprise change in risk view of October 19, 1987 is supported by the time-series behavior of implied risk estimates calculated on the Standard & Poor's (S&P) 500 Index Option for the September–November daily trading period. The highest implied risk estimate for stocks in the pre-crash period was 18.5% and occurred on October 15, 1987 [174]. This was still below the 22% annualized standard deviation of return calculated during 1974, the most volatile recent year before 1987, and significantly below the

46% recorded on Monday, October 19, 1987, and the 88% recorded on Monday, October 26, 1987. As we shall show in Figure 7.4, during November 1987, market volatility as measured by the implied annual return standard deviation fell to about 30%, which was still much higher than the highest implied risk value observed immediately prior to Black Monday [174].

The October 19, 1987, stock-market crash stunned Wall Street professionals, hacked about $1 trillion off the value of all U.S. stocks, and elicited predictions of another Great Depression. On Black Monday, the Dow Jones industrial average plummeted 508 points, or 22.6%, to 1,738.74. It was the largest one-day point and percentage loss ever for the blue-chip index. The broader markets followed the Dow downward. The S&P 500 index lost more than 20%, falling 57.86 to 224.84. The Nasdaq composite index dived 46.12 to 360.21. No Dow components emerged unscathed from Black Monday. Even market stalwarts suffered massive share losses. IBM shed $31 - 3/4$ to close at $103 - 1/3$, while USX lost $12 - 1/2$ to $21 - 1/2$ and Eastman Kodak fell $27 - 1/4$ to $62 - 7/8$. The crash splattered technology stocks as well. On the Nasdaq, Apple Computer lost $11 - 3/4$ to close at $36 - 1/2$, while Intel dropped 10 to 42.

Stocks descended quickly on Black Monday, with the Dow falling 200 points soon after the opening bell to trade at around 2,046. Yet by 10 a.m., the index had crept back up above 2,100, beginning a pattern of rebound and retreat that would continue for most of the day. Later, with 75 minutes left in the trading day, it looked like the Dow would escape with a loss of "only" about 200 points. But the worst was yet to come. Starting at about 2:45 p.m., a massive sell-off began, eventually ripping 300 more points off the Dow. At the closing bell, the Dow appeared to have suffered an amazing loss of about 400 points. However, heavy volume kept the NYSE's computers running hours behind trading. Only about two hours later would investors realize that the day's total loss exceeded 500 points. Reaction to the crash varied from sentiments that the market was due for a correction to feelings of outright despair.

President Ronald Reagan sought to reassure investors, saying: "All the economic indicators are solid. There is nothing wrong with the economy." And the day after the crash, Federal Reserve Chairman Alan Greenspan gave a lucid one-sentence statement indicating the Fed would provide sufficient funds to banks, allowing them to provide credit to securities firms. "The Federal Reserve, consistent with its responsibilities as the nation's central bank, affirmed today its readiness to serve as a source of liquidity to support the economic and financial system," the statement said. The NYSE did end up opening for business as usual on October 20, and the Dow rose 102.27—its largest one-day gain ever up to that time—to close at 1,841.01. But making up the full extent of Black Monday's losses would take longer. The Dow only returned to its pre-crash levels in January 1989, 15 months after Black Monday. The broader S&P 500 index took 21 months to fully recover.

It is interesting to quantify the relative weight of various participants during these volatile times. Based on the Federal Reserve's Flow of Funds Accounts of the US analyzed by Fung and Hsieh [146], the market value of U.S. corporate equities stood at U.S.$3,511 billion at the end of September 1987. The major owners were households (49%), private pension funds (21%), mutual funds (7%), state and local government retirement funds (6%), bank personal trusts and estates (6%), foreigners (6%), insurance companies (5%), and brokers and dealers (<1%). In the last quarter of 1987, households had been the largest sellers, with sells worth U.S.$19.6 billion, followed by the rest of the world, with sells worth U.S.$7.5 billion, brokers and dealers, U.S.$4.8 billion, and mutual funds, U.S.$3.0 billion. These sells were almost fully balanced by purchases of equities back from investors by U.S. corporations for the amount of U.S.$30.2 billion.

The net sells thus amounted to less than 1% of the total value of U.S. corporate equities. Studies carried out by the Investment Company Institute (ICI) confirm the following specific findings about mutual fund shareholders and their reactions to market volatility:

- The largest net outflow within a short period occurred during and immediately after the October 1987 stock market break and amounted to only 4.5% of total equity fund assets.

- An estimated 95% of stock fund owners did not redeem shares immediately after the 1987 stock market break.

- The responses of shareholders to other sharp drops in stock prices since 1945 were considerably more restrained than the reaction in 1987.

The Investment Company Institute [207] is the national association of the American investment company industry. Founded in 1940, its membership in 2000 included 8,414 mutual funds, 489 closed-end funds, and 8 sponsors of unit investment trusts. Its mutual fund members represent more than 83 million individual shareholders and manage approximately $7 trillion.

PRECURSORY PATTERN

In the sequel, time is often converted into decimal year units: for nonleap years, 365 days = 1.00 year, which leads to 1 day = 0.00274 years. Thus 0.01 year = 3.65 days and 0.1 year = 36.5 days or 5 weeks. For example, October 19, 1987 corresponds to 87.800.

Figure 7.1 shows the evolution of the NYSE index S&P 500 from July 1985 to the end of October 1987 after the crash. The plusses (+) represent the best fit to an exponential growth obtained by assuming that the market is given an average return of about 30% per year. This first representation does not describe the apparent overall acceleration before the crash, occurring more than a year in advance. This acceleration (*cusp*-like

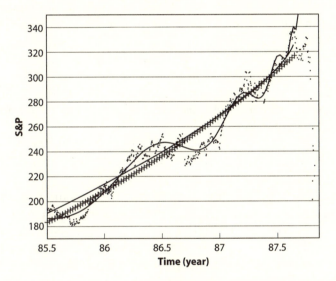

FIG. 7.1. Evolution as a function of time of the NYSE S&P 500 index from July 1985 to the end of October 1987 (557 trading days). The + represent a constant return increase of ≈30%/year and gives $var(F_{exp}) \approx 113$ (see text for definition). The best fit to the power law (14) gives $A_1 \approx 327$, $B_1 \approx -79$, $t_c \approx 87.65$, $m_1 \approx 0.7$, and $var_{pow} \approx 107$. The best fit to expression (15) gives $A_2 \approx 412$, $B_2 \approx -165$, $t_c \approx 87.74$, $C \approx 12$, $\omega \approx 7.4$, $T = 2.0$, $m_2 \approx 0.33$, and $var_{lp} \approx 36$. One can observe four well-defined oscillations fitted by the expression (15) before finite size effects limit the theoretical divergence of the acceleration, at which point the bubble ends in the crash. All the fits are carried over the whole time interval shown, up to 87.6. The fit with (15) turns out to be very robust with respect to this upper bound, which can be varied significantly. Reproduced from [401].

shape) is better represented by using power law functions that chapters 5 and 6 showed to be signatures of critical behavior of the market. The monotonic line corresponds to the following power law parameterization:

$$F_{pow}(t) = A_1 + B_1(t_c - t)^{m_1}, \tag{14}$$

where t_c denotes the time at which the power law fit of the S&P 500 presents a (theoretically) diverging slope, announcing an imminent crash. In order to qualify and compare the fits, the variances (denoted var, equal to the mean of the squares of the errors between theory and data) or its square-root (called the root-mean-square [r.m.s.]) are calculated. The ratio of two variances corresponding to two different hypotheses is taken as a qualifying statistic. The ratio of the variance of the constant rate hypothesis to that of the power law is equal to $\text{var}_{exp}/\text{var}_{pow} \approx 1.1$, indicating only a slightly better performance of the power law in capturing the acceleration, the number of free variables being the same and equal to 2.

However, to the naked eye, the most striking feature in this acceleration is the presence of systematic oscillatory-like deviations. Inspired by the insight given in chapter 5 and especially chapter 6, the oscillatory continuous line is obtained by fitting the data by the following mathematical expression:

$$F_{lp}(t) = A_2 + B_2(t_c - t)^{m_2}[1 + C\cos(\omega\log((t_c - t)/T))]. \tag{15}$$

This equation is the simplest example of a log-periodic correction to a pure power law for an observable exhibiting a singularity at the time t_c at which the crash has the highest probability. The log-periodicity here stems from the cosine function of the logarithm of the distance $t_c - t$ to the critical time t_c. Due to log-periodicity, the evolution of the financial index becomes (discretely) scale invariant close to the critical point.

As shown in chapter 6, the log-periodic correction to scaling implies the existence of a hierarchy of characteristic time intervals $t_c - t_n$, given by expression (11) on page 215, with a preferred scaling ratio denoted g or λ. For the October 1987 crash, we find $\lambda \simeq 1.5 - 1.7$ (this value is remarkably universal and is found approximately the same for other crashes, as we shall see). We expect a cut-off at short time scales (i.e., above $n \sim$ a few units) and also at large time scales due to the existence of finite size effects. These time scales $t_c - t_n$ are not universal but depend upon the specific market. What is expected to be universal are the ratios $\frac{t_c - t_{n+1}}{t_c - t_n} = \lambda$. For details on the fitting procedure, we refer to [401].

It is possible to generalize the simple log-periodic power law formula used in Figure 7.1 by using a mathematical tool, called bifurcation theory, to obtain its generic nonlinear correction, which allows one to account quantitatively for the behavior of the Dow Jones and S&P 500 indices up to eight years prior to October 1987 [397]. The result of this theory, presented in [397], is used to generate the new fit shown in Figure 7.2. One sees clearly that the new formula accounts remarkably well for almost eight years of market price behavior compared to only a little more than two years for the simple log-periodic formula shown in Figure 7.1. The nonlinear theory developed in [397] leads to "log-frequency modulation," an effect first noticed empirically in [128]. The remarkable quality of the fits shown in Figures 7.1 and 7.2 have been assessed in [214].

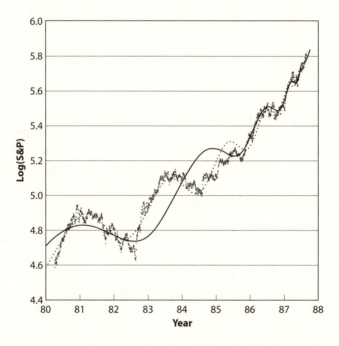

FIG. 7.2. Time dependence of the logarithm of the NYSE S&P 500 index from January 1980 to September 1987 and best fit by the improved nonlinear log-periodic formula developed in [397] (dashed line). The exponent and log-periodic angular frequency are $m_2 = 0.33$ and $\omega^{1987} = 7.4$. The crash of October 19, 1987 corresponds to 1987.78 decimal years. The solid line is the fit by (15) on the subinterval from July 1985 to the end of 1987 and is represented on the full time interval starting in 1980. The comparison with the thin line allows one to visualize the frequency shift described by the nonlinear theory. Reproduced from [397].

In a recent reanalysis, J. A. Feigenbaum [127] examined the data in a new way by taking the first differences for the logarithm of the S&P 500 from 1980 to 1987. The rationale for taking the price variation rather than the price itself is that the fluctuations, noises, or deviations are expected to be more random and thus more innocuous than for the price, which is a cumulative quantity. By rigorous hypothesis testing, Feigenbaum found that the log-periodic component cannot be rejected at the 95% confidence level: in plain words, this means that the probability that the log-periodic component results from chance is about or less than 0.05.

D. S. Bates [34] has studied the transaction prices of the S&P 500 futures options over 1985–87 and found evidence of expectations prior to October 1987 of an impending stock market crash in this data. These expectations are based on patterns of intermittent accelerating "fears," possibly related to the evidence presented so far. S&P 500 futures options are contracts that derive from the underlying S&P 500 index and whose price depends on three main variables, (1) the so-called exercise or strike price of the option, (2) the interval of time between the present and the maturity date of the option, and (3) a measure of the perceived volatility of the underlying S&P 500 index. So-called "put" (respectively, "call") options have increasing value the smaller (respectively, larger) is the expected future index price at the maturity date and the larger is the perceived volatility. Put options are thus direct probes of the sentiment of traders on the downside risk of the underlying market, that is, of the risk of a large drop of the market that would make these put options very valuable. Symmetrically, call options are direct probes of the sentiment of traders on the upside risk of the underlying market, i.e., of the possibility of a large rally of the market which would make these call options very valuable. Figure 7.3 summarizes how this idea can be used concretely for a quantification of the perceived asymmetry between large downside and upside risks. It shows the percentage deviation $(C - P)/P$ between call and put option prices (which Bates called a "skewness premium"). The curve at the bottom, called "at-the-money options," quantifies the percentage deviation $(C - P)/P$ of put and call options, which take a significant value as soon as the price deviates from the present price (so-called at-the-money options). Since the at-the-money options are mostly sensitive to price variations around zero, they do not provide a good measure of the perceived risks of large moves. The curve at the top called, "4% OTM [out-of-money] options," corresponds to put (respectively, call) options that become valuable only when the price has decreased (respectively, increased) by at least 4%.

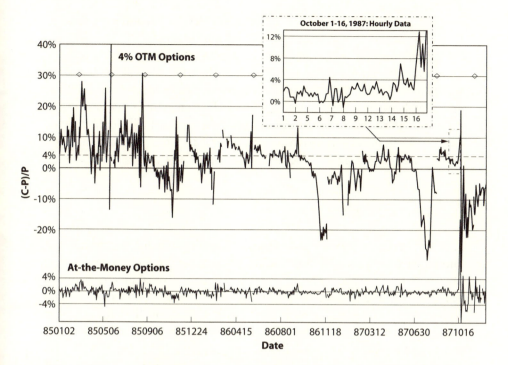

F IG. 7.3. Percentage deviation $(C - P)/P$ of call from put prices (skewness premium) for options at-the-money and 4% out-of-the-money, over 1985–87. The percentage deviation $(C - P)/P$ is a measure of the asymmetry between the perceived distribution of future large upward moves compared to large downward moves of the S&P 500 index. Deviations above (below) 0% indicate optimism (fear) for a bullish market (of large potential drops). The inset shows the same quantity $(C - P)/P$ calculated hourly during October 1987 prior to the crash: ironically, the market forgot its "fears" close to the crash. Reproduced from [34].

Such put and call options thus sample the perceived tails of the potential distribution of price variations. Figure 7.3 shows that, most of the time in the 1985–87 period, call options were more expansive than put options, corresponding to an optimistic view of the market felt to be oriented positively, with small risks of a market drop. However, stronger and stronger bursts of "fear" can be observed, first at the end of 1985, then in November 1986, and finally in August 1987. These bursts of fear correspond to a very significant overpricing of the put options (negative spikes on Figure 7.3), quantifying a perceived risk of a probably significant drop of the market. Notice a contraction of the time intervals between the spikes of "fear," reminiscent of the log-periodic acceleration towards a critical point t_c (see the section titled "Nonparametric Test of Log-Periodicity" later in this chapter and the section titled "The Shank's Transformation on a Hierarchy of Characteristic Times" in chapter 9). Quantitatively, however, the contraction of the time intervals between the spikes is not sufficiently fast to converge to a date close to the crash time and overshoots it by about a year and a half. Bates noted that his results are fully consistent with the model of rational expectation bubbles (see chapter 5) with an explosive divergence away from the fundamentals which is sustained by an expected sudden drop [34].

AFTERSHOCK PATTERNS

If the concept of a crash as a kind of critical point has any value, we should be able to identify post-crash signatures of the underlying cooperativity. In fact, we should expect an at least qualitative symmetry between patterns before and after the crash. In other words, we should be able to document the existence of a critical exponent as well as log-periodic oscillations on relevant quantities after the crash. Such a signature in the volatility of the S&P 500 index, implied from the price of S&P 500 options (which are derivative assets with price varying as a function of the price of the S&P 500), can indeed be seen in Figure 7.4.

The term "implied volatility" has the following meaning. First, one must recall what an option is: this financial instrument is nothing but an insurance that can be bought or sold on the market to insure oneself against unpleasant price variations. The price of an option on the S&P 500 index is therefore a function of the volatility of the S&P 500. The more volatile and the more risky is the S&P 500, the more expensive is the option. In other words, the price of an option on the market reflects the value of the variance of the stock as estimated by the market with its offer-and-demand rules. In practice, it is very difficult to have a good model for market price volatilities or even to measure it reliably. The standard procedure is then to see what the market forces decide for the option price and then determine the implied volatility by inversion of the Black and Scholes formula for option pricing [294]. Basically, the implied volatility is a measure of the market risks perceived by investors.

Figure 7.4 presents the time evolution of the implied volatility of the S&P 500, taken from [84]. The perceived market risk is small prior to the crash, jumps up abruptly at the time of the crash, and then decays slowly over several months. This decay to "normal times" of perceived risks is compatible with a slow power law decay decorated by log-periodic

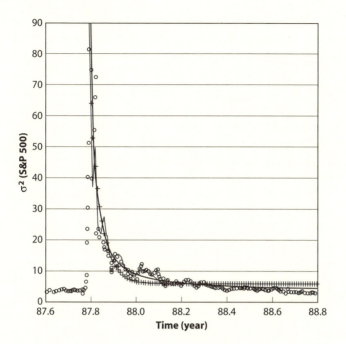

FIG. 7.4. Time evolution of the implied volatility of the S&P 500 index (in loga-rithmic scale) after the October 1987 crash, taken from [84]. The $+$ represent an exponential decrease with $var(F_{exp}) \approx 15$. The best fit to a power law, represented by the monotonic line, gives $A_1 \approx 3.9$, $B_1 \approx 0.6$, $t_c = 87.75$, $m_1 \approx -1.5$, and $var_{pow} \approx 12$. The best fit to expression (15) with $t_c - t$ replaced by $t - t_c$ gives $A_2 \approx 3.4$, $B_2 \approx 0.9$, $t_c \approx 87.77$, $C \approx 0.3$, $\omega \approx 11$, $m_2 \approx -1.2$, and $var_{lp} \approx 7$. One can observe six well-defined oscillations fitted by (15). Reproduced from [401].

oscillations, which can be fitted by expression (15) on page 232 with $t_c - t$ (before the crash) replaced by $t - t_c$ (after the crash). Our analysis of expression (15) with $t_c - t$ replaced by $t - t_c$ again gives an estimation of the position of the critical time t_c, which is found correctly within a few days. Note the long time scale covering a period of the order of a year involved in the relaxation of the volatility after the crash to a level comparable to the one before the crash. This implies the existence of a "memory effect": market participants remain nervous for quite a long time after the crash, after being burned out by the dramatic event.

It is also noteworthy that the S&P 500 index as well as other mar-kets worldwide have remained close to the after-crash level for a long time. For instance, by February 29, 1988, the world index stood at 72.7 (reference 100 on September 30, 1987). Thus, the price level established in the October crash seems to have been a virtually unbiased estimate of

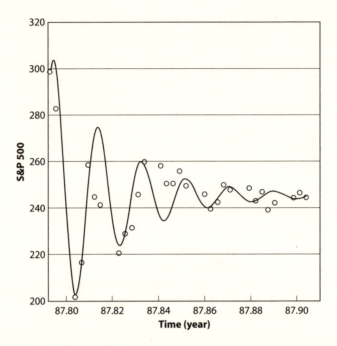

F<small>IG</small>. 7.5. Time evolution of the S&P 500 index over a time window of a few weeks
after the October 19, 1987 crash. The fit with an exponentially decaying sinusoidal
function shown in the continuous line suggests that a good model for the short-time
response of the U.S. market is a *single* dissipative harmonic oscillator or damped
pendulum. Reproduced from [401].

the average price level over the subsequent months (see also Figure 7.5).
Note also that the present value of the S&P 500 index is much larger
than it was even before the October 1987 crash, showing again that nothing fundamental happened then. All this is in support of the idea of a
critical point, according to which the event is an intrinsic signature of a
self-organization of the markets worldwide.

There is another striking signature of the cooperative behavior of the
U.S. market, found by analyzing the time evolution of the S&P 500 index
over a time window of a few weeks after the October 19, 1987 crash.
A fit shown in Figure 7.5 with an exponentially decaying sinusoidal
function suggests that the U.S. market behaved, for a few weeks after
the crash, as a *single* dissipative harmonic oscillator, with a characteristic
decay time of about one week equal to the period of the oscillations.
In other words, the price followed the trajectory of a pendulum moving
back and forth with damped oscillations around an equilibrium position.

This signature strengthens the view of a market as a cooperative self-organizing system. The basic story suggested by these figures is the following. Before the crash, imitation and speculation were rampant and led to a progressive "aggregation" of the multitude of agents into a large effective "superagent," as illustrated in Figures 7.1 and 7.2; right after the crash, the market behaved as a single superagent, rapidly finding the equilibrium price through a return to equilibrium, as shown in Figure 7.5. On longer time scales, the superagent progressively was fragmented and diversity of behavior was rejuvenated, as seen in Figure 7.4.

THE CRASH OF OCTOBER 1929

The crash of October 1929 is the other major historical market event of the twentieth century on the U.S. market. Notwithstanding the differences in technologies and the absence of computers and other modern means of information transfer, the October 1929 crash exhibits many similarities with the October 1987 crash—so much so, as shown in Figures 7.6 and 7.7, that one wonders about the similitudes: what has remained unchanged over the history of mankind is the interplay between the human craving for exchanges and profits, and our fear of uncertainty and losses.

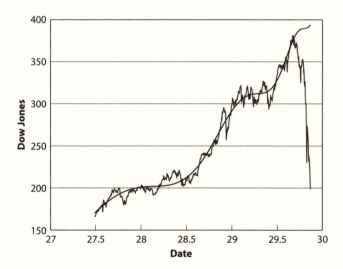

FIG. 7.6. The DJIA prior to the October 1929 crash on Wall Street. The fit shown as a continuous line is the equation (15) with $A_2 \approx 571$, $B_2 \approx -267$, $B_2C \approx 14.3$, $m_2 \approx 0.45$, $t_c \approx 1930.22$, $\omega \approx 7.9$, and $\phi \approx 1.0$. Reproduced from [212].

FIG. 7.7. Time dependence of the logarithm of the DJIA from June 1921 to September 1929 and best fit by the improved nonlinear log-periodic formula developed in [397]. The crash of October 23, 1929 corresponds to 1929.81 decimal years. The parameters of the fit are: r.m.s.= 0.041, t_c = 1929.84 year, m_2 = 0.63, ω = 5.0, $\Delta\omega$ = −70, Δt = 14 years, A_2 = 61, B_2 = −0.56, C = 0.08. $\Delta\omega$ and Δt are two new parameters introduced in [397]. Reproduced from [397].

The similarity between the situations in 1929 and 1987 was in fact noticed at a qualitative level in an article in the *Wall Street Journal* on October 19, 1987, the very morning of the day of the stock market crash (with a plot of stock prices in the 1920s and the 1980s). See the discussion in [374].

The similarity between the two crashes can be made quantitative by comparing the fit of the Dow Jones index with formula (15) from June 1927 until the maximum before the crash in October 1929, as shown in Figure 7.6, to the corresponding fit for the October 1987 crash shown in Figure 7.1. Notice the similar widths of the two time windows, the similar acceleration and oscillatory structures, quantified by similar exponents m_2 and log-periodic angular frequency ω: m_2^{1987} = 0.33 compared to m_2^{1929} = 0.45; ω^{1987} = 7.4 compared to ω^{1987} = 7.9. These numerical values are remarkably close and can be considered equal to within their uncertainties.

Figure 7.7 for the October 1929 crash is the analog of Figure 7.2 for the October 1987 crash. It uses the improved nonlinear log-periodic formula developed in [397] over a much larger time window starting in June 1921. Also according to this improved theoretical formulation, the values of the exponent m_2 and of the log-periodic angular frequency ω for the two great crashes are quite close to each other: $m_2^{1929} = 0.63$ and $m_2^{1987} = 0.68$. This is in agreement with the universality of the exponent m_2 predicted from the renormalization group theory exposed in chapter 6. A similar universality is also expected for the log-frequency, albeit with a weaker strength, as it has been shown [356] that fluctuations and noise will modify ω differently depending on their nature. The fits indicate that $\omega_{1929} = 5.0$ and $\omega_{1987} = 8.9$. These values are not unexpected and fall within the range found for other crashes (see below). They correspond to a preferred scaling ratio equal, respectively, to $\lambda_{1929} = 3.5$ compared to $\lambda_{1987} = 2.0$.

The October 1929 and October 1987 crashes thus exhibit two similar precursory patterns on the Dow Jones index, starting, respectively, 2.5 and 8 years before them. It is thus a striking observation that essentially similar crashes have punctuated the twentieth century, notwithstanding tremendous changes in all imaginable ways of life and work. The only thing that has probably changed little are the ways humans think and behave. The concept that emerges here is that the organization of traders in financial markets leads intrinsically to "systemic instabilities," which probably result in a very robust way from the fundamental nature of human beings, including our gregarious behavior, our greediness, our instinctive psychology during panics and crowd behavior, and our risk aversion. The global behavior of the market, with its log-periodic structures that emerge as a result of the cooperative behavior of traders, is reminiscent of the process of the emergence of intelligent behavior at a macroscopic scale that individuals at the microscopic scale cannot perceive. This process has been discussed in biology, for instance in animal populations such as ant colonies or in connection with the emergence of consciousness [8].

There are, however, some differences between the two crashes. An important quantitative difference between the great crash of 1929 and the collapse of stock prices in October 1987 was that stock price variability in the year following the crash was much higher in 1929 than in 1987 [351]. This has led economists to argue that the collapse of stock prices in October 1929 generated significant temporary increased uncertainty about future income that led consumers to forego purchases of durable goods. Forecasters were then much more uncertain about the course of future income following the stock market crash than was typical even for unsettled times. Contemporary observers believed that consumer uncertainty was an important force depressing consumption, which may have been an important factor in the strengthening of the great depression. The increase of uncertainty after the October 1987 crash has led to a smaller effect, as no depression ensued. However, Figure 7.4 clearly quantifies an increased uncertainty and risk, lasting months after the crash.

Actually, this phenomenon, known as the "leverage effect," is a robust property of markets observed for losses that are not necessarily of a crash amplitude: after a drop of an equity's value, the return volatility tends to increase more than after a gain. In other words, negative unanticipated returns result in an upward revision of conditional volatility, whereas positive unanticipated returns appear to result in a downward revision of the conditional volatility [242, 160, 86, 11].

Naively, this property seems in contradiction with the risk-driven model described in chapter 5 in which the price goes up because the risk of a crash increases. If the price goes up, the volatility should go down according to the "leverage effect." Since the volatility is usually taken as the measure of risks, this seems in contradiction with the increasing crash risk driving the underlying price increase in the risk-driven model. Actually, this contradiction is easily resolved by noting that the risk for a crash to occur is very different from the risk captured by the volatility. The former is sensitive to the most extreme possible yet unrealized price fluctuation, while the latter is an average estimation of small- and medium-size fluctuations of prices.

The negative correlation, quantified by the leverage effect, between the volatility of equity's rate of return and the value of equity reflects a larger perceived risk and uncertainty after a loss and might relate to a fundamental psychological trait of humans. Indeed, it is well documented that people perform better after initial success compared to initial failure. Failure or events perceived as unlucky undermine confidence in people's abilities and in the future [125].

THE THREE HONG KONG CRASHES
OF 1987, 1994, AND 1997

THE HONG KONG CRASHES

Hong Kong has a strong free-market attitude, characterized by very few restrictions on either residents or nonresidents, private persons or companies, to operate, borrow, and repatriate profit and capital. This continued even after Hong Kong reverted to Chinese sovereignty on July 1, 1997 as a Special Administrative Region (SAR) of the People's Republic of China, as it was promised a "high degree of autonomy" for at least 50 years from that date according to the terms of the Sino-British Joint Declaration. The SAR is ruled according to a miniconstitution, the Basic Law of the Hong Kong SAR. Hong Kong has no exchange controls, and cross-border remittances are readily permitted. These rules have not changed since China took over sovereignty from the U.K. Capital can thus flow in and out of the Hong Kong stock market in a very fluid manner. There are no restrictions on the conversion and remittance of dividends and interest. Investors bring their capital into Hong Kong through the open exchange market and remit it the same way.

Accordingly, we may expect speculative behavior and crowd effects to be free to express themselves in their full force. Indeed, the Hong Kong stock market provides perhaps the best textbook-like examples of speculative bubbles decorated by log-periodic power law accelerations followed by crashes. Over just the last fifteen years, one can identify three major bubbles and crashes. They are indicated as I, II, and III in Figure 7.8.

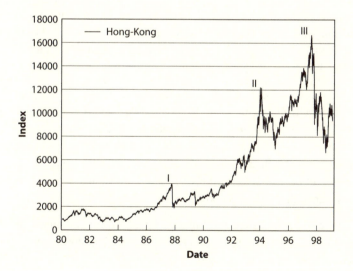

FIG. 7.8. The Hong Kong stock market index as a function of time. Three extended bubbles followed by large crashes can be identified. The approximate dates of the crashes are October 87 (I), January 94 (II), and October 97 (III). Reproduced from [218].

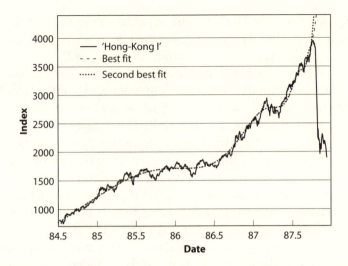

FIG. 7.9. Hong Kong stock market bubble ending with the crash of October 1987. On October 19, 1987, the Hang Seng index closed at 3362.4. On October 26, it closed at 2241.7, corresponding to a loss of 33.3%. See Table 7.1 for the parameter values of the fit with equation (15). Note that the two fits are almost indistinguishable except at the very end of the bubble. Reproduced from [218].

1. The first bubble and crash are shown in Figure 7.9 and are synchronous to the worldwide October 1987 crash already discussed. On October 19, 1987, the Hang Seng index closed at 3,362.4. On October 26, it closed at 2,241.7, corresponding to a cumulative loss of 33.3%.

2. The second bubble ends in early 1994 and is shown in Figure 7.10. The bubble ends with what we could call a "slow crash": on February 4, 1994, the Hang Seng index topped at 12,157.6 and, a month later on March 3, 1994, it closed at 9,802, corresponding to a cumulative loss of 19.4%. It went even further down over the next two months, with a close at 8,421.7 on May 9, 1994, corresponding to a cumulative loss since the high on February 4 of 30.7%.

3. The third bubble, shown in Figure 7.11, ended in mid-August 1997 by a slow and regular decay until October 17, 1997, followed by an abrupt crash: the drop from 13,601 on October 17 to 9,059.9 on October 28 corresponds to a 33.4% loss. The worst daily plunge of 10% was the third biggest percentage fall following the 33.3% crash in October 1987 and the 21.75% fall after the Tiananmen Square crackdown in June 1989.

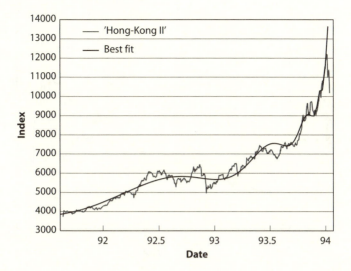

FIG. 7.10. Hong Kong stock market bubble ending with the crash of early 94. On February 4, 1994, the Hang Seng index topped at 12,157.6. A month later, on March 3, 1994, it closed at 9,802, corresponding to a cumulative loss of 19.4%. It went even further down two months later, with a close at 8,421.7 on May, 9, 1994, corresponding to a cumulative loss since the high on February 4 of 30.7%. See Table 7.1 for the parameter values of the fit with equation (15) shown as the continuous line. Reproduced from [218].

Table 7.1 gives the parameters of the fits with equation (15) of the bubble phases of the three events I, II, and III shown in Figures 7.9–7.11. It is quite remarkable that the three bubbles on the Hong Kong stock market have essentially the same log-periodic angular frequency ω within $\pm 15\%$. These values are also quite similar to what has been found for bubbles on the U.S. market and for the FOREX (see below). In particular, for the October 1997 crash on the Hong Kong market, we have $m_2^{1987} = 0.33 < m_2^{HK1997} = 0.34 < m_2^{1929} = 0.45$ and $\omega^{1987} = 7.4 < \omega^{HK1997} = 7.5 < \omega^{1929} = 7.9$; the exponent m_2 and the log-periodic angular frequency ω for the October 1997 crash on the Hong Kong Stock Exchange are perfectly bracketed by the two main crashes on Wall Street! Figure 7.12 demonstrates the "universality" of the log-periodic component of the signals in the three bubbles preceding the three crashes on the Hong Kong market.

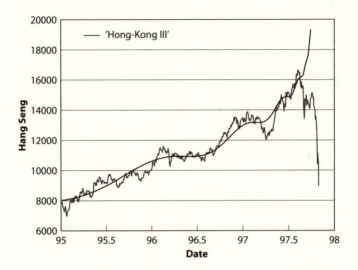

FIG. 7.11. The Hang Seng index prior to the October 1997 crash on the Hong Kong Stock Exchange. The index topped at 16,460.5 on August 11, 1997. It then regularly decayed to 13,601 reached on October 17, 1997. It then crashed abruptly, reaching a close of 9,059.9 on October 28, 1997, with an intraday low of 8,775.9. The amplitude of the total cumulative loss since the high on August 11 is 45%. The amplitude of the crash from October 17 to October 28 is 33.4%. The fit, shown as the solid line, is equation (15) with $A_2 \approx 20077$, $B_2 \approx -8241$, $C \approx -397$, $m_2 \approx 0.34$, $t_c \approx 1997.74$, $\omega \approx 7.5$, and $\phi \approx 0.78$. Reproduced from [212] and [218].

THE CRASH OF OCTOBER 1997 AND ITS RESONANCE ON THE U.S. MARKET

The Hong Kong market crash of October 1997 has been presented as a textbook example of contagion and speculation taking a course of their own. When Malaysian Prime Minister Dr. Mahathir Mohamad made his now-famous address to the World Bank International Monetary Fund seminar in Hong Kong in September 1997, many critics pooh-poohed his proposal to ban currency speculation as an attempt to hide the fact that Malaysia's economic fundamentals were weak. They pointed to the fact that the currency turmoil had not affected Hong Kong, whose economy was basically sound. Thus, if Malaysia and other countries were affected, that's because their economies were weak. At that time, it was easy to point out the deficits in the then-current accounts of Thailand, Malaysia, and Indonesia. In contrast, Hong Kong had a good current account situation and, moreover, had solid foreign reserves worth U.S.$88 bil-

TABLE 7.1

Stock market	A_2	B_2	B_2C	m_2	t_c	ω	ϕ
Hong Kong I	5523; 4533	−3247; −2304	171; −174	0.29; 0.39	87.84; 87.78	5.6; 5.2	−1.6; 1.1
Hong Kong II	21121	−15113	−429	0.12	94.02	6.3	−0.6
Hong Kong III	20077	−8241	−397	0.34	97.74	7.5	0.8

Fit parameters of the three speculative bubbles on the Hong Kong stock market shown in Figures 7.9–7.11 leading to a large crash. Multiple entries correspond to the two best fits. Reproduced from [218].

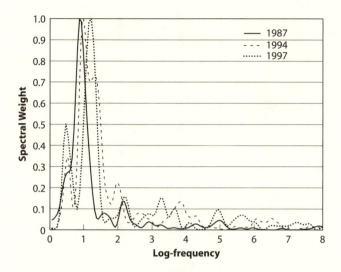

FIG. 7.12. The Lomb spectral analysis of the three bubbles preceding the three crashes on the Hong Kong market shown in Figures 7.9–7.11. See the section titled "Nonparametric Test of Log-Periodicity" later in this chapter. All three bubbles are characterized by almost the same "universal" log-frequency $f \approx 1$ corresponding to a preferred scaling ratio of the discrete scale invariance equal to $\lambda = \exp(1/f) \approx 2.7$. Courtesy of A. Johansen.

lion. This theory of the strong-won't-be-affected had already suffered a setback when the Taiwan currency's peg to the U.S. dollar had to be removed after Taiwanese authorities spent U.S.$5 billion to defend their currency from speculative attacks, and then gave up. The *coup de grace* came with the meltdown in Hong Kong in October 1997, which shocked analysts and the media, as this high-flying market was considered the safest haven in Asia. Notwithstanding the meltdown in Asia's lesser markets, as country after country, led by Thailand in July 1997, succumbed to economic and currency problems, Hong Kong was supposed to be different. With its Western-style markets, the second largest in Asia after Japan, it was thought to be immune to the financial flu that had swept through the rest of the continent. It is clear from our analysis in chapters 4 and 5 and from the lessons of the two previous bubbles ending in October 1987 and in early 1994 that those assumptions naively overlooked the contagion, leading to overinvestments in the build-up period preceding the crash and resulting instability, which left the Hong Kong market vulnerable to so-called speculative attacks. Actually, hedge funds in particular are known to have taken positions consistent with a possible crisis on the currency and on the stock market, by "shorting" (selling) the currency to drive it down, forcing the Hong Kong government to raise interest rates to defend it by increasing the currency liquidity, but as a consequence making equities suffer and making the stock market more unstable.

As we have already emphasized, one should not confuse the "local" cause with the fundamental cause of the instability. As the late George Stigler—Nobel laureate economist from the University of Chicago— once put it, to blame "the markets" for an outcome we don't like is like blaming restaurants waiters for obesity. Within the framework defended in this book, crashes occur as possible (but not necessary) outcomes of long preparation, which we term "herding," which pushes the market into increasingly unstable regimes. When in this state, there are many possible "local" causes that may cause it to stumble. Pushing the argument to the extreme to make it crystal clear, let us compare this to laying responsibility for the collapse of the infamous Tacoma Narrows Bridge that once connected mainland Washington with the Olympic peninsula on strong wind. It is true that, on November 7, 1940, at approximately 11:00 a.m., the bridge suddenly collapsed after developing a remarkably "ordered" sway in response to a strong wind [418] after it had been open to traffic for only a few months. However, the strong wind of that day was only the "local" cause, while there was a more fundamental cause: The bridge, like most objects, has a small number of characteristic vibration frequencies, and one day the wind was exactly the strength needed to excite one of them. The bridge responded by vibrating at this characteristic frequency so strongly, that is, by "resonating," that it fractured the supports holding it together. The fundamental cause of the collapse of the Tacoma Narrows Bridge thus lies in an error of conception that enhanced the role of one specific mode of resonance. In sum, the collapse of the Tacoma Narrows Bridge as well as that of many stock markets during crashes, is the result of built-in or acquired instabilities. These instabilities are in turn revealed by "small" perturbations that lead directly to the collapse.

The speculative attacks in periods of market instabilities are sometimes pointed to as possible causes of serious potential hazards for developing countries when allowing the global financial markets to have free play, especially when these countries come under pressure to open up their financial sectors to large foreign banks, insurance companies, stock-broking firms, and other institutions, under the World Trade Organization's financial services negotiations. We argue that the problem comes in fact fundamentally from the overenthusiastic initial influx of capital as a result of herding, which initially profits the country, but carries the risk of future instabilities: developing countries as well as investors "can't have their cake and eat it too!" From an efficient market viewpoint, the speculative attacks are nothing but the revelation of the instability and the means by which markets are forced back to a more stable dynamical state.

Interestingly, the October 1997 crash on the Hong Kong market caused important echos in other markets worldwide, and in particular in the U.S. markets. The story is often told as if a "wave of selling," starting in Hong Kong, spread first to other southeast Asian markets based on negative sentiment—which served to reaffirm the deep financial problems of the Asian "tiger" nations—then to the European markets, and finally to the U.S. market. The shares that were hardest hit in Western markets were the multinational companies that receive part of their earnings from the southeast Asian region. The reason for their devaluation is that the region's economic slowdown would lower corporate profits. It is estimated that the 25 companies that make up one-third of Wall Street's S&P 500 index of market capitalization earn roughly half of their income from non-U.S. sources. Lower growth in southeast Asia heightened one of the biggest concerns of Wall Street investors. To carry on the then-present bull run, the market needed sustained corporate earnings; if they were not forthcoming, the cycle of rising share prices would whither into one of falling share prices. Concern over earnings might have proved to be the straw that broke Wall Street's six-year bull run.

Fingerprints of herding and of incoming instability were detected by several groups independently and announced publicly. According to our theory, the turmoil on the U.S. financial market in October 1997 should not be seen only as a passive reaction to the Hong Kong crash. The log-periodic power law signature observed on the U.S. market over several years before October 1997 (see Figure 7.13) indicates that a similar herding instability was also developing simultaneously. In fact, the detection of log-periodic structures and a prediction of a stock market correction or a crash at the end of October 1997 was formally issued jointly ex ante on September 17, 1997 by A. Johansen and the current author, to the French office for the protection of proprietary softwares and inventions, with registration number 94781. In addition, a trading strategy was been devised using put options in order to provide an experimental test of the theory. A 400% profit had been obtained in a two-week period covering the minicrash of October 28, 1997. The proof of this profit is available from a Merrill Lynch client cash management account released in November 1997. Using a variation [435] of our theory, which turns out to be slightly less reliable (see comparative tests in [214]), a group of physicists and economists also made a public announcement published on September 18, 1997 in a Belgian journal [115] and communicated their methodology in a scientific publication afterwards [433]. Two other groups have also analyzed, after the fact, the possibility of having predicted this event. Feigenbaum and Freund analyzed the log-periodic oscillations in the S&P 500 and the NYSE in relation to the October 27 "correction" seen on Wall Street [129]. Gluzman and Yukalov proposed a new approach based on the algebraic self-similar renormalization group to analyze the time series corresponding to the October 1929 and 1987 crashes and the October 1997 correction of the NYSE [161].

The prices of stocks and their convertible bonds also gave a clear signal of the market reversal and of the minimum range of the stock price change during the Hong Kong stock market bubble of 1997 and its subsequent crash [82]. Recall that convertible bonds are debt instruments that can be converted into equities at a certain price, which is called the conversion price. A convertible bond is essentially a bond plus a call (buy) option on the equity. Because of the call option on the equity, convertible bonds usually pay lower coupon than the straight bonds. When the share price trades below the conversion price, the call option has very little value and the convertible bond behaves mostly like a straight bond. When the share prices trade higher than the conversion price, the convertible bond behaves more and more like an equity because the possibility of conversion is very high. For most convertible bonds, the issuers can call back the bonds and force the conversion when the underlying stocks reach a certain price, which is called the call price. So a convertible bond is a hybrid of debt and equity. Since a convertible bond contains a call option on the equity and the value of an option is always positive, a convertible bond should always trade at a premium over the share price; that is, the price of the convertible bond should always be higher than the corresponding share price. If a convertible is traded at a discount, this usually indicates that either there are some restrictions on the convertible bonds that reduce their values or some additional information has been revealed by this pricing anomaly, which is the effect documented for the end of the Hong Kong bubble [82]. There is thus additional information to be found in the relationship between underlying stocks and their derivatives during market bubbles.

The best fit of the logarithm of the S&P 500 index from January 1991 until September 4, 1997 by the improved nonlinear log-periodic formula developed in [397], already used in Figures 7.2 and 7.7, is shown in Figure 7.13. This result and many other analyses led to the prediction

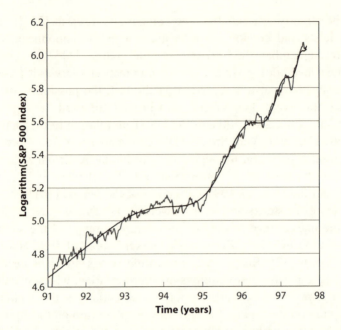

F<small>IG</small>. 7.13. The best fit shown as the smooth continuous line of the logarithm of the S&P 500 index from January 1991 until September 4, 1997 (1997.678) by the improved nonlinear log-periodic formula developed in [397], already used in Figures 7.2 and 7.7. The exponent m_2 and log-periodic angular frequency ω are, respectively, $m_2 = 0.73$ (compared to 0.63 for October 1929 and 0.33 for October 1987) and $\omega = 8.93$ (compared to 5.0 for October 1929 and 7.4 for October 1987). The critical time predicted by this fit is $t_c = 1997.948$, that is, mid-December 1997. Courtesy of A. Johansen.

alluded to above, which will be further discussed in chapter 9. It turned out that the crash did not really occur. What happened was that the Dow plunged 554.26 points, finishing the day down 7.2%, and Nasdaq posted its biggest-ever (up to that time) one-day point loss. In accordance with a new rule passed after the October 1987 Black Monday, trading was halted on all major U.S. exchanges. Private communications from professional traders to the author indicate that many believed that a crash was coming, but this turns out to be incorrect. This sentiment must also be put into the perspective of the earlier sell-off at the beginning of the month triggered by Greenspan's statement that the boom in the U.S. economy was unsustainable and that the current rate of gains in the stock market was unrealistic.

It is actually interesting that the critical time t_c identified around this data (see chapter 9) indicated a change of regime rather than a real crash: after this turbulence, the U.S. market remained more or less flat, thus breaking the previous bullish regime, with large volatility until the end of January 1998, and then started a new bull phase that was later stopped in its course in August 1998, which we shall analyze below. The observation of a change of regime after t_c is in full agreement with the rational expectation model of a bubble and crash described in chapter 5: the bubble expands, the market believes that a crash may be increasingly probable, the prices develop characteristic structures of speculation and herding, but the critical time passes without the crash happening. This can be interpreted as the nonzero probability scenario also predicted by the rational expectation model of a bubble and crash described in chapter 5, that it is possible that no crash occurs over the whole lifetime of the bubble including t_c.

What could be additional reasons for the abortion of the crash predicted in October 1997 on the U.S. market? One origin may be found in the behavior of household investors. U.S. households own the majority of the mutual fund industry, with an ownership of $2.626 trillion, or 74.2% of the $3.539 trillion of mutual fund assets (value at the end of 1996), while banks and individuals serving as trustees, guardians, or administrators and other institutional investors hold the remaining $913 billion, or 25.8%. As shown in Figure 7.14, the purchase of equities by households has evolved over the last decade by being more and more concentrated on mutual funds. An analysis of the Investment Company Institute covering more than 50 years, including fourteen major market contractions and several sharp market sell-offs, found no historical evidence of mass redemptions from stock mutual funds during U.S. stock market contractions. Even the severe market break of October 19, 1987 failed to trigger substantial outflows from mutual funds. This analysis is consistent with evidence from shareholder surveys suggesting that mutual fund owners have a long-term investment horizon and basic understanding of risk. Thus a larger share of the market by these long-term horizon investors provides more stability and less reactivity to local turn-downs. The limited drop in October 1997 that stopped just short of cascading in a crash might be due to this stabilizing effect, which was stronger in 1997 than in 1987 as a result of the larger market share owned by households.

The simultaneity of the critical times t_c of the Hong Kong crash and of the end of the U.S. and European speculative bubble phases at the end of October 1997 are neither a lucky occurrence nor a signature of a causal impact of one market (Hong Kong) onto others, as has often

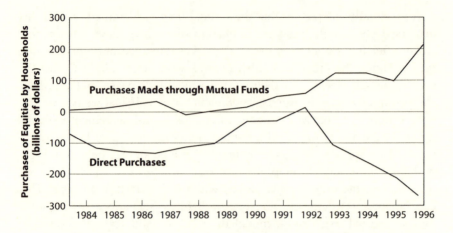

FIG. 7.14. Reproduced from a report of the Investment Company Institute based on sources from the Federal Reserve Board, the Employee Benefit Research Institute, and the Investment Company Institute (http://www.ici.org/). The ICI is the national association of the American investment company industry. Founded in 1940, its 2001 membership includes 8,414 mutual funds, 489 closed-end funds, and 8 sponsors of unit investment trusts. Its mutual fund members represent more than 83 million individual shareholders and manage approximately $7 trillion. The negative "Direct Purchases" correspond to sales.

been discussed too naively. This simultaneity can actually be predicted in a model of rational expectation bubbles allowing the coupling and interactions between stock markets. For general interactions, if a critical time appears in one market, it should also be present in other markets as a result of the nonlinear interactions existing between the markets [219]. This will be discussed further in chapter 10 in relation to the interaction between the world population, its global economic output, and global market indices.

In sum, two lessons can be taken home from the Hong Kong October 1997 crash: the trend-setting power of the "global village" and the might of the general investor sentiment forged by forces of imitation and herding.

CURRENCY CRASHES

Currencies can also develop bubbles and crashes. The bubble on the dollar starting in the early 1980s and ending in 1985 is a remarkable example, as shown in Figure 7.15.

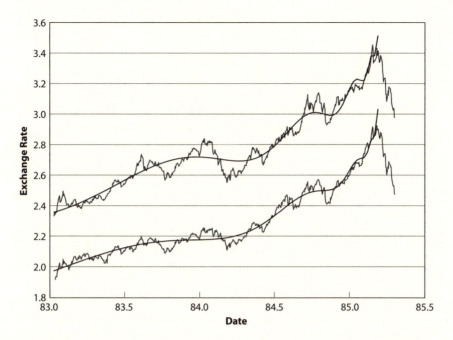

FIG. 7.15. The U.S. dollar expressed in German Mark DEM (top curve) and in Swiss franc CHF (bottom curve) prior to its collapse on mid-1985. The fit to the DEM currency against the U.S. dollar with equation (15) is shown as the continuous and smooth line and gives $A_2 \approx 3.88$, $B_2 \approx -1.2$, $B_2C \approx 0.08$, $m_2 \approx 0.28$, $t_c \approx$ 1985.20, $\omega \approx 6.0$, and $\phi \approx -1.2$. The fit to the Swiss franc against the U.S. dollar with equation (15) gives $A_2 \approx 3.1$, $B_2 \approx -0.86$, $B_2C \approx 0.05$, $m_2 \approx 0.36$, $t_c \approx 1985.19$, $\omega \approx 5.2$, and $\phi \approx -0.59$. Note the small fluctuations in the value of the scaling ratio $2.2 \leq \lambda \leq 2.7$, which constitute one of the key tests of our "critical herding" theory. Reproduced from [212].

To understand what happened, we need to retrace a piece of exchange rate history. In 1975, the U.S. Treasury Secretary informed the International Monetary Fund annual meeting that "We strongly believe that countries must be free to choose their own exchange rate system." Both these developments were the successful culmination of "campaigns" led by the economist Milton Friedman during the previous quarter-century. Friedman's case for flexible exchange rates was transformed from heresy to majority academic recommendation and from there (via two U.S. treasury secretaries) to become the cornerstone of the post-1973 international "monetary order" [261]. As flexible exchange rates were legitimized, several leading countries began to experiment with monetary targeting, with the idea that a flexible exchange rate is a precondition for independent national monetary policy. This was the death of the previous 1944 Bretton Woods agreement, designed to provide postwar international stability to facilitate the approach towards both free trade and full employment. It turned out that fixed-exchange rates led to numerous crises and problems: indeed, the whole point of going from a world fixed-exchange rate to floating exchanges between local currencies was to give governments the ability to have independent monetary policies so they could fight their local recessions when necessary. The flexibility to develop an independent monetary policy thus gives a country an essential additional degree of freedom to stabilize its economy. However, a country cannot simultaneously print money to fight a recession and maintain the value of its currency on the foreign exchange market. A country can also improve its competitive position by devaluing. But hints that a devaluation might be looming can cause massive speculation against the vulnerable currency, as we shall discuss in chapter 8. See also [248] for an eye-opening description of the conundrums of monetary policies.

With the end of Bretton Woods in the early 1970s, the market for foreign currency grew rapidly in both size and instability. The liberalization of capital flows that followed the adoption of floating-exchange rates brought vastly larger flows of capital between nations. The first naive presumption is that the exchange rate between two currencies, say the U.S. dollar and the European euro (since January 1999), would be determined by the needs of trade: by North Americans trading with Europeans for euros in order to buy European goods, and conversely. However, there is another important population, the investors: people who are buying and selling currencies in order to purchase stocks and bonds in the U.S. and/or the European markets. Since these investment demands are highly variable, including a fluctuating component of speculation, currency values prove volatile and prone to the same forces as described in chapters 4 and 5 for stocks and general financial markets. Such forces proved to be at the origin of the speculative bubble on the dollar in the first half of the 1980s [340].

The role of monetary policy allowed by the floating-exchange rate was particularly clear in the context of the large deficit of the U.S. federal budget in the early 1980s, which led to fears that inflation would go sky-high. According to supporters of monetary policy, the key to controlling inflation was that the Federal Reserve did not pump up the money supply too much. Indeed, by allowing a strong dollar (which slows the U.S. economy) and restricting the money supply, the Federal Reserve chopped inflation from 13.3% in 1979 to 4.4% in 1987 to about 2% at the end of the twentieth century. Many even believed that the value of the

U.S. dollar has been high because of large U.S. budget deficits. Indeed, the large U.S. budget deficit of the early 1980s had to be financed in particular by foreign investors encouraged by a high interest rate to buy U.S. Treasury bonds and securities. A high interest rate automatically makes the dollar attractive and thus in strong demand, raising it up. Statistical tests over several periods of whether the dollar appreciates when the federal budget deficit increases showed results globally counter to the held belief [121]. The Economic Recovery Tax Act of 1981 constituted the origin of the megadeficits, as it was designed to increase savings and investment and thus increase real economic growth; that increased growth would in turn offset a tax cut. It turned out that the act has not produced the increase in revenues necessary to reduce the budget deficit, in turn augmenting the foreign trade deficit linked to the federal deficit by high U.S. interest rates, which encourage foreign investors to buy U.S. securities. This is why there is general belief in the importance of a gradual and steady reduction of the federal deficit as the best long-term solution to reducing the high interest rates and the trade deficit.

In fact, the relationship between exchange rates and economic health is more complex due to other factors as well as the role of investor expectations and anticipations. As anything in the economic sphere, exchange rates are first determined by the interaction of supply and demand forces. For example, if the prices of products increase in the United States relative to those in France, the value of U.S. currency should decrease. Indeed, if initially, a bottle of wine, which is valued at $1 in the United States and 1 euro in France, later costs $2 in the United States and still 1 euro in France, the effective exchange rate $1 = 1$ euro based on the bottle of wine taken as a reference has become $2 = 1$ euro. Due to travel costs and other "frictions," the adjustment of the exchange rate does not, however, closely follow this relationship. If the exchange rate remains at $1 = 1$ euro for other reasons, the price increase is also felt in France: 1 bottle of wine $= \$2 = 2$ euros. The French will stop buying any wine from the United States, as it is twice as expensive as their homemade brands.

Actually, a more significant determinant of exchange rate is the (inflation-adjusted) real interest rate. If real interest rates increase in a country, the value of its currency should increase, as investors will get a larger return by owning the currency with the largest real interest rate. This currency is thus in strong demand, driving its price up. But this is not always the case: short-term data on exchange rates and interest rates during the 1980s shows a negative correlation, which probably occurred because most analysts anticipated higher inflation, even though interest rates were relatively high [35].

The U.S. dollar experienced an unprecedented cumulative appreciation against the currencies of the major industrial countries starting around 1980, with several consequences: loss of competitiveness, with important implications for domestic industries, and increase of the U.S. merchandise trade deficit by as much as $45 billion by the end of 1983, with export sales about $35 billion lower and the import bill $10 billion higher. For instance, in 1982, it was already expected that, through its effects on export and import volume, the appreciation would reduce real gross national product by the end of 1983 to a level 1% to 1.5% lower than the third-quarter 1980 preappreciation level [130]. The appreciation of the U.S. dollar from 1980–84 was accompanied by substantial decline in prices for the majority of manufactured imports from Canada, Germany, and Japan. However, for a substantial minority of prices, the imported items' dollar prices rose absolutely and in relation to the general U.S. price level. The median change was a price decline of 8% for imports from Canada and Japan and a decrease of 28% for goods from Germany [133]. As a positive effect, the impact on the U.S. inflation outlook was to improve it very significantly. There is also evidence that the strong dollar in the first half of the 1980s forced increased competition in U.S. product markets, especially vis a vis continental Europe [240].

As we explained in chapter 5, according to the rational expectation theory of speculative bubbles, prices can be driven up by an underlying looming risk of a strong correction or crash. Such a possibility has been advocated as an explanation for the strong appreciation of the U.S. dollar from 1980 to early 1985 [230]. If the market believes that a discrete event may occur when the event does not materialize for some time, this may have two consequences: drive price up and lead to an apparent inefficient predictive performance of forward exchange rates. (Forward and future contracts are financial instruments that closely track "spot" prices, as they embody the best information on the expectation of market participants on near-term spot price in the future.) Indeed, from October 1979 to February 1985, forward rates systematically underpredicted the strength of the U.S. dollar. Two discrete events could be identified as governing market expectations [230]: (1) change in monetary regime in October 1979 and the resulting private sector doubts about the Federal Reserve's commitment to lower money growth and inflation; (2) private sector anticipation of the dollar's depreciation beginning in March 1985, that is, anticipation of a strong correction, exactly as in the bubble-crash model of chapter 5. The corresponding characteristic power law acceleration of bubbles decorated by log-periodic oscillations is shown in Figure 7.15.

Expectations of future exchange rate have been shown to be excessive in the posterior period from 1985.2 to 1986.4, indicating bandwagon effects at work and the possibility of a rational speculative bubble [278]. As usual before a strong correction or a crash, analysts were showing overconfidence, and there was much reassuring talk about the absence of significant danger of collapse of the dollar, which had risen to unprecedented heights against foreign currencies [199]. In the long term, however, it was clear that such a strong dollar was unsustainable, and there were indications that the dollar was overvalued, in particular because foreign exchange markets generally hold that a nation's currency can remain strong over the longer term only if the nation's current account is healthy. By constrast, for the first half of 1984, the U.S. current account suffered a seasonally adjusted deficit of around $44.1 billion.

A similar but somewhat attenuated bubble of the U.S. dollar expressed, respectively, in Canadian dollar and Japanese Yen, extending over slightly less than a year and bursting in the summer of 1998, is shown in Figure 7.16. Paul Krugman, a professor of economics at the Massachusetts Institute of Technology, has suggested that this run-up on the Yen and the Canadian dollar, as well as the near collapse of U.S. financial markets at the end of the summer of 1998, which is discussed in the next section, are the unwanted "byproduct of a vast get-richer-quick scheme by a handful of shadowy financial operators" which backfired [246]. The remarkable quality of the fits of the data with our theory does indeed give credence to the role of speculation, imitation, and herding, be them spontaneous, self-organized, or manipulated in part. Actually, Frankel and Froot have found that, over the period 1981–85, the market shifted away from the fundamentalists and toward the chartists [139, 140].

THE CRASH OF AUGUST 1998

From its top in mid-June 1998 (1998.55) to its bottom in the first days of September 1998 (1998.67), the U.S. S&P 500 stock market lost 19%. This "slow" crash, and in particular the turbulent behavior of stock markets worldwide starting in mid-August, are widely associated with and even attributed to the plunge of the Russian financial markets, the devaluation of its currency, and the default of the government on its debt

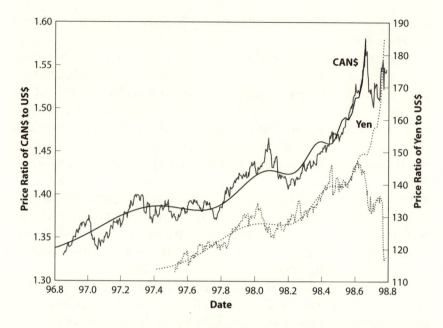

FIG. 7.16. The U.S. dollar expressed in Canadian dollars and Yen currencies prior to its drop starting in August 1998. The fit with equation (15) to the two exchange rates gives $A_2 \approx 1.62$, $B_2 \approx -0.22$, $B_2C \approx -0.011$, $m_2 \approx 0.26$, $t_c \approx 98.66$, $\phi \approx -0.79$, $\omega \approx 8.2$ and $A_2 \approx 207$, $B_2 \approx -85$, $B_2C \approx 2.8$, $m_2 \approx 0.19$, $t_c \approx 98.78$, $\phi \approx -1.4$, $\omega \approx 7.2$, respectively. Reproduced from [221].

obligations (see chapter 8 for information and analysis of other crises on the Russian market).

The analysis presented in Figure 7.17 suggests a different story: the Russian event may have been the triggering factor, but not the fundamental cause! One can observe clear fingerprints of a kind of speculative herding, starting more than three years before, with its characteristic power law acceleration decorated by log-periodic oscillations. Table 7.2 gives a summary of the parameters of the log-periodic power law fit to the main bubbles and crashes discussed until now. The crash of August 1998 is seen to fit nicely in the family of crashes with "herding" signatures.

This indicates that the stock market was again developing an unstable bubble which would have culminated at some critical time $t_c \approx 1998.72$, close to the end of September 1998. According to the rational expectation bubble models of chapter 5, the probability for a strong correction or a crash was increasing as t_c was approached, with a rising susceptibility to "external" perturbations, such as news or financial difficulties occur-

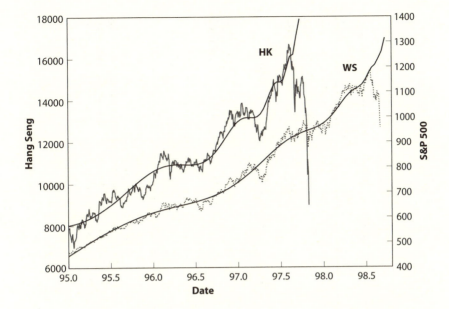

FIG. 7.17. The Hang Seng index prior to the October 1997 crash on the Hong Kong Stock Exchange already shown in Figure 7.11 and the S&P 500 stock market index prior to the crash on Wall Street in August 1998. The fit to the S&P 500 index is equation (15) with $A_2 \approx 1321$, $B_2 \approx -402$, $B_2C \approx 19.7$, $m_2 \approx 0.60$, $t_c \approx 98.72$, $\phi \approx 0.75$, and $\omega \approx 6.4$. Reproduced from [221].

ring somewhere in the "global village." The Russian meltdown was just such a perturbation. What is remarkable is that the U.S. market somehow contained the information of an upcoming instability through its unsustainable accelerated growth and structures! The financial world being an extremely complex system of interacting components, it is not farfetched to imagine that Russia was led to take actions against its unsustainable debt policy at the time of a strongly increasing concern by many about risks on investments made in developing countries. This concept is further developed in the section on the Russian crashes in chapter 8.

The strong correction starting in mid-August was not specific to the U.S. markets. Actually, it was much stronger in some other markets, such as the German market. Indeed, within the period of only nine months preceding July 1998, the German DAX index went up from about 3,700 to almost 6,200 and then quickly declined over less than one month to below 4,000. Precursory log-periodic structures have been documented for this event over the nine months preceding July 1998 [111], with the addition that analogous log-periodic oscillations also occurred on smaller

TABLE 7.2

Crash	t_c	t_{max}	t_{min}	drop	m_2	ω	λ	A_2	B_2	B_2C	Var
1929 (WS)	30.22	29.65	29.87	47%	0.45	7.9	2.2	571	−267	14.3	56
1985 (DEM)	85.20	85.15	85.30	14%	0.28	6.0	2.8	3.88	−1.16	0.08	0.0028
1985 (CHF)	85.19	85.18	85.30	15%	0.36	5.2	3.4	3.10	−0.86	+0.055	0.0012
1987 (WS)	87.74	87.65	87.80	30%	0.33	7.4	2.3	411	−165	12.2	36
1997 (HK)	97.74	97.60	97.82	46%	0.34	7.5	2.3	20077	−8241	−397	190360
1998 (WS)	98.72	98.55	98.67	19%	0.60	6.4	2.7	1321	−402	19.7	375
1998 (YEN)	98.78	98.61	98.77	21%	0.19	7.2	2.4	207	−84.5	2.78	17
1998 (CAN$)	98.66	98.66	98.71	5.1%	0.26	8.2	2.2	1.62	−0.23	−0.011	0.00024
1999 (IBM)	99.56	99.53	99.81	34%	0.24	5.2	3.4				
2000 (P&G)	00.04	00.04	00.19	54%	0.35	6.6	2.6				
2000 (Nasdaq)	00.34	00.22	00.29	37%	0.27	7.0	2.4				

Summary of the parameters of the log-periodic power law fit to the main bubbles and crashes discussed in this chapter (see Figures 7.22, 7.23, and 7.24 for the April 2000 crash on the Nasdaq and the two crashes on IBM and on Procter & Gamble). t_c is the critical time predicted from the fit of each financial time series to the equation (15) on page 232. The other parameters of the fit are also shown. $\lambda = \exp[\frac{2\pi}{\omega}]$ is the preferred scaling ratio of the log-periodic oscillations. The error Var is the variance between the data and the fit and has units of $price \times prices$. Each fit is performed up to the time t_{max} at which the market index achieved its highest maximum before the crash. t_{min} is the time of the lowest point of the market after the crash, disregarding smaller "plateaus." The percentage drop is calculated as the total loss from t_{max} to t_{min}. Reproduced from [221].

time scales as precursors of smaller intermediate decreases, with similar preferred scaling ratio λ at the various levels of resolution. However, the reliability of these observations at smaller time scales established by visual inspection in [111] remain to be established with rigorous statistical tests.

NONPARAMETRIC TEST OF LOG-PERIODICITY

Until now, the evidence presented in support of the "critical crash" concept is based on so-called parametric fits of financial prices with the formula of the power law decorated by log-periodic oscillations. Fitting data with sufficiently complex formulas with a rather large number of adjustable parameters is a delicate problem. In particular, one could question the explanatory power of a formula with too many parameters. The following sentence, often attributed to the famous Italian physicist Enrico Fermi, epitomizes (actually, exaggerates) the problem: "Give me five parameters and I will describe an elephant." In order to address this possible criticism, we have emphasized the remarkable robustness and quasi-universality of the two key meaningful parameters across the 10 crashes analyzed so far, the exponent m_2 controlling the acceleration close to the critical time and the preferred scale ratio λ quantifying the hierarchical organization in the time domain. If the log-periodic power law acceleration were the result of noise or luck, these parameters should vary wildly from one crash to the next.

As we emphasized in chapter 6 and in the present chapter, the log-periodic component is a key signature of discrete scale invariance, taken as a crucial witness of the critical self-organization of financial markets. This suggests another *non-parametric* test, specifically aimed at detecting the log-periodic component of the financial signals. A first example is shown in Figure 7.18 for the October 1987 crash. A simple and robust method is used to quantify the amplitude of the deviation from the overall growth of the DJIA [434]. This deviation is then seen to be close to an oscillation accelerating with the approach to the critical crash time, in agreement with the log-periodic prediction.

Another formulation of the same idea has been developed to quantify in addition the statistical significance of the putative log-periodicity [221]. As in Figure 7.18, the idea is first to detrend the financial time series to remove the trend and acceleration and keep only the noisy oscillatory residue shown in Figure 7.19. In the implementation shown

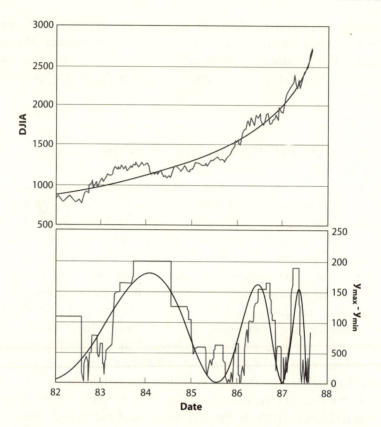

FIG. 7.18. Top panel: Evolution of the DJIA from January 1982 to August 1987; the continuous curve represents a fit with a pure power law with small exponent. Actually, Vandewalle et al. [434] use the limit of a vanishing exponent corresponding to a fit with a logarithmic acceleration $-\ln(t_c - t)$. This method provides inferior fits [214] but has the advantage of decreasing by one the number of adjustable parameters. The pattern in the bottom panel is a measure of the detrended oscillatory component. At any given time t, it is obtained by measuring the difference between the running maximum until time t and the running minimum from t to the end of the time series. The zeros of this difference correspond to new records since the maximum of the past is equal to the minimum of the future. The continuous oscillatory line is a pure log-periodic cosine $\cos(\omega \ln(t_c - t))$. Reproduced from [434] with permission from Elsevier Science.

in the figures, the detrending is performed by substracting and normalizing by the pure power law fit. The residual is then analyzed by a spectral analysis as a function of the variable $\ln(t_c - t)$ (specifically here the so-called Lomb periodogram method adapted to nonequidistant

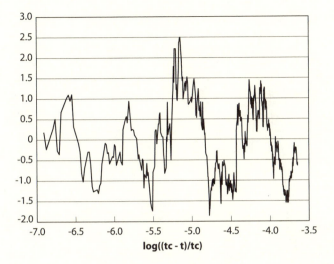

FIG. 7.19. The residual as defined by the transformation explained in the text as a function of $\log(\frac{t_c-t}{t_c})$ for the October 1987 crash. Reproduced from [221].

sampled data points), which should give a pure angular frequency ω if the log-periodicity was perfect. In Figure 7.20, a peak around the log-frequency $f = \omega/2\pi \approx 1.1$ (corresponding to the angular frequency $\omega_1 = 2\pi f \approx 7$) is obtained consistently for all eight cases reported in Table 7.2 and shown in previous figures (excluding the two companies and the Nasdaq index). This is in remarkable agreement with the results on ω listed in Table 7.2 that were obtained by the parametric log-periodic power law fits. If the noise was the standard white Gaussian process, the confidence given by the Lomb periodograms would be well above 99.99% for all cases shown [338]; that is, the probability that the log-frequency peaks observed in the bubble data could result from chance would be less than one in ten thousand (10^{-4}) *for each of the events*; for ten events supposed to be independent, it would be $(10^{-4})^{10} = 10^{-40}$ or one in ten thousand billion billion billion billion! However, since the "noise" spectrum is unknown and very likely different for each crash, we cannot estimate precisely the confidence interval of the peak in the usual manner [338] and compare the results for the different crashes. Therefore, to be conservative, only the relative level of the peak for each separate periodogram can be taken as a measure of the significance of the oscillations, and the periodograms have hence been normalized. In all cases, the mean peak is well above the background and is consistent across the crashes. Therefore, this spectral analysis demonstrates that the

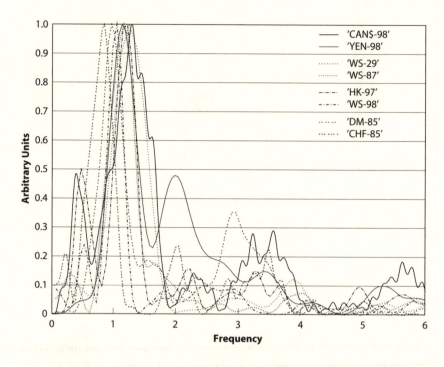

FIG. 7.20. The Lomb periodogram for the 1929, 1987, and 1998 crashes on Wall Street, the 1997 crash on the Hong Kong Stock Exchange, the 1985 U.S. dollar currency crash in 1985 against the DM and CHF and in 1998 against the Yen and the 5.1% correction against the Canadian dollar. For each periodogram, the significance of the peak should be estimated against the noise level. Reproduced from [221].

observed log-periodic oscillations have a very strong power spectrum, much above noise level. It would be very difficult and much less parsimonious to account for these structures by another model.

THE SLOW CRASH OF 1962 ENDING
THE "TRONICS" BOOM

In order to investigate further the statistical significance of these results, fifty 400-week intervals in the period 1910 to 1996 of the Dow Jones average were picked at random and fitted with the log-periodic power law formula [209]. The approximate end-dates of the 50 data sets are 1951, 1964, 1950, 1975, 1979, 1963, 1934, 1960, 1936, 1958, 1985, 1884, 1967, 1943, 1991, 1982, 1972, 1928, 1932, 1946, 1934, 1963, 1979, 1993, 1960, 1935, 1974, 1950, 1970, 1980, 1940, 1986, 1923,

1963, 1964, 1968, 1975, 1929, 1984, 1944, 1994, 1967, 1924, 1974, 1954, 1956, 1959, 1926, 1947, and 1965.

The motivation was to see whether the method has many false alarms, in other words, if the formula can find periods where it detects a speculative regime interpreted as a precursor of a critical time corresponding to a high probability for a strong correction or a crash, while in fact nothing of the sort happens. If a substantial fraction of the random intervals exhibit similar patterns as for the ten cases discussed above, there is no value in such a method with no discriminating power. On the other hand, if only the pre-crash periods are characterized by the log-periodic power law–like fits, we have a method to characterize, detect, identify, and maybe forecast critical times (more on this in chapters 9 and 10).

The results reported in [209] were as follows. Out of the fifty time intervals, only eleven had a quality of fit comparable with that of the other crashes, and only six of them produced values for the exponent m_2 and log-periodic angular frequency ω which were in the same range. This criterion embodies the expected "universality" of the critical cooperative regime underlying the critical point, as discussed in chapters 4–6. Among the six fits, five belonged to the periods prior to the crashes of 1929 and 1987. The sixth was identifying a speculative regime culminating in the spring of 1962, an event that we did not expect, as we were unaware of any crash during these times. The existence of a "crash" in 1962 was unknown to us before these results, and the identification of this crash naturally strengthens the case. After this discovery, a little search in the history of economic booms and busts (see, for instance, [282]) taught us that, indeed, the late 1950s and early 1960s had their "new industry" and "growth stocks," with soaring stock prices ending with the slow 1962 crash. Growth stocks in the new electronic industry like Texas Instruments and Varian Associates, expected to exhibit a very fast rate of earning growth, were highly prized and far outdistanced the standard blue-chip stocks. Many companies associated with the esoteric high-tech of space travel and electronics sold in 1961 for over 200 times their previous year's earning. Previously, the traditional rule had been that the price should be a multiple of 10 to 15 times their earnings. This is a story all too familiar! The "tronics boom," as it was called, actually has remarkably similar features to the New Economy boom preceding the October 1929 crash or the New Economy boom of the late 1990s, ending in the April 2000 crash on the Nasdaq index.

The best fit of the DJIA from 1954 to the end of 1961 by the log-periodic power law formula is shown in Figure 7.21. This period of time was followed by a "slow crash," in the sense that the stock market

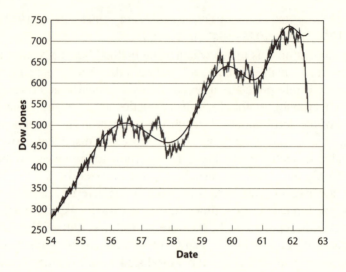

FIG. 7.21. The DJIA prior to the 1962 slow "crash" on Wall Street. The fit (solid line) is equation (15) with $A_2 \approx 960$, $B_2 \approx -120$, $B_2C \approx -14.9$, $m_2 \approx 0.68$, $t_c \approx 1964.83$, $\omega \approx 12.1$, and $\phi \approx 4.1$. Reproduced from [209].

declined approximately 27% in three months, not in one or two weeks as for the other crashes. In terms of the rational expectation model presented in chapters 5 and 6, some external shock may have provoked this slow crash before the stock market was "ripe." Indeed, within the rational expectation model, a bubble that starts to "inflate" with some theoretical critical time t_c can be perturbed and not go to its culmination due to the influence of external shocks. Recall that the critical time t_c of the power law is the time at which the crash is the most probable, but this does not prevent the bubble from crashing or stoping before a crash, albeit with a smaller probability. If this happens, as seems to have been the case in 1962, this does not prevent the log-periodic structures from developing up to the time when the course of the bubble evolution is modified by these external shocks. These structures are the signatures of a strong speculative phase announcing a coming unstable phase.

A recurring theme of this book is that bubbles and crashes result from speculation. The objects of speculation differ from boom to boom, as we have seen in the first chapters of this book, including metallic coins, tulips, selected companies, import commodities, country banks, foreign mines, building sites, agricultural and public lands, railroad shares, copper, silver, gold, real estate, derivatives, hedge-funds, and new industries [236]. The euphoria derived from the infatuation with new industries especially marked the bubble preceding the great crash of October 1929 as well as the "tronics boom" before the slow crash of 1962 or the Internet/Information technology (IT) boom before the Nasdaq crash of April 2000 discussed below. As the euphoria of a boom gives way to the pessimism of a bust, one ought to wonder what really happens to the buying plans and business projects of overextended consumers and businesspeople.

THE NASDAQ CRASH OF APRIL 2000

In the last few years of the second millenium, there was a growing divergence in the stock market between New Economy and Old Economy stocks, between technology and almost everything else. Over 1998 and 1999, stocks in the Standard & Poor's technology sector rose nearly fourfold, while the S&P 500 index gained just 50%. And without technology, the benchmark would be flat. In January 2000 alone, 30% of net inflows into mutual funds went to science and technology funds, versus just 8.7% into S&P 500 index funds. As a consequence, the average price-over-earnings ratio (P/E) for Nasdaq companies was above 200 (corresponding to a ridiculous earnings yield of 0.5%), a stellar value above anything that serious economic valuation theory would consider reasonable. It is worth recalling that the very same concept and wording of a so-called New Economy was hot in the minds and mouths of investors in the 1920s and in the early 1960s, as already mentioned. In the 1920s, the new technologies of the time were General Electric, ATT, and other electric and communication companies, and they also exhibited impressive price appreciations of the order of hundreds of percentage points in an eighteen-month time intervals before the 1929 crash.

The Nasdaq composite index (see chapter 2 for definition) dropped precipitously, with a low of 3,227 on April 17, 2000, corresponding to a cumulative loss of 37% counted from its all-time high of 5,133 reached on March 10, 2000. The Nasdaq composite consists mainly of stock related to the New Economy, that is, the Internet, software, computer hardware, telecommunication, and so on. A main characteristic of these companies is that their P/Es, and even more so their price-over-dividend ratios, often came in three digits prior to the crash. Some companies, such as VA LINUX, actually had a *negative* earnings/share of -1.68. Yet they were traded around $40 per share, which is close to the price of Ford in early March 2000. Opposed to this, so-called Old Economy companies, such as Ford, General Motors, and DaimlerChrysler, had

P/Es $\approx$ 10. The difference between Old Economy and New Economy stocks is thus the expectation of *future earnings* [395]: investors, who expect an enormous increase in, for example, the sale of Internet and computer-related products rather than in car sales, are hence more willing to invest in Cisco than in Ford notwithstanding the fact that the earning-per-share of the former is much smaller than for the latter. For a similar price per share (approximately $60 for Cisco and $55 for Ford), the earning per share is $0.37 for Cisco compared to $6.00 for Ford (Cisco had a total market capitalization of $395 billions [close of April, 14, 2000] compared to $63 billion for Ford). In the standard fundamental valuation formula, in which the expected return of a company is the sum of the dividend return and of the growth rate, New Economy companies are supposed to compensate for their lack of present earnings by fantastic potential growth. In essence, this means that the bull market observed in the Nasdaq in 1997–2000 was fueled by expectations of increasing future earnings rather than economic fundamentals (and by the expectation that others will expect the same thing and will help increase the capital gains): the price-over-dividend ratio for a company such as Lucent Technologies with a capitalization of over $300 billion prior to its crash on January 5, 2000 was over 900, which means that you get a higher return on your checking account (!) unless the price of the stock increases. Opposed to this, an Old Economy company such as DaimlerChrysler gave a return that was more than thirty times higher. Nevertheless, the shares of Lucent Technologies rose by more than 40% during 1999, whereas the shares of DaimlerChrysler declined by more than 40% in the same period. The recent crashes of IBM, Lucent, and Procter & Gamble shown in chapter 1 correspond to a loss equivalent to the state budgets of many countries. This is usually attributed to a "business-as-usual" corporate statement of a slightly revised, smaller-than-expected earnings!

These considerations make it clear that it is the *expectation* of future earnings and future capital gains rather than present economic reality that motivates the average investor, thus creating a speculative bubble. It has also been proposed [289] that better business models, the network effect, first-to-scale advantages, and real options effect could account for the apparent overvaluation, providing a sound justification for the high prices of dot.com and other New Economy companies. In a nutshell, the arguments are as follows.

1. The better business models refer to the fact that dot.com companies such as Amazon require little capital investment compared to their

brick-and-mortar competitors. In addition, the reduced delay in receiving electronic payments from customers compared to sending payments to suppliers means that, as the business grows, it actually generates cash from working capital.

2. Usually, positive feedback stems from economies of scale: the largest companies sustain the lowest unit costs. Economies of scale are driven by the "supply side," and consequently, may run into natural limitations and wane at a point well below market dominance. In the Internet economy, in contrast, positive feedback is fueled by the network effect, whose fundamental principle is that a network becomes more valuable to each user as incremental users are added. More specifically, the value of the network grows exponentially as the number of members grows arithmetically. A network of users is very valuable and becomes more so as it grows over time, locking in the customer base and enhancing the sustainability of excess returns. As companies start to enjoy the virtuous cycle, their revenue growth often meaningfully outstrips their cost increases.

3. First-to-scale advantages describe those companies that establish user bases large enough to launch them into the previously described virtuous cycle. According to this concept, it may often make sense for companies to forego current profits in an effort to build their network of users. Being first in a given space is important, as it offers the opportunity to establish a brand, set industry standards, and increase switching costs.

4. The real option effect refers to the concept that New Economy companies can use their already developed networks to grasp new opportunities as they unfold in the future. In other words, their customer network and their strong intellectual capital allow them to move rapidly in new markets, providing the potential for new gains. Their present structure thus gives them an "option" for the future, similar to a financial option: a financial option gives its owner the right, but not the obligation, to purchase or sell a security at a given price. Analogously, a company that owns a real option has the possibility, but not the obligation, to make a potentially value-accretive investment to enter a new market. The remarkable consequence is that, the larger the "volatility," that is, the larger the uncertainty of future market developments, the greater is the value of this option, because volatility and uncertainty highlight the value of future opportunities. For example, Amazon's e-commerce expertise and customer franchise in the book market gave it a "real option" to invest in the e-commerce markets for music, movies, and gifts.

These interesting views expounded in early 1999 were in synchrony with the bull market of 1999 and preceding years. They participated in the general optimistic view and added to the strength of the herd by a mechanism analogous to that exemplified in Figure 1.4. They seem less attractive in the context of the bearish phase of the Nasdaq market that has followed its crash in April 2000 and that is still running more than two years later. For instance, Koller and Zane [241] argued that the traditional triumvirate of earnings growth, inflation, and interest rates explains most of the growth and decay of U.S. indices (while not excluding the existence of a bubble of hugely capitalized new-technology companies).

Indeed, as already emphasized in chapter 1, history provides many examples of bubbles, driven by unrealistic expectations of future earnings, followed by crashes [454, 236]. The same basic ingredients are found repeatedly: fueled by initially well-founded economic fundamentals, investors develop a self-fulfilling enthusiasm by an imitative process or crowd behavior that leads to an unsustainable accelerating overvaluation. The fundamental origin of the crashes on the U.S. markets in 1929, 1962, 1987, 1998, and 2000 belongs to the same category, the difference being mainly in which sector the bubble was created: in 1929, it was utilities; in 1962, it was the electronic sector; in 1987, the bubble was supported by a general deregulation and new private investors with high expectations; in 1998, it was fueled by strong expectation regarding investment opportunities in Russia that ultimately collapsed; in 2000, it was powered by expectations regarding the Internet, telecommunication, and the rest of the New Economy sector. However, sooner or later, investment values always revert to a fundamental level based on real cash flows.

> This fact did not escape U.S. Federal Reserve chairman Alan Greenspan, who said: Is it possible that there is something fundamentally new about this current period that would warrant such complacency? Yes, it is possible. Markets may have become more efficient, competition is more global, and information technology has doubtless enhanced the stability of business operations. But, regrettably, history is strewn with visions of such "new eras" that, in the end, have proven to be a mirage. In short, history counsels caution [176].

Figure 7.22 shows the logarithm of the Nasdaq composite fitted with the log-periodic power law equation (15) on page 232. The data interval to fit was identified using the same procedure as for the other crashes: the first point is the lowest value of the index prior to the onset of the bubble, and the last point is that of the all-time high of the index. There exists

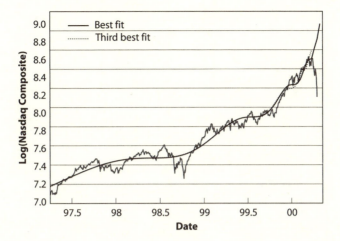

FIG. 7.22. Best (r.m.s. $\approx$ 0.061) and third best (r.m.s. $\approx$ 0.063) fits with equation (15) to the natural logarithm of the Nasdaq composite. The parameter values of the fits are $A_2 \approx 9.5$, $B_2 \approx -1.7$, $B_2 C \approx 0.06$, $m_2 \approx 0.27$, $t_c \approx 2000.33$, $\omega \approx 7.0$, $\phi \approx -0.1$ and $A_2 \approx 8.8$, $B_2 \approx -1.1$, $B_2 C \approx 0.06$, $m_2 \approx 0.39$, $t_c \approx 2000.25$, $\omega \approx 6.5$, $\phi \approx -0.8$, respectively. Reproduced from [217].

some subtlety with respect to identifying the onset of the bubble, the end of the bubble being objectively defined as the date when the market reached its maximum. A bubble signifies an acceleration of the price. In the case of Nasdaq, it tripled from 1990 to 1997. However, the increase was a factor 4 in the three years preceding the current crash, thus defining an "inflection point" in the index. In general, the identification of such an "inflection point" is quite straightforward on the most liquid markets, whereas this is not always the case for the emergent markets that we shall discuss in chapter 8. With respect to details of the methodology of the fitting procedure, we refer the reader to [221].

Undoubtedly, observers and analysts have forged post mortem stories linking the April 2000 crash with the effect of the crash of Microsoft Inc., which resulted from the breaking off of its negotiations with the U.S. federal government on the antitrust issue during the weekend of April 1, as well as from many other factors. Here, we interpret the Nasdaq crash as the natural death of a speculative bubble, antitrust or not, the results presented here strongly suggesting that the bubble would have collapsed anyway. However, according to our analysis based on the probabilistic model of bubbles described in chapters 5 and 6, the exact timing of the death of the bubble is not fully deterministic and allows for stochastic

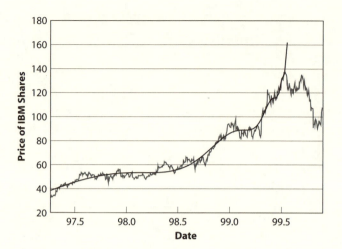

FIG. 7.23. Best (r.m.s. $\approx$ 3.7) fit, shown as solid line, with equation (15) to the price of IBM shares. The parameter values of the fits are $A_2 \approx 196$, $B_2 \approx -132$, $B_2 C \approx -6.1$, $m_2 \approx 0.24$, $t_c \approx 99.56$, $\omega \approx 5.2$, and $\phi \approx 0.1$. Reproduced from [217].

influences, but within the remarkably tight bound of about one month (except for the slow 1962 crash).

Log-periodic critical signatures can also be detected on individual stocks, as shown in Figures 7.23 for IBM and 7.24 for Procter & Gamble.

FIG. 7.24. Best (r.m.s. $\approx$ 4.3) fit (solid line) with equation (15) to the price of Procter & Gamble shares. The parameter values of the fit are $A_2 \approx 124$, $B_2 \approx -38$, $B_2 C \approx 4.8$, $m_2 \approx 0.35$, $t_c \approx 2000.04$, $\omega \approx 6.6$, and $\phi \approx -0.9$. Reproduced from [217].

These two figures extend Figures 1.7 and 1.9 of chapter 1 by offering a quantification of the precursory signals. The signals are more noisy than for large indices but are nevertheless clearly present. There is a weaker degree of generality for individual stocks as the valuation of a company is also a function of many other idiosyncratic factors associated with the specific course of the company. Dealing with broad market indices averages out all these specificities to mainly keep track of the overall market "sentiment" and direction. This is the main reason why the log-periodic power law precursors are stronger and more significant for aggregated financial series in comparison with individual assets. If speculation, imitation, and herding become at some time the strongest forces driving the price of an asset, we should then expect the log-periodic power law signatures to emerge again strongly above all the other idiosyncratic effects.

"ANTIBUBBLES"

We now summarize the evidence that imitation between traders and their herding behavior not only lead to speculative bubbles with accelerating overvaluations of financial markets possibly followed by crashes, but also to "antibubbles" with decelerating market devaluations following all-time highs [213]. There is thus a certain degree of symmetry between the speculative behavior of the "bull" and "bear" market regimes. This behavior is documented on the Japanese Nikkei stock index from January 1, 1990 until December 31, 1998 and on gold future prices after 1980, both after their all-time highs.

The question we ask is whether the cooperative herding behavior of traders might also produce market evolutions that are symmetric to the accelerating speculative bubbles that often end in crashes. This symmetry is performed with respect to a time inversion around a critical time t_c such that $t_c - t$ for $t < t_c$ is changed into $t - t_c$ for $t > t_c$. This symmetry suggests looking at *decelerating* devaluations instead of accelerating valuations. A related observation has been reported in Figure 7.4 in relation to the October 1987 crash showing that the implied volatility of traded options relaxed *after* the October 1987 crash to its long-term value, from a maximum at the time of the crash, according to a decaying power law with decelerating log-periodic oscillations. It is this type of behavior that we document now, but for real prices.

The critical time t_c then corresponds to the culmination of the market, with either a power law increase with accelerating log-periodic oscillations preceding it or a power law decrease with decelerating log-periodic oscillations after it. In chapter 8 we shall show an example using the Russian market where both structures appear simultaneously for the same t_c. This is, however, a rather rare occurrence, probably because accelerating markets with log-periodicity almost inevitably end up in a crash, a market rupture that thus breaks down the symmetry ($t_c - t$ for $t < t_c$ into $t - t_c$ for $t > t_c$). Herding behavior can occur and progressively weaken from a maximum in "bearish" (decreasing) market phases, even if the preceding "bullish" phase ending at t_c was not characterized by a strengthening imitation. The symmetry is thus statistical or global in general and holds in the ensemble rather than for each single case individually.

THE "BEARISH" REGIME ON THE NIKKEI STARTING FROM JANUARY 1, 1990

The most recent example of a genuine long-term depression comes from Japan, where the Nikkei decreased by more than 60% in the nine years following the all-time high of December 31, 1989. In Figure 7.25, we see (the logarithm of) the Nikkei from January 1, 1990 until December 31, 1998. The three fits, shown as the undulating lines, use three mathematical expressions of increasing sophistication: the dotted line is the simple log-periodic formula (15) on page 232; the continuous line is the improved nonlinear log-periodic formula developed in [397] and already used for the 1929 and 1987 crashes over eight years of data; the dashed line is an extension of the previous nonlinear log-periodic formula (19) on page 336 to the next order of description, which was developed in [213]. This last most sophisticated mathematical formula (25) on page 339 predicts the transition from the log-frequency ω_1 close to t_c to $\omega_1 + \omega_2$ for $T_1 < \tau < T_2$ and to the log-frequency $\omega_1 + \omega_2 + \omega_3$ for $T_2 < \tau$, where T_1 and T_2 are characteristic time scales of the model. The correspondence of notations is $\alpha = m$, $\Delta_t = T_1$, $\Delta'_t = T_2$, $\Delta_w = w_2$, and $\Delta'w = w_3$. Using indices 1, 2, and 3, respectively, for the simplest to the most sophisticated formulas, the parameter values of the first fit of the Nikkei are $A_1 \approx 10.7$, $B_1 \approx -0.54$, $B_1C_1 \approx -0.11$, $m_1 \approx 0.47$, $t_c \approx 89.99$, $\phi_1 \approx -0.86$, and $\omega_1 \approx 4.9$ for equation (15). The parameter values of the second fit of the Nikkei are $A_2 \approx 10.8$, $B_2 \approx -0.70$, $B_2C_2 \approx -0.11$, $m_2 \approx 0.41$, $t_c \approx 89.97$, $\phi_2 \approx 0.14$, $\omega_1 \approx 4.8$, $T_1 \approx 9.5$, $\omega_2 \approx 4.9$. The third fit uses the entire time interval and is performed by adjusting only T_1, T_2, ω_2, and ω_3, while $m_3 = m_2$, t_c and ω_1 are fixed at the values obtained from the previous fit. The values obtained for these four parameters are $T_1 \approx 4.3$, $T_2 \approx 7.8$, $\omega_2 \approx -3.1$, and $T_2 \approx 23$. In all these fits, T_1 and T_2

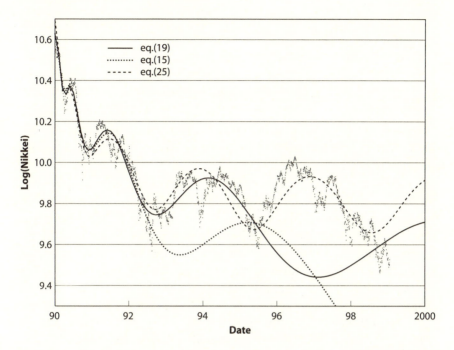

FIG. 7.25. Natural logarithm of the Nikkei stock market index after the start of the decline from January 1, 1990 until December 31, 1998. The dotted line is the simple log-periodic formula (15) on page 232 used to fit adequately the interval of ≈2.6 years starting from January 1, 1990. The continuous line is the improved nonlinear log-periodic formula (19) on page 336 developed in [397] and already used for the 1929 and 1987 crashes over 8 years of data. It is used to fit adequately the interval of ≈5.5 years starting from January 1, 1990. The dashed line is the extension (25) on page 339 of the previous nonlinear log-periodic formula to the next order of description, which was developed in [213] and is used to fit adequately the interval of ≈9 years starting from January 1, 1990. Reproduced from [213].

are given in years unit. Note that the values obtained for the two time scales T_1 and T_2 confirms their ranking. This last fit predicts a change of regime and that the Nikkei should increase in 1999. The value of this prediction will be analyzed in detail in chapter 9.

Not only do the first two equations agree remarkably well with respect to the parameter values produced by the fits, but they are also in good agreement with previous results obtained from stock market and Forex bubbles with respect to the values of exponent m_2. What lends credibility to the fit with the most sophisticated formula is that, despite its complex form, we get values for the two crossover time scales T_1, T_2 which correspond very nicely to what is expected from the ranking and from the nine-year interval of the data. We refer to [213] for a detailed and rather technical discussion.

THE GOLD DEFLATION PRICE STARTING IN MID-1980

Another example of log-periodic decay is that of the price of gold after the burst of the bubble in 1980, as shown in Figure 7.26. The bubble has an *average* power law acceleration, as shown in the figure, but *without* any visible log-periodic structure. A pure power law fit will, however, not lock in on the true date of the crash, but insists on an earlier date than the last data point. This suggests that the behavior of the price might be different in some sense in the last few weeks prior to the burst of the bubble. Again, we obtain a reasonable agreement with previous results for the exponent m_2 with a good preferred scaling ratio $\lambda \approx 1.9$ for the anti-bubble. In this case, the strength of the log-periodic oscillations compared to the leading behavior is $\approx 10\%$. The parameter values of the fit to the anti-bubble after the peak are $A_2 \approx 6.7$, $B_2 \approx -0.69$, $B_2 C \approx 0.06$, $m_2 \approx 0.45$, $t_c \approx 80.69$, $\phi \approx 1.4$, and $\omega \approx 9.8$. The line before the

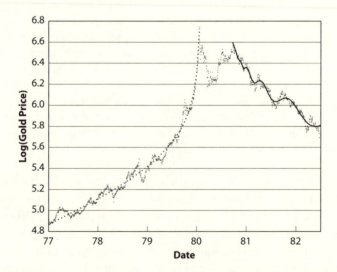

FIG. 7.26. Natural logarithm of the gold 100 Oz Future price in U.S. dollars after the decline of the price in the early 1980s. The dotted line before the peak is expression (15) fitted over an interval of almost 3 years. The continuous line after the peak is expression (15) with $t_c - t$ changed into $t - t_c$, fitted over an interval of 2 years. Reproduced from [213].

peak is expression (15) fitted over an interval of ≈ 3 years. The parameter values of the fit to the bubble before the peak are $A_2 \approx 8.5$, $B_2 \approx -111$, $B_2 C \approx -110$, $m_2 \approx 0.41$, $t_c \approx 80.08$, $\phi \approx -3.0$, $\omega \approx 0.05$.

SYNTHESIS: "EMERGENT" BEHAVIOR OF THE STOCK MARKET

In this chapter, we have shown that large stock market crashes are analogous to so-called critical points studied in the statistical physics community in relation to magnetism, melting, and similar phenomena. Our main assumption is the existence of cooperative behavior among traders imitating each other, as described in chapters 4–6. A general result of the theory is the existence of log-periodic structures decorating the time evolution of the system. The main point is that the market anticipates the crash in a subtle self-organized and cooperative fashion, hence releasing precursory "fingerprints" observable in the stock market prices. In other words, this implies that market prices contain information on impending crashes. If the traders were to learn how to decipher and use this information, they would act on it and on the knowledge that others act on it; nevertheless, the crashes would still probably happen. Our results suggest a weaker form of the "weak efficient market hypothesis" [122], according to which the market prices contain, in addition to the information generally available to all, subtle information formed by the global market that most or all individual traders have not yet learned to decipher and use. Instead of the usual interpretation of the efficient market hypothesis in which traders extract and consciously incorporate (by their action) all information contained in the market prices, we propose that the market as a whole can exhibit "emergent" behavior not shared by any of its constituents. In other words, we have in mind the process of the emergence of intelligent behaviors at a macroscopic scale that individuals at the microscopic scale cannot perceive. This process has been discussed in biology, for instance in animal populations such as ant colonies or in connection with the emergence of conciousness [8, 198]

Let us mention another realization of this concept, which is found in the information contained in options prices on the fluctuations of their underlying assets. Despite the fact that the prices do not follow geometrical Brownian motion, whose existence is a prerequisite for most options pricing models, traders have apparently adapted to empirically incorporating subtle information in the correlation of price distributions with fat tails [337]. In this case and in contrast to the crashes, the traders have had time to adapt. The reason is probably that traders have been exposed for decades to options trading in which the characteristic time scale for option lifetime is in the range of month to years at most. This is sufficient for an extensive learning process to occur. In contrast, only a few great crashes occur typically during a lifetime and this is certainly not enough to teach traders how to adapt to them. The situation may be compared to the ecology of biological species, which constantly strive to adapt. By the forces of evolution, they generally succeed in surviving by adaptation under slowly varying constraints. In constrast, life may exhibit successions of massive extinctions and booms probably associated with dramatically fast-occuring events, such as meteorite impacts and massive volcanic eruptions. The response of a complex system to such extreme events is a problem of outstanding importance that is just beginning to be studied [89].

Most previous models proposed for crashes have pondered the possible mechanisms for explaining the collapse of the price at very short time scales. Here, in contrast, we propose that the underlying cause of the crash must be searched years before it in the progressive accelerating ascent of the market price, reflecting an increasing build-up of the market cooperativity. From that point of view, the specific manner by which prices collapsed is not of real importance since, according to the concept of the critical point, any small disturbance or process may have triggered the instability, once ripe. The intrinsic divergence of the sensitivity and the growing instability of the market close to a critical point might explain why attempts to unravel the local origin of the crash have been so diverse. Essentially all would work once the system was ripe. Our view is that the crash has an endogenous origin and that exogenous shocks only serve as triggering factors. We propose that the origin of the crash is much more subtle and is constructed progressively by the market as a whole. In this sense, this could be termed a systemic instability.

CHAPTER 8

BUBBLES, CRISES, AND CRASHES IN EMERGENT MARKETS

SPECULATIVE BUBBLES IN EMERGING MARKETS

In periods of optimistic consensus, emerging markets have the favor of investors looking for opportunities to leverage their returns. Bubbles may ensue, and their demise is often associated with large swings and extreme corrections leading to financial crises [271].

Holdings of foreign stock by U.S. residents reached 10% of all equity holdings, or $876 billion by the end of 1996. More than one-third of that, $336 billion, was held through U.S. mutual funds specializing in international (non-U.S.) and global markets. Global and international mutual funds now represent 12.1% of net assets in long-term equity and bond funds. In addition, public and corporate U.S. pension funds report that on average they hold 10% and 9%, respectively, of their portfolios in non-U.S. assets. Trading in non-U.S. stocks on U.S. markets exceeded $1 trillion in 1996. Foreign investors are also increasingly actively in the U.S., with a trading volume of $1.2 trillion in 1996. Worldwide international trading of equities amounted to $5.9 trillion in 1996 according to NYSE estimates [422].

The record flows of capital towards emerging markets (essentially those in Asia and Latin America) in the 1990s were stimulated by three factors [136]. First, there was the search for higher yields leading to a strong increase in the demand for high-yield sovereign and corporate bonds issued by emerging market countries. Second, the continuing drive by institutional managers to increase their exposure to emerging markets and to achieve greater diversification of portfolios provided an important stimulus for flows to emerging markets. In November 1997, institutional investors (pension funds, insurance companies, and mutual funds in the Organisation for Economic Co-operation and Development [OECD] countries) had under management over $20 trillion in assets, only a small portion of which was invested in emerging markets. If institutional investors had reallocated just 1% of total assets under management toward the emerging markets, this shift would have constituted a capital flow of $200 billion. Third, the resurgence of capital flows also reflected the clear recognition by investors that the economic fundamentals in most emerging markets in the 1990s had vastly improved over those that prevailed in the late 1970s.

Since 1987, both the direct barriers, such as capital controls, and the indirect barriers, such as difficulties in evaluating corporate information, that prevented the free flow of capital had gradually been reduced. As capital controls were gradually lifted, global investors with more diversified portfolios began to influence stock prices, particularly in emerging markets [422]. This trend of opening up financial markets meant that firms from emerging markets were able to raise capital, both domestically and internationally, at a lower cost. In fact, firms from emerging markets were able to raise long-term equity and debt capital in global markets at unprecedented rates [422]. The capital infusion from foreign investors made it possible for emerging market firms to capitalize on their growth opportunities in a way that would have been impossible had they been restricted to raising funds in domestic markets. Moreover, previously state-owned assets were successfully sold off to both domestic and foreign investors, raising much-needed revenue for governments in both developed and emerging markets. The world financial markets are now on the road to becoming internationally integrated, but are still far from being there [422].

The story of financial bubbles and crashes has repeated itself over the centuries and in many different locations since the famous tulip bubble of 1636 in Amsterdam, almost without any alteration in its main global characteristics [152].

1. The bubble starts smoothly with some increasing production and sales (or demand for some commodity) in an otherwise relatively optimistic market.

2. The attraction to investments with good potential gains then leads to increasing investments, possibly with leverage coming from novel sources, often from international investors. This leads to price appreciation.

3. This in turn attracts less sophisticated investors and, in addition, leveraging is further developed with small downpayment (small margins), which leads to the demand for stock rising faster than the rate at which real money is put in the market.

4. At this stage, the behavior of the market becomes weakly coupled or practically uncoupled from real wealth (industrial and service) production.

5. As the price skyrockets, the number of new investors entering the speculative market decreases and the market enters a phase of larger nervousness, until a point when the instability is revealed and the market collapses.

This scenario applies essentially to all market crashes, including old ones such as October 1929 on the U.S. market, for which the U.S. market was considered to be at that time an interesting "emerging" market with good investment potentialities for national as well as international investors. In addition, the concept of a New Economy was used profusely in the medias of the time, reminiscent of several other New Economy phases in more recent times, including the recent crash of the Internet bubble documented in chapter 7. The robustness of this scenario is presumably deeply rooted in investor psychology and involves a combination of imitative/herding behavior and greediness (for the development of the speculative bubble) and overreaction to bad news in periods of instabilities.

There is also a simple mechanical effect which tends to sustain bubbles and then make them crash abruptly, stemming from the so-called buying on margin, that is, buying stocks on borrowed money. If there are huge amounts of borrowed money in the market, then it is no longer possible to slow things down. Prices must constantly increase, faster and faster. If they don't, the interest payments on all the borrowed money invested in the market will not be get paid. Money will be withdrawn to settle debts, leading to lower prices, leading to more money getting withdrawn, and so on in a vicious circle. This may lead to total market collapse and bank failure. This mechanism was active during the bubble preceding the Nasdaq crash of April 2000 discussed in chapter 7. Indeed, the economist, Kurt Richebacher [344], warned:

> There is something unique and unprecedented about the recent U.S. bubble: the phenomenal magnitude of the credit excesses. Credit creation is completely out of control in relation to economic activity and domestic savings. For each dollar added to gross domestic product (at current prices), there have been 4.5 of additional debt in 1999. By this measure, the U.S. stock market's bull run does not only rank as a bubble, but as the biggest and the worst of its kind in history. Bubbles and booms often continue much longer than anyone thinks possible. Nevertheless, all bubbles eventually burst with a vengeance, and the current one will not be any exception.

In addition, the constant effort to set a price with the available information, and in particular with the rational valuation formula, drives corporate managers to adopt policies aimed at producing a return for shareholders. There is thus an asymmetry in stock market variation: many more profit from an increase than from a decrease, in contrast with the symmetry between buyers and sellers of commodities traded nonspeculatively. The same mechanism is discussed by Franklin Allen and Douglas Gale [3, 4], who documented that bubbles may be caused by relationships between investors and banks: investors use money borrowed from banks to invest in risky assets, which are relatively attractive because investors can avoid losses in low-payoff states by defaulting on the loan. This risk shifting leads investors to bid up the asset prices. Such risk can originate in both the real and the financial sectors. Financial fragility occurs when the positive credit expansion eventually becomes insufficient to prevent a crisis.

The purpose of this chapter, based in large part on [218], is to extend the empirical basis for the observations presented in chapter 7 on major financial markets by analyzing a wide range of emerging markets. Eighteen significant bubbles followed by large crashes or severe corrections in Latin-American and Asian stock markets are identified. With very few exceptions, these speculative bubbles can be quantitatively described by the rational expectation model of bubbles presented in chapters 5 and 6, which predicts a specific power law acceleration as well as log-periodic geometric patterns. This study indicates that such large downward movements in the markets are nothing but depletions of the preceding bubble, thus bringing the market back towards a state closer to "rational" pricing via a relaxation process following the crash that may take hours, days, weeks, or longer (see, for instance, Figure 7.5).

METHODOLOGY

The methodology presented here follows the one previously used for major financial markets in chapter 7, which consists of a combination of parametric fits using the log-periodic formula (15) on page 232 as well as a so-called spectral analysis in the variable $\log(t_c - t)/t_c$ aiming at quantifying the oscillating part of the market prices (see the section on "Nonparametric Test of Log-Periodicity" in chapter 7). For such a "spectral" analysis, a so-called Lomb periodogram was used, which consists in a local fit of an oscillatory cosine function (with a phase) using some user-chosen range of frequencies. The relative level of the peak *for each separate* "periodogram" can be taken as a measure of the significance of the oscillations.

The use of the same methodology allows us to test the hypothesis that emerging markets exhibit bubbles and crashes with similar log-periodic signatures as in the major financial markets. It is very important for confirmation of the theory that no or little parameter tuning be done, as the danger of overfitting is always looming in this kind of analysis.

Identifying a speculative bubble is very difficult because there are several conceptual problems that obscure the economic interpretation of bubbles, starting with the absence of a general definition: bubbles are model specific and generally defined from a rather restrictive framework [1]. It is therefore difficult to avoid a subjective bias, especially since the very existence of bubbles is still hotly debated [459, 411, 229, 144, 120, 342, 108, 187, 109, 359, 453, 185, 320]. A major problem with arguments in favor of bubbles is also that apparent evidence for bubbles can be reinterpreted in terms of market fundamentals that are unobserved by the researcher [120, 135, 185].

We have thus taken a pragmatic and very straightforward approach consisting in selecting "bubbles" based on the following three criteria:

- the existence of a sharp peak in the spirit of [348],

- the existence of a preceding period of increasing price that extends over at least six months and that should preferably be comparable with those of the larger crashes discussed in chapter 7,

• the existence of a fast price decrease following the peak over a time interval much shorter than the accelerating period.

A bubble is defined as a period of time going from a pronounced minimum to a large maximum by a prolonged price acceleration, followed by a crash or a large decrease. As for the major financial markets, such a bubble is defined unambiguously by identifying its end with the date t_{max}, where the highest value of the index is reached prior to the crash/decrease. For the bubbles prior to the largest crashes on the major financial markets, the beginning of a bubble is clearly identified as coinciding always with the date of the lowest value of the index prior to the change in trend. However, this identification is not as straightforward for some of the emerging markets discussed below. In approximately half the cases, the date of the first data point used in defining the beginning of the bubble had to be moved forward in order to obtain fits with nonpathological values for the exponent and of the angular log-frequency. This may well be an artifact stemming from the restrictions in the fitting imposed by using a single cosine as the periodic function in expression (15). In order to filter out fits, the exponent m_2 has been chosen consistently between zero and one and it should be not too close to either zero or one: too small an m_2 implies a flat bubble with a very sudden acceleration at the end. Too large an m_2 corresponds to a nonaccelerating bubble. The angular frequency ω of the log-periodic oscillations must also not be too small or too large. If it is too small, less than one oscillation occurs over the whole interval and the log-periodic oscillation has little meaning. If it is too large, the oscillations are too numerous and they start to fit the high-frequency noise.

We refer to [218] for more details of the procedures.

LATIN-AMERICAN MARKETS

In Figures 8.1–8.6, the evolution of six Latin-American stock market indices (Argentina, Brazil, Chile, Mexico, Peru, and Venezuela) is shown as a function of time in the 1990s.

For these six Latin American stock market indices, four Argentinian bubbles, one Brazilian bubble, two Chilean bubbles, two Mexican bubbles, two Peruvian bubbles, and a single Venezuelan bubble were identified [218], with a subsequent large crash/decrease, as shown in Figures 8.1 to 8.6.

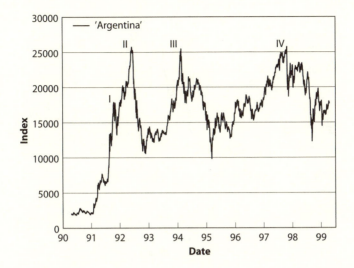

FIG. 8.1. The Argentinian stock market index as a function of time. Four bubbles with a subsequent very large drawdown can be identified. The approximate dates are in chronological order: mid-91 (I), early 93 (II), early 94 (III), and late 97 (IV). Reproduced from [218].

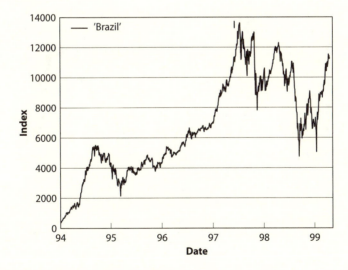

FIG. 8.2. The Brazilian stock market index as a function of time. One bubble with a subsequent very large drawdown can be identified. The approximate date is mid-97 (I). Reproduced from [218].

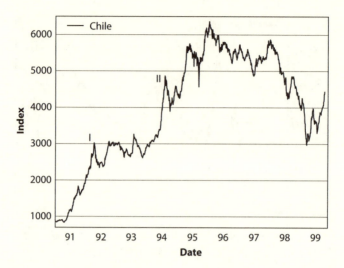

FIG. 8.3. The Chilean stock market index as a function of time. Two bubbles with a subsequent very large drawdown can be identified. The approximate dates are in chronological order: mid-91 (I) and early 94 (II). Reproduced from [218].

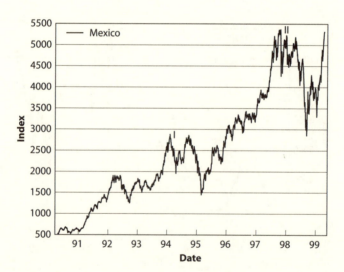

FIG. 8.4. The Mexican stock market index as a function of time. Two bubbles with a subsequent very large drawdown can be identified. The approximate dates are in chronological order: early 94 (I) and mid-97 (II). Reproduced from [218].

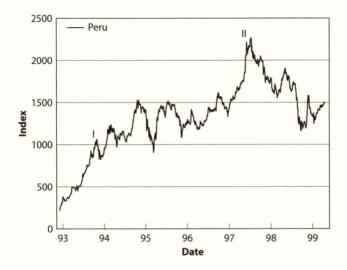

FIG. 8.5. The Peruvian stock market index as a function of time. Two bubbles with a subsequent very large drawdown can be identified. The approximate dates are in chronological order: late 93 (I) and mid-97 (II). Reproduced from [218].

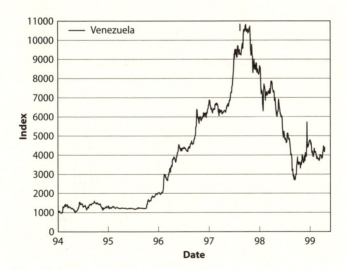

FIG. 8.6. The Venezuelan stock market index as a function of time. One bubble with a subsequent very large drawdown can be identified. The approximate date is mid-97 (I). Reproduced from [218].

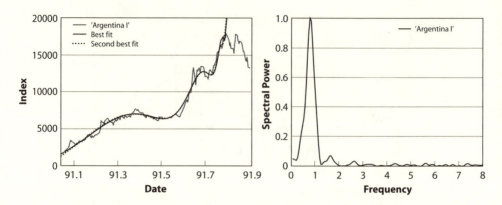

FIG. 8.7. Left panel: The Argentinian stock market bubble of 1991. See Table 8.1 for the main parameter values of the fits with equation (15). Right panel: Only the best fit is used in the Lomb periodogram. Reproduced from [218].

Figures 8.7–8.20 show the fits of the bubbles indicated in Figures 8.1–8.6 as well as the spectral Lomb periodogram of the difference between the indices and the pure power law, which quantifies the strength of the log-periodic component. The overall quality of these fits is good, and both the acceleration and the accelerating oscillations are rather well captured by the log-periodic power law formula. However, these fits do not have the same excellent quality as for those obtained for the major financial markets reported in chapter 7 as well as for the Russian stock market [221] (see below). A plausible interpretation is that these

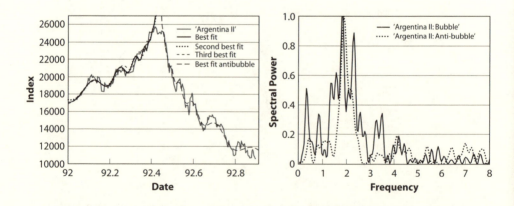

FIG. 8.8. Left panel: The Argentinian stock market bubble and antibubble of 1992. See Table 8.1. Right panel: Only the best fit is used in the Lomb periodograms. Reproduced from [218].

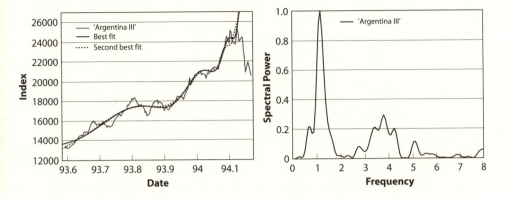

FIG. 8.9. Left panel: The Argentinian stock market bubble ending in 1994. See Table 8.1 for the main parameter values of the fit. Right panel: Only the best fit is used in the Lomb periodogram. Reproduced from [218].

are relatively small markets in terms of capitalization and number of investors, for which *finite size effects*, in the technical sense given in statistical physics [70], are expected and thus may blur out the signal with systematic distortions and unwanted fluctuations. See chapters 5 and 6 for a discussion.

In Table 8.1, the main parameters of the fits are given as well as the beginning and ending dates of the bubble and the size of the

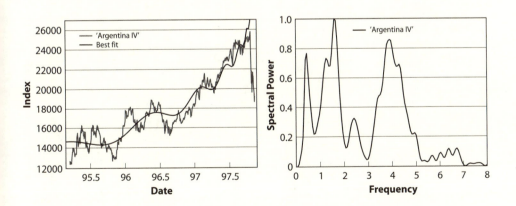

FIG. 8.10. Left panel: The Argentinian stock market bubble ending in 1997. See Table 8.1 for the main parameter values of the fit. Right panel: Only the best fit is used in the Lomb periodogram. Reproduced from [218].

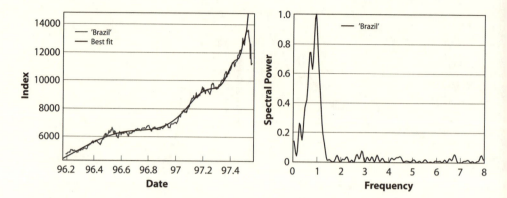

Fig. 8.11. Left panel: The Brazilian stock market bubble ending in 1997. See Table 8.1 for the main parameter values of the fit. Right panel: Only the best fit is used in the Lomb periodogram. Reproduced from [218].

crash/correction, defined as

$$\text{drop } \% = \frac{I(t_{max}) - I(t_{min})}{I(t_{max})}. \tag{16}$$

Here, t_{min} is defined as the date after the crash/correction where the index $I(t)$ achieves its lowest value before a clear novel market regime is observed. The duration $t_{max} - t_{min}$ of the crash/correction is found to

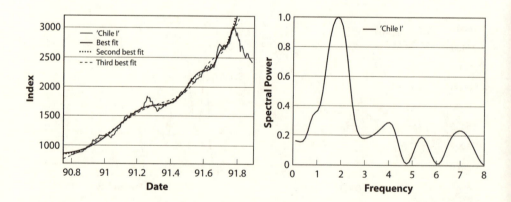

Fig. 8.12. Left panel: The Chilean bubble ending in 1991. See Table 8.1 for the main parameter values of the fit. Right panel: Only the best fit is used in the Lomb periodogram. Reproduced from [218].

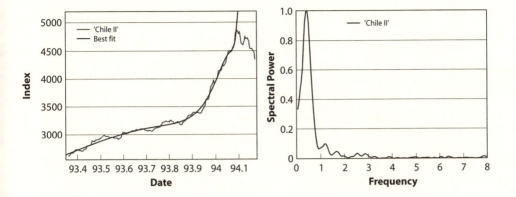

FIG. 8.13. Left panel: The Chilean bubble of 1993. See Table 8.1 for the main parameter values of the fit. Right panel: Lomb periodogram of the oscillatory component of the market price shown in the left panel. Reproduced from [218].

range from a few days (a crash) to a few months (a less abrupt change of regime).

Table 8.1 shows that the fluctuations in the parameter values m_2 and ω obtained for the eleven Latin-American crashes are considerable. The lower and upper values for the exponent m_2 are 0.12 and 0.62, respectively. For ω, the lower and upper values are 2.9 and 11.4, corresponding to a range of λ's in the interval 1.8–8.8. Removing the two largest values for λ reduces the fluctuations to 2.8 ± 1.1, which is still a much larger

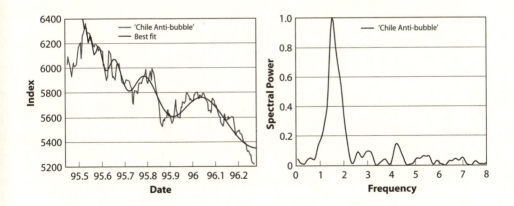

FIG. 8.14. Left panel: The Chilean antibubble beginning in 1995 fitted by the log-periodic power law with $m_2 = 0.36$, $t_c = 1,995.51$, and $\omega = 9.7$. Right panel: Lomb periodogram of the oscillatory component of the market price shown in the left panel. Reproduced from [218].

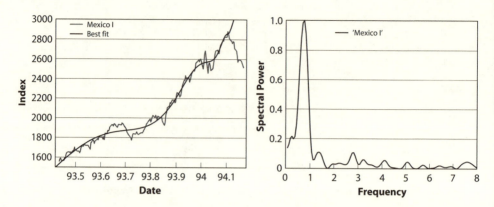

FIG. 8.15. Left panel: The Mexican bubble ending in 1994. See Table 8.1 for the main parameter values of the fit. Right panel: Lomb periodogram of the oscillatory component of the market price shown in the left panel. Reproduced from [218].

interval than the 2.5 ± 0.3 previously seen on major financial markets discussed in chapter 7. Three cases of antibubbles could be identified for the Latin-American markets analyzed here; see Figures 8.8, 8.14, and 8.20. Quite remarkably, the first and the last are preceded by a bubble, thus exhibiting a qualitative symmetry around comparable critical times t_c. Similar behavior will be shown later in this chapter for the Russian market in 1996–97 [221].

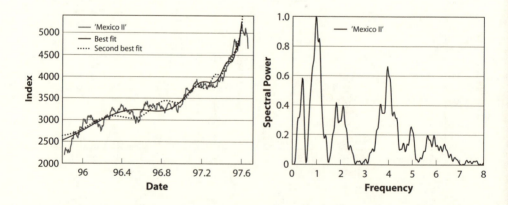

FIG. 8.16. Left panel: The Mexican bubble ending in 1997. See Table 8.1 for the main parameter values of the fit. Right panel: Only the best fit is used in the Lomb periodogram. Reproduced from [218].

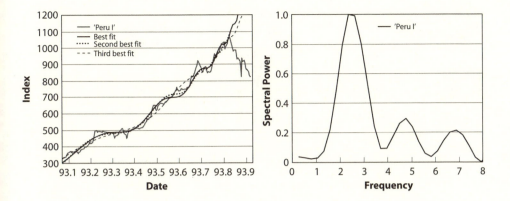

FIG. 8.17. Left panel: The Peruvian bubble of 1993. See Table 8.1 for the main parameter values of the fit. Right panel: Lomb periodogram of the oscillatory component of the market price shown in the left panel. Reproduced from [218].

ASIAN MARKETS

In Figures 8.21–8.25, the evolution of five Asian stock market indices (Indonesia, Korea, Malaysia, Philippines, and Thailand) is shown as a function of time from 1990 to February 1999. Two bubbles on the Indonesian stock market and one each on the Korean, the Malaysian, the Philippine, and the Thai markets are detected with subsequent crashes/decreases, as indicated in Figures 8.21–8.25.

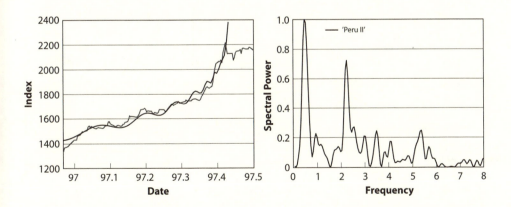

FIG. 8.18. Left panel: The Peruvian bubble ending in 1997. See Table 8.1 for the main parameter values of the fit. Right panel: Lomb periodogram of the oscillatory component of the market price shown in the left panel. Reproduced from [218].

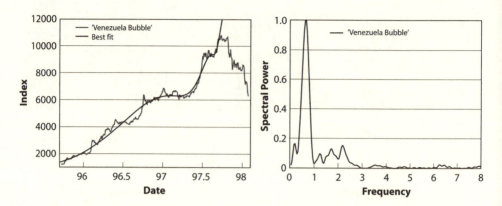

Fig. 8.19. Left panel: The Venezuelan bubble ending in 1997. See Table 8.1 for the main parameter values of the fit. Right panel: Lomb periodogram of the oscillatory component of the market price shown in the left panel. Reproduced from [218].

In Figures 8.26–8.31, the fits of the bubbles indicated in Figures 8.21–8.25 are given, as well as the spectral Lomb periodogram of the difference between the indices and the pure power law. Similarly to the Latin-American markets, somewhat larger fluctuations in the values for the exponent m_2 and the angular log-frequency ω can be observed compared to the major financial markets.

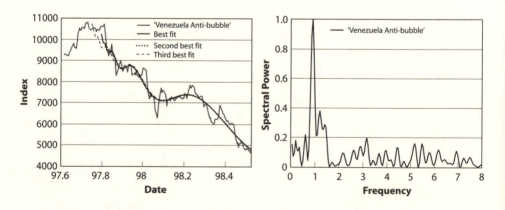

Fig. 8.20. Left panel: The Venezuelan antibubble starting in 1997 fitted by the log-periodic power law with $m_2 = 0.58, 0.35$, $t_c = 97.75, 97.75$ and $\omega = 6.7, 3.9$ (two best fits). Right panel: Only the best fit is used in the Lomb periodogram. Reproduced from [218].

TABLE 8.1

Crash and fit characteristics of the various speculative bubbles on the Latin-American market leading to a large drawdown in the 1990s

Stock market	t_c	t_{max}	t_{min}	% drop	m_2	ω	λ
Argentina I	91.80	91.80	91.90	26%	0.37	4.8	3.7
Argentina II	92.43	92.42	92.90	59%	0.22	11.4	1.7
Argentina III	94.13	94.13	94.30	30%	0.19	7.2	2.4
Argentina IV	97.89	97.81	97.87	27%	0.20	10.1	1.9
Brazil	97.58	97.52	97.55	18%	0.49	5.7	3.0
Chile I	91.77	91.75	91.94	22%	0.50	7.2	2.4
Chile II	94.10	94.09	94.26	20%	0.30	2.9	8.8
Mexico I	94.10	94.09	94.30	32%	0.12	4.6	3.9
Mexico II	97.93	97.80	97.82	21%	0.50	6.1	2.8
Peru I	93.84	93.83	93.88	22%	0.62	11.2	1.8
Peru II	97.43	97.42	98.15	30%	0.14	14.0	1.6
Venezuela	97.75	97.73	98.07	42%	0.35	3.9	5.0

t_c is the critical time predicted from the fit of the market index to equation (15) on page 232. When multiple fits exist, the fit with the smallest difference between t_c and t_{max} is chosen. Typically, this will be the best fit, but occasionally it is the second best fit. The other parameters m_2, ω, and λ of the fit are also shown. The fit is performed up to the time t_{max}, at which the market index achieved its highest maximum before the crash. The percentage drop is calculated from the total loss from t_{max} to t_{min}, where the market index achieved its lowest value as a consequence of the crash.

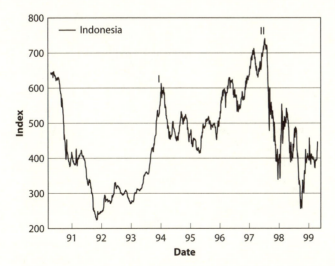

FIG. 8.21. The Indonesian stock market index as a function of time. Two bubbles with a subsequent very large drawdown can be identified. The approximate dates for the drawdowns are early 94 (I) and mid-97 (II). Reproduced from [218].

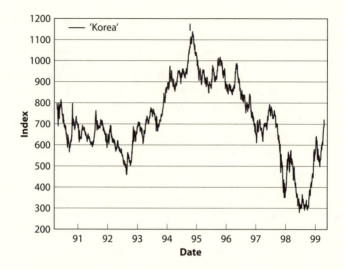

FIG. 8.22. The Korean stock market index as a function of time. One bubble with a subsequent very large drawdown can be identified culminating at the end of 1994. Reproduced from [218].

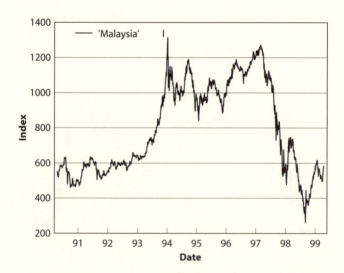

FIG. 8.23. The Malaysian stock market index as a function of time. One extended bubble with a subsequent very large drawdown occurring early in 1994 can be identified. Reproduced from [218].

FIG. 8.24. The Philippines stock market index as a function of time. One bubble with a subsequent very large drawdown occurring early in 1994 can be identified. Reproduced from [218].

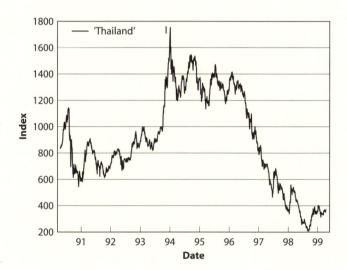

FIG. 8.25. The Thai stock market index as a function of time. One bubble with a subsequent very large drawdown occurring early in 1994 can be identified. Reproduced from [218].

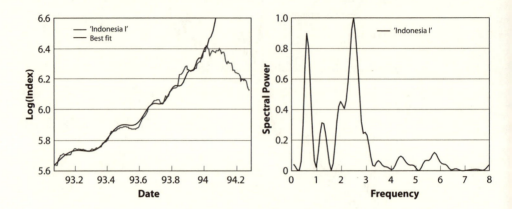

FIG. 8.26. Left panel: Indonesian stock market bubble ending in January 1994 with log-periodic power law fit with parameters $m_2 = 0.44$, $t_c = 1994.09$, and $\omega = 15.6$. Right panel: Lomb periodogram of the log-periodic oscillatory component of the price shown in the left panel. The abscissa is the log-frequency f defined as $f = \omega/2\pi$. Reproduced from [218].

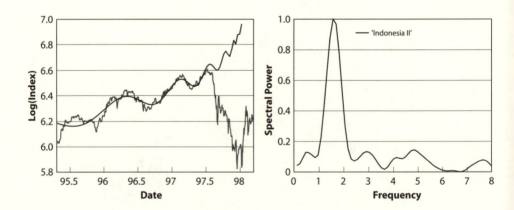

FIG. 8.27. Left panel: Indonesian stock market bubble ending in 1997 with log-periodic power law fit with parameters $m_2 = 0.23$, $t_c = 1998.05$, and $\omega = 10.1$. Right panel: Lomb periodogram of the log-periodic oscillatory component of the price shown in the left panel. Reproduced from [218].

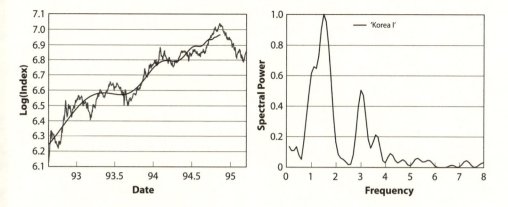

FIG. 8.28. Left panel: Korean stock market bubble ending in 1994 fitted by the log-periodic power law formula with main parameters $m_2 = 1.05$, $t_c = 1,994.87$, and $\omega = 8.15$. Right panel: Lomb periodogram of the log-periodic oscillatory component of the price shown in the left panel. Reproduced from [218].

A crisis is not always preceded by the log-periodic power law pattern. For instance, the log-periodic precursory behavior of the crisis of 1997 is clearly visible in the Asian markets only for Hong Kong and Indonesia. However, it is strongly present in the Argentinian, Brazilian, Mexican, Peruvian, and Venezuelan stock markets, as described in the previous

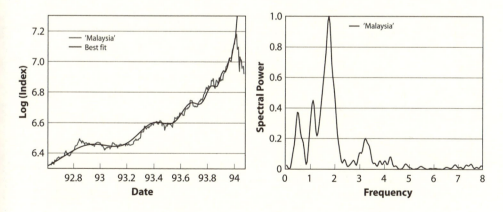

FIG. 8.29. Left panel: Malaysian stock market bubble ending with the crash of January 1994 fitted by the log-periodic power law formula with main parameters $m_2 = 0.24$, $t_c = 1,994.02$, and $\omega = 10.9$. Right panel: Lomb periodogram of the log-periodic oscillatory component of the price shown in the left panel. Reproduced from [218].

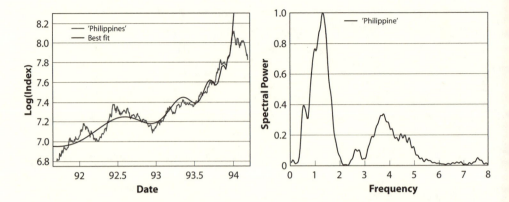

FIG. 8.30. Left panel: Philippine stock market bubble ending with the crash of January 1994 fitted by the log-periodic power law formula with main parameters $m_2 = 0.16$, $t_c = 1{,}994.02$, and $\omega = 8.2$. Right panel: Lomb periodogram of the log-periodic oscillatory component of the price shown in the left panel. Reproduced from [218].

section. The reason lies in the highly interconnected economic and market dynamics of these multiple countries. As a consequence, an adequate modeling requires a multidimensional approach. It can be shown that such multidimensional bubbles, which are extensions of the models of chapter 5, exhibit both synchronized and asynchronous crashes.

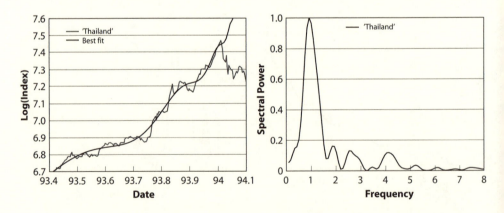

FIG. 8.31. Left panel: Thai stock market bubble ending with the crash of January 1994 fitted by the log-periodic power law formula with main parameters $m_2 = 0.48$, $t_c = 1{,}994.07$, and $\omega = 6.1$. Right panel: Lomb periodogram of the log-periodic oscillatory component of the price shown in the left panel. Reproduced from [218].

Recall that the 1997 crisis began in July in Southeast Asia when foreign bankers, investors, currency speculators, and market analysts lost confidence in Thailand's ability to cope with a deteriorating economic situation, including a rising trade deficit and a growing international debt that had reached 50% of gross domestic product. In the face of falling profits and mounting bankruptcies on the part of companies and financial institutions in Southeast Asia and South Korea, foreign investors dumped regional stocks and foreign lenders stopped rolling over their short-term loans. After depleting its hard currency reserves to counter speculative attacks on the baht, which had been pegged to the U.S. dollar, the Thai government had little choice but to adopt a managed float of its currency. The resultant plunge in the baht led to a series of forced currency devaluations that soon swept through Indonesia, Malaysia and the Philippines, and then spread to South Korea and, to a lesser extent, Singapore, Taiwan, and Japan.

The main causes of the 1997 Asian crisis involved the following ingredients: excessive reliance on foreign borrowing by business enterprises and banks and, especially, overdependence on short-term debt; overinvestment in real estate and excess manufacturing capacity; inadequate supervision of financial institutions and politically influenced allocations of credit to unsound companies; overly expansive fiscal and macroeconomic policies in several countries; and declining terms of trade for countries whose currencies have been pegged closely to the U.S. dollar, which had been strengthening against the Japanese yen.

Companies, banks, and governments unwisely piled up short-term debt on the unfounded assumption of never-ending growth. Since the mid-1990s these excesses were substantially facilitated by the easy availability of low-cost foreign capital, often at lower interest rates than domestically available credit. Such a credit distortion is an important mechanism helping the development of bubbles and their ensuing crises. In the period of the bubble growth, Asian government agencies have implicitly or explicitly guaranteed the credit risk of foreign loans, thus leading to lower interest rates compared to domestic loans (a smaller remuneration is required on foreign loans which bear less risk) [83]. As a consequence, there is an incentive to borrow from foreign sources on a great scale, even if savings are large: these foreign loans can be used in many different ways domestically to provide remunerations larger than the cost of the loan. Thus, heavy foreign borrowing and overinvestment in real estate are rational consequences when a particular currency is overvalued and cheap credit is available. This fuels lending to poorly managed local banks, a real estate boom while the economy has slowed down considerably, and consistent domestic real exchange appreciation while the currency becomes weaker.

Many of the excesses on the part of Asian governments, banks, and corporations would not have been possible except for the comparatively recent globalization of capital markets, including the relaxation of previous controls in Asian countries on international borrowing by banks and private corporations. By one estimate, 90% of international transactions were accounted for by trade before 1970, and only 10% by capital flows. Today, despite a vast increase in global trade, that ratio has been reversed, with 90% of transactions accounted for by financial flows not directly related to trade in goods and services [96]. Most of these capital flows are accounted for by highly volatile portfolio investment and short-term loans.

Vast outflows of investor funds from the strong U.S. economy in search of higher returns and the recycling of huge Japanese trade surpluses (Japanese lending to Asia alone rose from $40 billion in 1994 to $265 billion in 1997, i.e., 40% of their total foreign lending) contributed to a dangerous build-up of debt and excessive property development and manufacturing capacity. In testimony before the House Banking and Financial Services Committee, Federal Reserve Chairman Alan Greenspan noted with understatement that "In retrospect, it is clear that more investment monies flowed into these economies than could be profitably employed at modest risk" [96].

THE RUSSIAN STOCK MARKET

After the collapse of the Soviet Union in December 1991, following the highly symbolic destruction of the Berlin wall in 1990, the Russian stock market developed as an emerging market open to foreign investments. It is thus interesting to analyze whether the same patterns observed for essentially all emerging markets are also found there. As can be expected from the universal behavior of investors, the answer is positive. The post-crisis special 1999 report of the *St. Petersburg Times* is particularly instructive on the interplay between hypes of fast gains, for instance in Russian telecoms and other state-owned industries, and the psychology of political and financial risks permeating this chaotic period [412]. Indeed, in mid-1997, Russia benefitted from billions of dollars of International Monetary Fund (IMF), World Bank, and bilateral aid that initially permitted the Russian Central Bank to accumulate reserves at a pace of $1.5 billion a month. The Russian stock market

became the world's leading developing country stock market, as speculators chased stratospheric investment returns. This hid many problems
[408]: the early corruption of the nonmarket "privatization" to insiders;
the spread of organized crime; the impending complete collapse of the
Russian economy in 1998; the rise of weapons proliferation as a means
of generating hard currency; and the increasing estrangement of Russia
from the United States, essentially reversing the trends that existed in
1992. Russia's total economic collapse in 1998, following the bubble,
inflicted pain, suffering, and disruption on millions of Russians.

Due to the difficulty in getting a reliable measure of the Russian stock
market, it is useful to analyze four Russian stock market indices: The
Russian Trading System Interfax Index (IRTS), The Agence Skate Press
Moscow Times Index (ASPMT), The Agence Skate Press General Index
(ASPGEN), and The Credit Suisse First Boston Russia Index (ROSI).
The ROSI is generally considered the best of the four. As the Russian
stock market is highly volatile, companies go in and out of the indices
and it is difficult to maintain a representative stock market index. Using
four different indices mitigates this problem if the results turn out to be
robust.

In Figure 8.32, we see the ROSI fitted with equation (15) on page
232 in the interval [96.21 : 97.61]. The interval is chosen by identifying
the start of the bubble and the end represented by the date of the highest
value of the index before the crash, similarly to the major market crashes

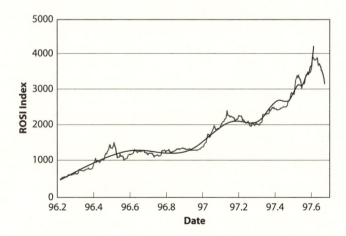

FIG. 8.32. The ROSI Index fitted with equation (15). The parameter values of the
fit with equation (15) are $A_2 \approx 4254$, $B_2 \approx -3166$, $B_2C \approx 246$, $m_2 \approx 0.40$, $t_c \approx$
97.61, $\phi \approx 0.44$, and $\omega \approx 7.7$. Reproduced from [221].

discussed previously. For all four indices, the same start-day and end-day can be identified to within a day.

As can be seen from Table 8.2, the nondimensional parameters m_2, ω, and λ as well as the predicted time of the crash t_c for the fit to the different indices agree very well except for the exponent m_2 obtained from the ASPGEN index. In fact, the value obtained for the preferred scaling ratio λ is fluctuating by no more than 5% for the four fits showing good numerical stability.

The origin of this bubble is well known. In 1996, large international investors (U.S., German, and Japanese) began to invest heavily in the Russian markets believing that the financial situation of Russia had finally stabilized. Nothing was further from the truth [206, 281], but the belief and hope in a new investment haven with large returns led to herding and bubble development. This means that the same herding that created the log-periodic bubbles on Wall Street (1929, 1987, 1998), Hong Kong (1997), and the Forex (1985, 1998), entered an emerging market and brought along the same log-periodic power law pattern characterizing the global markets. The fact that the consistent values of λ obtained for the four indices of the Russian market are comparable to that of the Wall Street, Hong Kong, and Forex crashes supports this interpretation. Furthermore, it supports the idea of the stock market as a self-organizing complex system of surprising robustness in one of its most dramatic behaviors.

Inspired by this clear evidence of log-periodic oscillations decorating the power law acceleration signaling a bubble in the Russian stock market, it is natural to search for possible log-periodic signatures in the antibubble that followed the log-periodic bubble described above.

As described in chapter 7, the decay of the Japanese Nikkei index starting January 1, 1990 and lasting until the present can be excellently modeled by a log-periodically decorated power law. In Figure 8.33, the ROSI index for the antibubble is fitted with equation (15), where t_c and t have been interchanged. The "symmetry" around t_c is rather striking.

It may seem odd to argue for the log-periodic power law precursory patterns while one can forcefully argue that the market is largely reflecting the vagaries of the Russian political institutions. For instance, in the antibubble case, February–April 1998 was a revival period for the market characterized by the returning of Western investors after the post-crash calm-down. This can be followed by studying the dynamics of the Russian external reserves. The timing of the return can be argued to be dictated by the risk policies of larger investors more than anything else. The next large drop of the Russian index in April 1998 originated

TABLE 8.2

Bubble	t_c	t_{max}	t_{min}	drop	m_2	ω	λ	A_2	B_2	B_2C	Var
ASPMT	97.61	97.61	97.67	17%	0.37	7.5	2.3	1280	−1025	59.5	907
IRTS	97.61	97.61	97.67	17%	0.39	7.6	2.3	633	−483	38.8	310
ROSI	97.61	97.61	97.67	20%	0.40	7.7	2.3	4254	−3166	246	12437
ASPGEN	97.62	97.60	97.67	8.9%	0.25	8.0	2.2	2715	−2321	72.1	1940
Anti-bubble	t_c	t_{max}	t_{min}	drop	m_2	ω	λ	A	B	C	Var
ROSI	97.72	97.77	98.52	74%	0.32	7.9	2.2	4922	−3449	472	59891
Nikkei (15)	89.99	90.00	92.63	63%	0.47	4.9	3.6	10.7	−0.54	−0.11	0.0029
Nikkei (Nonlinear log-periodic eq.)	89.97	90.00	95.51	63%	0.41	4.8	3.7	10.8	−0.70	−0.11	0.0600

t_c is the predicted time of the crash from the fit of the market index to equation (15). The other parameters of the fits to the preceding bubble are also given. The error Var is the variance between the data and the fit and has units $price^2$ except for the Nikkei, where the units are $[\log(price)]^2$. The fit to the bubble is performed up to the time at which the market index achieved its highest maximum before the crash. The parameters t_c, m_2, ω, and λ correspond to the fit with equation (15), where t_c and t have been interchanged. Here t_{max} and t_{min} represent the endpoints of the interval fitted.

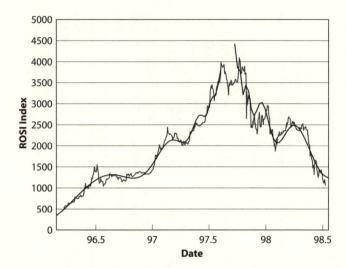

FIG. 8.33. Symmetric "bubble" and "antibubble": in addition to the ascending part of the ROSI Index, which is reproduced from Figure 8.32 with the same fit, we show the deflating part fitted with equation (15) by changing $t_c - t$ into $t - t_c$. The parameter values are $A_2 \approx 4922$, $B_2 \approx -3449$, $B_2C \approx 472$, $m_2 \approx 0.32$, $t_c \approx 97.72$, $\phi \approx 1.4$, and $\omega \approx 7.9$. Reproduced from [221].

by the decision of Mr. Yeltsin to sack Mr. Chernomyrdin's government, which destabilized the political situation and created uncertainty. Further political disturbance was introduced twice by the Duma when it rejected Mr. Yeltsin's candidates for the prime minister's office and put itself on the brink of dissolution.

The August 1998 crash, which had such a large effect on the markets of the rest of the world (see chapter 7), was often attributed to a devaluation of the ruble and to events on the Russian political scene. While we do not underestimate the effect of "news," we observe that markets are constantly bombarded by news, and it will always be possible to attribute the crash to a specific one, *after the fact*. In contrast, we view markets' reactions more often than not as reflecting their underlying stability (or instability). In the case of the August 1998 crash, the market was ripe for a major crisis and the "news" made it occur. If nothing had occurred on the Russian scene, other news would probably have triggered the event anyway [221], within a time scale of about a month, which seems to be the relevant lifetime of a market instability associated with the burst of a bubble.

We emphasize again that one must not mistake a systematically unstable situation for the specific historical action that triggered the instability.

Consider a ruler put vertically on a table. Being in an unstable position, the stick will fall in some direction and the specific air current or slight initial imperfection in the initial condition are of no real importance. What *is* important is the intrinsically unstable initial state of the stick. We argue that a similar situation applies for crashes. They occur because the market has reached a state of global instability. Of course, there will always be specific events that may be identified as triggers of market motions, but they simply reveal the instability rather than being its deep sources. Furthermore, political events must also be considered as indicators of the state of the dynamical system which includes the market. There is, in principle, no decoupling between the different events. Specifically, the 1997 Russian crash may have been triggered by the Asian crises, but it was to a large extent fueled by the collapse of a banking system, which in the course of the bubble had created an outstanding debt of $19.2 billion [281].

CORRELATIONS ACROSS MARKETS: ECONOMIC CONTAGION AND SYNCHRONIZATION OF BUBBLE COLLAPSE

It is well known that the October 1987 crash was an international event, occurring within a few days in all major stock markets worldwide [30]. It is also often noted that smaller western European stock markets as well as other markets around the world are influenced by dominating trends on the U.S. market.

There are counterexamples. An instance of a pronounced synchronization unrelated to a U.S. event is the rash of crashes/corrections on most emerging stock markets in early 1994. These crises occurred from January to June 1994 and concerned the currency markets (Mexico, South Africa, Turkey, Venezuela) and the stock markets (Chile, Hungary, India, Indonesia, Malaysia, Philippines, Poland, South Africa, Turkey, Venezuela, Germany, Hong Kong, Singapore, U.K.) [271]. In terms of the bubbles discussed above, the corresponding maxima of the stock markets occurred on 1994.13 (Argentina III), 1994.09 (Chile II), 1994.09 (Mexico I), Peru (1993.83), 1994.01 (Hong Kong II), 1994.01 (Indonesia I), 1994.01 (Malaysia), 1994.01 (Philippines), and 1994.01 (Thailand). The crises were particularly severe in Latin-American countries, the worst of which was felt in Mexico. The United States, helped by Canada and Europe, came to its rescue twice, first in April 1994 and then in early 1995 with a massive rescue fund of $50 billion [236].

Similarly, another rash of several crises evolved from the troubles in Thailand, which spilled over worldwide. This set of crises can be seen already contained in the death of the bubbles previously analyzed. The maximum of the bubbles was 1997.81 (Argentina IV), 1997.51 (Brazil), 1997.80 (Mexico II), 1997.42 (Peru II), 1997.73 (Venezuela), 1997.60 (Hong Kong III), and 1997.52 (Indonesia II). These maxima are followed by sharp corrections triggered by and following the abandonment by Thailand of the fixed-exchange rate system after strong attacks on its currency. When the Thailand domino fell, three other Asian countries immediately got caught up in the turmoil: the Philippines, Indonesia, and Malaysia. None had situations as bad as Thailand, but they all had currencies pegged to a strong dollar, so they were hit hard.

Such financial contagion is based on the same mechanisms as that leading to speculative bubbles. Investors' and lenders' moods follow regime shifts: when times are good, they think less about risk and focus on potential gain. When something bad happens, they start worrying about risk again, and the whole structure of hope and greed that had driven the market up collapses. Such sudden shifts in market psychology are nowadays amplified by the internationalization of investments: the same fund managers and bankers who got burned in Thailand also had money in Malaysia, Indonesia, and other emerging markets. In addition, they share much of the same information from similar channels. As a consequence, they often collectively reevaluate the risks they faced all over the globe particularly where economies and financial systems resemble Thailand's. In particular, the real economic adversity, the fundamentals, surfaces again with its interconnection across national borders by real economic ties.

There are also simple technical reasons for such cascades. The main players in emerging markets are the hedge funds and mutual funds. The former borrow money from banks to leverage their investments. If the value of these investments drops far enough, the bank calls in the loan and the hedge fund has to sell other securities to pay back the loan. The same mechanism can then operate on those securities that have been sold, as they also drop from the wave of selling. Mutual funds do not use leverage, but they have to keep a cushion of cash in case retail investors want their money back. They do it by selling securities from countries that have not been hit by the crisis yet.

The causes of currency crises such as the 1997–98 Asian currency crises, can probably be traced back to the interplay of countries' structural imbalances and weak policies with shifts in market expectations, both amplifying each other to provide the principal source of instability [332]. In other words, the crisis resulted from the interaction of structural weaknesses and volatile international capital markets, as well as inadequate supervision of the banking and financial sectors and the rapid transmission of the crisis across countries linked by trade and common credit sources. Using a panel of annual data for over 100 developing countries from 1971 through 1992, it is found that currency crashes tend to occur when output growth is low, the growth of domestic credit is high, and the level of foreign interest rates are high [141].

In the theoretical framework developed in chapter 5, it is possible to incorporate a feedback loop whereby prices affect the probability of a crash and vice versa. The higher the price, the higher the hazard rate or the increase rate of the crash probability. This process reflects the phenomenon of a self-fulfilling crisis, a concept that has recently gained wide attention, in particular with respect to the crises that occurred in seven countries (Mexico, Argentina, Thailand, South Korea, Indonesia, Malaysia, and Hong Kong) [245]. They have all experienced severe economic recessions, worse than anything the United States had seen since the 1930s. It is believed that this is due to the feedback process associated with the gain and loss of confidence from market investors. Playing the confidence game forced these countries into macroeconomic policies that exacerbated slumps instead of relieving them [245]. For instance, when the Asian crisis struck, countries were told to raise interest rates, not to cut them, in order to persuade some foreign investors to keep their money in place and thereby limit the exchange-rate plunge. In effect, countries were told to forget about macroeconomic policy; instead of trying to prevent or even alleviate the looming slumps in their economies, they were told to follow policies that would actually deepen those slumps, all this for fear of speculators. Thus, it is possible that a loss of confidence in a country can produce an economic crisis that justifies that loss of confidence: countries may be vulnerable to what economists call self-fulfilling speculative attacks. If investors believe that a crisis may occur in the absence of certain actions, they are surely right, because they themselves will generate that crisis. In other words, because their growth has been predicated on access to foreign capital, the Asian countries faced a kind of Hobson's choice between economic policies that reassure the financial markets and policies that might produce better results in the domestic economy and create less stress on social stability. One side is concerned with creating the right response in the financial markets. The other is more concerned with the impact of the IMF's reforms on the domestic economies and political stability of the affected countries.

In the same spirit, the Joint Economic Committee of the Congress of the United States recently released a new study finding a combination of perverse incentives as a key contributing factor to recent financial crises in Asian emerging economies [362]. The report, entitled "Financial Crises in Emerging Markets: Incentives and the IMF," finds that incentives to overextend credit (created by a combination of government guarantees, risky lending opportunities, and low levels of owner-contributed equity capital) often produce conditions resulting in financial crises. The impact of these incentives is similar to what troubled U.S. savings and loan and banking industries in the 1980s and early 1990s. The study demonstrates that recent IMF lending and prospects for its future lending serve to reinforce existing counterproductive incentives and create an additional layer of risk subsidies at the international level. The corresponding moral hazard problem is that investors take unreasonable risks because they know that the IMF will act as a lender of last resort. The imitation and herding mechanisms are thus unleashed without much restraint.

Another example of a pronounced synchronization between western European stock markets, unrelated to a U.S. event, comes from the period following the crashes/corrections on most emerging stock markets in early 1994. This time period is associated with sharply rising U.S. interest rates. Whereas the S&P 500 dipped less than 10% and recovered within a few months, the effect of the emergent market crisis was much more profound on smaller Western stock markets worldwide. The toll on a range of Western countries resembled that of a minirecession, with drops between 18% (London) and 31% (Hong Kong) over a period from about five months (London) to about thirteen months (Madrid), as summarized in Table 8.3. For each stock market, the decline in the logarithm of the index has been fitted with the log-periodic power law equation. In Figures 8.34–8.37, the decreases in all the stock markets analyzed can be quantified as log-periodic antibubbles.

From Table 8.3, we observe that the value of the preferred scaling ratio $\lambda = e^{2\pi/\omega}$ is very consistent with $\lambda \approx 2.0 \pm 0.3$. This is remarkable considering that these stock markets belong to three very different geographical regions of the world (Europe, Asia, and the Pacific). With respect to the value of the exponent m_2, the fluctuations are, as usual, much larger. However, excluding New Zealand and Hong Kong, we obtain $m_2 \approx 0.4 \pm 0.1$, which again is quite reasonable compared to the major financial markets [209]. The amplitudes of the log-periodic oscillations are remarkably similar with $B_2 C \approx 0.03 - 0.04$, except for London ($\approx 0.02$) and Milan ($\approx 0.05$).

TABLE 8.3
Characteristics of the fits of the 1994 antibubble on the Western financial markets plus Hong Kong following the emerging markets collapse in early 1994

Stock market	t_c	t_{max}	t_{min}	% drop	m_2	ω	λ
United Kingdom	94.08	94.09	94.48	18%	0.25	7.6	2.3
Hong Kong	94.09	94.09	94.53	31%	0.03	11	1.8
Australia	94.08	94.09	95.11	22%	0.46	8.0	2.2
New Zealand	94.08	94.09	94.95	23%	0.09	7.7	2.3
France	94.06	94.09	95.20	27%	0.51	12	1.7
Spain	94.08	94.09	95.23	27%	0.28	13	1.6
Italy	94.36	94.36	95.21	28%	0.35	9.2	2.0
Switzerland	94.08	94.08	94.54	22%	0.45	12	1.7

t_c is the critical time predicted from the fit of the market index to equation (15). When multiple fits exist, the fit with the smallest difference between t_c and t_{max} is chosen. Typically, this will be the best fit, but occasionally it is the second best fit. The other parameters m_2, ω, and λ of the fit are also shown. The fit is performed from the time t_{max}, at which the market index achieved its highest maximum before the decrease, to the time t_{min}, which is the time of the lowest point of the market before a shift in the trend. The percentage drop is calculated from the total loss from t_{max} to t_{min}. Reproduced from [218].

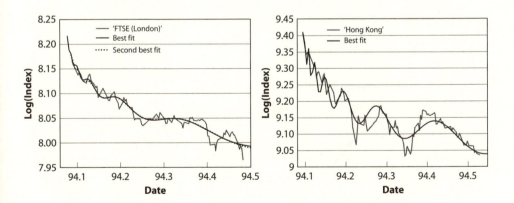

FIG. 8.34. Left panel: FTSE (London). The two lines are the best and the second best fit with equation (15). Right panel: Hong Kong. Note the small value for the exponent m_2 given in Table 8.3. This is presumably due to the undersampling of the data in the very first part of the data set. Reproduced from [218].

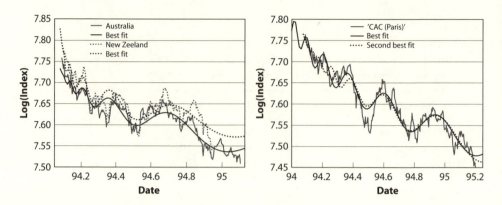

FIG. 8.35. Left panel: The Australian and New Zealand stock market indices. Right panel: The French CAC40. The two lines are the best and the second best fit with equation (15). Reproduced from [218].

IMPLICATIONS FOR MITIGATIONS OF CRISES

Several notable economists, J. E. Stiglitz and, recently, P. Krugman in particular as well as financier George Soros, have argued that markets should not be left completely alone. The mantra of the free-market purists requiring that markets should be totally free may not always be the best solution, because it overlooks two key problems: (1) the tendency of investors to develop strategies that may destabilize markets in a fundamental way and (2) the noninstantaneous adjustment of possible imbalance between countries. Soros has argued that real-world interna-

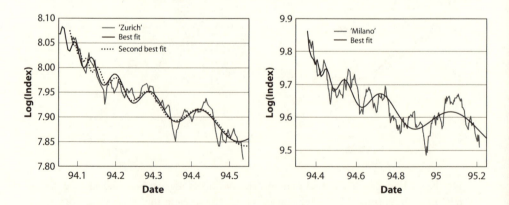

FIG. 8.36. Left panel: The Swiss stock market index. The lines are the two best fits with equation (15). Right panel: Italian stock market index. Reproduced from [218].

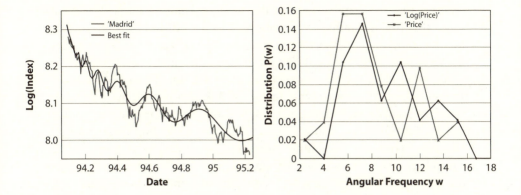

FIG. 8.37. Left panel: The Spanish (Madrid) stock market index. Right panel: Distribution of the log-periodic angular frequency ω for the fits of the previous antibubbles using the price (dashed line) and the logarithm of the price (continuous line). Reproduced from [218].

tional financial markets are inherently volatile and unstable since "market participants are trying to discount a future that is itself shaped by market expectations." This question is of course at the center of the debate on whether local and global markets are able to stabilize on their own after a crisis such as the Asian crisis, which started in 1997. In this example, to justify the intervention of the IMF, U.S. Treasury Secretary Rubin warned in January 1998 that global markets would not be able to stabilize in Asia on their own and that a strong role on the part of the IMF and other international institutions and governments was necessary, lest the crisis spread to other emerging markets in Latin America and Eastern Europe.

The following analogy with forest fires is useful to illustrate the nature of the problem: In many areas around the world, the dry season sees numerous large wildfires, sometimes with deaths of firefighters and other people and the destruction of many structures and large forests. It is widely accepted that livestock grazing, timber harvesting, and fire suppression over the past century have led to unnatural conditions, such as excessive biomass (too many trees without sufficient biodiversity and dead woody material) and altered species mix, in the pine forests of the western United States, in the Mediterranean countries, and elsewhere. These conditions make the forests more susceptible to drought, insect and disease epidemics, and other forest-wide catastrophes, and in particular large wildfires [167]. Interest in fuel management to reduce fire control costs and damage has been renewed due to the numerous, destructive wildfires that have spread across the western United States. The most frequently used technique of fuel management is fire suppression. Recent reviews comparing southern California on the one hand, where management has been active since 1900, and Baja California (northern Mexico) on the other hand, where management is essentially absent (a "let-burn" strategy) highlight a remarkable fact [301, 308]: only small and relatively moderate patches of fires occur in Baja California, compared to a wide distribution of fire sizes in southern California, including huge destructive fires. The selective elimination of small fires (those that can be controlled) in normal weather in southern California restricts large fires to extreme weather episodes, a process that encourages broad-scale high spread rates and intensities. It is found that the danger of fire suppression is the inevitable development of coarse-scale bush fuel patchiness and large-instance fires, in contradistinction with the natural self-organization of small patchiness in let-burn areas. Taken at face value, the let-burn theory seems paradoxically the correct strategy for maximizing the protection of property and of resources, at minimal cost.

This conclusion seems to be correct when the fuel is left on its own to self-organize in a way consistent with the dynamics of fires. In other words, the fuel-fire constitutes a complex nonlinear system with negative and positive feedbacks that may be close to optimal: more fuel favors fire; fires decrease the instantaneous level of fuel but may accelerate its future production; many small fires create natural barriers for the development and extension of large fires; fires produce rich nutrients in the soil; fires have other benefits, for instance, a few species, notably lodgepole pine and jack pine, are serotinous: their cones will only open and spread their seeds when they have been exposed to the heat of a wildfire. The possibility for complex nonlinear systems to find the "optimal" or to be close to the optimal solution has been stressed before in several contexts [97, 300, 404]. Let us mention, for instance, a model of fault networks interacting through the elastic deformation of the crust and rupturing during earthquakes, which finds that faults are the optimal geometrical structures accommodating the tectonic deformation: they result from a global mathematical optimization problem that the dynamics of the system solves in an analog computation, that is, by following its self-organizing dynamics (as opposed to digital computation performed by digital computers). One of the notable levels of organization is called self-organized criticality [26, 394] and has been applied in particular to explain forest fire distributions [280].

Baja California could be a representative of this self-organized regime of the fuel-fire complex left to itself, leading to many small fires and few big ones. Southern California could illustrate the situation where interference both in the production of fuel and also in its combustion by fires (by trying to stop fires) leads to a very broad distribution, with many small and moderate controlled fires and too many uncontrollable very large ones.

Where do stock markets stand in this picture? The proponents of the "let-alone" approach could get ammunition from the Baja/southern California comparison, but they would forget an essential element: stock markets and economies are more like southern California than Baja California. They are not isolated. Even if no government or regulation interferes, they are "forced" by many external economic, political, and climatic influences that impact them and on which they may also have some impact. If the example of the wildland fires has something to teach us, it is that we must incorporate into our understanding both the self-organizing dynamics of the fuel-fire complex as well as the different exogenous sources of randomness (weather and wind regimes, natural lightning strike distribution, etc.).

The question of whether some regulation could be useful is translated into whether southern California fires would be better left alone. Since the management approach fails to function fully satisfactorily, one may wonder whether the let-burn scenario would not be better. This has in fact been implemented in Yellowstone Park as the "let-burn" policy but was abandoned following the huge Yellowstone fires of 1988. Even the let-burn strategy may turn out to be unrealistic from a societal point-of-view because allowing a specific fire to burn down may lead to socially unbearable risks or emotional sensitivity, often discounted over a very short time horizon (as opposed to the long-term view of land management implicit in the let-burn strategy).

We suggest that the most momentous events in stock markets, the large financial crashes, can indeed be seen as the response of a self-organized system forced by a multitude of external factors in the presence of regulations. The external forcing is an essential element to consider and it modifies the perspective on the "let-alone" scenario. For instance, during the recent Asian crises, the IMF and the U.S. government considered that controls on the international flow of capital were counterproductive or impractical. J. E. Stiglitz, the chief economist of the IMF until 2000, has argued that in some cases it was justified to restrict short-term flows of money in and out of a developing economy and that industrialized countries sometimes pushed developing nations too fast to deregulate their financial systems. The challenge remains, as always, to encourage and work with countries that are ready and able to implement strong corrective actions and to cooperate toward finding the financial solutions best suited to the needs of the individual case and the broader functioning of the global financial system when difficulties arise [81].

In 1987, economist and Nobel prize winner James Tobin suggested two possible routes for reform of the international monetary system in order to control the world's speculative financial system and the "casino economy" [439]:

1. The first route consists in making currency transactions more costly to reduce capital mobility and speculative exchange rate pressures. This approach, which has become known as the "Tobin tax," has become most popular among many new economists in the form of an internationally uniform tax on all spot conversions of one currency into another, proportional to the size of the transaction. Conventional anti–Tobin tax arguments include that it will dry up liquidity, be impossible to collect, and invite offshore forex operations.

2. The second route consists in a greater world economic integration, implying eventual monetary union and a World Central Bank. This could take the form of an International Currency Unit administered by a World Central Bank and based on an equivalent "basket" of goods in each country. The value of these "baskets" in domestic currency would determine relative exchange rates, which would therefore depend on real domestic economic conditions rather than short-term currency movements [439]. Another form of integration could take the form of coordination of interest-rate policies among the United States, the European Union, and Japan, thereby enabling countries to pursue their own interest-rate objectives without destabilization from competing interest rate policies induced by foreign exchange rate transmissions and speculation. Another proposition is to establish a not-for-profit global foreign exchange facility (FXE) to perform foreign currency exchange transactions. It could be set up as a public utility, possibly franchised by a group of governments and the United Nations (UN) to offer a little competition to private forex banks, and in partnership with the UN, IMF, and BIS (Bank for International Settlements) [439]. Currency market "circuit-breaker fees," analogous to a similar fee on Wall Street, could also be used in conjunction with halts in trading (common on all stock exchanges) if a currency came under speculative attack. This would represent an important social innovation because it offers national governments and central banks a new domestic macromanagement tool to insulate their currencies and economies

from attack without having to raise interest rates and subject their citizens and businesses to a recession [439].

At present, it seems that the proposals and measures taken for combating risks inherent in the global financial system have no real chance for success.

CHAPTER 9

PREDICTION OF BUBBLES,

CRASHES, AND

ANTIBUBBLES

THE NATURE OF PREDICTIONS

The time arrow is inexorably projecting us towards the undetermined future. Predicting the future captures the imagination of all and is perhaps the greatest challenge. "Prophets" have historically terrified or inspired the masses by their visions of the future. Until recently, science has mostly avoided this question by focusing on another kind of prediction, that of novel phenomena such as the prediction by Einstein of the deviation of light by the sun's gravitation field, the prediction of the elusive particles called neutrinos by Pauli, and the prediction of the intermediate bosons within the electroweak theory by Weinberg and Salam, to cite just a few examples. Scientifically based predictions of the future, typically using computerized mathematical models, is a more recent phenomenon which is becoming pervasive in a modern society trying to control its environment and mitigate risks. In the real world, efforts to predict are frustrated because scientists have not nailed down all the physical workings and because a substantial measure of uncertainty remains in the characterization of the system, present and future. The result is a considerable range of uncertainty. Therefore, while mathematical modeling and computer simulations made

TREND REVERSALS?

reasonable predictions possible, they are always uncertain; results are, by definition, a model of reality, not reality itself.

Predictions of trend-reversals, changes of regime, or "ruptures" is extraordinarily difficult and unreliable in essentially all real-life domains of applications, such as economics, finance, weather, and climate. It is possibly the most difficult challenge and arguably the most interesting and useful. The two known strategies for modeling, namely analytical theories and brute-force numerical simulations of resulting large algebraic systems, are both unable to offer effective solutions for most concrete problems. Simulation studies of ruptures suffer from numerous sources of error, including model misspecifications and inaccurate numerical representation of the mathematical models, which are especially important for rare extreme events [232].

The following example borrowed from the field of climatology illustrates the point. In view of the growing concensus on global warming, it is instructive to remember that in the 1970s there was growing concern among scientists that the earth was cooling down and might enter a new ice-age similar to the previous little 1400–1800 ice age or even worse [61, 368, 429, 155]! Now that global warming is almost universally recognized, we can appreciate in hindsight how short-sighted was this "prediction." The situation is essentially the same nowadays: estimations of future modest changes of economic growth rates are rather good, but predictions of strong recessions and of crashes are utterly unreliable most of the time. For instance, the almost overwhelming concensus on the reality and magnitude of global warming is based on a clear trend over the twentieth century that has finally emerged above the uncertainty level. We stress that this concensus is not based on the prediction of a reversal or regime switch. In other words, scientists are good at recognizing a trend once already deeply immersed in it: we needed a century of data to extract a clear signal of a trend on global warming. In contrast, the techniques presently available to scientists are bad at predicting most changes of regime.

In economics and finance, the situation may be even worse, as the people's expectation of the future, their greediness, and their fear intertwine to construct the indeterminate future. On this question of prediction, Federal Reserve Chairman Alan Greenspan [177] said: "Learn everything you can, collect all the data, crunch all the numbers before making a prediction or a financial forecast. Even then, accept and understand that nobody can predict the future when people are involved. Human behavior hasn't changed; people are unpredictable. If you're wrong, correct your mistake and move on." The fuzziness resulting from the role of the expectation and discount of the future on present investor decisions may be captured by another famous quote from Greenspan before the Senate Banking Committee, June 20, 1995: "If I say something which you understand fully in this regard, I probably made a mistake."

Uncertainty in predictions is inherent in the complexity of the task. Nevertheless, predictions are useful. For instance, weather forecasts retain a large degree of uncertainty. Nevertheless, they are useful because they are better than pure chance once users know their shortcomings and take those into consideration. Predictions can be compared with observations and corrected for new improved predictions, a process called assimilation of data into the forecast. It is thus essential to use "error bars" and quantify uncertainties associated with any given prediction: hard numbers on predictions are misleading; only their probability distribution of success carries the relevant information. The flood of Grand Forks, ND, by the Red River of the North is a case in point. When it was rising to record levels in the spring of 1997, citizens and officials relied on scientists' predictions about how high the water would rise. A 49-foot forecast lulled the town into a false sense of security, because more precision was assigned to the forecast than was warranted. Actually, there was a wider range of probabilities; the river ultimately crested at 54 feet, forcing 50,000 people to abandon their homes fast. Had the full range of scenarios and probabilities been appreciated by the citizens, countermeasures could probably have been taken, allowing more people to preserve their possessions. The important message here is that the 49-foot forecast was not necessarily wrong. The possible deviations from this best guess were sorely missing. A probabilistic forecast allowing for at least two scenarios would have been much more instructive. It could have been phrased, for instance, as "there is a 50% probability that the river will crest at a level no larger than 49 foot and a 90% probability that the river will crest at a level no larger than 52 foot." Note that the first part of this statement carries the same information about the best guess (in the median sense) of the crest, while the second part provides a quantification of the uncertainty. With that, it is then possible in principle to weigh the cost of mitigation measures to respond to any given fluctuations from the best guess. The message here is to keep in mind the coexistence of several possible scenarios (and not of a best one or an average one) with their associated estimated likelihood.

The importance of working with several scenarios is illustrated in Figure 9.1, which represents the evolution of an ensemble of trajectories obeying a set of equations (now called the Lorenz system) proposed by the meteorologist Lorenz [270] as a parody of atmospheric dynamics.

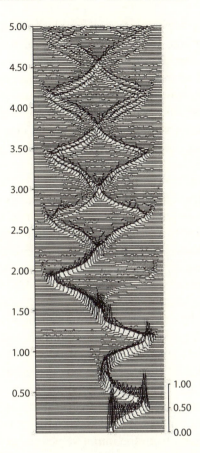

FIG. 9.1. Evolution of the probability density function represented in perspective for the variable v in a perfect ensemble under the Lorenz equations, which provide a simplified model of atmospheric dynamics. The variable v is plotted along the horizontal axis such that the center of symmetry is the initial condition. Time t is plotted along the vertical. As time increases (upwards), the initially sharp distribution at $t = 0$ decays and widens, but then shows true return of skill (at $t = 0.4$) by growing and sharpening. Later, the distribution bifurcates in two branches: the variable v is either largely above or below the initial value, while an average prediction predicts a value at the center, which in reality is almost never observed. This illustrates the fundamental limits of forecasts based on one representative value. Reproduced from [388].

Note that the study of this system was instrumental in the development of the theory of chaos in the 1970s and 1980s. The horizontal axis represents the proxy for a meteorological variable, say wind velocity v. The vertical axis is time, which goes from 0 to 5 in this plot. For each time, the third dimension in perspective shows the probability distribution of the wind velocity v: the maximum of the initial bell-shape distribution corresponds to the best initial guess of what is the present state of the system. The width of the bell-shape curve quantifies the initial uncertainty of our observations: we perform an initial measurement of the wind velocity and we know that any measure has some uncertainty, here quantified by the probability that the true initial condition deviates from the best estimate corresponding to the peak. To evolve this distribution, each of 4,096 initial conditions chosen at random is evolved according to the Lorenz equations of motion. Each of the 4,096 initial conditions thus defines a possible trajectory. At each time of interest, the value of v for each trajectory is measured and the aggregation of the 4,096 measures provides the statistics to construct the distribution of v. At early times, the distribution spreads out: notice that the peak decreases in amplitude and the distribution widens. This reflects an increasing uncertainty in the value of v after some time and thus a loss of prediction skill. Up to time $t = 1.5$, we observe alternative deterioration and improvement of prediction skill, as the distribution function widens and sharpens again periodically. This is the first rather nonintuitive lesson: regions of decreasing uncertainty may exist in a chaotic dynamics [388]. Increasing the forecast horizon does not always lead to a degradation of the prediction, in contrast to standard views on chaotic dynamics. Beyond $t = 1.5$, the distribution function bifurcates into two separate branches. At $t = 2.5$, it is clear that the velocity will have either a large positive or large negative deviation from the initial value, yet the optimal prediction made by averaging over all possible trajectories is close to the initial value. This is a fundamental shortcoming of such standard forecasting techniques for nonlinear systems [388]. It underscores the importance of thinking in terms of distributions or ensembles of scenarios, as opposed to a mean, an average, a median, or a representative forecast. At time $t = 2.5$, no single trajectory is a reliable representative of the complexity of the dynamics. Because of the structure of the dynamics in this example, as least two leading scenarios must be envisaged.

Thinking of predictions as intrinsically linked to their associated uncertainty is even more important when taking into account the combination of observational uncertainty and model error. Model error refers to the fact that, in general, we do not know the exact equations of the dynamics of the system we are interested in forecasting. We have only an approximate understanding of its complexity, and the models used for prediction by force capture only a part of all ingredients. This model error obviously places severe limits on what we can say about the future of a system. Working with an ensemble of trajectories for each model belonging to an ensemble of models is advocated as one way to mitigate these fundamental limitations [386].

We describe below how these ideas can be put into concrete form for the prediction of financial crashes. The different models will correspond to different implementations of the theory of critical points with log-periodic power laws. Different scenarios will be generated for each model by the different solutions obtained by the fitting procedure.

HOW TO DEVELOP AND INTERPRET STATISTICAL TESTS OF LOG-PERIODICITY

Before studying the issue of prediction, the question of a possible selection bias of the fitted financial time series presented in chapters 7 and 8 must be addressed. By selecting time windows on the basis of the existence of (1) a change of regime and acceleration of the market price and of (2) a crash or large correction at their end, we may have pruned the data so that, by chance alone, the fits with the log-periodic power law formula may have been qualified. This issue has to be raised each time a pattern is proposed as an indicator with some predictive skill. There is a fundamental mathematical reason for this: the English mathematician F. P. Ramsey proved that complete disorder is an impossibility [173, 172]. Every large set of numbers, such as an ensemble of financial price series or points or objects, necessarily contains highly regular patterns. For instance, the night sky appears to be filled with constellations in the shape of straight lines, rectangles and pentagons, which bear suggestive names such as the lion, the bull, or the scorpion, given by ancient astronomers. Could it be that such geometric patterns arise from unknown forces in the cosmos? In 1928, Ramsey proved that such patterns are implicit in any large structure. Given enough stars, one can always find a group that very nearly forms a particular pattern. Given a sufficiently long series of numbers, you will find any pattern in it, such as your birthdate or any other number of special interest to you. Intuitively, the argument underlying this theorem is that if it was not the case that any pattern could be approximately found in a random set, this set would not be really random. Randomness is such that any pattern can occur.

The relevant question is, then, to figure out just how many stars, numbers, or figures are required to guarantee a certain desired pattern. In other words, how probable is it to observe a desired substructure in a given set? Answering this question is the domain of statistics and its economic application, econometrics. If one can show that the number of stars needed to obtain a particular pattern is not much larger than the observed number, we can ask with reason whether this particular pattern may not result from chance alone in this particular set. This is the essence of the method of statistical hypothesis testing which constructs so-called "statistical confidence levels": if the confidence level of a phenomenon is, say, 99%, this means that there is only a remote probability of 1 in 100 that the phenomenon in question is due to chance.

In the present context, we first refer to the computer experiment summarized in the section titled "The Slow Crash of 1962 Ending the 'Tronics' Boom" of chapter 7, in which fifty 400-week intervals in the period 1910–1996 of the DJIA were chosen at random [209]. This experiment shows that fits, which in terms of the fitting parameters correspond to the three crashes of 1929, 1962, and 1987, are not likely to occur "accidentally." Feigenbaum and Freund have also looked at randomly selected time widows in the real data and generally found no evidence of log-periodicity in these windows unless they were looking at a time period in which a crash was imminent [128]. More recently, Feigenbaum has examined the first differences for the logarithm of the S&P 500 from 1980 to 1987 and finds that he cannot reject the log-periodic component at the 95% confidence level [127]: in plain words, this means that the probability that the log-periodic component results from chance is about or less than one in twenty.

To test furthermore the solidity of the advanced log-periodic hypothesis, Johansen, Ledoit, and I [209] tested whether the null hypothesis that a standard statistical model of financial markets, called the GARCH(1,1) model with Student-distributed noise, could "explain" the presence of log-periodicity. In the 1,000 surrogate data sets of length 400 weeks generated using this GARCH(1,1) model with Student-distributed noise and analyzed as for the real crashes, only two 400-week windows qualified. This result corresponds to a confidence level of 99.8% for rejecting the hypothesis that GARCH(1,1) with Student-distributed noise can generate meaningful log-periodicity. There is no reference to a crash; the question is solely to test if log-periodicity of the strength observed before the 1929 and 1987 crashes can be generated by one of the standard benchmarks of financial time series used intensively by both academics and practitioners. If in addition, we add that the two spells of significant log-periodicity generated in the simulations using GARCH(1,1) with Student-distributed noise were not followed by crashes, then the case is even stronger for concluding that real markets exhibit behaviors that are dramatically different from the one predicted by one of the most fundamental benchmarks of the industry. Indeed, the frequency of crashes in the Monte Carlo simulations was much smaller than the frequency of crashes in real data: if one of the most frequently used benchmarks of the industry is incapable of reproducing the observed frequency of crashes, this indeed means that there is something to explain that may require new concepts and methods.

We should stress, however, that no truth is ever demonstrated in science; the only thing that can be done is to construct models and reject them at a given level of statistical significance. Those models that are not rejected when pitted against more and more data progressively acquire the status of theory (think, for instance, of quantum mechanics, which is repeatedly put to tests). In the present context, it is clear that, in a purist sense, we shall never be able to "prove" the existence of a log-periodicity genuinely associated with specific market mechanisms. The next best thing we can do is to take one by one the best benchmarks of the industry and test them to see if they can generate the same structures as we document. It would, of course, be interesting to test more sophisticated models in the same way as for the GARCH(1,1) model with Student-distributed noise. However, we caution that rejecting one model after another will never prove that log-periodicity exists. This is outside the realm of statistical and econometric analysis. If more and more models are unable to "explain" the observed log-periodicity, this means, however, that log-periodicity is an important fact that needs to be understood.

Another worry is that integrated processes, like a random walk which sums up random innovations over time, can generate log-periodic patterns from pure chance. Actually, Huang et al. [203] specifically tested the following problem: Under what circumstances can an integrated process produce spurious log-periodicity? The answer obtained after lengthy and thorough Monte Carlo tests is twofold. (1) For approximately regularly sampled time series, as in the case of the financial time series, taking the integral of a noisy log-periodic function *destroys* the log-periodic signal! (2) Only when sampling rates increase exponentially or as a power law of $t_c - t$ can spurious log-periodicity in integrated processes be observed. The name "Monte Carlo" refers to the notion that random (as in a casino) series with prescribed properties are used to test the probability that a given pattern can occur by chance: if this probability is very small, the corresponding pattern is probably not due to chance. The consequence is that it may result from a causal set of effects that can be understood and used.

Ultimately, only forward predictions can demonstrate the usefulness of a theory (see the section below titled "Forward Predictions"), thus only time will tell. However, as we have suggested by the many examples reported in chapters 7 and 8 and from the discussion offered below, the analysis points to an interesting predictive potential. However, a fundamental question concerns the use of a reliable crash prediction scheme, if any. Assume that a crash prediction is issued stating that a crash of an amplitude between 20% and 30% will occur between one and two months from now. At least three different scenarios are possible [217]:

- Nobody believes the prediction, which was then futile, and, assuming that the prediction was correct, the market crashes. One may consider this as a victory for the "predictors" but as we have experienced in relation to our quantitative prediction of the change in regime of the Nikkei index [213, 216], this would only be considered by some critics just another "lucky one" without any statistical significance (see the section below entitled "Estimation of the Statistical Significance of the Forward Predictions" [216] and below for an alternative Bayesian approach).

- Everybody believes the warning, which causes panic, and the market crashes as consequence. The prediction hence seems self-fulfilling and the success is attributed more to the panic effect than to real predictive power.

- Sufficiently many investors believe that the prediction *may* be correct, investors make reasonable adjustments, and the steam goes off the bubble. The prediction hence disproves itself.

None of these scenarios is attractive. In the first two, the crash is not avoided, and in the last scenario the prediction disproves itself and as a consequence the theory looks unreliable. This seems to be the inescapable lot of scientific investigations of systems with learning and reflective abilities, in contrast with the usual inanimate and unchanging physical laws of nature. Furthermore, this touches upon the key problem of scientific responsibility. Naturally, scientists have a responsibility to publish their findings. However, when it comes to the practical implementation of those findings in society, the question becomes considerably more complex, as history has taught us. We believe, however, that increased awareness of the potential for market instabilities, offered in particular by our approach, will help in constructing a more stable and efficient stock market.

FIRST GUIDELINES FOR PREDICTION

Time is converted into decimal year units: for nonleap years, 365 days = 1.00 year, which leads to 1 day = 0.00274 years. Thus 0.01 year = 3.65 days and 0.1 year = 36.5 days or 5 weeks. For example, October 19, 1987 corresponds to 87.800.

WHAT IS THE PREDICTIVE POWER OF EQUATION (15) ON PAGE 232?

Table 9.1 presents a summary of equation (15)'s predictive power for the 1929, 1987, and 1998 crashes on Wall Street and the 1987, 1994, and 1997 crashes on the Hong Kong stock exchange as well as the collapse of the U.S. dollar in 1985 and the crash on the Nasdaq in April 2000, all cases previously discussed in chapter 7.

We see that, in all nine cases, the market crash started at a time between the date of the last point and the predicted t_c. And with the exception of the October 1929 crash, in all cases the market ended its decline less than approximately one month from the predicted t_c. These results suggest that predictions of crashes with equation (15) is indeed possible.

TABLE 9.1

Crash	t_c	t_{max}	t_{min}	% drop	m_2	ω	λ
1929 (DJ)	30.22	29.65	29.87	47%	0.45	7.9	2.2
1985 (DM)	85.20	85.15	85.30	14%	0.28	6.0	2.8
1985 (CHF)	85.19	85.18	85.30	15%	0.36	5.2	3.4
1987 (S&P)	87.74	87.65	87.80	30%	0.33	7.4	2.3
1987 (HK)	87.84	87.75	87.85	50%	0.29	5.6	3.1
1994 (HK)	94.02	94.01	94.04	17%	0.12	6.3	2.7
1997 (HK)	97.74	97.60	97.82	42%	0.34	7.5	2.3
1998 (S&P)	98.72	98.55	98.67	19.4%	0.60	6.4	2.7
1999 (IBM)	99.56	99.53	99.81	34%	0.24	5.2	3.4
2000 (P&G)	00.04	00.04	00.19	54%	0.35	6.6	2.6
2000 (Nasdaq)	00.34	00.22	00.29	37%	0.27	7.0	2.4

t_c is the critical time predicted from the fit of the financial time series to the equation (15). The other parameters m_2, ω, and λ of the fit are also shown. The fit is performed up to the time t_{max} at which the market index achieved its highest maximum before the crash. t_{min} is the time of the lowest point of the market before rebound. The percentage drop is calculated from the total loss from t_{max} to t_{min}. Several of these crashes have also been listed in Table 7.2. Reproduced from [218].

How Long Prior to a Crash Can One Identify the Log-Periodic Signatures?

Not only would one like to predict future crashes, but it is important to further test how robust the results are. Obviously, if the log-periodic structure of the data is purely accidental, then the parameter values obtained should depend heavily on the size of the time interval used in the fitting. The systematic testing procedure reported in [209] using a second-order expansion of the crash hazard rate [397] and a time interval of eight years prior to the two crashes of 1929 and 1987 consists in the following.

For each of these two crashes, the time interval used in the fitting has been truncated by removing points and relaunching the fitting procedure for each truncated data set. Specifically, the logarithm of the S&P 500 was truncated down to an end-date of approximately 1985 and fitted. Then, 0.16 years was added consecutively and the fitting was relaunched until the full time interval was recovered. Table 9.2 reports the number of minima obtained for the different time intervals. This number is to some extent rather arbitrary since it naturally depends on the number of points used in the preliminary scan as well as the size of the time interval used for t_c. Specifically, 40,000 points were used and the search on t_c was chosen in the interval from 0.1 years from the last data point used to 3 years forward. What is more interesting is the number of solutions of these fits (each "solution" corresponds to a minimum of the error between the data and the theoretical function) with reasonable parameters referred to as "physical" especially for the values of t_c, m_2, ω, and Δ_t, where Δ_t is an additional time parameter quantifying the size of the critical region. The general picture to be extracted from this Table 9.2 is that a year or more before the crash, the data is not sufficient to give any conclusive results at all. This point corresponds to the end of the fourth oscillation. Approximately a year before the crash, the fit begins to lock in on the date of the crash with increasing precision. In fact, in four of the last five time intervals, a fit exists with a t_c, which differs from the true date of the crash by only a few weeks.

In order to better investigate this, Table 9.3 shows the corresponding parameter values for the other three pertinent variables m_2, ω, and Δ_t. The scenario resembles that for t_c. This suggests that the fitting procedure of [397] is rather robust up to approximately one year prior to the crash. However, if one wants to actually predict the time of the crash, a major obstacle is the fact that the fitting procedure produces several possible dates for the date of the crash, even for the last data set.

TABLE 9.2

Number of minima obtained by fitting different truncated versions of the S&P 500 time series shown in Figure 7.2 to predict the October 1987 crash using the procedure described in the text. Note that the predicted times for the crash are progressively postponed as the end-date increases. However, the correct time is identified early (in hindsight) and is recurrent in the set of solutions as the end-date increases. Reproduced from [397]

End-date	Total # minima	"Physical" minima	t_c of "physical" minima
85.00	33	1	86.52
85.14	25	4	4 in [86.7 : 86.8]
85.30	26	7	5 in [86.5 : 87.0], 2 in [87.4 : 87.6]
85.46	29	8	7 in [86.6 : 86.9],1 with 87.22
85.62	26	13	12 in [86.8 : 87.1],1 with 87.65
85.78	23	7	87.48, 5 in [87.0 − 87.25], 87.68
85.93	17	4	87.25, 87.01, 87.34, 86.80
86.09	18	4	87.29, 87.01, 86, 98, 87.23
86.26	28	7	5 in [87.2 : 87.4], 86.93, 86.91,
86.41	24	4	87.26, 87.36, 87.87, 87.48
86.57	20	2	87.67, 87.34
86.73	28	7	4 in [86.8 : 87.0], 87.37, 87.79, 87.89
86.88	22	1	87.79
87.04	18	2	87.68, 88.35
87.20	15	2	87.79, 88.03
87.36	15	2	88.19, 88.30
87.52	14	3	88.49, 87.92, 88.10
87.65	15	3	87.81, 88.08, 88.04

TABLE 9.3

End-date	t_c	m_2	ω	Δ_t
86.88	87.79	0.66	5.4	7.8
87.04	87.68, 88.35	0.61, 0.77	4.1, 13.6	12.3, 10.2
87.20	87.79, 88.03	0.76, 0.77	9.4, 11.0	10.0, 9.6
87.36	88.19, 88.30	0.66, 0.79	7.3, 12.2	7.9, 8.1
87.52	88.49, 87.92, 88.10	0.51, 0.71, 0.65	12.3, 9.6, 10.3	10.2, 9.8, 9.8
87.65	87.81, 88.08, 88.04	0.68, 0.69, 0.67	8.9, 10.4, 10.1	10.8, 9.7, 10.2

For the last five time intervals shown in Table 9.2, the corresponding parameter values for the other three variables m_2, ω, Δ_t are shown. Reproduced from [397].

TABLE 9.4

The average of the values listed in Table 9.3. Reproduced from [397].

End-date	t_c	m_2	ω	Δ_t
86.88	87.79	0.66	5.4	7.8
87.04	88.02	0.69	8.6	11.3
87.20	87.91	0.77	10.20	9.8
87.36	88.25	0.73	9.6	8.0
87.52	88.17	0.62	10.7	9.9
87.65	87.98	0.68	9.8	10.2

As a naive solution to this problem, Table 9.4 shows the average of the different minima for t_c, m_2, ω, and Δ_t. The values for m_2, ω, and Δ_t are within 20% of those for the best prediction, but the prediction for t_c has not improved significantly. The reason for this is that the fit in general "overshoots" the true day of the crash. This overshooting is consistent with the rational expectation models of a bubble and crash described in chapter 5. Indeed, the critical time t_c is *not* the time of the crash but only its most probable value, that is, the time for which the asymmetric distribution of the possible times of the crash peaks. The occurrence of the crash is a biased random phenomenon which occurs with a probability that increases as time approaches t_c. Thus, we expect that fits will give values of t_c which are in general close to but *systematically* later than the real time of the crash: the critical time t_c is included in the log-periodic power law structure of the bubble, whereas the crash is randomly triggered with a biased probability increasing strongly close to t_c.

The same procedure was used on the logarithm of the Dow Jones index prior to the crash of 1929 shown in Figure 7.7 and the results are shown in Tables 9.5, 9.6, and 9.7. One has to wait until approximately four months before the crash before the fit locks in on the date of the crash, but from that point the picture is the same as for the crash in 1987. The reason for the fact that the fit "locks-in" at a later time for the 1929 is obviously the difference in the transition time Δ_t for the two crashes which means that the index prior to the crash of 1929 exhibits fewer distinct oscillations.

Feigenbaum [127] has recently confirmed that, for the October 1987 crash, "excluding the last year of data, the log-periodic component is no longer statistically significant." This should not be a surprise for specialists of critical phenomena, and it is naive to expect otherwise. The

TABLE 9.5
Same as Table 9.2 for the October 1929 crash. Reproduced from [397].

End-date	Total # minima	"Physical" minima	t_c of "physical" minima
27.37	12	1	31.08
27.56	14	2	30.44, 30.85
27.75	24	1	30.34
27.94	21	1	31.37
28.13	21	4	29.85, 30.75, 30.72, 30.50
28.35	23	4	30.29, 30.47, 30.50, 36.50
28.52	18	1	31.3
28.70	18	1	31.02
28.90	16	4	30.40, 30.72, 31.07, 30.94
29.09	19	2	30.52, 30.35
29.28	33	1	30.61
29.47	24	3	29.91, 30.1, 29.82
29.67	23	1	29.87

TABLE 9.6
Same as Table 9.3 for the October 1929 crash. Reproduced from [397].

End-date	t_c	m_2	ω	Δ_t
28.90	30.40, 30.72, 31.07, 30.94	0.60, 0.70, 0.70, 0.53	7.0, 7.6, 10.2, 13.7	12.3, 9.5, 9.0, 11.6
29.09	30.52, 30.35	0.54, 0.62	11.0, 7.8	12.6, 10.2
29.28	30.61	0.63	9.5	9.5
29.47	29.91, 30.1, 29.82	0.60, 0.67, 0.69	5.8, 6.2, 4.5	15.9, 11.0, 10.9
29.67	29.87	0.61	5.4	15.0

TABLE 9.7
The average of the values listed in Table 9.6. Reproduced from [397].

End-date	t_c	m_2	ω	Δ_t
28.90	30.78	0.63	9.6	10.6
29.09	30.44	0.58	9.4	11.4
29.28	30.61	0.63	9.5	9.5
29.47	29.94	0.65	5.5	12.6
29.67	29.87	0.61	5.4	15.0

determination of a power law $B_2(t_c - t)^{m_2}$ is indeed very sensitive to noise and to the distance from t_c of the data used in the estimation. This is well known by experimentalists and numerical scientists working on critical phenomena who have invested considerable efforts in developing reliable experiments that could probe the system as closely as possible to the critical point t_c, in order to get reliable estimations of t_c and m_2. A typical rule of thumb is that an error of less than 1% in the determination of t_c can lead to tenth-of-a-percent errors in the estimation of the critical exponent m_2. While the situation is improved by the addition of the log-periodic component because the fit can lock in on the oscillations, the problem remains qualitatively the same. Being one year before the critical time corresponds to the situation in which a worker on critical phenomena would be trying to get a reliable estimation of t_c and m_2 by trashing the last 15% of the data, which are of course the most relevant—an almost impossible task in general.

We thus caution the reader that jumping into the prediction game may be hazardous and misleading: one deals with a delicate optimization problem that requires extensive backward and forward testing. Furthermore, the formulas discussed here are only "first-order" approximations, and novel improved methods have been developed that are not published. Finally, one must never forget that the crash has to remain in part a random event in order to exist! This is according to the rational expectation models described in chapter 5.

A HIERARCHY OF PREDICTION SCHEMES

THE SIMPLE POWER LAW

The concept that a crash is associated with a critical point suggests fitting a simple power law

$$\log[p(t)] = A + B(t_c - t)^\beta \tag{17}$$

to the price or the logarithm of the price. A fit of the logarithm of the S&P 500 index before the October 87 crash gives $t_c = 87.65$, $\beta = 0.72$, $\chi^2 = 107$, $A = 327$, and $B = -79$ when using data from 1985.7 to 1987.65. Note that the value of t_c obtained from the fit is completely dominated by the last values used in the fit. The reason is that the information on t_c is contained essentially in or is dominated by the

acceleration in the last points. In contrast, the log-periodic structures contain the information on t_c in their oscillations that develop much before
t_c.

All attempts to use this formula (17) for prediction have been unsuccessful, because it is virtually impossible to distinguish this law (17)
from a noncritical exponential growth when data are noisy. A smooth
increase like (17) is well known to constrain very poorly the time t_c in
noisy time series. This is why all our empirical efforts were focused on
the log-periodic formulas.

The "Linear" Log-Periodic Formula

We rewrite here the equation (15) that was used before for fitting the
price of a financial time series in terms of the logarithm of the price:

$$\log[p(t)] = A + B(t_c - t)^\beta \left\{ 1 + C \cos[\omega \log(t_c - t) + \phi] \right\}. \quad (18)$$

It turns out that, for time scales of about two years or less, the amplitude
of the price variation in such periods is not large enough for detecting a
significant difference between the goodness-of-fit of the fits of $p(t)$ and
of $\log[p(t)]$.

For practical implementation of the fit of such a formula to a financial
time series, it is important to stress that the variables A, B, and C enter
linearly once the other four variables t_c, β, ω, and ϕ are fixed. The
best procedure is to determine them analytically through so-called least
squares minimization and to plug them into the objective function to
derive a *concentrated* objective function that depends only on t_c, β, ω,
and ϕ.

Due to the noisy nature of the data and the fact that we are performing
a highly nonlinear four-parameter fit, there are several local minima. The
best strategy is to perform a first grid search and then start an optimizer
(for instance the Levenberg–Marquardt) from all the local optima of the
grid. The best of the resulting convergence points is taken as the global
optimum.

A priori restrictions are imposed on parameter values, which ensure
that they are plausible. The exponent β needs to be between 0 and 1
for the price to accelerate and to remain finite. The more stringent criterion $0.2 < \beta < 0.8$ has been found useful to avoid the pathologies
associated with the endpoints 0 and 1 of the interval. Recall that the
angular log-periodic frequency ω determines the ratio λ of successive

time intervals between local maxima through the following relationship: $\lambda = e^{2\pi/\omega}$. Experience across many disciplines and some theoretical arguments [392] suggest that this ratio λ should typically lie in the range 2–3. In practice, we have often used the constraint $5 < \omega < 15$, which corresponds to $1.5 < \lambda < 3.5$. Obviously, t_c must be greater than the last date in the sample data being fitted. The phase ϕ cannot be meaningfully restricted.

THE "NONLINEAR" LOG-PERIODIC FORMULA

The nonlinear log-periodic formula used to fit the longest financial time series discussed in chapters 7 and 8 is [397]

$$\log[p(t)] = A + B \frac{(t_c - t)^{\beta}}{\sqrt{1 + \left(\frac{t_c - t}{\Delta_t}\right)^{2\beta}}} \left\{ 1 + C \cos\left[\omega \log(t_c - t) \right.\right.$$

$$\left.\left. + \frac{\Delta_\omega}{2\beta} \log\left(1 + \left(\frac{t_c - t}{\Delta_t}\right)^{2\beta}\right)\right] + \phi\right\}. \quad (19)$$

Using the same least-squares method as for the linear log-periodic formula allows one to concentrate away the linear variables A, B, and C and form an objective function depending only on t_c, β, ω, and ϕ as before, with the addition of two parameters Δ_t and Δ_ω. Since Δ_t is a transition time between two regimes, this transition should be observed in the data set, and therefore we require it to be between 1 and 20 years. As before, the nonlinearity of the objective function creates multiple local minima, and the preliminary grid search is used to find starting points for the optimizer.

THE SHANK'S TRANSFORMATION ON A HIERARCHY OF CHARACTERISTIC TIMES

The fundamental idea behind the appearance of log-periodicity is the existence of a hierarchy of characteristic scales. Reciprocally, any log-periodic pattern implies the existence of a hierarchy of characteristic time scales. This hierarchy of time scales is determined by the local positive maxima of the function such as $\log[p(t)]$. They are given by

$$t_c - t_n = \tau \lambda^{\frac{n}{2}}, \quad (20)$$

where

$$\tau \propto \exp\left(-\frac{\log \lambda}{2\pi} \tan^{-1} \frac{2\pi}{\beta \log \lambda}\right) \tag{21}$$

with

$$\lambda = e^{\frac{2\pi}{\omega}}. \tag{22}$$

The spacing between successive values of t_n approaches zero as n becomes large and t_n converges to t_c. This hierarchy of scales $t_c - t_n$ is not universal but depends upon the specification of the system. What is expected to be universal are the ratios $\frac{t_c - t_{n+1}}{t_c - t_n} = \lambda^{\frac{1}{2}}$. From three successive observed values of t_n, say t_n, t_{n+1}, and t_{n+2}, we have

$$t_c = \frac{t_{n+1}^2 - t_{n+2}t_n}{2t_{n+1} - t_n - t_{n+2}}. \tag{23}$$

This relation applies the so-called Shanks transformation to accelerate the convergence of series. In the case of an exact geometrical series, three terms are enough to converge exactly to the asymptotic value t_c. Notice that this relation is invariant with respect to an arbitrary translation in time. In addition, the next time t_{n+3} is predicted from the first three ones by

$$t_{n+3} = \frac{t_{n+1}^2 + t_{n+2}^2 - t_n t_{n+2} - t_{n+1}t_{n+2}}{t_{n+1} - t_n}. \tag{24}$$

The weakness of this method lies in the identification of the characteristic times t_n's which may be quite subjective.

Application to the October 1929 Crash.
Looking at the Dow Jones index by eye, we can try to identify the "characteristic" times as those of the successive "coarse-grained" local maxima that form a geometrical series. We propose $t_1 = 1926.3$, $t_2 = 1928.2$, and $t_3 = 1929.1$. Inserting into (23), we get a prediction $t_c = 1929.91$. This prediction is less than a month off the true date. Notwithstanding this positive result, this method is rather unstable, as a change of one month or about 0.1 of one of these dates t_1, t_2, t_3 may move the predicted date by one month or more. This is why this can be no more than an indication that must be taken with a grain of salt. Compared to

fitting with a complete mathematical formula, this method focuses only on specific times and thus loses what may be an important part of the information.

Application to the October 1987 Crash.
Looking at the S&P 500 index, we identify the characteristic times as those of the successive coarse-grained local maxima that form a geometrical series. We find $t_1 = 1986.5$, $t_2 = 1987.2$, and $t_3 = 1987.5$ or 1987.55. Inserting into (23), we get the prediction $t_c = 87.725$ and 87.900, respectively. These predictions correctly bracket the true date, 87.800.

FORWARD PREDICTIONS

As we said earlier, only forward predictions provide a reliable test, avoiding the many traps of statistical bias and data snooping.

We are now going to narrate the forward predictions that A. Johansen and the present author have made in the last few years. Specifically, we have examined a few of the major indices in real time, essentially continuously since 1996, and have tried to apply the methodology described before in order to predict a crash, a severe correction, or even a depression (called an antibubble in chapter 7). Here, the word "prediction" is taken with its full meaning, since the future was unknown at the time when each prediction was performed. The term "forward" prediction stresses this fact. In contrast, "post-dictions" or retroactive predictions are performed by artificially cutting a part of the most recent past in recorded time series to perform a prediction of this hidden past. Such post-dictions, which were described in the previous section, are very useful for testing the skills of a forecasting system by providing much faster a larger testing set than would be otherwise available by waiting for the future to confirm or disprove a given prediction. However, they never completely reproduce the real-time and real-life situations of forward predictions.

We report all cases, successes, and failures, so that the reader can judge for himself or herself. We report three successes (U.S. market August 1998, Nikkei Japanese market 1999, Nasdaq April 2000), two failures (U.S. market December 1997, Nasdaq October 1999), and one "semifailure" (U.S. market October 1997).

Of the successes, only the Nikkei 1999 prediction was publicly announced in advance and published. The two others (U.S. market

August 1998 and Nasdaq April 2000) were made about one month in advance but were not published.

The semifailure concerns the prediction of a crash on the U.S. market in October 1997 which was registered by an official agency about a month in advance. As we showed in chapter 7, this prediction may actually be counted as a semifailure or semisuccess depending on taste, since something did happen as far as investors and market commentators are concerned (the main U.S. market indices dropped about 7% in a day), as can be seen from the many available reports on this event, but it was not of sufficient magnitude to qualify as a crash, as the market quickly recovered. Other groups have also analyzed this event [129] and predicted it [433] with a similar log-periodic analysis.

Successful Prediction of the Nikkei 1999 Antibubble

Following the general guidelines described above (see also [214]), a prediction was made public on January 25, 1999 by posting a preprint on the Los Alamos Internet server; see http://xxx.lanl.gov/abs/cond-mat/9901268. The preprint was later published as [213]. The prediction stated that the Nikkei index should recover from its 14-year low (13,232.74 on January 5, 1999) and reach $\approx$20,500 a year later, corresponding to an increase in the index of $\approx$50%. This prediction was mentioned in a wide-circulation journal in physical sciences which appeared in May 1999 [413].

Specifically, based on a third-order "Landau" expansion generalizing the nonlinear log-periodic formula (19), the following formula was established:

$$\log(p(t)) \approx A' + \frac{\tau^{\alpha}}{\sqrt{1 + \left(\frac{\tau}{\Delta_t}\right)^{2\alpha} + \left(\frac{\tau}{\Delta_t'}\right)^{4\alpha}}}$$

$$\times \left\{ B' + C' \cos\left[\omega \log \tau + \frac{\Delta_{\omega}}{2\alpha} \log\left(1 + \left(\frac{\tau}{\Delta_t}\right)^{2\alpha}\right) \right.\right.$$

$$\left.\left. + \frac{\Delta_{\omega}'}{4\alpha} \log\left(1 + \left(\frac{\tau}{\Delta_t'}\right)^{4\alpha}\right) + \phi \right] \right\}, \tag{25}$$

describing the time evolution of the Nikkei index $p(t)$, where $\tau \equiv t - t_c$, and $t_c =$ December 31, 1989 is the time of the all-time high of the Nikkei index. Equation (25) was then fitted to the Nikkei index in the time interval from the beginning of 1990 to the end of 1998, that is, a total of nine years. Extending the curve beyond 1998 thus provided us with a quantitative prediction for the future evolution of the Nikkei. The original figure published in [213], which formed the basis for the prediction, is Figure 7.25 of chapter 7.

In Figure 9.2, the actual and predicted evolution of the Nikkei over 1999 and later are compared [216]. Not only did the Nikkei experience a trend reversal as predicted, but it has also followed the quantitative prediction with rather impressive precision. In particular, the prediction of the 50% increase at the end of 1999 is validated accurately. The prediction of another trend reversal is also accurately predicted, with the correct time for the reversal occuring at the beginning of 2000: the predicted maximum and the observed maximum match closely. It is impor-

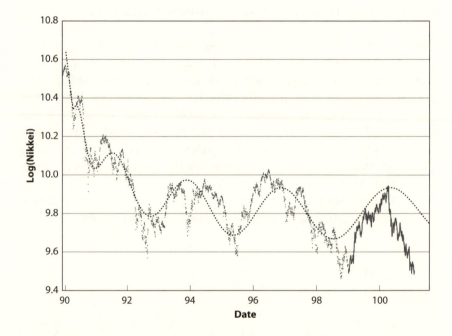

FIG. 9.2. Natural logarithm of the Nikkei stock market index after the start of the decline from January 1, 1990 until February 2001. The continuous smooth line is the extended nonlinear log-periodic formula (25), which was developed in [213] and is used to fit adequately the interval of ≈9 years starting from January 1, 1990. The Nikkei data is separated into two parts. The dots show the data used to perform the fit with formula (25) (dotted line) and to issue the prediction in January 1999 (see Figure 7.25). Its continuation as a continuous line gives the behavior of the Nikkei index after the prediction has been made. Reproduced from [216].

tant to note that the error between the curve and the data has not grown after the last point used in the fit over 1999. This tells us that the prediction has performed well for more than a year. Furthermore, since the relative error between the fit and the data is within ±2% over a time period of ten years, not only has the prediction performed well, but so has the underlying model.

The fulfillment of this prediction is even more remarkable than the comparison between the curve and the data indicates, because it included a change of trend: at the time when the prediction was issued, the market was declining and showed no tendency to increase. Many economists were at that time very pessimistic and could not envision when Japan and its market would rebound. For instance, the well-known economist P. Krugman wrote on July 14, 1998, at the time of the banking scandal:

"The central problem with Japan right now is that there just is not enough demand to go around—that consumers and corporations are saving too much and borrowing too little.... So seizing these banks and putting them under more responsible management is, if anything, going to further reduce spending; it certainly will not in and of itself stimulate the economy.... But at best this will get the economy back to where it was a year or two ago—that is, depressed, but not actually plunging [247].

Then, on January 20, 1999, Krugman wrote: "The story is starting to look like a tragedy. A great economy, which does not deserve or need to be in a slump at all, is heading for the edge of the cliff—and its drivers refuse to turn the wheel" [249]. In an October 1998 poll of thirty economists performed by Reuters (one of the major news and finance data providers in the world), only two economists predicted growth for the fiscal year of 1998–99. For the year 1999–2000 the prediction was a meager 0.1% growth. This majority of economists said that "a vicious cycle in the economy was unlikely to disappear any time soon as they expected little help from the government's economic stimulus measures.... Economists blamed moribund domestic demand, falling prices, weak capital spending and problems in the bad-loan laden banking sector for dragging down the economy" [315].

It is in this context that we predicted an approximately 50% increase of the market in the 12 months following January 1999, assuming that the Nikkei would stay within the error-bars of the fit. Predictions of trend reversals is notably difficult and unreliable, especially in the linear framework of autoregressive models used in standard economic analyses. The present nonlinear framework is well adapted to the forecasting of changes of trends, which constitutes by far the most difficult challenge posed to forecasters. Here, we refer to our prediction of a trend reversal within the strict confines of equation (25): trends are limited periods of time when the oscillatory behavior shown in Figure 9.2 is monotonous. A change of trend thus corresponds to crossing a local maximum or minimum of the oscillations. Our formula seems to have predicted two changes of trends, bearish to bullish at the beginning of 1999 and bullish to bearish at the beginning of 2000.

SUCCESSFUL PREDICTION OF THE NASDAQ CRASH OF APRIL 2000

This prediction was performed by using equation (18). The last point used in the fitted data interval was March 10, 2000. The predicted time of the crash was May 2, 2000 for the best fit and March 31, 2000 for the third best fit. The second best fit had a rather small value for $\beta \approx 0.08$ and was not considered. Except for slight gains on March 31 and April 5, 6, and 7, the closing of the Nasdaq composite had been in continuous decline since March 24 and lost over 25% in the week ending on Friday, April 14. Consequently, the crash occured approximately in between the predicted date of the two fits. The best fit is shown in Figure 7.22 in the section entitled "The Nasdaq Crash of April 2000" of chapter 7.

Table 7.2 reports the main characteristics of the fit of the Nasdaq index as well as ten other cases. Observe that, in all cases, the market crash started at a time between the date of the last point and the predicted t_c. And with the exception of the October 1929 crash and using the third best fit of the Nasdaq crash (this fit had $\omega/2\pi \approx 1$), in all cases, the market ended its decline less than approximately one month after the predicted t_c.

THE U.S. MARKET, DECEMBER 1997 FALSE ALARM

The shock at the end of October 1997 on the U.S. markets might be considered as an aborted crash. Private polling of professional investors indeed suggests that many traders were actually afraid that a crash was coming at the end of October 1997. After this event, we continued to monitor the market closely to detect a possible resurgent instability. An analysis using data up to Friday, November 21, 1997 using the three methods based on the log-periodic formula (18), its nonlinear extension (19), and the Shank formula (23) suggested a prediction for a decrease of the price approximately mid-December 1997, with an error bar of about two weeks.

Table 9.8 shows an attempt at predicting a critical time t_c with the linear log-periodic formula using data ending at the "last date" given in the first column, in order to test for robustness. The last "last date" 97.8904 corresponds to Friday, November 21, 1997 and the data includes the close of this Friday. In the fit on the data going up to Friday, November 21, 1997, ten solutions are found. The first eight all give $25 \leq \omega \leq 38$, which is quite large. Since large values of ω correspond to fast oscillations, there is the danger of fitting "noise," that is, extracting information where there is none. It was thus considered safe to reject these solutions, which were all proposing $t_c = 98.6 \pm 0.1$. The last two solutions are those that are reported in Table 9.8. Their square error χ^2 is only 7% above the very best fast oscillating solution. Thus the χ^2 is not a parameter that allows one to qualify an acceptable or nonacceptable solution. Taking the two predictions obtained for the past dates of 97.719[1] and of 97.678[1] (the superscript [1] means that we select here the best fit of the formula to the data) as the values that should bracket the true t_c, this suggested $97.922 \leq t_c \leq 97.985$, which corresponds to December 3, 1997 $\leq t_c \leq$ December 25, 1997.

In hindsight and knowing what happened in August 1998 (see the section titled "The Crash of August 1998" in chapter 7), the best eight

TABLE 9.8

Prediction of the next crash by the linear log-periodic formula (18) on the S&P 500 index using time intervals from 1994.9 to "last date."

Last date	t_c	β	ω	χ^2	A	B	C
97.8904[1]	98.06	0.28	6.4	8.884	998	−858	0.105
97.8904[2]	98.04	0.25	6.1	8.886	989	−793	0.103
97.719[1]	97.985	0.23	8.3	113.4	897	−622	0.026
97.678[1]	97.922	0.24	7.9	108.8	838	−573	0.028
97.633[1]	97.678	0.42	6.3	103.9	514	−280	0.054
97.633[2]	97.845	0.27	7.3	105.0	753	−499	0.032
97.588[1]	97.796	0.30	7.0	102	670	−422	0.038
97.543[1]	97.756	0.36	6.8	95.2	579	−337	0.046
97.498[1]	97.702	0.44	6.4	90.3	501	−265	0.056
97.453[1]	97.676	0.50	6.3	88.2	461	−227	0.061
97.408[1]	97.674	0.52	6.2	88.7	452	−218	0.062
97.408[2]	97.864	0.74	16	160	414	−154	0.031
97.363[1]	97.734	0.53	6.6	88.7	458	−217	0.059

The superscripts [1] and [2] refer, respectively, to the best and second best fits of the formula to the data. Unpublished results obtained in collaboration with A. Johansen.

solutions may have actually been relevant as indicating possible scenarios for the future further ahead. Here is a lesson to learn in connection with Figure 9.1: it may be that several scenarios are possible for the future evolution. The stock market dynamics will select one, but another branch may have occurred with some slight modifications of the different perturbations acting on the system. This brings us back to the beginning of this chapter, where we emphasized the importance of a view of prediction involving multiple scenarios. As used in a different context in [6], predictive patterns and their associated forecasts should be defined in probabilistic terms, allowing for multiple scenarios evolving from the same past evolution. Deeply imbedded in this approach is the view of the future as a set of potentially acceptable trajectories that can branch and bifurcate at special times. At certain times, only one main trajectory extrapolates with high probability from the past making the future depend almost deterministically (albeit possibly in a nonlinear and chaotic manner) on the past. At other times, the future is much less certain, with multiple almost equivalent choices. In this case, we return to an almost random walk picture. The existence of a unique future must not be taken as the signature of a single dynamical system but as the collapse of the large distribution of probabilities. This is the concept learned, for instance, from the famous Polya urn problem discussed in chapter 4 in which the historical trajectory appears to converge to a certain outcome, which is, however, solely controlled by the accumulation of purely random choices; a different outcome might have been selected by history with equal probability [20]. It is fundamental to view any forecasting program as essentially a quantification of probabilities for possible competing scenerios. This view has been vividly emphasized by Asimov in his famous science fiction *Foundation* series [23, 22].

Table 9.9 shows an attempt at predicting a critical time t_c with the nonlinear log-periodic formula (19) using data going from "first date" (first column) to "last date" (second column), in order to test for robustness. There seems to be a clear prediction toward 1997.94 ± 0.01. Some of the fits give a value for t_c very close to the "last date" and must thus be rejected. This is the case for the rows marked by an asterisk *. The preferred prediction date was $t_c \approx$ December 12, 1997.

The last attempt consisted in using the Shank formula (23). The difficulty here is to identify the "characteristic" times t_n. For this, we used the successive "coarse-grained" local maxima. A rough estimation by eye gave $t_1 = 94.05$, $t_2 = 96.15$, $t_3 = 97.1$. Inserting in (23) provided a prediction $t_c^{(1)} = 97.884$. Expression (24) predicts $t_4 = 97.53$, while we observed $t_4 = 97.55$, providing a rather good confirmation. Using t_2, t_3,

TABLE 9.9

First date	Last date	t_c	β	ω	Δ_ω	Δ_t	χ^2	A	B	C
1991	97.8904[1]	98.07	0.82	10.5	−11.2	5.2	0.02483	6.33	−0.338	−0.085
1991	97.678[2]	98.13	0.52	12.3	−58.6	29	0.02576	6.51	−0.510	−0.076
1991	97.678[1]	97.948	0.73	8.9	−14.1	9.3	0.03916	6.26	−0.505	−0.091
1991	97.678[2]	97.942	0.61	9.1	−33.8	23.0	0.03930	6.33	−0.584	−0.089
1991	97.606[1]	97.709	0.69				0.039	6.15		
1991	97.516[1]	97.819	0.80				0.039	6.13		
1991	97.444[1]	97.780	0.885				0.039	6.06		
1988	97.392[1]	97.982	0.94				0.076	6.17		
1992.4	97.392[1]	97.990	0.48				0.102	9.83		
1995*	97.392[1]	97.481	0.247				0.019	7.14		
1991	97.372[1]	97.818	0.94				0.0393	6.05		
1987.9	97.304[1]	98.788	0.86	9.9	−6.6	7.1	0.102	596	−134	0.066
1988	97.286[1]	99.479	0.135	6.6	−14.9	10.4	0.088	17.0	−24.8	0.488
1992.2	97.268[1]	98.962	0.39	8.5	−76.7	16.4	0.100	11.5	−4.63	0.034
1991	97.242[1]	97.966	0.62	10.4	−20.2	9.5	0.016	6.73	−0.367	0.074
1988*	97.242[1]	98.280	0.84	12.6	−35.9	9.5	0.026	6.63	−0.212	0.113
1988	97.242[2]	97.361	0.79	7.0	−34.1	13.9	0.026	6.46	−0.196	0.158
1991	97.229[1]	97.894	0.925				0.03915	6.10		
1988*	97.215[1]	98.229	0.88	12.6	−10.5	3.3	11.3	786	−173	0.055
1991	97.157[1]	97.851	0.927				0.03935	6.08		
1991	97.085[1]	98.412	0.43				0.0405	7.40		
1988	97.055[1]	97.760	0.47	10.1	−15.9	7.5	232	6.26	−0.505	−0.091

Attempt to predict a crash by the nonlinear log-periodic formula using time intervals from the "first date" to the "last date" to fit the logarithm of the S&P 500 index. The exponents [i] indicate the order of the minima found for the same "last date." Unpublished results obtained in collaboration with A. Johansen.

and t_4 in (23) gives the prediction $t_c^{(2)} = 97.955$. This was taken as the preferred value because it uses the log-periodicity in the last two years for which the log-frequency shift described by the nonlinear log-periodic formula is not present. This again predicted $t_c \approx$ December 15, 1997, in agreement with the two other methods.

THE U.S. MARKET, OCTOBER 1999 FALSE ALARM

Following a similar methodology, we also closely monitored several U.S. markets and found that significant log-periodic power behavior could be detected in September 1999, suggesting the end of a bubble in October 1999. The world markets were actually sent into turmoil by a speech by Alan Greenspan, and the Dow Jones for the first time since April 8, 1999 dipped below 10.000 on October 15 and 18, 1999. However, the market did not crash and instead quickly recovered and later started a renewed and strengthened bullish phase. In hindsight, we see that, similarly to October 1997, this may have been an aborted event, which turned into a precursor of the large crash in April 2000, which we correctly detected.

PRESENT STATUS OF FORWARD PREDICTIONS

We have just discussed in some detail two of the three successful predictions (U.S. market August 1998, Nikkei Japanese market 1999, Nasdaq April 2000) and the two false alarms (U.S. market December 1997, Nasdaq October 1999).

Several remarks are in order.

THE FINITE PROBABILITY THAT NO CRASH WILL OCCUR
DURING A BUBBLE

We stress again that the fact that markets are approximately efficient and that investors try to arbitrage away gain opportunities lead to the fundamental constraint that crashs are stochastic events. The rational expectation model described in chapter 5 provides a benchmark for such behavior. It tells us that we should not expect all speculative bubbles to end in a crash: the crux of the theory is that there is always a finite probability that the bubble will deflate smoothly without a crash. Hence, according to this theory, the two false alarms may just correspond to this scenario of a smooth death of the bubble. The sample is not large, but without better knowledge, the existence of these two false alarms interpreted in this context suggests that the total probability for a crash to occur conditioned on the existence of a bubble is approximately $3/5 = 60\%$. Thus, there is a probability of 40% for living through a speculative bubble safely without crash.

In other words, the two cases of bubbles landing more or less smoothly are completely consistent with the theory of rational bubbles and crashes developed in [221] and reported in chapter 5. This also illustrates the difficulties involved in developing a crash-prediction scheme based on the critical point theory. According to the rational expectation model, the critical time t_c is not necessarily the time of the crash, only its most probable time.

ESTIMATION OF THE STATISTICAL SIGNIFICANCE OF THE FORWARD PREDICTIONS

Statistical Confidence of the Crash "Roulette."
Let us now be conservative and consider that the two false alarms are real failures. How can we quantify the statistical significance of the predictions? Let us formulate the problem precisely. First, we divide time into monthly intervals and ask what the probability is that a crash will occur in a given month interval. Let us consider N month intervals. The recent out-of-sample period over which we carried out our analysis goes from January 1996 to December 2000, corresponding to $N = 60$ months. In these $N = 60$ months, $n_c = 3$ crashes occurred while $N - n_c = 57$ monthly periods were without crash. Over this 5-year time interval, we made $r = 5$ predictions, and $k = 3$ of them where successful while $r - k = 2$ were false alarms. What is the probability P_k of achieving such success by chance?

This question has a clear mathematical answer and reduces to a well-known combinatorial problem leading to the so-called hypergeometric distribution.

As explained in the book of W. Feller [131], this problem is the same as the following game. In a population of N balls, n_c are red and $N - n_c$ are black. A group of r balls is chosen at random. What is the probability p_k that the group so chosen will contain exactly k red balls?

To make progress, we need to define a quantity called $C(n, m)$, which is the number of distinct ways to choose m elements among n elements, independently of the order with which we choose the m elements. The combinatorial factor $C(n, m)$ has a simple mathematical expression $C(n, m) = n!/m!(n - m)!$ where $m!$, called the factorial of m, is defined by $m! = m \times (m - 1) \times (m - 2) \times \cdots \times 3 \times 2 \times 1$. $C(n = 52, m = 13) = 635{,}013{,}559{,}600$ gives, for instance, the number of possible different hands at the game of bridge, and $C(n = 52, m = 5) = 2{,}598{,}960$ gives the number of possible different hands at the game of poker.

We can now use $C(n, m)$ to estimate the probability p_k. If, among the r chosen balls, there are k red ones, then there are $r - k$ black ones. There are thus $C(n_c, k)$ different ways of choosing the red balls and $C(N - n_c, r - k)$ different ways of choosing the black balls. The total number of ways of choosing r balls among N is $C(N, r)$. Therefore, the probability p_k that the group of r balls so chosen will contain exactly k red balls is the product $C(n_c, k) \times C(N - n_c, r - k)$ of the number of ways corresponding to the draw of exactly k red balls among r divided by the total possible number $C(N, r)$ of ways to draw the r ball (here we simply use the so-called "frequentist" definition of the probability of an event as the ratio of the number of states corresponding to that event divided by the total number of events):

$$p_k = \frac{C(n_c, k) \times C(N - n_c, r - k)}{C(N, r)}. \tag{26}$$

p_k is the so-called hypergeometric function. In order to quantify a statistical confidence, we must ask a slightly different question: what is the probability P_k that, out of the r balls, there are at least k^* red balls? Clearly, the result is obtained by summing p_k over all possible values of k's from k^* up to the maximum of n_c and r; indeed, the number of red balls among r cannot be greater than r, and it cannot be greater than the total number n_c of available red balls.

In the case of interest here, the number of monthly periods is $N = 60$, the number n_c of real crashes is equal to the number k of correct predictions $n_c = k = 3$, $N - n_c = 57$, the total number of issued prediction is $r = 5$, and the number of false alarms is $r - k = 2$. Since $n_c = k$, $P_{k=3} = p_{k=3} = \frac{C(3,3) \times C(57,2)}{C(60,5)} = 0.03\%$: the probability that this result is due to chance is a very small value 0.03%, corresponding to an exceedingly strong statistical significance of 99.97%. We conclude that our track record, while containing only few cases, is highly suggestive of real significance.

To obtain a feeling for the sensitivity of this estimation on the reported number of successes and failures, let us assume that instead of correctly predicting $k = 3$ crashes, we had predicted only two out of the five alarms that we declared. This corresponds to $N = 60$, $n_c = 3$, $N - n_c = 57$, $r = 5$, $k = 2$, and $r - k = 3$. The probability that this result is due to chance is $P_{k=2} = p_2 + p_3 = \frac{C(3,2) \times C(57,3)}{C(60,5)} + \frac{C(3,3) \times C(57,2)}{C(60,5)} = 1.9\% + 0.03\%$; the probability that this result would be due to chance is still very small and approximately equal to 2%, corresponding to a still strong statistical significance of 98%. While less overwhelming, two correct predictions and three false alarms is still strongly significant. We conclude that the statistical confidence level of our track record is robust.

What will happen if we issue a sixth prediction in the following year, which turns out to be incorrect? The track record would then be such that $N = 72$, $n_c = 3$, $N - n_c = 69$, $r = 6$, $k = 3$, and $r - k = 3$. The probability that this result is due to chance is $P_{k=3} = \frac{C(3,3) \times C(69,3)}{C(72,6)} = 0.033\%$, which gives a small degradation of the statistical significance: three correct predictions and three failures in a set of seventy-two targets remains highly nonrandom. We are thus justified in claiming that these results are nonrandom with high significance.

We should stress that this contrasts with the view that three successes and two failures, or vice versa, would correspond to approximately one chance in two of being right, giving the impression that the prediction skill is no better than deciding that a crash will occur by random coin tosses. This conclusion would be very naive because it forgets an essential element of the forecasting approach, which is to identify a (short) time window (one month) in which a crash is probable: the main difficulty in making a prediction is indeed to identify the few monthly periods among the sixty in which there is the risk of a crash.

Statistical Significance of a Single Successful Prediction via Bayes's Theorem.

Consider our prediction in January 1999 of the trend reversal of the Nikkei index in its antibubble regime. This is a single case of a prediction of an antibubble regime. In the standard "frequentist" approach to probability [224] and to the establishment of statistical confidence, this bears essentially no weight and should be discarded as storytelling. However, the "frequentist" approach is unsuitable for assessing the quality of such a unique experiment of the prediction of a global financial indicator. The correct framework is Bayesian. Within the Bayesian framework, the probability that the hypothesis is correct given the data can be estimated, whereas this is excluded by construction in the standard "frequentist" formulation, in which one can only calculate the probability that the null-hypothesis is wrong, not that the alternative hypothesis is correct (see also [279, 98] for recent introductory discussions). We now present a simple application of Bayes's theorem to quantify the impact of our prediction [216].

Bayes's view of the prediction skill given one successful prediction:
We can approach the problem of the significance of a single successful prediction by using a fundamental result in probability theory, known as Bayes' theorem. This theorem states that

$$P(H_i|D) = \frac{P(D|H_i) \times P(H_i)}{\sum_j P(D|H_j)P(H_j)}, \tag{27}$$

where the sum in the denominator runs over all the different conflicting hypotheses. In words, equation (27) estimates that the probability that hypothesis H_i is correct given the data D is proportional to the probability $P(D|H_i)$ of the data given the hypothesis H_i multiplied with the prior belief $P(H_i)$ in the hypothesis H_i divided by the probability of the data. Consider our prediction in January 1999 of the trend reversal of the Nikkei index. Translated in this context, we use only the two hypotheses H_1 and H_2 that our model of a trend reversal is correct or that it is wrong. For the data, we take the change of trend from bearish to bullish. We now want to estimate whether the fulfillment of our prediction was a "lucky one." We quantify the general atmosphere of disbelief that Japan would recover by the value $P(D|H_2) = 5\%$ to the probability that the Nikkei will change trend while disbelieving our model. We estimate the classical confidence level of $P(D|H_1) = 95\%$ to the probability that the Nikkei will change trend while believing our model.

Let us consider a skeptical Bayesian with prior probability (or belief) $P(H_1) = 10^{-n}$, $n \geq 1$, that our model is correct. From (27), we get

$$P(H_1|D) = \frac{0.95 \times 10^{-n}}{0.95 \cdot 10^{-n} + 0.05 \times (1 - 10^{-n})}. \tag{28}$$

For $n = 1$, we see that her posterior belief in our model has been amplified compared to her prior belief by a factor ≈ 7 corresponding to $P(H_1|D) \approx 70\%$. For $n = 2$, the amplification factor is ≈ 16 and hence $P(H_1|D) \approx 16\%$. For large n (very skeptical Bayesian), we see that her posterior belief in our model has been amplified compared to her prior belief by a factor $0.95/0.05 = 19$.

Alternatively, consider a neutral Bayesian with prior belief $P(H_1) = 1/2$; that is, a priori she considers it equally likely that our model is correct or incorrect. In this case, her prior belief is changed into the posterior belief equal to

$$P(H_1|D) = \frac{0.95 \cdot \frac{1}{2}}{0.95 \cdot \frac{1}{2} + 0.05 \cdot \frac{1}{2}} = 95\%. \tag{29}$$

This means that this single case is enough to convince the neutral Bayesian.

We stress that this specific application of Bayes's theorem only deals with a small part of the model; the trend-reversal. It does not establish the significance of the quantitative description of *ten years* of data (of which the last one was unknown at the time of the prediction) by the proposed model within a relative error of $\approx \pm 2\%$.

The Error Diagram and the Decision Process.
In evaluating predictions and their impact on (investment) decisions, one must weigh the relative cost of false alarms with respect to the gain resulting from correct predictions. The Neyman-Pearson diagram, also called the decision quality diagram, is used in optimizing decision strategies with a single test statistic. The assumption is that samples of events or probability density functions are available both for correct signals (the crashes) and for the background noise (false alarms); a suitable test statistic is then sought which optimally distinguishes between the two. Using a given test statistic (or discriminant function), one can introduce a cut that separates an acceptance region (dominated by correct predictions) from a rejection region (dominated by false alarms). The Neyman-Pearson diagram plots contamination (misclassified events, that is, classified as predictions, which are in fact false alarms) against losses (misclassified signal events, that is, classified as background or failure-to-predict), both as fractions of the total sample. An ideal test statistic corresponds to a diagram where the "acceptance of prediction" is plotted as a function of the "acceptance of false alarm" in which the acceptance is close to 1 for the real signals and close to 0 for the false alarms. Different strategies are possible: a "liberal" strategy favors minimal loss (i.e., high acceptance of signal, i.e., almost no failure to catch the real events but many false alarms), a "conservative" one favors minimal contamination (i.e., high purity of signal and almost no false alarms but many possible misses of true events).

Molchan has shown that the task of predicting an event in continuous time can be mapped onto the Neyman-Pearson procedures. He has introduced "error diagram" which plots the rate of failure-to-predict (the number of missed events divided by the total number of events in the total time interval) as a function of the rate of time alarms (the total time of alarms divided by the total time, in other words the fraction of time we declare that a crash is looming) [303, 304]. The best predictor corresponds to a point close to the origin in this diagram, with almost no failure-to-predict and with a small fraction of time declared as dangerous: in other words, this ideal strategy misses no event and does not declare false alarms! These considerations teach us that making a prediction is one thing, but using it is another, which corresponds to solving a control optimization problem [303, 304].

Decision theory provides useful guidelines. Let c_1 represent the cost of mispredicting a crash as a noncrash and c_2 the cost of mispredicting a normal time as a crash. Let us assume that, conditioned on past data X, our model provides the probability $\pi = \Pr(Y = 1|X)$ for a crash to occur ($Y = 1$). If a crash occurs, the average cost is $C_1 = c_2(1 - \pi)$, which represents the possibility that we may have mispredicted it. If the crash does not occur, the average cost is $C_2 = c_1\pi$, which represents the possibility that we may have predicted a crash anyway. By comparing these two costs, it is clear that $C_1 > C_2$ if $\pi < 1/(1 + (c_1/c_2))$ and $C_1 \leq C_2$ if $\pi \geq 1/(1 + (c_1/c_2))$. Thus, the optimal prediction (in the sense of minimizing total expected cost) is "crash" ($Y = 1$) when $\Pr(Y = 1|X) > 1/(1 + (c_1/c_2))$ and "no-crash" ($Y = 0$) otherwise (see also [345, pp. 19, 58]). Hence, if the two possible mispredictions are equally costly, $c_1/c_2 = 1$, we would predict that a crash will occur when $\Pr(Y = 1|X) > 0.5$. However, if mispredicting a crash is, say, twice as costly as mispredicting a no-crash, $c_1/c_2 = 2$, an optimal decision process would predict a crash whenever $\Pr(Y = 1|X) > 1/3$. By applying decision theory like this, we can compare model outputs to the data and judge our success in prediction. The key, however, is that the value of c_1/c_2 must be decided independently of the data and of the development of the model. The model should also be able to provide a prediction in a probabilistic language. There is thus much to do in future research.

PRACTICAL IMPLICATIONS ON DIFFERENT TRADING STRATEGIES

A significant fraction of professional investors and managers, and in particular hedge fund managers, use a variety of strategies in order to improve their performance. It is clear that the two broad classes of strategies, trend following and market timing, would profit from ex ante detections of impending crashes.

Fung and Hsieh [147] have recently provided a useful and simple classification scheme for strategies which we borrow here. They considered so-called buy-and-hold, market-timing, and trend-following strategies.

Both market-timers and trend-followers attempt to profit from price movements. Roughly speaking, a market-timer forecasts the direction of an asset, buying to capture a price increase, and selling to capture a price decrease. A trend-follower attempts to capture trends, that is, serial correlations in price changes that make prices move persistently, mainly in one direction over a given time interval (for positive price correlations).

A simple model of such strategies is as follows. Let p_i, p_f, p_{max}, and p_{min} be the initial asset price, the final price, the maximum price, and the minimum price achieved over a given time interval. Let us consider strategies that complete a single trade over the given time interval.

The buy-and-hold strategy consists in buying at the beginning at the price p_i and selling at the end at the price p_f, pocketing or losing $p_f - p_i$.

In this example, the market-timing strategy attempts to capture the price movement between p_i and p_f. If p_f is expected to be higher (lower) than p_i, the trader buys (sells) an asset. The trade is reversed at the end of the period, to exit the market. Thus, the optimal payout of the market-timing strategy is $p_f - p_i$ if $p_f > p_i$, or $p_i - p_f$ if $p_f < p_i$, which can be noted $|p_f - p_i|$, where the vertical bars correspond to taking the absolute value. In other words, such an ideal market-timing strategy works like an electric rectifier, changing negative price changes into positive gains.

In this example, the perfect trend-following strategy attempts to capture the largest price movement during the time interval. Therefore, the optimal payout is $p_{max} - p_{min}$. It is clear that this strategy would profit the most from a crash prediction.

Let us in addition mention investment strategies using financial derivatives, such as "put" and "call" options. A put option is the natural tool for leveraging a prediction on an incoming crash. Recall that a put (also called sell) option gives the right (but not the obligation) obtained from a counterparty (say a bank) to sell a stock at a prechosen price, called the exercise price, during a given time period. When the real price becomes much smaller than the exercise price, the put option becomes very valuable because the investor can buy at a low price on the market and sell at the high exercise price to the bank, thus pocketing the difference. The leveraging embedded in the put option stems from the fact that its initial price may be very small if the exercise price is initially chosen "out-of-the-money," that is, much below current price, since the trader does not get much from the possibility of selling at a price below market price. If a crash occurs before the option comes to maturity and as a consequence the price plunges close to or below the exercise price, the initially almost valueless option suddenly acquires a large value. Its price may jump by factors of up to hundreds for large crashes, corresponding to potential gains of tens of thousands of percentage points! But this is more easily said than done, as precise timing is of the essence.

Understandably, traders regard their trading systems to be proprietary and are reluctant to disclose them. We are no exception: while we have taken an open view by describing our underlying theory in great detail and by providing explicit examples of some past implementations, key recent progress has not been divulged yet. Recent theoretical studies indeed suggest that new strategies coevolving with older ones may surpass them if used only by a limited number of players.

CHAPTER 10

2050: THE END OF THE GROWTH ERA?

STOCK MARKETS, ECONOMICS, AND POPULATION

How will the stock markets of the world behave in the months, years, or even decades ahead of us? This question underlies much of our economic future and well-being. As discussed in previous chapters, countries around the world are relying increasingly on the stock market for the retirement of their elders, for quantifying the value of companies, and for characterizing the health of the economy in general. In addition, the stock market has become a powerful engine of both developed and emerging economies as the principal source of liquidity and capital for investment.

At the end of the twentieth century, several authors, emboldened by the seemingly endless bull market of the time, proposed that the Dow Jones index will climb to 36,000 [158], 40,000 [118], or even 100,000 [225] in the next two or three decades from the flat range 10,000–11,000 in which it has hovered from mid-1999 to the time of writing (mid-2001). Are these predictions realistic or overblown? More generally, what possible scenarios are ahead of us?

To address these questions, we generalize our approach by analyzing financial as well as economic and population times series over the longest time scales for which reliable data is available. The rationale for this multivariate approach is that the future of the stock market cannot be decoupled from that of the economy, which itself is linked to the productivity of the labor, and hence to the dynamics of the population. This leads us naturally to ask broader questions, such as whether the present pace of human population growth and of its associated economic development can continue along its accelerating path in the indefinite future. Or, as a growing number of scholars threaten, are they bound to stop catastrophically if mankind is not able to soon achieve a regime of long-term sustainable development?

Indeed, contrary to common belief, both the global human population as well as its economic output have grown faster than exponentially for most of known history, and most strikingly in the last two centuries. Recall that an exponential growth corresponds to a constant growth rate, such as the interest rate one gets on a CD account or from a government bond. A faster-than-exponential growth thus means that the growth rate is itself growing with time (see the "Intuitive Explanation of the Creation of a Finite-Time Singularity at t_c" in chapter 5). We shall show below that this observed accelerating growth rate is consistent with a spontaneous apparent divergence at the same critical time around 2050, with the same self-similar log-periodic patterns in three data sets: human population, gross domestic product, and financial indices. This result can be explained by the interplay between the dynamics of the growth of population, of capital, and of technology, producing an "explosion" in the economic output, even when the individual isolated dynamics do not have strong enough positive feedbacks to do the same by their single action. Interestingly, in the 1950s, two famous mathematicians and computer scientists, S. Ulam and J. von Neumann (the father of modern computing as well as game theory in economics) were aware of this possibility. Indeed, in [428], Ulam recalled a conversation with von Neumann: "One conversation centered on the ever accelerating progress of technology and changes in the mode of human life, which gives the appearance of approaching some essential singularity in the history of the race beyond which human affairs, as we know them, could not continue."

The tremendous pace of accelerated growth observed until now has led to increasing worries about its sustainability. It has also led to rising concerns that the human culture as a result may cause severe and irreversible damage to ecosystems, global weather systems, and so on. On the other hand, optimists expect that the innovative spirit of mankind will be able to solve such problems and the economic development of the world will continue as a succession of revolutions, for example, the Internet, bio-technological, and other yet unknown major innovations replacing the agricultural, industrial, medical, and information revolutions of the past. The observed acceleration of economic development seems to support the optimistic point of view.

However, the spontaneous apparent divergence around 2050, which we shall document below, has the surprising consequence that even the optimistic view needs to be revised, since an acceleration of the growth rate contains endogenously its own limit in the form of a singularity. The singularity is a mathematical idealization of a transition to a qualitatively new behavior. The degree of abruptness of the transition to the new regime can be inferred from the fact that the maximum of the world population growth rate was reached in 1970, about 80 years before the predicted singular time, corresponding to approximately 4% of the 2,000 years over which the acceleration is documented below. This rounding-off of the finite-time singularity is probably due to a combination of well-known finite-size effects and drag effects that are bound to become dominant close to the singularity. It suggests that we have already entered the transition region to a new regime, as we shall discuss in more detail in this chapter.

As a bonus, we also offer the prediction that the U.S. market is in a period of consolidation, or stagnation, which may last up to a full decade. This period will be followed by renewed accelerated growth. We attempt to unearth the origins of this behavior on the basis of macroeconomic reasoning.

THE PESSIMISTIC VIEWPOINT OF "NATURAL" SCIENTISTS

The rapid growth of the world population is a quite recent phenomenon compared to the total history of modern homo sapiens. It is estimated that 2,000 years ago the population of the world was approximately 300 million. It took more than 1,600 years for the world population to double to 600 million, and since then the growth has accelerated. It reached 1 billion in 1804, 2 billion in 1927 (123 years later), 3 billion in 1960 (33 years later), 4 billion in 1974 (14 years later), 5 billion in 1987 (13 years later), and 6 billion in 1999 (12 years later) (see Table 10.1).

Representatives of national academies of sciences from throughout the world met in New Delhi in October 1993 at a "Science Summit" on world population. The participants issued a statement, signed by representatives of 58 academies on population issues, related to development, notably on the determinants of fertility and the effect of demographic

TABLE 10.1

Year	Population (billions)	Source
0	0.30	Durand
1000	0.31	Durand
1250	0.40	Durand
1500	0.50	Durand
1750	0.79	D & C
1800	0.98	D & C
1850	1.26	D & C
1900	1.65	D & C
1910	1.75	Interp.
1920	1.86	WPP63
1920	1.86	WPP63
1930	2.07	WPP63
1940	2.30	WPP63
1950	2.52	WPP94
1960	3.02	WPP94
1970	3.70	WPP94
1980	4.45	WPP94
1990	5.30	WPP94
1994	5.63	WPP94
1999	6.00	WPP94
2001	6.14	WPP01

Data from the United Nations Population Division, Department of Economic and Social Information and Policy Analysis. *Durand:* J.D. Durand, 1974. *Historical Estimates of World Population: An Evaluation* (University of Pennsylvania, Population Studies Center, Philadelphia), mimeo. *D & C:* United Nations, 1973. *The Determinants and Consequences of Population Trends*, Vol. 1 (United Nations, New York). *WPP63:* United Nations, 1966. *World Population Prospects as Assessed in 1963* (United Nations, New York). *WPP94:* United Nations, 1993. *World Population Prospects: The 1994 Revision* (United Nations, New York). *Interp:* Estimate interpolated from adjacent population estimates.

growth on the environment and the quality of life. The statement asserted that "continuing population growth poses a great risk to humanity," and proposed a demographic goal: "In our judgment, humanity's ability to deal successfully with its social, economic, and environmental problems will require the achievement of zero population growth within the lifetime of our children," and "Humanity is approaching a crisis point with respect to the interlocking issues of population, environment and development because the Earth is finite" [366]. Accordingly, "Excessive peopling of the world is contributing to major environmental trauma, including famine, rain forest destruction, global warming, acid rain, pollution of air, water, overflow and even to the AIDS epidemic" [366].

There are many documented cases of irreversible damage to ecosystems, global weather system perturbations, as well as increasing concerns about a severe shortage of water. Extrapolating present trends, it is estimated that, by 2025, two-thirds of the world population will live in water-stressed conditions [119]. These problems all have one common root: the fast-increasing human population and its associated economic development. The worry about human population size and growth is shared by many natural scientists, including the Union of Concerned Scientists (comprising 99 Nobel Prize winners), which asks nations to "stabilize population."

THE OPTIMISTIC VIEWPOINT
OF "SOCIAL" SCIENTISTS

At what may be considered the other extreme, optimists expect that the innovative spirit of mankind will be able to solve the problems associated with a continuing increase in the growth rate [441, 380, 306]. Specifically, as we said above, they believe that world economic development will continue as a successive unfolding of revolutions, for example, the Internet, bio-technological, and other yet unknown innovations replacing the prior agricultural, industrial, medical, and information revolutions of the past.

Indeed, by 1990, most of the economics profession has turned almost completely away from the previous view that population growth is a negative factor in economic development (see, however, [94, 145, 99]). In fact, they now consider it to be a positive factor: more people implies greater wealth, more resources, and a healthier environment. The argument goes: "Additional persons produce more than they consume in the long run, and natural resources are not an exception" [380, 306]. "Without exception, the relevant data, i.e., the long-run economic trends, and the appropriate measures of scarcity, i.e., the costs of natural resources in human labor and their prices relative to wages and to other goods, all suggest that natural resources have been becoming less scarce over the long run, right up to the present" [380]. On essentially all accounts, the optimists thus argue that the situation has improved compared to past decades and will continue to improve in the coming decades [380, 306]:

1. **Pollution**: Pollution has always been a problem since the beginning of time, but we now live in a more healthy and less dirty environment than in earlier centuries. Life expectancy, which is the best overall index of the pollution level, has improved markedly as the world's population has grown.

2. **Food**: Food production per capita has been increasing over the half-century since World War II. Famine has progressively diminished for at least the past century (quantified in relative values, as the fraction of the total population). There is compelling reason to believe that human nutrition will continue to improve into the indefinite future, even with continued population growth.

3. **Land**: The amount of agricultural land has been increasing substantially, and it is likely to continue to increase where needed. For rich countries (United States, for instance), the quantity of land under cultivation has been decreasing. The amount of land used for forests, recreation, and wildlife has been increasing rapidly in the United States!

4. **Natural resources**: Our supplies are not finite in any economic sense, nor does past experience give reason to expect natural resources to become more scarce. Natural resources will progressively become less costly, hence less scarce, and will constitute a smaller proportion of our expenses in future years. Population growth is likely to have a long-run beneficial impact on the natural-resource situation.

5. **Energy**: The long-run future of our energy supply is at least as bright as that of other natural resources, though government intervention can temporarily boost prices from time to time. Finiteness is no problem here either. And the long-run impact of additional people is likely to speed the development of cheap energy supplies that are almost inexhaustible.

6. **The standard of living**: In the short run, additional children imply additional costs, as all parents know. In the longer run, per capita income is likely to be higher with a growing population than with a stationary one, both in more-developed and less-developed countries.

7. **Human fertility**: The contention that poor and uneducated people breed without constraint is demonstrably wrong, even for the poorest and most "primitive" societies [380, 306]. Well-off people who believe that

the poor do not weigh the consequences of having more children are simply arrogant, or ignorant, or both.

8. **Future population growth**: Present trends suggest that even though total population for the world is increasing, the density of population on most of the world's surface will decrease. This is already happening in the developed countries. Though the total populations of developed countries increased from 1950 to 1990, the rate of urbanization was sufficiently great that population density on most of their land areas (say, 97% of the land area of the United States) has been decreasing. As the poor countries become richer, they will surely experience the same trends, leaving most of the world's surface progressively less populated, astonishing as this may seem.

ANALYSIS OF THE FASTER-THAN-EXPONENTIAL GROWTH OF POPULATION, GDP, AND FINANCIAL INDICES

Let us start from Malthus's exponential growth model, which assumes that the size of a population increases by a fixed proportion over a given period of time independently of the size of the population, and thus gives an exponential growth. Take, for instance, the proportion of 2.1% per year or 23.1% per decade corresponding to the all-time peak of the population growth rate reached in 1970. This leads to a population doubling time of forty-eight years. Starting from a population of, say 1,000, the population is 1.231 times $1,000 = 1,231$ after one decade, 1.231 times 1.231 times $1,000 = 1,515$ after two decades, and so on. As we see, such an exponential growth corresponds to the multiplication of the population by a constant factor, here 1.231, for each additional unit of time, here ten years. It is thus convenient to visualize it by presenting the population on a scale such that successive values of the multiplication by a constant factor are equally spaced, which defines the so-called "logarithmic scale" already encountered several times in this book; we will use this scale for all figures presented below.

In the Malthusian exponential model, the logarithm of the population should thus increase proportionally to, or linearly with, time. Figure 10.1 shows the estimated (logarithm of the) world population (obtained from the United Nations Population Division, Department of Economic and Social Affairs) as a function of time. In contrast to the expected Malthusian straight line, we clearly observe a strong upward curvature characterizing "superexponential" behavior. Similar faster-than-exponential

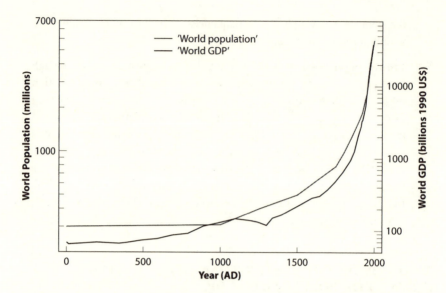

FIG. 10.1. World population and world GDP (gross domestic production) over 2,000 years from 0 to the present in logarithmic scale as a function of time (linear scale), such that a straight line would qualify as exponential growth. The upward curvature of both time series shows that their growth cannot be accounted for by the exponential model and is "superexponential."

growth is also observed in the estimated GDP (gross domestic product) of the world estimated by DeLong at the Department of Economics at U.C. Berkeley [105], for the year 0 up to 2000.

Over a shorter time period, a faster-than-exponential growth is also shown in Figure 10.2 for a number of financial indicators, such as the DJIA since 1790 obtained from the Foundation of the Study of Cycles (www.cycles.org/cycles.htm), the S&P 500 index since 1871, and a number of regional and global financial indices since 1920, including the Latin American index, the European index, the EAFE index, and the World index. The last five financial indices are obtained from Global Financial Data, Los Angeles (www.globalfindata.com). They are shown as their logarithm as a function of time, such that an exponential growth should be qualified by a linear increase.

Source of data: The several data sets analyzed here express the development of mankind on Earth in terms of size and economic impact. They are as follows.

- The human population data from 0 to 1998 was retrieved from the website of The United Nations Population Division, Depart-

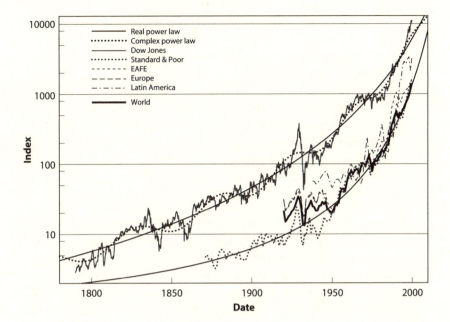

Fig. 10.2. Financial indices in logarithmic scale as a function of time (linear scale). The two largest time series, the Dow Jones extrapolated back to 1790 and the S&P (500) index from 1871, are fitted by a power law $A(t_c - t)^m$ shown as continuous lines. The log-periodic law (corresponding to a complex exponent of the power law) is shown only for the Dow Jones time series as a dashed line. A sophisticated power law analysis suggests an abrupt transition at around 2050 [219]. EAFE is the composite index regrouping Europe, Australia, and Far Eastern countries. Note again the upward curvature, which excludes exponential growth in favor of superexponential acceleration.

ment of Economic and Social Affairs (http://www.popin.org/pop1998/).

- The GDP of the world from 0 to 1998, estimated by J. Bradford DeLong at the Department of Economics, U.C. Berkeley [105], was given to us by R. Hanson [186].

- The financial data series include the DJIA from 1790 to 2000, the S&P index from 1871 to 2000, as well as a number of regional and global indices since 1920. The DJIA was constructed by The Foundation for the Study of Cycles (http://www.cycles.org/cycles.htm). It is the DJIA back to 1896, which has been extrapolated back to 1790 and further. The other indices are from Global Financial Data [159]. These indices are constructed as follows. For the S&P, the data from 1871 to 1918 are from the Cowles commission, which back-calculated the data using the *Commercial and Financial Chronicle*. From 1918, the data is the Standard and Poor's composite index (S&P) of stocks. The other indices use Global Financial Data's indices from 1919 through 1969 and Morgan Stanley Capital International's indices from 1970 through 2000. The EAFE index includes Europe, Australia, and the Far East. The Latin America index includes Argentina, Brazil, Chile, Colombia, Mexico, Peru, and Venezuela.

Demographers usually construct population projections in a disaggregated manner, filtering the data by age, stage of development, region, and so on. Disaggregating and controlling for such variables is thought to be crucial for demographic development and for any reliable population prediction. Here, we propose a different strategy based on aggregated data, which is justified by the following concept: in order to get a meaningful prediction at an aggregate level, it is often more relevant to study aggregate variables than "local" variables, which can miss the whole picture in favor of special idiosyncrasies. To take an example from material sciences, the prediction of the failure of heterogeneous materials subjected to stress can be performed according to two methodologies. Material scientists often analyze in exquisite details the wave forms of the acoustic emissions or other signatures of damage resulting from microcracking within the material. However, this is of very little help in predicting the overall failure, which is often a cooperative global phenomenon [193] resulting from the interactions and interplay between the many different microcracks nucleating, growing, and fusing within the materials. In this example, it has indeed been shown that aggregating all the acoustic emissions in a single aggregated variable is much better for prediction purpose [215]. Similarly, the economic and financial development of the United States and Europe and of other parts of the world are interdependent due to the existence of several coupling mechanisms (exchanges of goods, services, transfer of research and development, immigration, etc.)

The faster-than-exponential growths observed in Figures 10.1 and 10.2 correspond to nonconstant growth rates, which increase with population or with the size of economic factors.

Suppose, for instance, that the growth rate of the population doubles when the population doubles. For simplicity, we consider discrete time intervals as follows. Starting with a population of 1,000, we assume it grows at a constant rate of 1% per year until it doubles. We estimate the doubling time as proportional to the inverse of the growth rate, that is, approximately $1/1\% = 1/0.01 = 100$ years. Actually, there is a multiplicative correction term equal to $\ln 2 = 0.69$ such that the doubling time is $\ln 2/1\% = 69$ years. But we drop this proportionality factor $\ln 2 = 0.69$ for the sake of pedagogy and simplicity. Including it just multiplies all time intervals below by 0.69 without changing the conclusions. Thus, with this approximation, the first doubling time is one century.

When the population turns 2,000, we assume that the growth rate doubles to 2% and stays fixed until the population doubles again to reach 4,000. This takes only fifty years at this 2% growth rate. When the population reaches 4,000, the growth rate is doubled to 4%. The doubling time of the population is therefore approximately halved to twenty-five years and the scenario continues with a doubling of the growth rate every time the population doubles. Since the doubling time is approximately halved at each step, we have the following sequence (time = 0, population = 1,000, growth rate = 1%), (time = 100, population = 2,000, growth rate = 2%), (time = 150, population = 4,000, growth rate = 4%), (time = 175, population = 8,000, growth rate = 8%), and so on. We observe that the time interval needed for the population to double is shrinking very rapidly by a factor of 2 at each step. In the same way that $1/2 + 1/4 + 1/8 + 1/16 + \cdots = 1$, which was immortalized by the ancient Greeks as Zeno's paradox, the infinite sequence of doubling thus takes a finite time and the population reaches infinity at a finite "critical time" approximately equal to $100 + 50 + 25 + \cdots = 200$ (a rigorous mathematical treatment requires a continuous-time formulation, which does not change the qualitative content of the example). A spontaneous singularity has been created by the increasing growth rate!

This process is quite general and applies as soon as the growth rate possesses the property of being multiplied by some factor larger than 1 when the population is multiplied by some constant larger than 1. Such spontaneous singularities are quite common in mathematical descriptions of natural and social phenomena, even if they are often looked at as monstrosities. They are found in many physical and natural systems. Examples are flows of fluids, the formation of black holes, the rupture of structures, and material failure in models of large earthquakes and of stock market crashes, as we have seen in previous chapters. The mathematics of singularities is applied routinely in the physics of phase transitions to describe the transformations from ice to water or from a magnet to a demagnetized state when raising the temperature.

The empirical test of the existence of singularities in the dynamics of the population or the economic indices rest on the way they increase up to the critical time. It turns out that they do so in a self-similar or fractal manner: for a given fixed contraction of the distance in time from the singularity, the population is multiplied by a fixed given factor. Repeating the contraction to approach closer to the singularity leads to the same magnification of the population by the same factor. These properties are captured by the mathematical law called a power law, already discussed in previous chapters. Power laws describe the self-similar geometrical structures of fractals. As we have seen in chapter 6, fractals are geometrical objects with structures at all scales that describe many complex systems, such as the delicately corrugated coast of Brittany or of Norway, the irregular surface of clouds, or the branched structure of river networks. The exponent of the power law is the so-called fractal dimension and, in the present context, quantifies the regular multiplicative structure appearing on the population, on financial indices, and on the distance in time to the singularity.

Plotting the logarithm of the population as a function of the logarithm of the time from the singularity, a power law will appear as a straight line. This is shown in Figures 10.3 and 10.4 for the world population, the world GDP, and the financial indices shown in Figures 10.1 and 10.2. Since the power laws characterizing the population and economic growth are expressed as a function of the time to the singularity, a value has to be chosen for this critical time. In Figure 10.3, the year 2050 is used, which is close to the value obtained from a more sophisticated statistical analysis discussed later (see also [219]). For the financial indices, removing an average inflation of 4% or similar amounts does not change the results qualitatively, but the corresponding results are not quantitatively reliable as the inflation has varied significantly over history with quantitative impacts that are difficult to estimate. Correcting for inflation amounts to subtracting a linear term in the panel where the logarithm of the price is represented as a function of time. This will thus have no impact on the existence of the documented nonlinear upward curvature, qualified as an accelerated superexponential process.

The issue of detrending by inflation to get constant-value dollars and indices: For the United States, it is generally agreed that the inflation factor converting U.S. dollars at the end of the nineteenth century to the

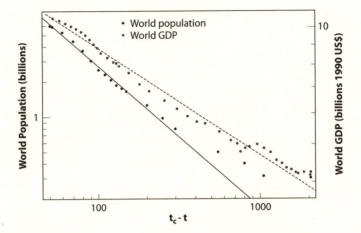

FIG. 10.3. World population and world GDP (with a logarithmic scale) as a function of the time to the critical time $t_c = 2050$ (with a logarithmic scale) such that time flows from right to left. The straight lines are the best fit of the data to power laws (see text) and suggest an abrupt transition at 2050.

end of the twentieth century is about 15: $1 in 1870 is equal approximately to $15 in 1995. This is small compared to France, for instance, where the conversion factor is already as large as 20 to convert 1959 francs into 1995 francs. An example of a detrending to account for inflation of the DJIA since 1885 can be found in [378]. The conversion is performed by using the CPI (consumer price index). The problem is that the definition and way of calculation of the CPI has evolved a lot since its creation. At its origin, it was the wholesale price index, for its ease of measurement. Another way to measure inflation is to use the value of gold in U.S. dollars (about $300 per ounce at present, compared to about 20$ at the end of the nineteenth century, retrieving the factor 15 discussed above). There are many detrending techniques; they all have advantages and problems, which we have chosen to avoid.

Inflation in the United States has undergone several phases:

1. Before 1914, inflation was essentially zero on average, except during the civil war (famous "greenbacks").

2. From 1914 to 1921, there was high inflation followed by deflation in 1921, and then during the depression of 1929–1932, which brought the CPI back to its pre-1914 level.

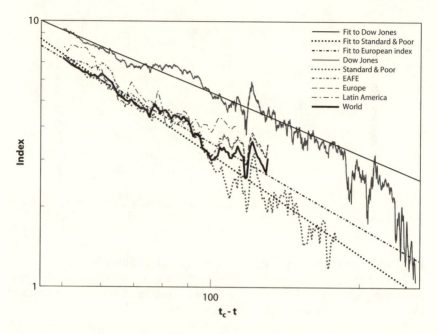

FIG. 10.4. Logarithm of financial indices as a function of the logarithm of the time to the critical time $t_c = 2050$, such that time flows from right to left. The straight lines are the best fits, which qualify as power law behavior, as explained in the text, and suggest an abrupt transition at 2050.

3. From 1933 to the present, there were some strong inflationary periods associated with World War II, the Cold War, the Korean war, the Vietnam war, as well as the oil shocks of the seventies.

The factor 15 thus corresponds approximately to an average annual inflation rate of 4% since 1933. We present in Figure 10.5, the long-term time evolution of the debt of the U.S. federal government. There seems to be a relationship (a factor 2, approximately) between the growth of this debt and inflation rates. This relationship is especially strong in times of war, when inflation is galloping and the debt is accumulating at a fast rate. This is expected since inflation is a simple way for government to leverage taxes, in effect to finance expenses. Due to the complexity in accounting for these intermittent inflationary periods, we have not corrected our data for inflation.

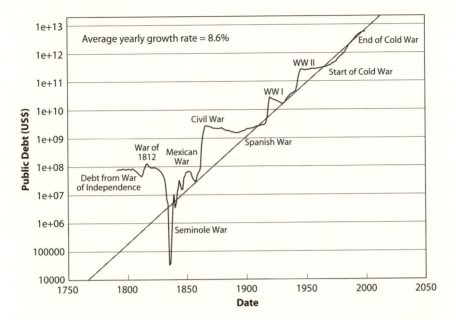

FIG. 10.5. The debt of the U.S. federal government since the war of independence in logarithmic scale as a function of time (linear scale). The notation 1e + 09 corresponds to $1 billion and 1e + 12 corresponds to $1 trillion. In 2000, the U.S. federal goverment debt was about $5.6 trillion. The straight line corresponds to an average exponential law with constant growth rate of 8.6% per year. Notice that the U.S. wars can be seen to punctuate the growth of the debt at many scales. U.S. wars seem to be the main large-scale features explaining the growth of the debt. The data is from the Bureau of the Public Debt (http://www.publicdebt.treas.gov/opd/opd.htm#history). Figure researched and prepared by A. Johansen.

REFINEMENTS OF THE ANALYSIS

COMPLEX POWER LAW SINGULARITIES

The message to be extracted from the analysis of the previous section is that the world population, as well as the major economic indices, have on average grown at an accelerating growth rate which is compatible with a singular behavior occurring within a finite time horizon.

Singularities and infinities were anathema for a long time until it was realized that they are often good mathematical idealizations of many natural phenomena. They are not fully present in reality; only the precursory acceleration can be observed and may announce an important transition. In the present context, they must be interpreted as a kind of "critical

2. 2050

point" signaling a fundamental change of regime. At this point in the analysis, there is still a relatively large uncertainty in the determination of the critical time t_c. As can be seen from the figures, an important reason lies in the existence of large fluctuations around the average power law behavior.

The mathematical theory of power laws, summarized in chapter 6, suggests an efficient way of taking these fluctuations into account by generalizing the concept of a real exponent into a complex exponent. As we have seen, this leads to so-called log-periodic oscillations, which decorate the overall power law acceleration. Fundamentally, this corresponds to replacing the continuous self-similar symmetry by a discrete self-similar symmetry. For instance, in the previous example, the population had a doubling growth rate each time it doubled. In this case, the dynamics is self-similar only under a change of times scales and a change of growth rate performed with a multiplication by a power of two. This leads to discreteness in the acceleration of the population such that the power law is modulated by steps in its slope occurring at each magnification by a factor of 2, that is, steps that are regularly spaced in the logarithmic representation. In reality, other factors than 2 can be selected by the dynamics. In addition, there are many other effects not taken into account in the analysis, which introduce some blurring of the steps and which then become smooth log-periodic oscillations as shown in Figure 10.2 in dashed lines for the DIJA. A nonparametric test of log-periodicity is shown in Figure 10.6, using the same approach as in chapters 7 and 8. One can observe a reliable log-periodic signal.

There are fundamental reasons for introducing log-periodic corrections and complex exponents, deriving from the very structure of the theories describing fundamental particles at the smallest level on one hand and the organization of complex systems on the other hand. Again, examples are fluid flows, formation of black holes, material failure, and stock market crashes, as we have shown in chapters 7–9. The presence of log-periodic oscillations derived from general theoretical considerations may provide a first step to account for the ubiquitous observation of cycles at many scales in population growth and in the economy. Sensitivity analysis of the power law fits shown in Figures 10.3 and 10.4 and of the log-periodic power law fit shown for the Dow Jones in Figure 10.2 as well as tests of the statistical significance all give a large improvement on the position of the critical time t_c. It is found to lie in the range 2042–2062, with 70% probability [219].

The best fit of equation (19) on page 336 to the 210 years of monthly quotes is shown in Figure 10.7, and its parameter values are given in

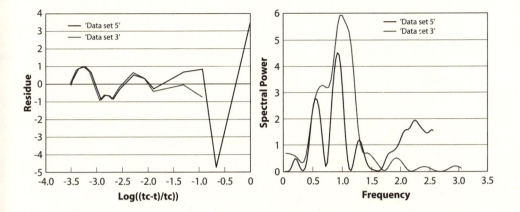

FIG. 10.6. Left panel: Residue between the best simple power law fit and the population data from 1250 to 1998 (called data set 3) and from 1500 to 1998 (called data set 5), performed to (i) check the sensitivity to the part of the demographic data in the past that is the most unreliable and (ii) detect the presence of log-periodicity. Right panel: Spectrum of the residues using a Lomb periodogram technique. For the population data from 1500 to 1998, the position of the peak corresponds to an angular log-frequency $\omega \approx 5.8$, which should be compared with $\omega \approx 6.5$ for the fit with the log-periodic power law formula. For the population data from 1250 to 1998, the peak corresponds to $\omega \approx 6.1$, which should be compared with $\omega \approx 6.5$ for the fit with the log-periodic power law formula. Reproduced from [219] .

the caption. Note the close agreement between the value of the angular log-frequency $\omega \approx 6.5$ compared to $\omega \approx 6.3$ for the world population, as well as the value for the position of the singularity $t_c \approx 2,053$ compared to $t_c \approx 2,056$ for the population. Furthermore, the crossover time scale between the two log-frequencies $\Delta t \approx 171$ years is perfectly compatible with the total time window of 210 years.

PREDICTION FOR THE COMING DECADE

Figure 10.8 shows the extrapolation of the nonlinear log-periodic fit for the DJIA shown in Figure 10.7 up to the critical time $t_c \approx 2053$. Note that the trajectory of the DJIA since the last point (December 1999) used in the fit is following our prediction remarkably well up to the time of proof reading (mid-2002): the log-periodic fit predicts a plateau or a slowdown that may last for about a decade; and since mid-1999, the DJIA has indeed been stagnant.

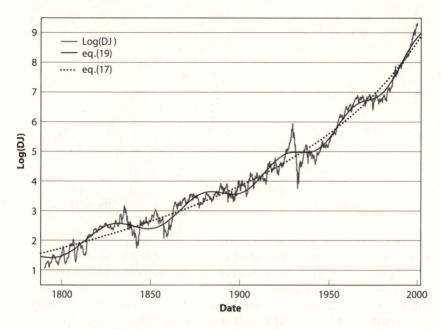

FIG. 10.7. The corrugated line is the (natural) logarithm of the monthly quotes of the DJIA index from December 1790 to December 1999, already shown in Figure 10.2. The upward trending dashed line is the best fit with the simple power law equation giving $\beta \approx +0.27$ (see definition with expression (17) on page 334) and $t_c \approx 2068$. The oscillating solid line is the best fit with the nonlinear log-periodic power law formula (19) giving an exponent $\beta \approx 0.39$, $t_c \approx 2053$, $\omega \approx 6.5$, and $\Delta t \approx 171$. Reproduced from [219].

In Figure 10.8, five other periods of stagnation of the DJIA can be observed. They fall into two classes: (1) weak fluctuations around an approximately constant level (1790–1810, 1880–1900, and 1970–1980), and (2) strong acceleration followed by a crash/depression followed by a recovery (1830–1850 and 1920–1945). Note that the crash of October 1987 belongs to an acceleration regime in this large-scale coarse-grained classification. Will the 2001–2010 decade be in the first or second class?

This prediction of a period of consolidation is in line with the analysis of W. Godley [162], a scholar at the Levy Institute and professor emeritus of applied economics at Cambridge University, England. Godley examined the origin of the remarkable growth of the U.S. economy in the last decade of the twentieth century, based on an analysis of fiscal policy, foreign trade, and private income expenditure and borrowing, and found that it is unsustainable over the following decade.

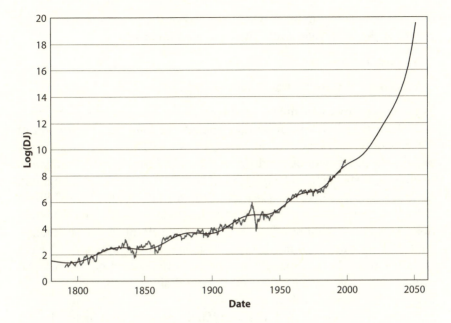

FIG. 10.8. Extrapolation of the nonlinear log-periodic fit for the DJIA shown in Figure 10.7 up to the critical time $t_c \approx 2,053$. The vertical axis is the (natural) logarithm of the DJIA. Note that the trajectory of the DJIA since the last point (December 1999) used in the fit is following our prediction remarkably well: the log-periodic fit predicts a plateau or a slowdown that may last for about a decade; from mid-1999 to mid-2002 (the time of proof-reading), the DJIA fluctuated between approximately 10,000 and 11,500 with no clear upward trend. Reproduced from [219].

To understand Godley's arguments, let us recall a few basic principles of wealth conservation and flux. We are all aware of these principles even unconsciously when we try to balance our expenses by income. From the point of view of the private sector in a given country (consumers and companies), we become instantaneously richer at the aggregate level if

- the government spends more as its spending translates into increasing income for companies and people, and

- exports to foreign countries increase,

as these two processes directly pump funds into the economy. Of course, an instantaneous measure of government spending, counted as a positive flow of funds for the private sector and for households on the short time scale, has to be funded by public borrowing (if deficit arises) whose

Gov Def + Exports = GDP Growth
But + For Debt

interests are paid from taxes which are part of the process that makes us poorer at the aggregate level. Thus, we are poorer if

- taxes increase, and

- imports increase for which we need to pay foreigners,

as these two processes siphon funds out of the economy.

If there is not growth of productivity, in the long run, the growth of the economy measured, for instance, by the GDP should thus follow one-to-one the growth of the difference between the amounts pumped in (government spending and exports) and siphoned out (taxes and imports). Godley shows that between 1961 and 1992 the GDP of the United States did indeed track this net balance of influx funds, within minor fluctuations. From the beginning of 1992 until 1999, GDP rose 3.3% per annum, while the net balance of influx funds rose only 0.6% per annum. The net spending from the government and net exports since 1992, which had been much weaker than in any other period since 1960, cannot be the cause of the large growth of the GDP.

Godley [162] suggested that the GDP growth was fueled by an increasing private financial deficit, that is, excess of personal consumption and housing investment over personal disposable income, which became much larger than ever before. This increase of private deficit can be derived from two sets of evidence. First, the deficit of private households can be inferred from the fact that it must mechanically be equal to the government surplus plus the balance-of-payment deficit. Conversely, a positive private balance is equal to the government deficit plus positive export-minus-import balance. The intuition is that public deficits and balance-of-payment surpluses create income and financial assets for the private sector, whereas budget surpluses and balance-of-payment deficits withdraw income and destroy financial assets. As the budget balance between 1992 and 1999 has changed by a larger amount than ever before (at least since the early 1950s) and has reached a record surplus (2.2% of GDP in the first quarter of 1999), and as the current balance of payments has deteriorated rapidly, the consequence is that the private sector balance has reached a record deficit (5.2% of GDP in the first quarter of 1999) [162]. The increase of private deficit can also be directly measured by comparing private income and expenditure: since 1993, the rise in private expenditure has been increasing much faster than the rise of income [162]. Data shows that most of the fall in private balance and the entire private deficit has taken place in the household sector, rather than by businesses, which financed most of their investment by internally generated funds.

Exponential Index Growth for went !! (handwritten annotation)

Thus, the private sector as a whole has become a net borrower of money (or a net seller of financial assets) on a record and growing scale. The annual rate of net lending rose from about 1% of disposable income ($40 billion) at the end of 1991 to 15% (over $1 trillion) in the first quarter of 1999. The private financial deficit measures the extent to which the flow of payments into the private sector arising from the production and sale of goods and services exceeds private outlays on goods and services and taxes, which have to be made in money.

Capital gains on the stock markets have probably been fueled by increasing borrowing invested in it and may also have fueled increasing consumption. In order to have a continuing influence, the stock market has to continue rising at an accelerating pace faster than exponential. Only a faster-than-exponential stock market growth makes private investors feel richer. They can sell a fraction of their stock without feeling poorer since the accelerating stock market compensates for the reduction in capital, providing a still rising capital. For instance, if investors are used to a stock market growth of 10% per year, they expect their capital to appreciate from $100 to $110 in a year. If during the following year, the growth rate rises to 20%, their capital rises to $120 instead of the expected $110. They can thus spend $10 without having the impression of eating their capital, a psychological process associated with mental accounting [423, 373] (see the section titled "Behavioral Economics" in chapter 4). On the other hand, if there is not acceleration of stock market prices, capital gain only makes a one-time addition to the stock of wealth without changing the future flow of income. If the market is not accelerating, capital gains have only a transitory effect on expenditure. But even a faster-than-exponential accelerating market is unsustainable, as we have seen in preceding chapters. It may take years for the effect of a large rise in the stock market to burn itself out, but over a strategic time period, say 5 to 10 years, it is bound to do so [162].

To summarize, the growth of the GDP and its associated stock market bubble can be associated with several unsustainable processes in the United States [162]: (1) the fall in private savings into ever deeper negative territory, (2) the rise in the flow of net lending to the private sector, (3) the rise in the growth rate of the real money stock, (4) the rise in asset prices at a rate that far exceeds the growth of profits (or of GDP), (5) the rise in the budget surplus, (6) the rise in the current account deficit, (7) the increase in the United States' net foreign indebtedness relative to GDP.

Godley concluded [162] that if spending were to stop rising relative to income without there being either a fiscal relaxation or a sharp recovery in net exports, the impetus that has driven the expansion so far would evaporate and output would not grow fast enough to stop unemployment from rising. If, as seems likely, private expenditure at some stage reverts to its normal relationship with income, there will be, given present fiscal plans, a severe and unusually protracted recession with a large rise in unemployment. Because its momentum has become so dependent on rising private borrowing and rising capital gains, the real economy of the United States is at the mercy of the stock market to an unusual extent. A crash would probably have a much larger effect on output and employment now than in the past [162].

However, there is one key ingredient that has been left out of this analysis: productivity gains. Recall that labor productivity is defined as real output per hour of work. Similarly, total factor productivity is defined as real output per unit of all inputs. Total factor productivity reflects, in part, the overall efficiency with which inputs are transformed into outputs. It is often associated with technology, but it also reflects the impact of a host of other factors, like economies of scale, any unaccounted inputs, resource reallocations, and so on. When productivity grows, the growth of the economy (GDP) can be larger than the growth of the difference between the amounts pumped in (government spending and exports) and siphoned out (taxes and imports), because more output per input creates internally new wealth at the aggregate level. As a consequence, it seems that Godley's arguments do not apply directly.

According to the official U.S. productivity statistics prepared by the U.S. Bureau of Labor Statistics, the average annual growth of total factor productivity was 2.7% between 1995 and 1999 (such a large growth rate implies that productivity would be 70% higher after 20 years). Clearly, the rate of productivity growth can have an enormous effect on real output and living standards. Productivity growth is a fundamental measure of economic health, and all of the major measures of aggregate labor and total factor productivity have recently shown improvements after long spells of sluggishness. If this improved performance continues, strong overall performance of real growth and low inflation may be sustained, although the short-run linkage of productivity to real income (and to output, after the very shortest period) is not as tight as some might expect [415]. Examination of the sources of productivity growth suggests that a major source of the better aggregate performance has been the remarkable surge of the high-technology sector (the New Economy argument!). A recent study of the link between information technology and the U.S. productivity revival in the late 1990s indeed shows that virtually all of the aggregate productivity acceleration can be traced to the industries that either produced information technology or used it most intensively, with essentially no contribution from the remaining industries that were less involved in the IT revolution [416]. Faster productivity growth in this rapidly growing sector has directly added to aggregate growth, and the massive wave of investment in high-technology capital by other sectors has been equally important.

This optimistic view should be tempered, however, by the fact that U.S. productivity growth shows a major cyclical component. In what amounts to a return to Godley's argument [162], it has been shown recently that much of the rebound in productivity growth in the late 1990s is a reflection of the strengthening of aggregate demand, rather than a fundamental improvement in the medium- or longer term productivity trend [165, 166]. The crash of the Nasdaq in April 2000, which reflects the collapse of the New Economy bubble, makes concrete that many New Economy industries have been far from delivering the enormous future incomes that were expected.

The Aging "Baby Boomers."

Summarizing the world demographic structure and its financial assets by single statistics, as we have done so far, is restrictive and may miss important dimensions of the problem. In particular, understanding the economic consequences of the demographic development of the world over future decades probably requires us to distinguish between different segments of the populations, typically the young segment, the "asset accumulating" population (typically in the 40–65 range), and the 65+ segment of the population. These population classes have different impacts in wealth creation, different consumption levels, they exert very different weights on society, and they have very different investment behaviors and needs.

In particular, there is a concern that the aging "Baby Boomers," the generation born in the two decades following the end of World War II, not only will exert an enormous strain on society due to retirement benefits but will correlatively cause a market meltdown as they start, in the decade of 2010, to sell their assets to finance their retirement. To appreciate why this may be of importance, let us recall that public and private pensions control almost a quarter of the United States' tangible wealth, which is roughly equivalent to all of the country's residential real estate. They account for most current savings in the country, are a crucial component of household retirement resources, and have significant effects on labor market mobility and efficiency. Collectively, they hold a tremendous proportion of all common stock. Similar figures hold for most developed industrial countries in Europe and Japan.

When the baby boomers retire, it is already clear that the Social Security system will require drastic changes to remain solvent. Will the stock market experience a similar meltdown as baby boomers withdraw their assets from pension plans [365]? The concern is that when the pension system begins to be a net seller of assets, roughly in the third decade of the century, this could depress stock prices.

J. Poterba [336] of the Massachussets Institute of Technology argued that this simple logic is flawed because it neglects several important dimensions of the problem. First, lower demand for financial assets can lower price only if supply remains relatively unaffected. It is unrealistic to assume that the supply of stocks and bonds will remain fixed. For instance, a more balanced budget will lead goverments to issue fewer bonds. Second and more importantly, large demographic changes can have a substantial effect on economic performance and productivity growth, which in turn will impact asset returns. As we have argued before in this chapter, the magnitude of such indirect effects can be very significant and actually drive the accelerated growth of the economy. This can thus overwhelm any direct effect that population structure may have on asset returns. Third, the possible dependence between asset returns and demographic structure may be weakened by the increasing integration of world capital markets. For open economies with significant foreign investments, it is the global demographic structure that should matter. Finally, empirical data suggests that assets are sold much more slowly during retirement years than they are accumulated during working years.

While not leading to a systematic meltdown, the stability of the markets and their susceptibility to external shocks may be significantly modified by the retirement of Baby Boomers. The impact of these Baby Boomers may also be one of the ingredients in the transition, by the middle of the twenty-first century, to another regime, which is discussed below.

RELATED WORKS AND EVIDENCE

Other authors have also documented a superexponential acceleration of human activity. Kapitza [231] recently analyzed the dynamical evolution of the human population, both aggregated and regionally, and also documented an overall acceleration until recent times, consistent with a power law singularity. He introduces an arbitrary saturation effect to limit the blow-up on the basis that an infinity is impossible. Note that we, in contrast, prefer not to add any parameter and we interpret the approaching singularity as the signature of a transition. Using data from the *Cambridge Encyclopedia*, Kapitza also argued that epochs of characteristic evolutions or changes shrink as a geometrical series. In other words, the epoch sizes are approximately equidistant in the logarithm of the time to present, in agreement with our own findings [219].

In a study of an important related human activity associated with research and development, A. van Raan [436] found that scientific production since the sixteenth century in Europe has accelerated much faster than exponentially [436]. Faster-than-exponential growth also occurs in computing power, as measured by the evolution of the number of MIPS per $1,000 of computer from 1900 to 1997 (see Figure 10.9). Thus, the so-called Moore's law is incorrect, since it implies only an exponential growth. This faster-than-exponential acceleration has been argued to lead to a transition to a new era, around 2030, corresponding to the epoch when we will have the technological means to create superhuman intelligence [438].

From a more standard viewpoint, macroeconomic models have also been developed that predict the possibility of accelerated growth [352]. Maybe the simplest model is that of M. Kremer [243], who noted that, over almost all of human history, technological progress has led mainly to an increase in population rather than an increase in output per person. Kremer developed a simple model in which the economic output per person is equal to a constant factor times the subsistence level, and is thus assumed fixed. The total output is supposed to increase with technology and knowledge and labor (proportional to population), for instance as proportional to their square root such that a multiplication of knowledge or of labor by 4 leads to a multiplication of output by only 2. The growth rate of knowledge and technology is taken proportional to population and to knowledge, embodying the concept that a larger population offers more opportunities for finding exceptionally talented people who will make important innovations and that new knowledge is obtained by leveraging existing knowledge. The resulting equation for the total population exhibits a growth rate, which is proportional to the population. Since the population growth rate grows as a positive power of population, this gives a finite-time singularity due to the positive feedback effects between population/labor, technology/knowledge, and output. Kremer tested this prediction by using population estimates extending back to 1 million B.C., constructed by archaeologists and anthropologists: he showed that the population growth rate is approximately linearly increasing with the

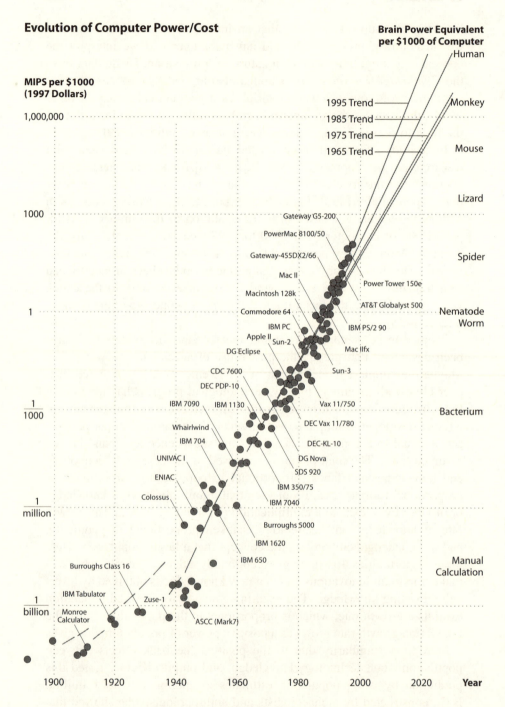

FIG. 10.9.

population [243], in agreement with his prediction. This theory also predicts, in agreement with historical facts, that in the historical times when regions were separated, technological progress was faster in regions with larger populations, thus explaining the differences between Eurasia-Africa, the Americas, Australia, and Tasmania. Our results extend and refine his by showing the consistency of the determination of the critical time, not only for the population but also for the world GDP and for major financial indices.

We have also generalized Kremer's economic model by combining labor, capital, technology/innovation, and output/production to show that the finite-time singularities can be created from the interplay of these simultaneously growing variables, even if the individual quantities do not carry such singularities [219]. This interplay also explains the observation that the population and the financial indices have the same approximate critical time around 2050. The key point of these models is that the long-run growth is created endogenously rather than by random exogenous technical progress. Thus, rather than suffering from diminishing returns and dependence on exogenous innovations, the growth view provides an endogenous mechanism for long-run growth, either by avoiding diminishing returns to capital or by explaining technological progress internally.

A complementary and very simple approach is to incorporate a feedback between the population and the increasing "carrying capacity" of

---

FIG. 10.9. Faster than exponential growth in computing power illustrated by the evolution of the number of MIPS (million of instructions per second) per $1,000 of computer from 1900 to 1997. Steady improvements in mechanical and electromechanical calculators before World War II had increased the speed of calculation a thousandfold over manual methods from 1900 to 1940. The pace quickened with the appearance of electronic computers during the war, and 1940 to 1980 saw a millionfold increase. Since then, the pace has been even quicker, a pace that would make humanlike robots possible before the middle of the twenty-first century. The vertical scale is logarithmic; the major divisions represent thousandfold increases in computer performance. Exponential growth would show as a straight line, and the upward curve indicates faster than exponential growth, an accelerating rate of innovation. The superexponential growth is also seen from the fact that the estimated exponential trends, represented as the straight lines, increase continuously from 1965 to 1995. The reduced spread of the data in the 1990s is probably the result of intensified competition: underperforming machines are more rapidly squeezed out. The animals listed on the right provide a scale of reference of their effective calculation power. Figure reproduced from [307].

the Earth within Malthus's model. Such feedback comes from techno-logical progress such as the use of tools and fire, the development of agriculture, the use of fossil fuels, and fertilizers, as well the expansion into new habitats and the removal of limiting factors by the development of vaccines, pesticides, antibiotics, and so on. If the carrying capacity increases sufficiently fast, a finite-time singularity is obtained in the equations. In reality, the singularity will be smoothed out because the Earth is not infinite.

The logistic equation of population growth and positive feedback on the earth's carrying capacity: As a standard model of population growth, Malthus's model assumes that the size of a population increases by a fixed proportion r over a given period of time independently of the size of the population and thus gives an exponential growth. The logistic equation attempts to correct for the resulting unbounded exponential growth by assuming a finite carrying capacity K such that the population instead evolves according to

$$\frac{dp}{dt} = rp(t)[K - p(t)]. \tag{30}$$

The carrying capacity K is not fixed and has no simple relation with other variables as it depends on the structure of production and consumption. It is contingent on the changing interactions between the physical and biotic environment. While a single number for human carrying capacity is certainly reductionist because of the difficulties in knowing human innovations and biological evolutions, Vitousek et al. [440] have provided a general index of the current intensity of the impact of humans on the biosphere: the total net terrestrial primary production of the biosphere currently appropriated for human consumption is around 40%. This puts the scale of the human presence on the planet in perspective [15].

Cohen and others (see [87] and references therein) have put forward idealized models taking into account interaction between the human population $p(t)$ and the corresponding carrying capacity $K(t)$ by assuming that $K(t)$ increases with $p(t)$ due to technological progress, as explained above. If $dK(t)/dt$ is sufficiently larger than $dp(t)/dt$ for all times, for instance if $K \propto p^{\delta}$ with $\delta > 1$, then $p(t)$ explodes to infinity after a finite time, creating a singularity. Indeed, in this case, the limiting factor $-p(t)$ can be dropped out and (30) becomes

$$\frac{dp}{dt} = r[p(t)]^{1+\delta}, \tag{31}$$

where the growth rate accelerates with time according to $r[p(t)]^\delta$. The generic consequence of a power law acceleration in the growth rate is the appearance of singularities in finite time:

$$p(t) \propto (t_c - t)^z, \text{ with } z = -\frac{1}{\delta} \text{ and } t \text{ close to } t_c. \tag{32}$$

Equation (31) is said to have a "spontaneous" or "movable" singularity at the critical time t_c [37], the critical time t_c being determined by the constant of integration, that is, the initial condition $p(t = 0)$.

Nottale (an astrophysicist), Chaline (a paleontologist), and Grou (an economist) [317, 318] have recently independently applied a log-periodic analysis to the main crises of different civilizations. They first noticed that historical events seem to accelerate. This was actually anticipated by Meyer, who used a primitive form of log-periodic acceleration analysis [295, 296]. Grou [181] has demonstrated that the economic evolution since the neolithic can be described in terms of various dominating poles, which are subjected to an accelerating crisis/no-crisis pattern.

The quantitative analysis of Nottale, Chaline, and Grou on the median dates of the main periods of economic crisis in the history of Western civilization (as listed in [181, 52, 156]) are as follows (the dominating pole and the date are given in years with respect to Jesus Christ): Neolithic: -6500, Egypt: -3000, Egypt: -900, Greece: -100, Rome: $+400$, Byzantium: $+800$, Arab expansion: $+1100$, Southern Europe: $+1400$, Netherlands: $+1650$, Great Britain: $+1775$, Great Britain: $+1830$, Great Britain: $+1880$, Great Britain: $+1935$, United States: $+1975$. A log-periodic acceleration with scale factor $\lambda = 1.32 \pm 0.018$ occurs towards $t_c = 2080 \pm 30$. Agreement between the data and the log-periodic law is statistically significant ($t_{student} = 145$; the probability that this results from chance is much less than 0.01%). It is striking that this independent analysis based on a different data set gives a critical time that is compatible with our own estimate, 2050 ± 10.

SCENARIOS FOR THE "SINGULARITY"

What could be the possible scenarios for mankind close to and beyond the critical time? As seems fitting for the apex of this essay, this last part is highly speculative in nature.

COLLAPSE

Contemporary thinkers foresee collapse from such catastrophes as nuclear war, resource depletion, economic decline, ecological crises, or sociopolitical disintegration (see [419] and references therein).

In such a gloomy scenario, humankind will enter a severe recession fed by the slow death of its host (the Earth). W. Hern [192], from the University of Colorado at Boulder, and other scientists have gone as far as comparing the human species with cancer: the sum of human activities, viewed over the past tens of thousand of years, exhibits all four major characteristics of a malignant process: rapid uncontrolled growth, invasion and destruction of adjacent tissues (ecosystems), metastasis (colonization and urbanization), and dedifferentiation (loss of distinctiveness in individual components as well as communities throughout the planet).

This worry about human population size and growth is shared by many scientists, as we summarized at the beginning of this chapter. Associated with predicted crises of overpopulation, possible scenarios involve a systematic development of terrorism and the segregation of mankind into at least two groups, a minority of wealthy communities hiding behind fortresses from the crowd of "have-nots" roaming outside, as discussed in a recent seminar of the National Academy of Sciences of the United States. This could occur both within developed countries as well as between them and developing countries.

In this respect, history tells us that civilizations are fragile, impermanent things. Our present civilization is a relative newborn, succeeding many others that have died. The fall of the Roman Empire is, in the West, the most widely known instance of collapse. Yet it is only one case of a common process. Collapse is a recurrent feature of human societies. The archeological and historical record is indeed replete with evidence for prehistoric, ancient, and premodern societal collapses. These collapses occurred quite suddenly and frequently involved regional abandonment, replacement of one subsistence base by another (such as agriculture by pastoralism), or conversion to a lower energy sociopolitical organization (such as local state from interregional empire).

Human history as a whole has been characterized by a seemingly inexorable trend toward higher levels of complexity, specialization, and sociopolitical control, processing of greater quantities of energy and information, formation of ever larger settlements, and development of more complex and capable technologies [419]. There is a growing body of research suggesting that the complexity caused by high technology could be humankind's undoing. For instance, the Maya of the southern Peten lowlands dominated Central America up to the ninth century. They built elaborate irrigation systems to support their booming population, which was concentrated in cities growing in size and power, with temples and palaces built and decorated, the arts flourishing, and the landscape being modified and claimed for planting. Overpopulation and the overreliance on irrigation was a major factor in making the Maya vulnerable to failure: the trigger event of their collapse appears to have been a long drought beginning about 840 A.D. (communication of V. Scarborough, an archaelogist from the University of Cincinnati [90]). Among many factors, such as war and plagues, that contributed to many of the collapses of ancient societies, there seem to be two main causes: too many people and too little fresh water. As a consequence, the civilization became vulnerable to environmental stress, for instance, a prolonged drought or a change in climate [90]. The societies themselves appear to have contributed to their own demise by encouraging growth of their population to levels that carried the seeds of their own decline through overexploitation of the land (communication of C. Scarre, an archaelogist from the Cambridge University in England [90]). Similarly, the Akkadian empire in Mesopotamia, the Old Kingdom of Egypt, the Indus Valley civilization in India, and early societies in Palestine, Greece, and Crete all collapsed in a catastrophic drought and cooling of the atmosphere between 2300 and 2200 B.C.

The accumulation of high-resolution paleoclimatic data that provide an independent measure of the timing, amplitude, and duration of past climate events shows that the climate during the past 11,000 years has been punctuated by many climatic instabilities [449]: multidecadal to multicentury-length droughts started abruptly, were unprecedented in the experience of the existing societies, and were highly disruptive to their agricultural foundations because social and technological innovations were not available to counter the rapidity, amplitude, and duration of changing climatic conditions. These climatic events were abrupt, involved new conditions that were unfamiliar to the inhabitants of the time, and persisted for decades to centuries. They were therefore highly disruptive, leading to societal collapse—an adaptive response to otherwise insurmountable stresses [449].

It is tempting to believe that modern civilization, with its scientific and technological capacity, its energy resources, and its knowledge of economics and history, should be able to survive whatever crises ancient and simpler societies found insurmountable. But how firm is this belief in view of the fact that our modern civilization has achieved the highest level of complexity known to humanity? This complexity comes with a high differentiation of human activities, a strong interdependence, and a reliance on environmental resources to feed concentrated populations. These ingredients seem to have been the roots of collapse of many previous civilizations. Tainter [420] suggested that the diminishing returns to problem solving due to increased complexity limited the ability of historical societies to resolve their challenges. To allow contemporary societies to address global change, he proposes encouraging and financing problem solving in the context of a system of evolving complexity. This view seems the opposite of our suggestion of a coming crisis announced by the acceleration of population growth fed by its associated economic growth, both relying on the unfolding of scientific and technological revolutions. The acceleration of innovations is the solution that Tainter requires to avoid the dead-ends confronted by previous civilizations. In contrast, we suggest that this acceleration carries the roots of its own collapse in its womb.

How can these two viewpoints be reconciled? To answer, we have to draw on recent research in optimization/remediation of complex systems, with applications in epidemiology, aeronautical and automotive design, forestry and environmental studies, the Internet, traffic, and power systems, which suggest that complex systems develop somewhat paradoxically a remarkable robustness as well as a fragility [71, 394]. Indeed, there is a tendency for interconnected systems to gain robustness against uncertainties in one area by becoming more sensitive in other areas. A system might attain robustness against common uncertainties and yet be hypersensitive to design flaws or rare events. For example, organisms and ecosystems exhibit remarkable robustness to large variations in temperature, moisture, nutrients, and predation, but can be catastrophically sensitive to tiny perturbations of a different kind, such as a genetic mutation, an exotic species, or a novel virus.

As an illustration, consider a forest in which spontaneous ignition (sparks and lightning) occurs preferentially in some part of the forest; in other words, the spatial distribution of sparks is not homogeneous. The management problem is to conceive an optimal array of firewalls that provides the highest possible yield of the forest, while taking into account the cost of building and keeping firewalls in good working order. To a given geometrical structure of firewalls corresponds a specific size and a specific spatial distribution of protected domains or tree clusters. When a spark falls on a tree within a cluster, the whole connected cluster of trees delimited by the firewalls bounding it is supposed to burn entirely. In other words, the fires are supposed to stop only at the fire-walls. We can thus reformulate the optimal management of the forest so that it consists of building firewalls that maximize the yield after fires, that is, that minimize the average destructive impact of fires, given the cost of building and keeping firewalls in good working order.

In the presence of a heterogeneous spatial probability density ρ of sparks, it is clear that the density r of firewalls should not be spatially uniform: more firewalls are needed in sensitive regions where the sparks are numerous. The density r of firewalls will thus not be constant according to the optimization process but will adjust to the predefined distribution ρ of sparks. This spatial distribution ρ of sparks determines the probability p_i that a spark ignites a fire in a given domain or cluster i bounded by the fire walls: p_i is the sum of ρ over the cluster. In the presence of a nonuniform distribution of sparks, it can be shown [71, 394] that the optimization of the yield, that is, the minimization of the average fire size, given the cost of firewalls, leads to a power distribution of domains delimited by firewalls. The optimization process provides robust performance despite the uncertainties quantified by the probabilities p_i. In the forest fire example, the optimal distribution of spatial firewalls is the result of the interplay between our a priori knowledge of the uncertainty in the distribution of sparks and the cost resulting from fires. The solutions are robust with respect to the existence of uncertainties, that is, to the fact that we do not know deterministically where sparks are going to ignite; we only know their probability distribution.

However, the optimal spatial geometry of firewalls is fragile with respect to an error in the quantification of the probabilities p_i, that is, to model errors, to use the terminology of chapter 9. It is not the uncertainty that is dangerous, but errors in quantifying this uncertainty: a different set of p_i would lead to a very different spatial distribution of firewalls. Thus, an optimized system of firewalls will be fragile, that is, poorly adapted to even a modest but long-term spatial redistribution of spark ignitions [71, 394].

Following this concept, we can rephrase the problem and say that the robustness of our modern society is derived from its adaptation to a model of growth relying on a succession of technological revolutions and its applications. However, our society may be fragile with respect to a global change that may require a different dynamical regime. The concept of a critical singularity suggests in addition that this fragility or susceptibility to global changes will rise as the optimization of society and its complexity increase. Following Tainter [420], we probably need to develop solutions for qualitatively different regimes. These solutions

(a)   (b)

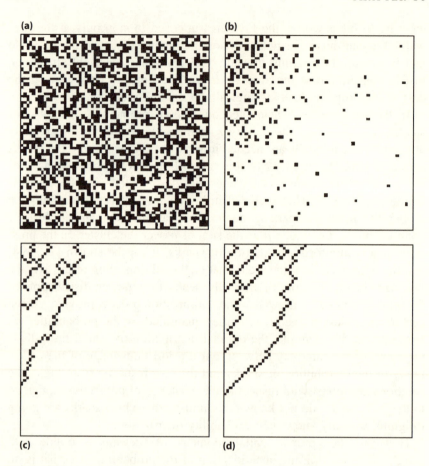

(c)   (d)

FIG. 10.10. Unoccupied sites are black, and occupied sites (trees) are white in a
system of $N = 64$ by $N = 64$ sites. The goal is to optimize the yield of the
model forest, that is, to optimize the number of trees minus the losses due to fires.
Sparks are assumed to be more probable in the top-left corner. The optimal tree
configurations of four different forest management strategies are compared in the
different panels. In panel (a), trees are grown at random step by step at previously
empty sites. The optimal tree configuration corresponds to the so-called percolation
critical density. This is the "laissez-faire" strategy. In panels (b)–(d), an optimization
is performed by calculating for each choice of an additional tree what would be the
resulting average yield, thus weighting the possible future impact of random sparks.
An increasing degree of sophistication is used from panel (b) to (d) according to
the "design parameter" D. D measures the number of tree configurations that are
considered upon the addition of a new tree in the calculation of the optimal tree
planting strategy. Panel (b) corresponds to $D = 2$; that is, only two tree positions
are examined and the best one is chosen. Panel (c) corresponds to $D = N = 64$
and panel (d) corresponds to $D = N^2 = 4096$; that is, all possible positions for the

NO HABITAT
TRACKING

may not emerge spontaneously from the accelerated innovation process and ensuing growth which feed on themselves while preventing exploration of other dynamical modes.

A disruption that is particularly predicted is that future climatic change will involve both natural and anthropogenic forces and will be increasingly dominated by the latter. Current estimates show that we can expect them to be large and rapid. Global temperature will rise and atmospheric circulation will change, leading to a redistribution of rainfall that is difficult to predict. These changes will affect a world population expected to increase from about 6 billion people today to about 10 billion by 2050. In spite of technological changes, most of the world's people will continue to be subsistence or small-scale market agriculturalists, who are similarly as vulnerable to climatic fluctuations as the late prehistoric/early historic societies. Furthermore, in an increasingly crowded world, habitat tracking as an adaptive response will not be an option. We do, however, have distinct advantages over societies in the past because we can anticipate the future somewhat. We must use this information to design strategies that minimize the impact of climate change on societies that are at greatest risk. This will require substantial international cooperation, without which the twenty-first century will likely witness unprecedented social disruptions [449].

TRANSITION TO SUSTAINABILITY

A more optimistic perspective is that "ecological" actions will grow in future decades, leading to a smooth transition towards an ecologically integrated industry and humanity. There are some signs that we are on this path: during the 1990s, the use of wind power grew at a rate of 26% a year, and solar photovoltaic power at 17%, compared to the growth

---

FIG. 10.10 *continued.* additional tree are studied with respect to their consequence on the danger of fires. This is reminiscent of playing chess, in which D is the number of combinations that the player examines. Note that, as the sophistication D of the optimization process increases, the optimal forest becomes denser and denser, with only a few empty sites remaining that are organized so as to form effective firewalls. These firewalls have been optimized to disconnect the forest in an optimal set of tree clusters, given the known distribution of dangerous sparks. Note that, if the sparks were suddenly to become more numerous in the lower right corner of the square, the optimal solution (d) would behave catastrophically, illustrating also the fragile nature of this optimization. Figure reproduced from [72].

in coal and oil at under 2%; governments have ratified more than 170 international environmental treaties, on everything from fishing to desertification.

However, there is serious resistance, in particular because there is no consensus on the seriousness of the situation, as described in the section on "The Optimistic Viewpoint of Social Scientists." The problem is not that this optimistic view is wrong. By economic accounting, the optimistic view is mostly right. The issues raised by the analysis presented here [219] and by others is that the approach to a finite-time singularity can be surprisingly fast in the last few decades preceding it. As a result, linear extrapolations will be grossly misleading, with catastrophic consequences. What our analysis shows is that the "optimistic viewpoint" contains endogenously its own death, in the form of a predicted singularity, precisely created by the acceleration feeding the optimistic viewpoint.

The transition to sustainability consists in the evolution from a growth regime to a balanced symbiosis with nature and with the Earth's resources. This would require the transition to a knowledge-based society, in which knowledge, intellectual, artistic, and humanistic values replace the quest for material wealth. Indeed, the main economic difference is that knowledge is "nonrival" [350]: the use of an idea or of a piece of knowledge in one place does not prevent it from being used elsewhere. In contrast, say an item of clothing used by an individual precludes its simultaneous use by someone else. Only the emphasis on nonrival goods will ultimately limit the plunder of the planet. The incentives that people need to work and to find meaning in their lives should be found beyond material wealth and power. Some so-called "primitive" societies seem to have been able to evolve into such a state.

Many researchers and environmental groups advocate a transition from our present energy systems, dominated by use of oil, gas, and coal, which are not sustainable, to a more direct use of solar energy in the form of radiation, wind, ocean motions, and biomass production (see, for instance, [148, 149, 151] and references therein). The sustainable production of food and biomass depends on a number of critical components, which include soil quality, water quality with adequate quantity, climate, air quality, agriculture technology, fertilizer technology, biotechnology, and biodiversity. Novel advances in plant biotechnology must be deployed for the benefits of the rising population of developing countries as the gains in food production provided by the "green" revolution have reached their ceilings while world population continues to rise [91].

QUANTITY
QUALITY SOIL

There is also a global problem of soil erosion, as almost 1% of the world's topsoil is lost annually [151] (at this rate, half the soil will be lost in less than 70 years). Soil erosion can be prevented by intelligent use of water and of vegetation. The quality of soil is also a crucial issue: soil is a very complex material formed by the action of the atmosphere, the hydrosphere, and the biosphere on rocky materials, collectively called "weathering." To reform a soil from its parent rock once the soil is removed takes many decades to millenia. There is a need for total soil chemistry with the development of a new agriculture based on diversity and integration of techniques for a multiplicity of fields. Water and soil are closely associated. The management of water supplies requires integration of knowledge from almost all sciences and engineering with major input coming from sustainable sociology and economics [148, 149, 151].

Extraction of ore and purification of minerals produce enormous amounts of toxic elements and pollution like arsenic, halogens (fluorine, chlorine, and bromine), mercury, lead, sulphur, and selenium. We need new engineering technologies to collect materials with minimal disturbance to the environment. As 75% of the population of industrial nations live in cities, there is a vast problem of waste management, including technologies leading to massive air and water pollution. We need good quality control at the source and recycling technology. To produce truly sustainable systems, all people must be educated and must understand our life support system [150].

Last but not least, we need the will to act rather than lip service [264]. The triumphalism around economic growth has left no time to spare for concern about the environment. For the major multinationals in the resource, energy, chemicals, and agriculture industries to work really concretely towards sustainability, the market forces do not seem sufficient [145] as long as the service really offered by the environment is not adequately priced and inserted into the accounting balance.

Ecosystems are capital assets: when properly managed, they yield a flow of vital goods and services [99]. The value of nature includes the production of goods (such as seafood and timber), life support processes (such as pollination, air and water purification, climate stabilization, mitigation of floods and droughts, pest control, generation of fertile soils), and life-fulfilling conditions (such as recreation, beauty, and serenity). Moreover, ecosystems have value in terms of the conservation of options (such as genetic diversity for future use). To take another example, the economic value of part of the Amazon rainforest is not limited to its financial value as a repository of future pharmaceutical products or as a location for ecotourism. That "use" value may only be a small part of the properly defined economic valuation. For decades, economists have recognized the importance of the "non-use" value of environmental amenities such as wilderness areas or endangered species. The public nature of these goods makes it particularly difficult to quantify these values empirically, as market prices do not exist [145]. Indeed, relative to other forms of capital, ecosystems are poorly understood, scarcely monitored, and (in many cases) undergoing rapid degradation and depletion.

It has been argued that the process of economic valuation could improve stewardship [99]. Individuals and societies already assess the value of nature implicitly in their collective decision making, too often treating ecosystem services as "free." Until recently, this was generally safe to do: relatively speaking, ecosystem capital was abundant, and the impacts of economic activity were minimal. Ecosystem capital is becoming ever scarcer, however, so that it is now critical to understand both how to value ecosystems and the limitations of such valuations [145]. R. Costanza of the University of Maryland and twelve coauthors have made one of the most controversial recent attempts to integrate economics and ecology to obtain the total monetary value for the world's "ecosystem services and natural capital" [94]: they obtained the figure of $33 trillion per year, which exceeds the sum of the world's gross national products. Costanza et al. described the $33 trillion per year as "a minimum estimate" for the "current economic value" of 17 ecosystem services (from atmospheric gas regulation to the provision of "cultural value") summed over 16 types of ecosystems (from the open ocean to urban centers). This work has raised much criticisms, from "a serious underestimate of infinity" by M. Toman of Resources for the Future, to "non-applicable as neoclassical economics measures value in the context of a specific exchange." In the neoclassical economics view, it is nonsensical to ask what the value of the world's ecosystem services is. A related requirement is that one can evaluate only small (or "marginal") changes from current conditions. However, what is important in our view is that this order of magnitude study corrects the result of 1% of GNP or less for the value of ecosystem services that many would have guessed. Having this number is better than no number at all, as it can foster the integration of environmental sustainability into industrial and economics approaches.

RESUMING ACCELERATING GROWTH BY OVERPASSING FUNDAMENTAL BARRIERS

The new regime announced by the finite-time singularity could be a renewed race for growth, an even stronger acceleration enhanced by new discoveries enabling mankind to fully exploit the vast resources of the oceans (mostly untapped yet) and even that of other planets, especially beyond our solar system. The conditions for this are rather drastic. For the planets, novel modes of much faster propulsions are required as well as revolutions in our control of the adverse biological effects of space on humans with its zero gravity and high radiation. New drugs and genetic engineering could prepare humans for the hardship of space, leading to a new era of enhanced accelerated growth after a period of consolidation, culminating in a new finite-time singularity, probably centuries in the future.

The growth rate of computer power (see Figure 10.9) followed more recently by the advent of the large-scale use of the Internet makes more probable a major evolution of human interactions with computers and networks than with any other machines. V. Vinge, [438] emeritus professor at the Department of Mathematical Sciences at San Diego State University and an author of science fiction books, proposes that the acceleration of technological progress will cause the creation by technology of entities with greater than human intelligence before 2030. He explored several routes by which science may achieve this breakthrough:

- There may be developed computers that are "awake" and superhumanly intelligent. (To date, there has been much controversy as to whether we can create human equivalence in a machine. But if the answer is "yes, we can," then there is little doubt that beings more intelligent can be constructed shortly thereafter.)

- Large computer networks (and their associated users) may "wake up" as a superhumanly intelligent entity.

- Computer–human interfaces may become so intimate that users may reasonably be considered superhumanly intelligent.

- Biological science may provide means to improve natural human intellect.

Vinge used the word "singularity" quite adequately in the present context to describe the point where our old models must be discarded and a new reality rules as a result of this transition to a superhuman intelligence. If or when greater-than-human intelligence will drive progress, this progress will be much more rapid and will probably involve the creation of still more intelligent entities, on a still-shorter time scale. In the evolutionary past, animals adapted to problems and made inventions, the world acting as its own simulator in the case of natural selection over time scales of millions of years. Superhuman intelligence can lead to a drastic acceleration of natural evolution by executing simulations at much higher speeds. Developments that before were thought to be possible in "a million years" (if ever) may happen in this or in the next century [438]. This accelerated evolution may have disturbing consequences. Superhumanly intelligent machines would not be humankind's "tools," any more than humans are the tools of rabbits or robins or chimpanzees. Will they treat us more kindly than we have treated animals?

There are several arguments opposing the possibility of human intelligence and consciousness, not to speak of superhuman. R. Penrose, professor of physics and mathematics at the University of Oxford and at Penn State University, develops an argument based on Gödel's incompleteness theorem that the mechanism for consciousness involves quantum gravitational phenomena, acting through microtubules in neurons [331]. J. Searle, professor of philosophy at U.C. Berkeley, holds that the syntactic manipulation of formal symbols by computers does not by itself constitute a semantics [367]. Computers are mindless manipulators of symbols, and they don't understand what they are "saying." It should be noted that Searle's biological naturalism does not entail that brains and only brains can cause consciousness. Searle is careful to point out that while it appears to be the case that certain brain functions are sufficient for producing conscious states, our current state of neurobiological knowledge prevents us from concluding that they are necessary for producing consciousness.

There is also the possibility that the computational competence of single neurons may be far higher than generally believed. If so, our present computer hardware might be as much as ten orders of magnitude short of the equipment we carry around in our heads. If this is true (or for that matter, if the Penrose or Searle critique is valid), we might never see the singularity [438]. But if the technological singularity can happen, it will. Vinge argues that we cannot prevent the singularity, that its coming is an inevitable consequence of humans' natural competitiveness and the possibilities inherent in technology.

Within this scenario, a central feature of strongly superhuman entities will likely be their ability to communicate at variable bandwidths, including ones far higher than speech or written messages. What happens when pieces of ego can be copied and merged, when the size

FASTER CORP
ADJUST = HAZARD
Economy ≈ MARKET

of a self-awareness can grow or shrink to fit the nature of the problems under consideration [438]? These are probably essential features of strong superhumanity, with time accelerated so much that it becomes unending and with the ability to truly know one another and to understand the deepest mysteries.

THE INCREASING PROPENSITY TO EMULATE
THE STOCK MARKET APPROACH

The immersion of our analysis of stock markets into this general demographic, environmental, and economic framework was a necessary step because, at long time scales, their future and, in particular, the occurrence of financial crashes cannot be decoupled from the many other components of the world in which they "live."

We would like to conclude this essay by pointing out that, reciprocally, the whole economy is progressively emulating the behavior of stock markets. In his testimony on monetary policy on the last Wednesday February 2001, Alan Greenspan, the chairman of the U.S. Federal Reserve, made the following argument: "The same forces that have been boosting growth in structural productivity seem also to have accelerated the pace of cyclical adjustment." In other words, the recent plunge in manufacturing is just a matter of nimble firms, reflexes speeded up by information technology, moving quickly to get rid of excess inventories [250]. This faster adjustment contains a caveat: firms' investment decisions are starting to emulate the hair-trigger behavior of financial investors. This was summarized in Greenspan's testimony as follows: "The hastening of the adjustment to emerging imbalances is generally beneficial ... But the faster adjustment process does raise some warning flags ... flags appear to be acting in far closer alignment with one another than in decades past."

This implies that a growing part of the economy may be starting to act like a financial market, with all that implies, like the potential for bubbles and panics. Indeed, Krugman has argued that, far from making the economy more stable, the rapid responses of today's corporations make their investment in equipment and software vulnerable to the kind of self-fulfilling pessimism that used to be possible only for investment in paper assets like stocks [250]. A typical behavior is that businesses are abruptly scaling back their investment plans, not because they are already hurt but because a developing climate of fear has convinced managers that it would be "prudent to be prudent." And since one company's invest-ment is another company's sales, such retrenchment can bring on the very slump that managers fear [250]. We argue that, symmetrically, opti-mistic views of the future can progressively transform into self-fulfilling bubbles which define corporations strategies, and their investment and recruitment objectives. If the bubbles inflate too much or for too long, they may collapse in "crashes."

Thus, far from being a thing of the past, it is probable that the spec-ulative and self-fulfilling bubble and antibubble behaviors are going to inhabit a larger and larger portion of economic and human activities. The phenomena and underlying mechanisms discussed in this book may thus become even more relevant to a larger and larger portion of human activ-ity. Understand their origin, and be prepared for subtle but significant precursors!

References

1. Adam, M. C. and Szafarz, A. (1992). Speculative bubbles and financial markets, *Oxford Economic Papers* **44**, 626–640.
2. Agent-Based Computational Economics, http://www.econ.iastate.edu/tesfatsi/ace.htm.
3. Allen, F. and Gale, D. (1999). Bubbles, crises, and policy, *Oxford Review of Economic Policy* **15** (3), 9–18.
4. Allen, F. and Gale, D. (2000). Bubbles and crises, *Economic Journal* **110** (460), 236–255.
5. Altes, R. A. (1976). Sonar for generalized target description and its similarity to animal echolocation systems, *Journal of the Acoustic Society of America* **59**, 97–105.
6. Andersen, J. V., Gluzman, S., and Sornette, D. (2000). Fundamental framework for technical analysis, *European Physical Journal B* **14**, 579–601.
7. Anderson, P. W. (1972). More is different, *Science* **177**, 393–396.
8. Anderson, P. W., Arrow, K. J., and Pines, D., Editors (1988). *The economy as an evolving complex system* (Addison-Wesley, New York).
9. Andrade, R. F. S. (1999). Thermodynamical behavior of aperiodic Ising models on hierarchical lattices, *Physical Review E* **59**, 150–157.
10. Andreassen, P. B. and Kraus, S. J. (1990). Judgemental extrapolation and the salience of change, *Journal of Forecasting* **9**, 347–372.
11. Ang, J. S. (1978). A note on the leverage effect on portfolio performance measures, *Journal of Financial & Quantitative Analysis* **13**, 567–571.
12. Anifrani, J.-C., Le Floc'h, C., and Sornette, D. (1999). Prédiction de la rupture de réservoirs composites de haute pression à l'aide de l'émission acoustique, *Contrôle Industriel* **220**, 43–45.
13. Anifrani, J.-C., Le Floc'h, C., Sornette, D., and Souillard, B. (1995). Universal log-periodic correction to renormalization group scaling for rupture stress prediction from acoustic emissions, *Journal of Physics I France* **5**, 631–638.

14. Arneodo, A., Bacry, E., Graves, P. V., and Muzy, J.-F. (1995). Characterizing long-range correlations in DNA sequences from wavelet analysis, *Physical Review Lett.* **74**, 3293–3296.

15. Arrow, K., Bolin, B., Costanza, R., Dasguptam, P., Folke, C., Holling, C. S., Jansson, B.-O., Levin, S., Mäler, K.-G., Perrings, C., and Pimentel, D. (1995). Economic growth, carrying capacity and the environment, *Science* **268**, 520–521.

16. Arrow, K. J. and Debreu, G. (1954). Existence of an equilibrium for a competitive economy, *Econometrica* **22**, 265–290.

17. Arthur, B. W. (1994). Inductive reasoning and bounded rationality (The El Farol Problem), *American Economic Review (Papers and Proceedings)* **84**.

18. Arthur, W., Lane, D., and Durlauf, S., Editors (1997). *The economy as an evolving complex system II* (Addison-Wesley, Redwood City).

19. Arthur, W. B. (1987). Self-reinforcing mechanisms in economics, *Center for Economic Policy Research* **111**, 1–20.

20. Arthur, W. B., Ermoliev, Y. M., and Kaniovsky, Y. M. (1984). Strong laws for a class of path-dependent stochastic processes with applications, in *Proceedings of the International Conference on Stochastic Optimization*, A. Shiryaev and R. Wets, editors (Springer-Verlag, New York), pp. 287–300.

21. Arthur, W. B., Holland, J. H., LeBaron, B., Palmer, R., and Taylor, P. (1997). Asset pricing under endogenous expectations in an artificial stock market, in *The Economy as an Evolving Complex System II*, W. Arthur, D. Lane, and S. Durlauf, editors (Addison-Wesley, Redwood City).

22. Asimov, I. (1982). *The Foundation Trilogy: Three Classics of Science Fiction* (Doubleday, Garden City, New York).

23. Asimov, I. (1983). *Foundation* (Ballantine Books, New York).

24. Assoe, K. G. (1998). Regime-switching in emerging stock market returns, *Multinational Finance Journal* **2**, 101–132.

25. Bachelier, L., Théorie de la speculation, 1900, *Annales de l'Ecole Normale Supérieure* (translated in the book *Random Character of Stock Market Prices*); Théorie des probabilités continues, 1906, *Journal des Mathematiques Pures et Appliquées*; Les Probabilités cinematiques et continues, 1913, *Annales de l'Ecole Normale Supérieure*.

26. Bak, P. (1996). How Nature Works: The Science of Self-Organized Criticality (Copernicus, New York).

27. Bak, P., Norrelykke, S. F., and Shubik, M. (1999). Dynamics of money, *Physical Review E* **60**, 2528–2532.

28. Barlevy, G. and Veronesi, P. (2000). Rational panics and stock market crashes, Working paper, http://gsb.uchicago.edu/.

29. Barnsley, M. (1988). *Fractals Everywhere* (Academic Press, Boston).

30. Barro, R. J., Fama, E. F., Fischel, D. R., Meltzer, A. H., Roll, R., and Telser, L. G. (1989). *Black Monday and the Future of Financial Markets*, R. W. Kamphuis, Jr., R. C. Kormendi, and J. W. H. Watson, editors (Mid American Institute for Public Policy Research, Inc. and Dow Jones-Irwin, Inc. Toronto, Canada).

31. Barton, C. C. and La Pointe, P. R., Editors (1995). *Fractals in the Earth Sciences* (Plenum Press, New York, London).

32. Basle Committee on Banking Supervision (1997). *Core Principles for Effective Banking Supervision*, Basle, September 1997. The Basle Committee on Banking Supervision is a Committee of banking supervisory authorities which was established by the central bank Governors of the Group of Ten countries in 1975. It

consists of senior representatives of bank supervisory authorities and central banks from Belgium, Canada, France, Germany, Italy, Japan, Luxembourg, Netherlands, Sweden, Switzerland, United Kingdom and the United States. It usually meets at the Bank for International Settlements in Basle, where its permanent Secretariat is located.

33. Batagelj, V. and Mrvar, A. (2000). Some analyses of Erdös collaboration graph, *Social Networks* **22**, 173–186.

34. Bates, D. S. (1991). The crash of '87: Was it expected? The evidence from options markets, *Journal of Finance* **46**, 1009–1044.

35. Batten, D. S. (1981). Foreign exchange markets: The dollar in 1980, *Federal Reserve Bank of St. Louis Review* **63**, 22–30.

36. Bauer, R. J. and Dahlquist, J. R. (1999). *Technical Market Indicators, Analysis and Performance* (Wiley, New York).

37. Bender, C. and Orszag, S. A. (1978). *Advanced Mathematical Methods for Scientists and Engineers* (McGraw-Hill, New York), p. 147.

38. Benford, F. (1938). The law of anomalous numbers, *Proceedings of the American Philosophical Society* **78**, 551–572.

39. Bikhchandani, S., Hirshleifer, D., and Welch, I. (1992). A theory of fads, fashion, custom, and cultural change as informational cascades, *Journal of Political Economy* **100**, 992–1026.

40. Black, F. (1986). Noise, *Journal of Finance* **41**, 529–543.

41. Black, F. and Scholes, M. (1973). The pricing of options and corporate liabilities, *Journal of Political Economy* **81**, 637–659.

42. Blackmore, S. (2000). *The Meme Machine* (Oxford University Press, Oxford, U.K.).

43. Blanchard, O. J. (1979). Speculative bubbles, crashes and rational expectations, *Economics Letters* **3**, 387–389.

44. Blanchard, O. and Fischer, S. (1989). *Lectures on Macroeconomics* (MIT Press, Cambridge, MA).

45. Blanchard, O. J. and Watson, M. W. (1982). Bubbles, rational expectations and speculative markets, in *Crisis in Economic and Financial Structure: Bubbles, Bursts, and Shocks*, P. Wachtel, editor (Lexington Books, Lexington, MA).

46. Bollerslev, T., Chou, R. Y., and Kroner, K. F. (1992). ARCH modeling in finance: A review of the theory and empirical evidence, *Journal of Econometrics* **51**, 5–59.

47. Bonanno, G. and Zeeman, E. C. (1988). Divergence of choices despite similarity of characteristics: An application of catastrophe theory, *European Journal of Operational Research* **36**, 379–392.

48. Boissevain, J. and Mitchell, J., Editors (1973). *Network Analysis: Studies in Human Interaction* (Mouton, The Hague).

49. Bouchaud, J.-P. and Cont, R. (1998). A Langevin approach to stock market fluctuations and crashes, *European Physics Journal B* **6**, 543–550.

50. Bouchaud, J.-P. and Potters, M. (2000). *Theory of Financial Risks: From Statistical Physics to Risk Management* (Cambridge [England]; New York, Cambridge University Press).

51. Boutchkova, M. K. and Megginson, W. L. (2000). Privatization and the rise of global capital markets, *Financial Management* **29** (4), 31–75.

52. Braudel, F. (1979). *Civilisation matérielle, économie et capitalisme* (A. Colin, Paris, France).

53. Brock, W., Lakonishok, J., and LeBaron, B. (1992). Simple technical trading rules and the stochastic properties of stock returns, *Journal of Finance* **47**, 1731–1764.

54. Brock, W. A. (1993). Pathways to randomness in the economy: Emergent nonlinearity and chaos in economics and finance, *Estudios Económicos* **8**, 3–55.

55. Brock, W. A. and Hommes, C. H. (1997). A rational route to randomness, *Econometrica* **65**, 1059–1095.

56. Brock, W. A. and Hommes, C. H. (1998). Heterogeneous beliefs and routes to chaos in a simple asset pricing model, *Journal of Economic Dynamics and Control* **22**, 1235–1274.

57. Brock, W. A. and Hommes, C. H. (1999). Rational animal spirits, in *The Theory of Markets*, P. J. J. Herings, G. van der Laan, and A. J. J. Talman, editors (North-Holland, Amsterdam), pp. 109–137.

58. Brock, W. A. and LeBaron, B. D. (1996). A dynamic structural model for stock return volatility and trading volume, *Review of Economics & Statistics* **78**, 94–110.

59. Broglia, R. A., Terasaki, J., and Giovanardi, N. (2000). The Anderson-Goldstone-Nambu mode in finite and in infinite systems, *Physics Reports* **335**, 2–18.

60. (The) Bubble Project at http://is.dal.ca/dmcneil/bubble.html.

61. Budyko, M. I. (1969). The effect of solar radiation variations on the climate of the earth, *Tellus* **21**, 611–619.

62. Burgess, C. P. (2000). Goldstone and pseudo-Goldstone bosons in nuclear, particle and condensed-matter physics, *Physics Reports* **330**, 194–261.

63. Cai, J. (1994). A Markov model of switching-regime ARCH, *Journal of Business & Economic Statistics* **12**, 309–316.

64. Callen, E. and Shapero, D. (1974). A theory of social imitation, *Physics Today* **July**, 23–28.

65. Camerer, C. (1992). The rationality of prices and volume in experimental markets, *Organizational Behavior & Human Decision Processes* **51**, 237–272.

66. Camerer, C. and Lovallo, D. (1999). Overconfidence and excess entry: An experimental approach, *American Economic Review* **89**, 306–318.

67. Camerer, C. and Weigelt, K. (1991). Information mirages in experimental asset markets, *Journal of Business* **64**, 463–493.

68. Campbell, J. Y., Lo, A. W., and MacKinlay, A. C. (1997). The Econometrics of Financial Markets. (Princeton University Press, Princeton, NJ).

69. Carbonara, P. (1999). What is the intrinsic value? *Money* **28**, 133.

70. Cardy, J. L. (1998). Finite-size scaling (North-Holland, New York).

71. Carlson, J. M. and Doyle, J. (1999). Highly optimized tolerance: A mechanism for power laws in designed systems, *Physical Review E* **60**, 1412–1427.

72. Carlson, J. M. and Doyle, J. (2000). Highly optimized tolerance: Robustness and design in complex systems, *Physical Review Letters* **84**, 2529–2532.

73. Chaitin, G. J. (1987). *Algorithmic Information Theory* (Cambridge University Press, Cambridge, New York).

74. Chaline, J., Nottale, L., and Grou, P. (1999). L'arbre de la vie a-t-il une structure fractale? *Comptes Rendus l'Académie des Sciences, Paris* **328**, 717–726.

75. Challet, D. Minority Game's web page: http://www.unifr.ch/econophysics/minority/minority.html.

76. Challet, D., Chessa, A., Marsili, M., and Zhang, Y.-C. (2001). From minority games to real markets, *Quantitative Finance* **1** (1), 168–176.

77. Challet, D. and Zhang, Y.-C. (1997). Emergence of cooperation and organization in an evolutionary game, *Physica A* **246**, 407–418.

78. Challet, D. and Zhang, Y.-C. (1998). On the minority game: Analytical and numerical studies, *Physica A* **256**, 514–532.

79. Chan, N. T., LeBaron, B., Lo, A. W., and Poggio, T. (1999). Agent-Based Models of Financial Markets: A Comparison with Experimental Markets, Working paper, MIT, Cambridge, MA; preprint at http://cyber-exchange.mit.edu/.

80. Chauvet, M. (1998). An econometric characterization of business cycle dynamics with factor structure and regime switching, *International Economic Review* **39**, 969–996.

81. Checki, T. J. and Stern, E. (2000). Financial crises in the emerging markets: The roles of the public and private sectors, *Current Issues in Economics and Finance* (Federal Reserve Bank of New York) **6** (13), 1–6.

82. Chen, J. (1999). When the bubble is going to burst, *International Journal of Theoretical and Applied Finance* **2**, 285–292.

83. Chen, J. (2000). *Credit Distortion and Financial Crisis*, Working paper, National University of Singapore.

84. Chen, N.-F., Cuny, C. J., and Haugen, R. A. (1995). Stock volatility and the levels of the basis and open interest in futures contracts, *Journal of Finance* 50, 281–300.

85. Chiang, R., Liu, P., and Okunev, J. (1995). Modelling mean reversion of asset prices towards their fundamental value, *Journal of Banking & Finance* **19**, 1327–1340.

86. Christie, A. A. (1982). The stochastic behavior of common stock variances: Value, leverage and interest rate effects, *Journal of Financial Economics* **10**, 407–432.

87. Cohen, J. E. (1995). Population growth and Earth's human carrying capacity, *Science* **269**, 341–346.

88. Coleman, P. H. and Pietronero, L. (1992). The fractal structure of the universe, *Physics Reports* **213**, 311–389.

89. Commission on Physical Sciences, Mathematics, and Applications, Computing and Communications in the Extreme Research for Crisis Management and Other Applications, Steering Committee, *Workshop Series on High Performance Computing and Communications*, Computer Science and Telecommunications Board, National Academy Press, Washington, D.C., 1990.

90. Conference on "The Collapse of Complex Societies," San Francisco, Feb. 2001.

91. Conway, G. and Toenniessen, G. (1999). Feeding the world in the twenty-first century, *Nature* **402**, c55–c58.

92. Cootner, P. H., Editor (1967). *The Random Character of Stock Market Prices* (Cambridge, MA, MIT Press).

93. Cosmides, L. and Tooby, J. (1994). Better than rational—evolutionary psychology and the invisible hand, *American Economic Review* **84**, 327–332.

94. Costanza, R., dArge, R., deGroot, R., Farber, S., Grasso, M., Hannon, B., Limburg, K., Naeem, S., O'Neill, R. N., Parvelo, J., Raskin, R. G., Sutton, P., and van den Belt, M. (1997). The value of the world's ecosystem services and natural capital, *Nature* **387**, 253–260.

95. Cox, J. C., Ingersoll, J. E., and Ross, S. A. (1985). A theory of the term structure of interest rates, *Econometrica* **53**, 385–407.

96. Cronin, R. P. (1998). *Asian Financial Crisis: An Analysis of U.S. Foreign Policy Interests and Options, Foreign Affairs and National Defense Division*, http://www.fas.org/man/crs/crs-asia.htm.

97. Crutchfield, J. P. and Mitchell, M. (1995). The evolution of emergent computation, *Proceedings of the National Academy of Science, U.S.A.* **92**, 10742–10746.

98. D'Agostini, G. (1999). Teaching statistics in the physics curriculum: Unifying and clarifying role of subjective probability, *American Journal of Physics* **67**, 1260–1268.

99. Daily, G. C., Sderqvist, T., Aniyar, S., Arrow, K., Dasgupta, P., Ehrlich, P. R., Folke, C., Jansson, A., Jansson, B.-O., Kautsky, N., Levin, S., Lubchenco, J., Mler, K.-G., Simpson, D., Starrett, D., Tilman, D., and Walker, B. (2000). The value of nature and the nature of value, *Science* **289**, 395–396.

100. Darke, P. R. and Freedman, J. L. (1997). Lucky events and beliefs in luck: Paradoxical effects on confidence and risk-taking, *Personality & Social Psychology Bulletin* **23**, 378–388.

101. Davis, D. and Holt, C. (1993). *Experimental Economics* (Princeton University Press, Princeton, NJ).

102. Dawkins, R. (1990). *The Selfish Gene* (Oxford University Press, Oxford, U.K.).

103. De Bandt, O. and Hartmann, P. (November, 2000). *Systemic Risk: A survey, Financial Economics and Internation Macroeconomics*, ECB Discussion paper series No. 35, European Central Bank.

104. De Bondt, W. F. M. and Thaler, R. H. (1995). Financial decision-making in markets and firms: A behavioral perspective, in *Finance*, R. A. Jarrow, V. Maksimovic, and W. T. Ziemba, editors, Handbooks in Operations Research and Management Science **9**, 385–410 (Elsevier Science, Amsterdam, New York).

105. DeLong, J. B. (1998). *Estimating World GDP, One Million B.C.–Present.* Working paper available at http://econ161.berkeley.edu/TCEH/1998_Draft/World_GDP/Estimating_World_GDP.html.

106. Derrida, B., De Seze, L., and Itzykson, C. (1983). Fractal structure of zeros in hierarchical models, *Journal of Statistical Physics* **33**, 559–569.

107. Devenow, A. and Welch, I. (1996). Rational herding in financial markets, *European Economic Review* **40**, 603–616.

108. Dezhbakhsh, H. and Demirguc-Kunt, A. (1990). On the presence of speculative bubbles in stock prices, *Journal of Financial & Quantitative Analysis* **25**, 101–112.

109. Diba, B. T. and Grossman, H. I. (1988). Explosive rational bubbles in stock prices? *American Economic Review* **78**, 520–530.

110. Driffill, J. and Sola, M. (1998). Intrinsic bubbles and regime-switching, *Journal of Monetary Economics* **42**, 357–373.

111. Drozdz, S., Ruf, F., Speth, J., and Wojcik, M. (1999). Imprints of log-periodic self-similarity in the stock market, *European Physical Journal* **10**, 589–593.

112. Dubrulle, B., Graner, F., and Sornette, D., Editors (1997). *Scale Invariance and Beyond* (EDP Sciences and Springer-Verlag, Berlin).

113. Dunbar, N. (1998). Plugging the holes in Black-Scholes, *Financial Products* **84**, 14–16.

114. Dunning, T. J. (1860). *Trades' Unions and Strikes: Their philosophy and intention.* T. J. Dunning, London.

115. Dupuis, H. (1997). Un krach avant Novembre, *Tendances*, September 18, p. 26.

116. Dyson, F. (1988). *Infinite in All Directions* (Penguin, London), pp. 258–259.

117. Edgar, G. A., Editor (1993). *Classics on Fractals* (Addison-Wesley, Reading, MA).

118. Elias, D. (1999). *Dow 40,000: Strategies for Profiting from the Greatest Bull-Market in History* (McGraw-Hill, New York).

119. Energy and Natural Environment Panel (2000). *Stepping Stones to Sustainability*, The Office of Science and Technology, Department of Trade and Industry, United Kingdom, http://www.foresight.gov.uk/.

120. Evans, G. W. (1991). Pitfalls in testing for explosive bubbles in asset prices, *American Economic Review* **81**, 922–930.

121. Evans, P. (1986). Is the dollar high because of large budget deficits? *Journal of Monetary Economics* **18**, 227–249.

122. Fama, E. F. (1991). Efficient capital markets. 2, *Journal of Finance* **46**, 1575–1617.

123. Farmer, J. D. (1998). *Market Force, Ecology and Evolution*, Preprint available at adap-org/9812005.

124. Farmer, J. D. and Joshi, S. (2000). The price dynamics of common trading strategies, to appear in the *Journal of Economic Behavior and Organization*; e-print at http://xxx.lanl.gov/abs/cond-mat/0012419.

125. Feather, N. T. (1968). Change in confidence following success or failure as a predictor of subsequent performance, *Journal of Personality and Social Psychology* **9**, 38–46.

126. Feder, J. (1988). *Fractals* (Plenum Press, New York).

127. Feigenbaum, J. A. (2001). A statistical analysis of log-periodic precursors to financial crashes, *Quantitative Finance* **1**, 346–360.

128. Feigenbaum, J. A. and Freund, P. G. O. (1996). Discrete scale invariance in stock markets before crashes, *International Journal of Modern Physics B* **10**, 3737–3745.

129. Feigenbaum, J. A. and Freund, P. G. O. (1998). Discrete scale invariance and the "second Black Monday," *Modern Physics Letters B* **12**, 57–60.

130. Feldman, R. A. (1982). Dollar appreciation, foreign trade, and the U.S. economy, *Federal Reserve Bank of New York Quarterly Review* **7**, 1–9.

131. Feller, W. (1971). *An Introduction to Probability Theory and Its Applications*, Vol. I (Wiley, New York), section 6 of chapter 2.

132. Fernando, C. S. and Herring, R. J. (2001). Liquidity shocks, systemic risk, and market collapse: Theory and application of the market for perps, Working paper of the Financial Institutions Center at the Wharton School of the University of Pennsylvania, Philadelphia. 01.34.

133. Fieleke, N. S. (1985). Dollar appreciation and U.S. import prices, *New England Economic Review* (Nov/Dec), 49–54.

134. Fisher, I. (1961). *The Theory of Interest as determined by impatience to spend income and opportunity to invest it*. A. M. Kelley, editor, New York.

135. Flood, R. P. and Hodrick, R. J. (1990). On testing for speculative bubbles, *Journal of Economic Perspectives* **4**, 85–101.

136. Folkerts-Landau, D., Mathieson, D. J., and Schinasi, G. J. (1997). *World Economic and Financial Surveys on International Capital Markets Developments, Prospects and Key Policy Issues*, International Monetary Fund (available at http://www.imf.org/external/pubs/ft/icm/97icm/icmcon.htm).

137. Forsythe, R., Palfrey, T. R., and Plott, C. R. (1982). Asset valuation in an experimental market, *Econometrica* **50**, 537–567.

138. Foundation for the Study of Cycles, http://www.cycles.org/.

139. Frankel, J. A. and Froot, K. A. (1988). Chartists, fundamentalists and the demand for dollars, *Greek Economic Review* **10**, 49–102.

140. Frankel, J. A. and Froot, K. A. (1990). Chartists, fundamentalists, and trading in the foreign exchange market, *American Economic Review* **80**, 181–185.

141. Frankel, J. A. and Rose, A. K. (1996). Currency crashes in emerging markets: An empirical treatment, *Journal of International Economics* **41**, 351–366.

142. Friedberg Mercantile Group, *The Collapse of Wall Street and the Lessons of History*, http://www.usastores.com/Consensus/longterm/fried.htm.

143. Friedman, D. and Sunder, S. (1994). *Experimental Methods: A primer for Economists* (Cambridge University Press, New York).

144. Froot, K. A. and Obstfeld, M. (1991). Intrinsic bubbles: The case of stock prices, *American Economic Review* **81**, 1189–1214.

145. Fullerton, D. and Stavins, R. (1998). How economists see the environment, *Nature* **395**, 433–434.

146. Fung, W. and Hsieh, D. A. (2000). Measuring the market impact of hedge funds, *Journal of Empirical Finance* **7**, 1–36.

147. Fung, W. and Hsieh, D. A. (2001). The risk in hedge fund strategies: Theory and evidence from trend followers, *The Review of Financial Studies* **14**, 313–341.

148. Fyfe, W. S. (1998). Towards 2050: The past is not the key to the future—Challenges for the science of geochemistry, *Environmental Geology* **33**, 92–95.

149. Fyfe, W. S. (1999). Clean energy for 10 billion humans in the 21st century: Is it possible? *International Journal of Coal Geology* **40**, 85–90.

150. Fyfe, W. S. (1999). Needed universal education and new systems for a positive 21st century, *Ecosystem Health* **5**, 181–182.

151. Fyfe, W. S. (2000). Truly sustainable development for a positive future: the role of the earth sciences, *Trends in Geochemistry* **1**, 125–132.

152. Galbraith, J. K. (1997). *The Great Crash, 1929* (Houghton Mifflin, Boston).

153. Garber, P. M. (2000). *Famous First Bubbles: The Fundamentals of Early Manias* (MIT Press, Cambridge, MA).

154. Gaunersdorfer, A. (2000). Endogenous fluctuations in a simple asset pricing model with heterogeneous agents, *Journal of Economic Dynamics & Control* **24**, 799–831.

155. Ghil, M. and Childress, S. (1987). *Topics in Geophysical Fluid Dynamics: Atmospheric Dynamics, Dynamo Theory and Climate Dynamics* (Springer-Verlag, New York, Berlin, London, Paris, Tokyo).

156. Gilles B. (1982). *Histoire des techniques* (Gallimard, Paris).

157. Gillette, D. and DelMas, R. (1992). *Psycho-Economics: Studies in Decision Making, Classroom Expernomics*, Newsletter published by Department of Economics, Management and Accounting, Marietta College, Marietta, Ohio, Fall 1992, 1, pp. 1–5.

158. Glassman, J. K. and Hassett, K. A. (1999). *DOW 36,000: The New Strategy for Profiting from the Coming Rise in the Stock Market* (Times Books, London).

159. Global Financial Data, Freemont Villas, Los Angeles, CA 90042. The data used are free samples available at http://www.globalfindata.com/.

160. Glosten, L. R., Jagannathan, R., and Runkle, D. E. (1993). On the relation between the expected value and the volatility of the nominal excess return on stocks, *Journal of Finance* **48**, 1779–1801.

161. Gluzman, S. and Yukalov, V. I. (1998). Booms and crashes in self-similar markets, *Modern Physics Letters B* **12**, 575–587.

162. Godley, W. (1999). *Seven Unsustainable Processes (Medium Term Prospects and Policies for the United States and the World)*, Special report of The Jerome Levy Economics Institute, available at http://www.levy.org/docs/sreport/sevenproc.html.

163. Goldberg, J. and von Nitzsch, R. (2001). *Behavioral Finance*, translated by A. Morris (Wiley, Chichester, U.K., New York).

164. Goldenfeld, N. (1992). *Lectures on Phase Transitions and the Renormalization Group* (Addison-Wesley, Reading, MA).

165. Gordon, R. J. (1999). *Has the New Economy Rendered the Productivity Slowdown Obsolete?*, Manuscript, Northwestern University, Evanston, IL.

166. Gordon, R. J. (2000). Does the New Economy measure up to the great inventions of the past?, *Journal of Economic Perspectives* **14**, 49–74.

167. Gorte, R. W. (1995). *Forest Fires and Forest Health*, Congressional Research Service Report, The Committee for the National Institute for the Environment, Washington, D.C.

168. Gould, S. J. and Eldredge, N. (1977). Punctuated equilibria: The tempo and mode of evolution reconsidered, *Paleobiology* **3**, 115–151.

169. Gould, S. J. and Eldredge, N. (1993). Punctuated equilibrium comes of age, *Nature* **366**, 223–227.

170. Graham, B. and Dodd, D. L. (1934). *Security Analysis*, 1st ed. (McGraw-Hill, New York).

171. Graham, J. R. (1999). Herding among investment newsletters: Theory and evidence, *Journal of Finance* **54**, 237–268.

172. Graham, R. L., Rothschild, B. L., and Spencer, J. H. (1990). *Ramsey Theory*, 2nd ed. (Wiley, New York).

173. Graham, R. L. and Spencer, J. H. (1990). Ramsey theory, *Scientific American* **July**, 112–117.

174. Grant, J. L. (1990). Stock return volatility during the crash of 1987, *Journal of Portfolio Management* **16**, 69–71.

175. Gray, S. F. (1996). Regime-switching in Australian short-term interest rates, *Accounting & Finance* **36**, 65–88.

176. Greenspan, A. (1997). Federal Reserve's semiannual monetary policy report, before the Committee on Banking, Housing, and Urban Affairs, U.S. Senate, February 26.

177. Greenspan, A. (1998). Is there a new economy? *California Management Review* **41** (1), 74–85.

178. Grossman, J. The Erdos Number Project, http://www.acs.oakland.edu/grossman/erdoshp.html.

179. Grossman, J. W. and Ion, P. D. F. (1995). On a portion of the well-known collaboration graph, *Congressus Numerantium* **108**, 129–131.

180. Grossman, S. and Stiglitz, J. E. (1980). On the impossibility of informationally efficient markets, *American Economic Review* **70**, 393–408.

181. Grou, P. (1987, 1995). *L'aventure économique* (L'Harmattan, Paris), p. 160.

182. Guare, J. (1990). *Six Degrees of Separation: A Play* (Vintage, New York).

183. Guild, S. E. (1931). *Stock Growth and Discount Tables* (Financial publishers).

184. Hamilton, J. B. (1989). A new approach to the economic analysis of nonstationary time' series and the business cycle, *Econometrica* **57**, 357–384.

185. Hamilton, J. D. (1986). On testing for self-fulfilling speculative price bubbles, *International Economic Review* **27**, 545–552.

186. Hanson, R. (2000). *Could It Happen Again? Long-Term Growth as a Sequence of Exponential Modes*, Working paper available at http://hanson.gmu.edu/longgrow.html.

187. Hardouvelis, G. A. (1988). Evidence on stock market speculative bubbles: Japan, the United States, and Great Britain, *Federal Reserve Bank of New York Quarterly Review* **13**, 4–16.

188. Harris, L. (1997). Circuit breakers and program trading limits: what have we learned?, in *The 1987 Crash, Ten Years Later: Evaluating the Health of the Financial Markets*, published in Volume II of the annual Brookings-Wharton Papers on Financial Services (The Brookings Institution Press, Washington, D.C.).

189. Heath, C. and Gonzalez, R. (1995). Interaction with others increases decision confidence but not decision quality: Evidence against information collection views of interactive decision making, *Organizational Behavior & Human Decision Processes* **61**, 305–326.

190. Heath, C. and Tversky, A. (1991). Preference and belief: Ambiguity and competence in choice under uncertainty, *J. Risk Uncertainty* **4**, 5–28.

191. Helbing, D., Farkas, I., and Vicsek, T. (2000). Simulating dynamical features of escape panic, *Nature* **407**, 487–490.

192. Hern, W. M. (1993). Is human culture carcinogenic for uncontrolled population growth and ecological destruction? *BioScience* **43**, 768–773.

193. Herrmann, H. J. and Roux, S., Editors (1990). *Statistical Models for the Fracture of Disordered Media* (North-Holland, Amsterdam, New York).

194. Hill, T. P. (1995). Base-invariance implies Benford's law, *Proc. Amer. Math. Soc.* **123**, 887–895.

195. Hill, T. P. (1998). The first digit phenomenon, *American Scientist* **86**, 358–363.

196. Hill, T. P. (1995). A statistical derivation of the significant-digit law, *Statistical Science* **10**, 354–363.

197. Hoffman, E. (1991). *Bibliography of Experimental Economics*, Department of Economics, University of Arizona, Tucson, 1991.

198. Holland, J. H. (1992). Complex adaptive systems, *Daedalus* **121**, 17–30.

199. Holmes, P. A. (1985). How fast will the dollar drop? *Nation's Business* **73**, 16.

200. Hommes, C. H. (2001). Financial markets as nonlinear adaptive evolutionary systems, *Quantitative Finance* **1**, 149–167.

201. Hsieh, D. A. (1989). Testing for nonlinear dependence in daily foreign exchange rates, *Journal of Business* **62**, 339–368.

202. Hsieh, D. A. (1995). Nonlinear dynamics in financial markets: evidence and implications, *Financial Analysts Journal* **July–August**, 55–62.

203. Huang, Y., Johansen, A., Lee, M. W., Saleur, H., and Sornette, D. (2000). Artifactual log-periodicity in finite-size data: Relevance for earthquake aftershocks, *Journal of Geophysics Research* **105**, 25451–25471.

204. Huberman, G. and Regev, T. (2001). Contagious speculation and a cure for cancer: A nonevent that made stock prices soar, *Journal of Finance* **56**, 387–396.

205. Ide, K. and Sornette, D. (2002). Oscillatory finite-time singularities in finance, population and rupture, *Physica A*, **307** (1–2), 63–106.

206. Intriligator, M. D. (1998). Russia: Lessons of the economic collapse, *New York Times*, Aug. 8; Paper presented to the World Bank, Sept. 4.

207. Investment Company Institute, http://www.ici.org/aboutici.html.

208. Johansen, A. (1997). *Discrete Scale Invariance and Other Cooperative Phenomena in Spatially Extended Systems with Threshold Dynamics*, Ph.D. Thesis, Niels Bohr Institute, available on http://www.nbi.dk/johansen/pub.html.

209. Johansen, A., Ledoit, O., and Sornette, D. (2000). Crashes as critical points, *International Journal of Theoretical and Applied Finance* **3**, 219–255.

210. Johansen, A. and Sornette, D. (1998). Evidence of discrete scale invariance by canonical averaging, *International Journal of Modern Physics C* **9**, 433–447.

211. Johansen, A. and Sornette, D. (1998). Stock market crashes are outliers, *European Physical Journal B* **1**, 141–143.

212. Johansen, A. and Sornette, D. (1999). Critical crashes, *Risk* **12** (1), 91–94.

213. Johansen, A. and Sornette, D. (1999). Financial "anti-bubbles": Log-periodicity in gold and Nikkei collapses, *International Journal of Modern Physics C* **10**, 563–575.

214. Johansen, A. and Sornette, D. (1999). Modeling the stock market prior to large crashes, *European Physics Journal B* **9**, 167–174.

215. Johansen, A. and Sornette, D. (2000). Critical ruptures, *European Physics Journal B* **18**, 163–181.

216. Johansen, A. and Sornette, D. (2000). Evaluation of the quantitative prediction of a trend reversal on the Japanese stock market in 1999, *International Journal of Modern Physics C* **11**, 359–364.

217. Johansen, A. and Sornette, D. (2000). The Nasdaq crash of April 2000: Yet another example of log-periodicity in a speculative bubble ending in a crash, *European Physical Journal B* **17**, 319–328.

218. Johansen, A. and Sornette, D. (2001). Bubbles and anti-bubbles in Latin-American, Asian and Western stock markets: An empirical study, *International Journal of Theoretical and Applied Finance* **4** (6), 853–920.

219. Johansen, A. and Sornette, D. (2001). Finite-time singularity in the dynamics of the world population and economic indices, *Physica A* **294**, 465–502.

220. Johansen, A. and Sornette, D. (2001). Large stock market price drawdowns are outliers, *Journal of Risk* **4** (2), 69–110 (2002).

221. Johansen, A., Sornette, D., and Ledoit, O. (1999). Predicting financial crashes using discrete scale invariance, *Journal of Risk* **1**, 5–32.

222. Johansen, A., Sornette, D., Wakita, G., Tsunogai, U., Newman, W. I., and Saleur, H. (1996). Discrete scaling in earthquake precursory phenomena: Evidence in the Kobe earthquake, Japan, *Journal of Physics I, France* **6**, 1391–1402.

223. Johnson, S. (2001). *Emergence: The Connected Lives of Ants, Brains, Cities* (Scribner, New York).

224. Jeffreys, H. (1961). *Theory of Probability*, 3rd ed. (Oxford University Press, Oxford, U.K.).

225. Kadlec, C. W. (1999). *Dow 100,000: Fact or Fiction* (Prentice-Hall, Englewood Cliffs, NJ).

226. Kagel, J. and Roth, A., Editors (1995). *Handbook of Experimental Economics* (Princeton University Press, Princeton, NJ).

227. Kahneman, D., Knetsch, J. K., and Thaler, R. (1986). Fairness as a constraint on profit seeking: Entitlements in the market, *American Economic Review* **76**, 447–464.

228. Kahneman, D., Knetsch, J. L., and Thaler, R. H. (1986). Fairness and the assumptions of economics/comments, *Journal of Business* **59**, S285–S300, S329–S354.

229. Kalyvitis, S. and Pittis, N. (1994). Testing for exchange rate bubbles using variance inequalities, *Journal of Macroeconomics* **16**, 359–367.

230. Kaminsky, G. and Peruga, R. (1991). Credibility crises: The dollar in the early 1980s, *Journal of International Money & Finance* **10**, 170–192.

231. Kapitza, S. P. (1996). Phenomenological theory of world population growth, *Uspekhi Fizichskikh Nauk* **166**, 63–80.

232. Karplus, W. J. (1992). *The Heavens Are Falling: The Scientific Prediction of Catastrophes in Our Time* (Plenum Press, New York).

233. Keller, E. F. (1985). *Reflections on Gender and Science* (Yale University Press, New Haven, CT).

234. Keller, E. F. and Segel, L. (1970). Initiation of slime mold aggregation viewed as an instability, *Journal of Theoretical Biology* **26** 399–415.

235. Keynes, J. M. (1936). *The General Theory of Employment, Interest and Money* (Harcourt, Brace, New York), chapter 12.

236. Kindleberger, C. P. (2000). *Manias, Panics, and Crashes: A History of Financial Crises*, 4th ed. (Wiley, New York).

237. Kindleberger, C. P. (2000). Review of Peter M. Garber's "Famous First Bubbles: The Fundamentals of Early Manias," *Economic History Services*, Aug. 15, http://www.eh.net/bookreviews/library/0281.shtml.

238. Kirman, A. (1991). Epidemics of opinion and speculative bubbles in financial markets, in *Money and Financial Markets* M. Taylor, editor (Macmillan, New York).

239. Kleidon, A. W. (1995). Stock market crashes, in *Finance*, R. A. Jarrow, V. Maksimovic, and W. T. Ziemba, editors, Handbooks in Operations Research and Management Science **9**, 465–495 (Elsevier Science, Amsterdam and New York).

240. Knetter, M. M. (1994). Did the strong dollar increase competition in U.S. product markets? *Review of Economics & Statistics* **76**, 192–195.

241. Koller, T. and Zane, D. W. (2001). What happened to the bull market? *The McKinsey Quarterly Newsletter* **4** (August), http://www.mckinseyquarterly.com.

242. Koutmos, G. and Saidi, R. (1995). The leverage effect in individual stocks and the debt to equity ratio, *Journal of Business Finance & Accounting* **22**, 1063–1075.

243. Kremer, M. (1993). Population growth and technological change: One million B.C. to 1990. *Quarterly Journal of Economics* **108**, 681–716.

244. Krugman, P. (1996). *The Self-Organizing Economy* (Blackwell, Malden, MA).

245. Krugman, P. (1998). The confidence game: How Washington worsened Asia's crash, *The New Republic*, October 5, available at http://web.mit.edu/krugman/www.

246. Krugman, P. (1998). I know what the hedgies did last summer, *Fortune*, December issue, available at http://web.mit.edu/krugman/www/xfiles.html.

247. Krugman, P. (1998). *A bridge to nowhere?* July 14. Shizuoka Shimbun, available at http://web.mit.edu/krugman/www/bridge.html.

248. Krugman, P. (1999). A monetary fable, *The Independent*, E-print at http://web.mit.edu/krugman/www/coyle.html.

249. Krugman, P. (1999, January 20). Japan heads for the edge, *Financial Times*, available at http://web.mit.edu/krugman/www.sakikab.html.

250. Krugman, P. (2001). Reckonings, *The New York Times*, March 4.

251. Laboratory for Financial Engineering at the Massachusetts Institute of Technology, http://cyber-exchange.mit.edu/.

252. L'vov, V. S., Pomyalov, A., and Procaccia, I. (2001). *Outliers, Extreme Events and Multiscaling*, Physical Review E 6305, 6118, U158–U166.

253. Laherrère, J. and Sornette, D. (1998). Stretched exponential distributions in Nature and Economy: "Fat tails" with characteristic scales, *European Physical Journal B* **2**, 525–539.

254. Laibson, D. (1997). Golden eggs and hyperbolic discounting, *Quarterly Journal of Economics* **112**, 443–477.

255. Laibson, D. (1998). Life-cycle consumption and hyperbolic discount functions. *European Economic Review* **42**, 861–871.

256. Lamont, O. (1988). Earnings and expected returns, *The Journal of Finance* **LIII**, 1563–1587.

257. LeBaron, B. (2000). Agent based computational finance: suggested readings and early research, *Journal of Economic Dynamics and Control* **24** (5–7), 679–702.

258. LeBaron, B., Arthur, W. B., and Palmer, R. (1999). Time series properties of an artificial stock market, *Journal of Economic Dynamics and Control* **23**, 1487–1516.

259. Le Bras, H. (1996). *Rumeur, troublante vérité du faux* (Rumors, troubling truth of the false) (Editions Odile Jacob, Paris).

260. Lee, C. M., Myers, J., and Swaminathan, B. (1999). What is the intrinsic value of the Dow? *Journal of Finance* **54**, 1693–1741.

261. Leeson, R. (1999). *The Decline and Fall of Bretton Woods*, Working Paper No. 178, Economics Department, Murdoch University, Perth, Western Australia, E-print at http://cleo.murdoch.edu.au/teach/econs/wps/178.html.

262. Levy, M., Levy, H., and Solomon, S. (1995). Microscopic simulation of the stock market—the effect of microscopic diversity, *Journal de Physique I* **5**, 1087–1107.

263. Levy, M., Levy, H., and Solomon, S. (2000). *The Microscopic Simulation of Financial Markets: From Investor Behavior to Market Phenomena* (Academic Press, San Diego).

264. Lewis, S. (2000). Politics, resources and the environment: A witches brew? In *Malthus and the Third Millenium*, W. Chesworth, M. R. Moss, and V. G. Thomas, editors, The Kenneth Hammond Lectures on Environment, Energy and Resources, Faculty of Environmental Sciences, University of Guelph, CBC Ideas, Toronto, ON, Canada.

265. Liggett, T. M. (1985). *Interacting Particle Systems* (Springer-Verlag, New York).

266. Liggett, T. M. (1997). Stochastic models of interacting systems, *The Annals of Probability* **25**, 1–29.

267. Lillo, F. and Mantegna, R. N. (2000). Symmetry alteration of ensemble return distribution in crash and rally days of financial markets, *European Physical Journal B* **15**, 603–606.

268. Lintner, J. (1965). The valuation of risk assets and the selection of risky investments in stock portfolios and capital budgets, *Review of Economics and Statistics* **47**, 13–37.

269. Lloyd, J. N. and Kotz, S. (1977). *Urn Models and Their Application: An Approach to Modern Discrete Probability Theory* (Wiley, New York).

270. Lorenz, E. N. (1963). Deterministic nonperiodic flow, *Journal of Atmospheric Science* **20**, 130–141.

271. Lowell, J., Neu, C. R., and Tong, D. (1998). *Financial Crises and Contagion in Emerging Market Countries*, RAND publication, Santa Monica, CA.

272. Lowenstein, R. (2001). Exuberance is rational, *New York Times*, February 11.

273. Lux, T. (1995). Herd behaviour, bubbles and crashes, *Economic Journal: The Journal of the Royal Economic Society* **105**, 881–896.

274. Lux, T. (1998). The socio-economic dynamics of speculative markets: Interacting agents, chaos, and the fat tails of return distributions, *Journal of Economic Behavior & Organization* **33**, 143–165.

275. Lux, T. and Marchesi, M. (1999). Scaling and criticality in a stochastic multi-agent model of a financial market, *Nature* **397**, 498–500.

276. Lux, T. and Marchesi, M. (2000). Volatility clustering in financial markets: a micro-simulation of interacting agents, *International Journal of Theoretical and Applied Finance* **3**, 675–702.

277. MacArthur Jr., J. (1997). Grace Community Church in Panorama City, CA. Sermon transcribed from the tape, GC 90-164, titled "Gambling: The Seductive Fantasy, Part 1" (Word of Grace, Panorama City, CA).

278. MacDonald, R. and Torrance, T. S. (1988). On risk, rationality and excessive speculation in the Deutschmark-US dollar exchange market: Some evidence using survey data, *Oxford Bulletin of Economics & Statistics* **50**, 107–123.

279. Malakoff, D. (1999). Bayes offers a "new" way to make sense of numbers, *Science* **286**, 1460–1464; A brief guide to Bayes theorem, *Science* **286**, 1461.

280. Malamud, B. D., Morein, G., and Turcotte, D. L. (1998). Forest fires: An example of self-organized critical behavior, *Science* **281**, 1840–1842.

281. Malki, E. (1999). *The Financial Crisis in Russia*, ewp-mac/9901001.

282. Malkiel, B. G. (1999). *A Random Walk Down Wall Street* (Norton, New York).

283. Mandelbrot, B. B. (1967). How long is the coast of Britain? Statistical self-similarity and fractional dimension, *Science* **155**, 636–638.

284. Mandelbrot, B. B. (1982). *The Fractal Geometry of Nature* (Freeman, San Francisco).

285. Mandelbrot, B. B. (1999). A multifractal walk down Wall Street, *Scientific American* **280**, 70–73(February).

286. Mantegna, R. N., Buldyrev, S. V., Goldberger, A. L., Halvin, S., and Stanley, H. E. (1995). Systematic analysis of coding and non-coding sequences using methods of statistical linguistics, *Physical Review E* **52**, 2939–2950.

287. Mantegna, R. and Stanley, H. E. (2000). An Introduction to Econophysics: Correlations and Complexity in Finance (Cambridge University Press, Cambridge, U.K. and New York).

288. Markowitz, H. (1959). *Portfolio Selection: Efficient Diversification of Investment* (Wiley, New York).

289. Mauboussin, M. J. and Hiler, R. (1999). *Rational Exuberance?* Equity research report of Credit Suisse First Boston, January 26.

290. Maug, E. and Naik, N. (1995). *Herding and Delegated Portfolio Management: The Impact of Relative Performance Evaluation on Asset Allocation*, Working paper, Duke University, Durham, NC.

291. McCarty, P. A. (1986). Effects of feedback on the self-confidence of men and women, *Academy of Management Journal* **29**, 840–847.

292. Meakin, P. (1998). *Fractals, Scaling, and Growth Far from Equilibrium* (Cambridge University Press, Cambridge, U.K. and New York).

293. Merton, R. (1973). An intertemporal capital asset pricing model, *Econometrica* **41**, 867–888.

294. Merton, R. C. (1990). *Continuous-Time Finance* (Blackwell, Cambridge, U.K.).

295. Meyer, F. (1947). *L'accélération évolutive. Essai sur le rythme évolutif et son interprétation quantique* (Librairie des Sciences et des Arts, Paris).

296. Meyer, F. (1954). *Problématique de l'évolution* (Presses Universitaires de France, Paris).

297. Milgram, S. (1967). The small world problem, *Psychology Today* **2**, 60–67.

298. Miller, M. (1991). *Financial Innovations and Market Volatility* (Basil Blackwell, Cambridge, MA).

299. Miller, M. H. and Modigliani, F. (1961). Dividend policy, growth and the valuation of shares, *Journal of Business* **34**, 411–433.

300. Miltenberger, P., Sornette, D., and Vanneste, C. (1993). Fault self-organization as optimal random paths selected by critical spatio-temporal dynamics of earthquakes, *Physics Review Letters* **71**, 3604–3607.

301. Minnich, R. A. and Chou, Y. H. (1997). Wildland fire patch dynamics in the chaparral of southern California and northern Baja California, *International Journal of Wildland Fire* **7**, 221–248.

302. Modigliani, F. and Miller, M. H. (1958). The cost of capital, corporation finance and the theory of investment, *American Economic Review* **48**, 655–669.

303. Molchan, G. M. (1990). Strategies in strong earthquake prediction, *Physics of the Earth and Planetary Interiors* **61**, 84–98 (1990).

304. Molchan, G. M. (1997). Earthquake prediction as a decision-making problem, *Pure and Applied Geophysics* **149**, 233–247 (1997).

305. Montroll, E. W. and Badger, W. W. (1974). *Introduction to Quantitative Aspects of Social Phenomena* (Gordon and Breach, New York).

306. Moore, S. and Simon, J. (2000). It's Getting Better All the Time: 100 Greatest Trends of the Last 100 Years (Cato Institute, Washington, D.C.).

307. Moravec, H. (1998). *ROBOT: Mere Machine to Transcendent Mind* (Oxford University Press, Oxford, UK).

308. Moreno, J. M., Editor (1998). *Large Forest Fires* (Backhuys, Leiden).

309. Morris, C. R. (1999). *Money, Greed, and Risk: Why Financial Crises and Crashes Happen* (Times Books, London).

310. Moss de Oliveira, S., de Oliveira, P. M., and Stauffer, D. (1999). *Evolution, Money, War and Computers* (Teubner, Stuttgart-Leipzig).

311. Mulligan, C. B. and Sala-i-Martin, X. (2000). Extensive margins and the demand for money at low interest rates, *Journal of Political Economy* **108**, 961–991.

312. Nature.com (1999). *Nature Debates, Is The Reliable Prediction of Individual Earthquakes a Realistic Scientific Goal?* http://helix.nature.com/debates/ earthquake/.

313. Newman, M. E. J. (2001). *The Struture of Scientific Collaboration Networks*, Proceedings of the National Academy of Sciences, USA 98, 404–409.

314. Newman, M. E. J. (2001). Scientific collaboration networks. I. Network construction and fundamental results—art. no. 016131, Physical Review E 6401, U249. U255; II. Shortest paths, weighted networks, and centrality,—art. 016132, Physical Review E 6401, U256–U261.

315. Nishikawa, Y. (1998, October 16). Japan economy seen shrinking 1.6%, *Financial Express, 1998 Indian Express Newspaper* (Bombay) Ltd., available at http://www.financialexpress.com/fe/daily/19981016/28955054.html.

316. Nison, S. (1991). *Japanese Candlestick Charting Techniques* (New York Institute of Finance, New York).

317. Nottale, L., Chaline, J., and Grou, P. (2000). *Les arbres de l'évolution* (Hachette Litterature, Paris).

318. Nottale, L., Chaline, J., and Grou, P. (2000). On the fractal structure of evolutionary trees. In *Fractals 2000 in Biology and Medicine*, Proceedings of Third International Symposium, Ascona, Switzerland, March 8–11, 2000, G. Losa, editor (Birkhauser Verlag, Basel).

319. O'Brien, J. and Srivastava, S. (1991). Dynamic stock markets with multiple assets, *Journal of Finance* **46**, 1811–38.

320. Obstfeld, M. and Rogoff, K. (1986). Ruling out divergent speculative bubbles, *Journal of Monetary Economics* **17**, 349–362.

321. Onsager, L. (1944). Crystal statistics. I. A two-dimensional model with an order-disorder transition, *Physics Review* **65**, 117–149.

322. Oreskes, N., Shraderfrechette, K., and Belitz, K. (1994). Verification, validation and confirmation of numerical models in the Earth Sciences, *Science* **263**, 641–646; The meaning of models—response, *Science* **264**, 331–331.

323. Orléan, A. (1984). Mimétisme et anticipations rationnelles: une perspective keynesienne, *Recherches Economiques de Louvain* **52** (1), 45–66.

324. Orléan, A. (1986). L'auto-référence dans la théorie keynesienne de la spéculation, *Cahiers d'Economie Politique* **14–15**.

325. Orléan, A. (1989). Comportements mimétiques et diversité des opinions sur les marchés financiers, in *Théorie économique et crises des marchés financiers*, H. Bourguinat and P. Artus, editors (Economica, Paris), chapter III, pp. 45–65.

326. Orléan, A. (1989). Mimetic contagion and speculative bubbles, *Theory and Decision* **27**, 63–92.

327. Orléan, A. (1991). Disorder in the stock market (in French), *La Recherche* **22**, 668–672.

328. Orléan, A. (1995). Bayesian interactions and collective dynamics of opinion—Herd behavior and mimetic contagion, *Journal of Economic Behavior & Organization* **28**, 257–274.

329. Palmer, R., Arthur, W. B., Holland, J. H., LeBaron, B., and Taylor, P. (1994). Artificial economic life—A simple model of a stock market, *Physica D* **75**, 264–274.

330. Pandey, R. B. and Stauffer, D. (2000). Search for log-periodicity oscillations in stock market simulations, *International Journal of Theoretical and Applied Finance* **3**, 479–482.

331. Penrose, R. (1989). *The Emperor's New Mind* (Oxford University Press, Oxford, UK).

332. Pesenti, P. and Tille, C. (2000). The economics of currency crises and contagion: An introduction, *Economic Policy Review* **6**, Federal Reserve Bank of New York, September, 3–16.

333. Plott, C. R. and Sunder, S. (1982). Efficiency of experimental security markets with insider information: An application of rational-expectations models, *Journal of Political Economy* **90**, 663–698.

334. Plott, C. R. and Sunder, S. (1988). Rational expectations and the aggregation of diverse information in laboratory settings, *Econometrica* **56**, 1085–1118.

335. Porter, D. P. and Smith, V. L. (1995). Futures contracting and dividend uncertainty in experimental asset markets, *Journal of Business* **68**, 509–541.

336. Poterba, J. M. (2001). Demographic structure and asset returns, *The Review of Economics and Statistics* **83**, 565–584.

337. Potters, M., Cont, R., and Bouchaud, J.-P. (1998). Financial markets as adaptative ecosystems, *Europhysics Letters* **41**, 239–244.

338. Press, W. H., Teulolsky, S. A., Vetterlong, W. T., and Flannery, B. P. (1994). *Numerical Recipies in Fortran* (Cambridge University Press, Cambridge, U.K.).

339. Quinn, D. (1999). *Beyond Civilization: Humanity's Next Great Adventure* (Harmony Books, New York).

340. Quinn, S. F. and Harvey, J. T. (1998). Speculation and the dollar in the 1980s, *Journal of Economic Issues* **32**, 315–323.

341. Rachlevsky-Reich, B., Ben-Shaul, I., Chan, N. T., Lo, A. W., et al. (1999). GEM: A global electronic market system, *Information Systems* **24**, 495–518.

342. Renshaw, E. (1990). Some evidence in support of stock market bubbles, *Financial Analysts Journal* **46**, 71–73.

343. Richardson, L. F. (1961). The problem of contiguity: An appendix of statistics of deadly quarrels, *General Systems Yearbook* **6**, 139–187.

344. Richebacher, K. (2000/2001). *The Richebacher Letter*, August 2000 and March 2001, the Fleet Street group, Baltimore, MD.

345. Ripley, B. D. (1996). *Pattern Recognition and Neural Networks* (Cambridge University Press, Cambridge, U.K.).

346. Roberts, J. C. and Castore, C. H. (1972). The effects of conformity, information, and confidence upon subjects' willingness to take risk following a group discussion, *Organizational Behavior & Human Performance* **8**, 384–394.

347. Roby, T. B. and Carterette, T. (1965). *The Measurement of Confidence and Trust*, United States Air Force Electronic Systems Division Technical Documentary Report **65–299**, 27.

348. Roehner, B. M. and Sornette, D. (1998). The sharp peak-flat trough pattern and critical speculation, *European Physical Journal B* **4**, 387–399.

349. Roehner, B. M. and Sornette, D. (2000). "Thermometers" of speculative frenzy, *European Physical Journal B* **16**, 729–739.

350. Romer, P. M. (1990). Endogeneous technological change. *Journal of Political Economy* **98**, S71–S102.

351. Romer, C. D. (1990). The great crash and the onset of the great depression, *Quarterly Journal of Economics* **105**, 597–624.

352. Romer, D. (1996). *Advanced Macroeconomics* (McGraw-Hill, New York).

353. Ross, S. A. (1976). The arbitrage theory of capital asset pricing, *Journal of Economic Theory* **13**, 341–360.

354. Rubinstein, M. (2001). Rational markets: Yes or no? The affirmative case, *Financial Analysts Journal* **57**, 15–29.

355. Saleur, H., Sammis, C. G., and Sornette, D. (1996). Discrete scale invariance, complex fractal dimensions and log-periodic corrections in earthquakes, *Journal of Geophysics Research* **101**, 17661–17677.

356. Saleur, H. and Sornette, D. (1996). Complex exponents and log-periodic corrections in frustrated systems, *Journal de Physique I France* **6**, 327–355.

357. Samuelson, P. A. (1965). Proof that properly anticipated prices fluctuate randomly, *Industrial Management Review* **6**, 41–49.

358. Samuelson, P. A. (1973). Proof that properly discounted present values of assets vibrate randomly, *The RAND Journal of Economics* **4**, 369–374.

359. Santoni, G. J. (1987). The great bull markets 1924–29 and 1982–87: Speculative bubbles or economic fundamentals? *Federal Reserve Bank of St. Louis Review* **69**, 16–30.

360. Sato, A. H. and Takayasu, H. (1998). Dynamic numerical models of stock market price: From microscopic determinism to macroscopic randomness, *Physica A* **250**, 231–252.

361. Savoy, C. and Beitel, P. (1997). The relative effect of a group and group/individualized program on state anxiety and state self-confidence, *Journal of Sport Behavior* **20**, 364–376.

362. Saxton, J. (1998). *Financial Crises in Emerging Markets: Incentives and the IMF*, http://www.house.gov/jec/imf/incentiv.htm.

363. Schaller, H. and van Norden, S. (1997). Regime switching in stock market returns, *Applied Financial Economics* **7**, 177–191.

364. Scharfstein, D. and Stein, J. (1990). Herd behavior and investment, *American Economic Review* **80**, 465–479.

365. Schieber, S. J. and Shoven, J. B. (1997). *Public Policy Toward Pensions* (MIT Press, Cambridge, MA).

366. Science Summit on World Population: A Joint Statement by 58 of the World's Scientific Academies (1994). *Population and Development Review* **20** 233–238.

367. Searle, J. R. (1980). Minds, brains, and programs, in *The Behavioral and Brain Sciences*, Vol. 3 (Cambridge University Press, Cambridge, U.K.). Reprinted in *The Mind's I* (1981), D. R. Hofstadter and D. C. Dennett, editors (Basic Books, New York).

368. Sellers, W. D. (1969). A climate model based on the energy balance of the earth-atmosphere system, *Journal of Applied Meteorology* **8**, 392–400.

369. Sharp, G. L., Cutler, B. L., and Penrod, S. D. (1988). Performance feedback improves the resolution of confidence judgments, *Organizational Behavior & Human Decision Processes* **42**, 271–283.

370. Sharpe, W. F. (1964). Capital asset prices: A theory of market equilibrium under conditions of risk, *Journal of Finance* **19**, 425–442.

371. She, Z. S. (1998). Universal law of cascade of turbulent fluctuations, *Progress of Theoretical Physics Supplement* **130**, 87–102.

372. Shefrin, H. (2000). Beyond Greed and Fear: Understanding Behavioral Finance and the Psychology of Investing (Harvard Business School Press, Boston, MA).

373. Shefrin, H. M. and Thaler, R. H. (1988). The behavioral life-cycle hypothesis, *Economic Inquiry* **26**, 609–643.

374. Shiller, R. J. (1989). *Market Volatility* (MIT Press, Cambridge, MA).

375. Shiller, R. J. (2000). *Irrational Exuberance* (Princeton University Press, Princeton, NJ).

376. Shleifer, A. (2000). *Inefficient Markets: An Introduction to Behavioral Finance* (Oxford University Press, New York).

377. Sieck, W. and Yates, J. F. (1997). Exposition effects on decision making: Choice and confidence in choice, *Organizational Behavior & Human Decision Processes* **70**, 207–219.

378. Siegel, J. J. (1998). *Stocks for the Long Run*, 2nd ed. (McGraw Hill, New York).

379. Simon, H. (1982). *Models of Bounded Rationality*, Vols. 1 and 2 (MIT Press, Cambridge, MA).

380. Simon, J. L. (1996). *The Ultimate Resource 2?* (Princeton University Press, Princeton, NJ).

381. Sircar, K. R. and Papanicolaou, G. (1998). General Black-Scholes models accounting for increased market volatility from hedging strategies, *Applied Mathematical Finance* **5**, 45–82.

382. Slater, M. D. and Rouner, D. (1992). Confidence in beliefs about social groups as an outcome of message exposure and its role in belief change persistence, *Communication Research* **19**, 597–617.

383. Small, P. (2000). *The Entrepreneurial Web* (Addison-Wesley, Reading, MA).

384. Smith, A. (1776). *An Inquiry into the Nature and Causes of the Wealth of Nations* (Printed for W. Strahan and T. Cadell, London); (1805) 11th ed. with notes, supplementary chapters, and a life of Dr. Smith, by William Playfair (Printed for T. Cadell and W. Davies, London).

385. Smith, J. Q., Harrison, P. J., and Zeeman, E. C. (1981). The analysis of some discontinuous decision processes, *European Journal of Operational Research* **7**, 30–43.

386. Smith, L. A. (2000). Disentangling uncertainty and error: On the predictability of nonlinear systems, in *Nonlinear Dynamics and Statistics*, A. Mees, editor, (Birkhauser, Boston), chapter 2.

387. Smith, L. A., Fournier, J.-D., and Spiegel, E. A. (1986). Lacunarity and intermittency in fluid turbulence, *Physics Letters A* **114**, 465–468.

388. Smith, L. A., Ziehmann, C., and Fraedrich, K. (1999). Uncertainty dynamics and predictability in chaotic systems, *Quarterly Journal of the Royal Meteorological Society* **125**, 2855–2886.

389. Smith, V. L. (1982). Microeconomic systems as an experimental science, *American Economic Review* **72**, 923–955.

390. Smith, V. L. (1991). *Papers in Experimental Economics* (Cambridge University Press, New York).

391. Smith, V. L. (1996). The handbook of experimental economics, *Journal of Economic Literature* **34**, 1950–1952.

392. Sornette, D. (1998). Discrete scale invariance and complex dimensions, *Physics Reports* **297**, 239–270.

393. Sornette, D. (1999). Complexity, catastrophe and physics, *Physics World* **12** (N12), 57–57.

394. Sornette, D. (2000). *Critical Phenomena in Natural Sciences, Chaos, Fractals, Self-organization and Disorder: Concepts and Tools*, Springer Series in Synergetics (Springer-Verlag, Heidelberg).

395. Sornette, D. (2000). Stock market speculation: Spontaneous symmetry breaking of economic valuation, *Physica A* **284**, 355–375.

396. Sornette, D. and Andersen, J. V. (2002). A nonlinear super-exponential rational model of speculative financial bubbles, *International Journal of Modern Physics C* **13** (2), 171–188.

397. Sornette, D. and Johansen, A. (1997). Large financial crashes, *Physica A* **245**, 411–422.

398. Sornette, D. and Johansen, A. (1998). A hierarchical model of financial crashes, *Physica A* **261**, 581–598.

399. Sornette, D. and Johansen, A. (2001). Significance of log-periodic precursors to financial crashes, *Quantitative Finance* **1** (4), 452–471.

400. Sornette, D., Johansen, A., Arnéodo, A., Muzy, J.-F., and Saleur, H. (1996). Complex fractal dimensions describe the internal hierarchical structure of DLA, *Physical Review Letters* **76**, 251–254.

401. Sornette, D., Johansen, A., and Bouchaud, J.-P. (1996). Stock market crashes, precursors and replicas, *Journal de Physique I, France* **6**, 167–175.

402. Sornette, D. and Knopoff, L. (1997). The paradox of the expected time until the next earthquake, *Bulletin of the Seismological Society of America* **87**, 789–798.

403. Sornette, D. and Malevergne, Y. (2001). From rational bubbles to crashes, *Physica A* **299**, 40–59.

404. Sornette, D., Miltenberger, P., and Vanneste, C. (1994). Statistical physics of fault patterns self-organized by repeated earthquakes, *Pure and Applied Geophysics* **142**, 491–527.

405. Sornette, D. and Sammis, C. G. (1995). Complex critical exponents from renormalization group theory of earthquakes: Implications for earthquake predictions, *Journal de Physique I, France* **5**, 607–619.

406. Sornette, D., Stauffer, D., and Takayasu, H. (2002). Market fluctuations: Multiplicative and percolation models, size effects and predictions, chapter 14 of "Theories of disaster: Scaling laws governing weather, body and stock market dynamics," A. Bunde, J. Kropp, and H.-J. Schellnhuber, editors, Springer Proceedings of Facets of Universality: Climate, Biodynamics and Stock Markets, Giessen University, June 1999, E-print at http://xxx.lanl.gov/abs/cond-mat/9909439.

407. Soros, G. (1998). Toward a global open society, *Atlantic Monthly* **22**,

408. Speaker's Advisory Group on Russia (1998). *Russia's Road to Corruption*, Report available at http://policy.house.gov/russia/contents.html.

409. Stanley, H. E. and Ostrowsky, N., Editors (1986). On growth and form: Fractal and non-fractal patterns in physics (M. Nijhoff, Dordrecht, the Netherlands and Boston).

410. Stanley, H. E. and Ostrowsky, N., Editors (1988). Random fluctuations and pattern growth: Experiments and models (Kluwer, Dordrecht, the Netherlands and Boston).

411. Stanley, T. D. (1994). Silly bubbles and the insensitivity of rationality testing: An experimental illustration, *Journal of Economic Psychology* **15**, 601–620.

412. St. Petersburg Times (1999). Post-crisis special '99, Timeline of economic collapse.

413. Stauffer, D. (1999). Monte-Carlo-Simulation mikroskopischer Börsenmodelle, *Physikalische Blätter* **55**, 49.

414. Stauffer, D. and Aharony, A. (1994). *Introduction to Percolation Theory*, 2nd ed. (Taylor & Francis, London).

415. Steindel, C. and Stiroh, K. J. (2001). *Productivity: What Is It, and Why Do We Care about It?* Working paper of the Federal Reserve Bank of New York.

416. Stiroh, K. J. (2001). *Information Technology and the U.S. Productivity Revival: What Do the Industry Data Say?* Working paper of the Federal Reserve Bank of New York.

417. Svenson, O. (1981). Are we less risky and more skillful than our fellow drivers? *Acta Psychol.* **47**, 143–148.

418. Tacoma Narrows Bridge historical film footage showing in 250 frames (10 seconds) the maximum torsional motion shortly before failure of this immense structure, http://cee.carleton.ca/Exhibits/Tacoma_Narrows/.

419. Tainter, J. A. (1988). *The Collapse of Complex Societies* (Cambridge University Press, Cambridge, U.K. and New York).

420. Tainter, J. A. (1995). Sustainability of complex societies, *Futures* **27**, 397–407.

421. Takayasu, H., Miura, H., Hirabayshi, T., and Hamada, K. (1992). Statistical properties of deterministic threshold elements—The case of the market price, *Physica A* **184**, 127–134.

422. Tesar, L. T. and Werner, I. M. (1997). *The Internationalization of Securities Markets Since the 1987 Crash*, Papers presented at the October 1997 conference, published in Vol. II of the annual Brookings-Wharton Papers on Financial Services, http://wrdsenet.wharton.upenn.edu/fic/wfic/papers/97/b6.html.

423. Thaler, R. H. (1985). Mental accounting and consumer choice, *Marketing Science* **4**, 199–214.

424. Thaler, R. H., Editor (1993). *Advances in Behavioral Finance* (Russell Sage Foundation, New York).

425. Thaler, R. H. and Johnson, E. J. (1990). Gambling with the house money and trying to break even: The effects of prior outcomes on risky choice, *Management Science* **36**, 643–660.

426. Toner, J. and Tu, Y. H. (1998). Flocks, herds, and schools: A quantitative theory of flocking, *Physical Review E* **58**, 4828–4858.

427. Trueman, B. (1994). Analyst forecasts and herding behavior, *The Review of Financial Studies* **7**, 97–124.

428. Ulam, S. (1959). Tribute to John von Neumann, *Bulletin of the American Mathematical Society* **64**, 1–49.

429. U.S. Committee of the Global Atmospheric Research Program (1975). *Understanding Climatic Change—A Program for Action* (National Research Council, National Academy of Sciences, Washington, D.C.).

430. U.S. Postage Release No. 99-045, May 21, 1999.

431. Van Norden, S. (1996). Regime switching as a test for exchange rate bubbles, *Journal of Applied Econometrics* **11**, 219–251.

432. Van Norden, S. and Schaller, H. (1993). The predictability of stock market regime: Evidence from the Toronto Stock Exchange, *Review of Economics & Statistics* **75**, 505–510.

433. Vandewalle, N., Ausloos, M., Boveroux, P., and Minguet, A. (1998). How the financial crash of October 1997 could have been predicted, *European Physical Journal B* **4**, 139–141.

434. Vandewalle, N., Ausloos, M., Boveroux, P., and Minguet, A. (1999). Visualizing the log-periodic pattern before crashes, *European Physical Journal B* **9**, 355–359.

435. Vandewalle, N., Boveroux, P., Minguet, A., and Ausloos, M. (1998). The crash of October 1987 seen as a phase transition: Amplitude and universality, *Physica A* **255**, 201–210.

436. van Raan, A. F. J. (2000). On growth, ageing and fractal differentitation of science, *Scientometrics* **47**, 347–362.

437. Varian, H. R. (1989). Difference of opinion in financial markets, in *Financial Risk: Theory, Evidence and Implications*, Proceedings of the Eleventh Annual Economic Policy Conference of the Federal Reserve Bank of St. Louis, Courtenay C. Stone, editor (Kluwer, Boston).

438. Vinge, V. (1993). *The Coming Technological Singularity: How to Survive in the Post-Human Era*, available at http://www.aleph.se/Trans/Global/Singularity/sing.html, presented at the VISION-21 Symposium sponsored by NASA Lewis Research Center and the Ohio Aerospace Institute, March 30–31, 1993.

439. Visser, W. (1997). Can the casino economy be tamed? *Money Values*, http://sane.org.za/moneyvalues/27-Oct-1997.html.

440. Vitousek, P. M., Mooney, H. A., Lubchenco, J., and Mellilo, J. M. (1997). Human domination of Earth's eco systems, *Science* **277**, 494–499.

441. von Foerster, H., Mora, P. M., and Amiot, L. W. (1961). Population density and growth, *Science* **133**, 1931–1937.

442. Von Neumann, J. (1938/1968). Uber ein ökonomisches Gleichungssystem und eine Verallgemeinerung des Brouwerschen Fixpunktsatzes (English translation, 1968, A Model of General Economic Equilibrium), in *Readings in Mathematical Economics*, Peter Newman, editor (John Hopkins University Press, Baltimore), pp. 221–229.

443. Von Neumann, J. and Morgenstern, O. (1947). *Theory of Games and Economic Behavior* (Princeton University Press, Princeton, NJ).

444. Voss, R. F. (1992). Evolution of long-range fractal correlations and 1/f noise in DNA base sequences, *Phys. Rev. Lett.* **68**, 3805–3808.

445. Watts, D. J. (1999). *Small Worlds* (Princeton University Press, Princeton, NJ).

446. Weber, M. and Camerer, C. F. (1998). The disposition effect in securities trading: An experimental analysis, *Journal of Economic Behavior & Organization* **33**, 167–184.

447. Weierstrass, K. (1895). Über continuirliche functionen eines reellen arguments, die für keiner Werth des letzteren einen bestimmten differential-quotienten besitzen, *Mathematische Werke* (Mayer & Muller, Berlin). (Proof first given in 1872.)

448. Weinberg, S. (1996). *The Quantum Theory of Fields* (Cambridge University Press, Cambridge, U.K. and New York).

449. Weiss, H. and Bradley, R. S. (2001). What drives societal collapse? *Science* **291**, 609–610.

450. Welch, I. (1992). Sequential sales, learning, and cascades, *Journal of Finance* **47**, 695–732; see also http://welch.som.yale.edu/cascades for an annotated bibliography and resource reference on "information cascades."

451. Welch, I. (2000). Herding among security analysts, *Journal of Financial Economics* **58** (3), 369–396.

452. Weron, R. (2000). Energy price risk management, *Physica A* **285**, 127–134.

453. West, K. D. (1987). A specification test for speculative bubbles, *Quarterly Journal of Economics* **102**, 553–580.

454. White, E. N. (1996). Stock market crashes and speculative manias. In *The International Library of macroeconomic and financial history* **13**. An Elgar Reference Collection, Cheltenham, U.K. and Brookfield, MA.

455. White, E. N. and Rappoport, P. (1995). The New York stock market in the 1920s and 1930s: Did stock prices move together too much?, in *Anglo-American Financial Systems: Institutions and Markets in the Twentieth Century*, M. Bordo and R. Sylla, editors (Burr Ridge Irwin), pp. 299–316.

456. Wigner, E. P. (1960). The (unreasonable) effectiveness of mathematics, *Communications in Pure and Applied Mathematics* **13**, February.

457. Williams, J. B. (1938). *The Theory of Investment Value* (Harvard University Press, Cambridge, MA).

458. Wilson, K. G. (1979). Problems in physics with many scales of length, *Scientific American* **241** (2), 158–179.

459. Wu, Y. (1995). Are there rational bubbles in foreign exchange markets? Evidence from an alternative test, *Journal of International Money & Finance* **14**, 27–46.

460. Youssefmir, M., Huberman, B. A., and Hogg, T. (1998). Bubbles and market crashes, *Computational Economics* **12**, 97–114.

461. Zajdenweber, D. (2000). *Economie des extrêmes*, collection Nouvelle Bibliothèque Scientifique (Flammarion Editor, Paris).

462. Zaslavsky, G. M. (2000). Multifractional kinetics, *Physica A* **288**, 431–443.

463. Zwiebel, J. (1995). Corporate conservatism and relative compensation, *Journal of Political Economy* **103**, 125.

464. Lo, A. W. and MacKinlay, A. C. (1999). *A Non-Random Walk Down Wall Street* (Princeton University Press, Princeton, NJ).

Index